Keep Reforming: China's Strategic Economic Transformation

Zhong Xu

Keep Reforming: China's Strategic Economic Transformation

Springer

Zhong Xu
National Association of Financial Market Institutional Investors
Beijing, China

ISBN 978-981-15-8005-5 ISBN 978-981-15-8006-2 (eBook)
https://doi.org/10.1007/978-981-15-8006-2

This Springer imprint is published by the registered company Springer Nature Singapore Pte Ltd.
The registered company address is: 152 Beach Road, #21-01/04 Gateway East, Singapore 189721, Singapore

For my wife and son

Contents

Chapter 1
China's Economic Transformation

1.1 Current Trends and Characteristics of the Chinese Economy

China's economy has now reached a stage in which the macro leverage ratio is effectively controlled, the central market interest rate (one-year fixed interest rate) has gone down, and liquidity is relatively abundant. However, financial institutions are generally reluctant to lend, the local governments are unwilling to act, and the fact that liquidity released by the central bank cannot be effectively transmitted to the real economy is leading to a contraction of credit and higher financing costs for private enterprises. Meanwhile, the downturn in the internal economic cycle has been exacerbated by the external shocks caused by frictions in Sino-US trade, and this set of circumstances has contributed to the polarization of expectations regarding China's real economic prospects, as seen for example in the discussions about policy trends relevant to the private economy. Indeed, one might claim that the current confusion of expectations even exceeds that of 2008, when the international financial crisis broke out.

From a dialectical perspective, the more pessimistic the expectation of economic trend, the easier it is to build consensus on reform, and the more remarkable are the actual effects of reform. However, that reform must be based on a comprehensive understanding of the phased characteristics of China's economic development.

1.1.1 Long-Term Trend

China is currently in a phase of diminishing demographic dividends. As a result, the economy is experiencing systematic changes in macroeconomic variables such as savings rate, current account balance, and social financing scale, and a transformation from high-speed growth to medium–high level growth is inevitable.

Z. Xu, *Keep Reforming: China's Strategic Economic Transformation*,
https://doi.org/10.1007/978-981-15-8006-2_1

Theoretically, when analyzing the long-term growth we should focus more on the supply side factors of capital, labor force, and technology progress, which drive economic growth, rather than the conventional "troika" method of "National Income = Consumption + Investment + Net Export," which is more relevant to short-term demand management.

With regard to demography, in 2004 China passed the Lewis point of economic development. In 2010, the proportion of China's working population aged between 15 and 64 reached a historical high of 74.5%; since then it has been declining, and the demographic dividend is gradually diminishing. The labor market is changing from a situation of oversupply to excess demand, and the demographic changes have added to economic moderation. Therefore, it is an objective fact of the new normal economic growth that high-level growth is turning into medium–high level growth. According to our assessment, China's real GDP growth will slow down in line with demographic changes. By 2050, the average growth rate of real GDP will be close to 3% and per capita GDP will be around 3.5%.

The diminishing demographic dividend and declining potential economic growth will bring about systematic changes in macroeconomic variables such as savings rate, current account balance and social financing scale. The change of natural interest rate is directly related to monetary policy. In 2012, China's economy began gradually to enter the new normal period characterized by medium–high economic growth, and the natural interest rate has declined accordingly, from more than 4% in the first half of 2004 to the average level of 2.4% in 2018, which is consistent with studies regarding the impact of population structure on potential output.

Because the natural interest rate is the real interest rate that accords with steady growth, it is mainly determined by technological progress. The average growth rate of technology during the period of rapid economic growth from 2004 to 2006 was 2.98%; in the crisis management period from 2007 to 2011 it was 1.4024%; and in the new normal period since 2012 it has been 2.0823%. Technological growth is closely related to natural interest rate and economic trend. However, in the second half of the global financial crisis management period, i.e. 2010 and 2011, there was a clear deviation between technological growth and natural interest rate, which may have been caused by the failing stimulus policies. This is consistent with previous research findings that the sharp increase in investment and continuous expansion of government after the global financial crisis led to declines in capital returns and productivity. From 2012, however, technological growth remained high and proved to be the determining factor for natural interest rates. Moreover, the fluctuation of technological growth was lower than it had been during the period of rapid economic growth and of crisis management. The standard deviations of technological growth in the three periods were 0.8657%, 1.2623%, and 0.3845%, respectively, reflecting the structural upgrading and innovation-driven characteristics of the new normal. In addition, several economic trends should be taken into account:

First of all, the national savings rate has been following a downward trend since 2008. Based on comparable data, from 2008 to 2015 the national savings rate fell from 51.91 to 47.16%, a decrease of 4.74% points. The enterprise savings rate dropped from 22.74 to 19.81%; the government savings rate from 5.89 to 4.51%; and the household savings rate from 23.28 to 22.85%, decreases of 2.93, 1.38 and 0.43% points respectively. Government and enterprise savings rates contributed most to the changes, while the household savings rate was relatively stable.

With regard to the age structure of the population, if the growth rate of the labor force exceeds the growth rate of the total population, the increase in the proportion of working population increases the total income and savings rate, and vice versa. It is estimated that more than half of China's savings rate changes can be explained by demographic factors. In terms of trend, with the decline of the working-age population, the acceleration of aging population and the increase of dependency ratio, the savings rate of residents will remain on a downswing. Our estimation shows that the national savings rate will drop to around 21% by 2050.

Second, the current account is significantly affected by aging population. According to our simulation, following a rapid decline from positive to negative the current account will remain at −1.3% in the long run, and will reach a low of −1.33% before rising around 2044.

Third, capital returns and total factor productivity (TFP) will decline in the long run. From 2007 to 2015, capital input per unit of GDP increased from 3.5 to 6.7; that is, the return on assets measured by capital output fell by half in eight years, with an average annual decline of 11.25%. The PBC DSGE simulation shows that, after reaching the lowest point in 2023–2025, the labor cost will continue to rise. TFP decreased from 3.039 in 2008 to 1.383 in 2017, and after recovering slightly it will stay stable at 1.5 in 2022.

These changes are due to be the rising costs faced by enterprises for raw materials, labor, land, capital, and environment protection. The cost of other factors is not so easy to pass on as the cost of capital. Enterprises always finance their operations through financial institutions. In fact, the rising cost of capital and the breaking of the capital chain are rooted in enterprises' operational failures, which lead to problems such as borrowing to repay, evading debts, and "zombie enterprises."

This is also true at the macro level. The financial risks of the macro economy are often characterized by liquidity risk. However, if we focus only on the liquidity risk but ignore the underlying structural factors and actual solvency; and if we propose monetary stimulus only, instead of structural reform, then while there might be an expansion of investment in the short term, in the long run we will see expansion of debt, a rise in leverage, asset bubbles, and even economic recession. Since the financial crisis, major economies have focused on monetary and fiscal stimulus rather than structural reforms, which has contributed to the rising leverage ratio in most countries. The "recovery" of stock and real estate markets is much better than the economic recovery. From the perspective of the financial system and monetary policy, in the context of a declining savings rate and high-quality economic development in China, the emphasis of finance serving the real economy should be shifted from increasing savings to improving financial allocation efficiency; that is, to enhancing total factor productivity.

1.1.2 Medium-Term Policies and Prospects

China's focus on deleverage, environment protection, and poverty alleviation is the active policy option not only for high-quality growth, but also for long-term sustainable growth. In order to contain financial risks, resources should be shifted from high-risk and low-efficiency sectors to low-risk and high-efficiency sectors, thus creating a virtuous circle within the finance and real economy, finance and real estate, and financial system. The process will be painful in the short run, but will lay the foundation for future sustainable growth. Meanwhile, environment protection is the key to high-quality development. Improving environmental standards will affect short-term output by increasing the technological input and production costs of enterprises. However, the development of green industry will create new economic growth points. Furthermore, a program of poverty alleviation, which would see all the people benefit from the achievements of reforms and developments, would place social equity as the foundation of sustainable economic development.

In the financial field, structural deleverage is the priority to fend off and defuse major risks. Here, the emphasis should be on achieving macro leverage stability and decline. Currently, China's macro leverage level is stabilizing. BIS data show that, after reaching a peak of 166.9% in Q2 2016, the leverage of non-financial enterprises in China has been declining. Although the data rebounded slightly in Q1 2018 as some off-balance sheet financing went back onto the balance sheet, the fact that BIS data do not include off-balance financing means that this rebounding did not indicate a reversal of the deleverage process, or debt expansion.

Moreover, the risks of China's high leverage ratio can be contained. When we examine debt risk, we look at both size and speed of debt expansion. In this regard, the overall leverage level in China is declining. When we examine the debt sustainability, net asset is more important, as sufficient net assets means strong debt repayment capacity. Although China's corporate leverage seems relatively high, most highly indebted firms are local government financial platforms and SOEs; hence, their debt should be considered government debt. China's government has strong repayment capacity, holding massive amounts of high-quality assets such as land and equity of firms, and these are more than enough to cover the existing debt. Another concern regarding local government debt is the implicit debt, which is being addressed through enhanced debt transparency and removal of the local government soft budget.

Attention should also be paid to the rising leverage ratio of the household sector. The latest BIS data show that at the end of Q1 2018, the leverage of households in China stood at 49.3% when excluding housing provident fund loans, and at 54.7% when including these loans. Considering the consumption habits of Chinese households and the particular stages of economic development, the leverage of households in China is in a reasonable range compared with the average level of 60.8% in G20 countries. Nevertheless, in recent years, the leverage has increased. From 2008 to 2017, the leverage of China's households increased by an average of 3.5% every year, significantly higher than in other countries. Horizontal comparison shows that the leverage of US households has risen from 20 to 50% over the past 40 years, while the same increase in China has taken less than 10 years. The global experience tells us that a rapid rise of debt in the short term always creates asset bubbles. Most household debt is concentrated in real estate. Indeed, it is estimated that the real estate debt may account for more than 70% of all debt in the household sector. Housing prices have a significant impact on the wealth of households, which may cause systemic risks and affect social stability.

1.1.3 Short-Term Trend

From a short-term perspective, the main economic indicators are in a reasonable range. The GDP growth rate for the first three quarters of 2018 was 6.7%, and it reached 6.5% for the whole year. The slowing investment growth rate is mainly due to stricter local government soft budget constraint and enhanced transparency. The rebounding of manufacturing investment reflects improving producer and investor confidence. Moreover, the consumption and disposable income growth rates are both stable.

Prices are in a reasonable range. The average inflation of China in 2018 was 2.07%. The increased CPI is mainly pushed by cost, such as oil price, pork price and environment protection cost. Core CPI has not risen. Moreover, unemployment is stable: in December of 2018 it stood at 4.9%.

We have observed improvements to economic structure, driven mainly by domestic demand, consumption and the service sector, while the current account surplus is falling. In the first three quarters, consumption accounted for 78% of GDP growth, and the service sector for 60.8% of overall GDP, 14 and 1.8% higher than for the same period last year. China even experienced a slight current account deficit, although for the whole year, a small surplus is expected.

The on-going economic moderation and financial market fluctuation are the results of the supply-side reform (including deleverage) and economic growth model upgrading. They are the inevitable costs of economic structure transformation.

The recent Sino-US trade friction has been a major factor affecting market sentiment. In the short term, Sino-US trade friction has limited impacts on Chinese exports and economic growth. From January to September 2018, China's trade surplus was $221.385 billion, a decrease of 23.76% YOY (year on year). However, China's trade surplus with the US was $225.79 billion, an increase of 15.2% YOY, and accounted for 102% of the total trade surplus, an increase of 34.5% YOY. Moreover, from June to September 2018, YOY growth of China's exports to the US was 13.5%, almost exactly the same as the 13.6% from January to May, before the trade frictions. From June to September 2018, China's trade surplus with the US rose by 17.3% YOY, an increase of 4.5% compared with January to May.

Not surprisingly, the trade friction has aggravated the effect of domestic factors and provoked internal contradictions. Our forecast shows that the trade friction will reduce China's GDP by 0.2 to 0.5%.

1.1.4 The High-Quality Growth Model Poses Challenges for the Monetary Policy Framework

Since 1984, when the PBC officially assumed the role of central bank, it has managed a major transition of the monetary policy framework from direct control to indirect control, with the intermediate objective of broad money supply and the ultimate objective of price stability. This quantitative framework for monetary policy control combines a variety of monetary policy tools. Furthermore, the role of the market in financial resources allocation and in the macro financial policies has been enhanced. The process of reform can be summarized as follows. First, in selecting monetary policy objectives, focus on price stability while also including other objectives. Second, develop a set of monetary policy tools to enhance indirect control. Third, select a combination of quantitative, pricing and macro-prudential tools according to China's development stage and economic status. Fourth, integrate short-term macroeconomic measures with medium- and long-term financial reform; attend to "online recovery" of the financial system, and promote reform of the interest rate and foreign exchange rate to improve the monetary transmission mechanism.

This monetary policy framework has been improving with our development and PBC practices. We have gone through the Asian financial crisis and the global financial crisis, as well as different economic cycles in China, and the monetary policies have been effective. Nevertheless, as the central bank for the largest emerging economy in transition, we face a more complicated environment, which has prevented us from copying the practices of western central banks. Currently, we are in the midst of drastic transition of the economic and financial environment, which has posed new challenges for our monetary policies.

As marketization has deepened and the decision-making capacity of economic entities has got stronger, the efficiency of traditional administrative and quantitative tools has weakened. Consequently, we need to adopt more market-oriented and pricing tools. First of all, high RRR should be reduced. Currently, the RRR for medium- and small-sized depository financial institutions is 12.5%, and for large ones, 14.5%. Further, in October 2015 we removed constraints from the deposit interest rate floating band, which can be viewed as the last step of interest marketization reform. However, the base rates for deposits and loans (as announced by the PBC) co-exist with monetary market rates and bond market rates. The double tracks need to be unified.

A further challenge is that the channels of base money have changed significantly with the changes of international capital flow, and liquidity has caused volatilities in the money market. To address these issues, the PBC has added, inter alia, Standing Lending Facility (SLF), Medium-term Lending Facility (MLF), and Pledge Supplementary Lending (PSL) to our liquidity innovation tools. These are intended to improve the PBC's pledge framework, and increase OMO from twice weekly to daily operation to stabilize the money market. However, new issues will continue to arise, as some interest rate signals may not be sufficiently transparent, or may conflict with each other, and cannot help to guide market expectation.

In addition, the foreign exchange rate formation mechanism requires further reform, and the depth and breadth of foreign exchange market are still limited. In order to avoid the "impossible trinity," in which the unstable corner solution is the only feasible option, the PBC adopts a middle solution. However, flexible and market-oriented foreign exchange rate is the safety valve and stabilizer of an economy, and the necessary condition for interest rate marketization and independent monetary policies. Even though RMB has a decent floating band, the harbinger of further foreign exchange rate reform will be enlargement of that band. Over the long run, the target of China's financial reform is a clean float of RMB and market-determined foreign exchange rate. For now, the requirement that foreign exchange derivative must be based on real demand remains as an impediment to be removed. This requirement has hampered the development of the foreign exchange market, because banks can conduct derivative transactions only at the request of firms; as banks are all risk averse, their transactions are all in the same direction. This prevents foreign exchange pricing discovery.

Finally, there remain many constraints upon financial market innovation and development, and the limited depth of the financial market undermines the efficiency of monetary policy transmission. The segregated money market and bond market, and the high credit risk premium and consequent yield level and volatility of the exchange market, have distorted market expectation and PBC liquidity management. Strict entry criteria for financial market transactions and the lagged interest rate derivative market represent further constraints. Entry criteria for the derivative market are particularly difficult to meet, and products for price discovery and risk management are lacking. In 2017, the value of interest rate derivative transactions reached RMB14.4 trillion, less than 20% of the bond market assets. There is also a need for enriched financial products. Currently, pledged repo requiring freezing of bond accounts for 80% of money market transactions, while the bond turnover ratio is very low; these do not support bond market price discovery. Moreover, the base assets of ABS are mostly corporate loans, posing massive information asymmetry. Finally, owing to the insufficient capacities of financial product pricing and risk management, de facto interest rate double tracking continues to exist. This also hampers the transmission of market interest rate to deposit and loan interest rates.

1.1.5 Policy Implications

At present, the decline of potential output growth is in line with the changes of labor factor endowment, and the economy is still in a reasonable range. China's economic fundamentals remain sound, and with its good resilience and new driving forces the economy will maintain soundness and stability over the long term. The problems we have observed are largely due to the contradiction of different systems and mechanisms and to the periodic adjustment of the economy, which is the cost of underlying reform and of the five priority tasks.[1] The short-term impact of Sino-US trade frictions and external changes on China's economy is relatively limited; however, its impact on market confidence and the medium- and long-term effects are causes for concern.

China's policy should be focused on internal demand. In the coming period, we need to persevere in the market orientation, step up reform and opening up, and create a favorable business environment. On macro policy:

(1) **We need to reach a common understanding of the medium and high economic growth, and avoid the dream of high growth.**

Demographic changes have eased employment pressure. That is, China no longer needs high growth: a growth rate of 6.0–6.5% may be sufficient to meet the employment demand. Reduced employment pressure provides a 3–5 year window to achieve economic growth model transformation.

(2) **The long-term and structural problems cannot be attributed to short-term and cyclical problems. We need to stick to supply-side structural reform, accelerate economic transformation and structural adjustment, and further unleash the reform dividends and growth potential.**

In this regard, it is necessary to create a level playing field through tax reduction, market access liberalization, and competition neutrality. Taking fiscal policy as a counter cyclical adjustment, the key is to cut the tax rate and simplify the tax system. Here the US fiscal stimulus plan, which guides a more intuitive understanding of tax cuts, thus enhancing market confidence, serves as an example. We will promote both opening up and domestic reform, and construct high-standard free-trade zones with TPP as the benchmark. Market access for energy, telecommunications, finance, health care, education, and pensions will be liberalized, and tolerance for private SMEs will be increased. The economic viability can be effectively enhanced on the ground that foreign, private and state-owned capital are treated equally.

It is important to break the administrative monopoly and reduce the cost of land, energy and water. Researches show that the costs of land, energy, communications, logistics, and financing in China are one or two times higher than those in developed countries such as the US. This is despite the fact that the per capita income in the US and other developed countries exceeds $40,000 to $50,000, while in China it is only about $8,000. The practical means to achieve cost reduction are to reduce government intervention, break administrative monopolies, and reduce various economic "rents." The priority is land system reform, which is essential for a long-term and sound development of real estate, and for benefiting those who create value rather than distribute value.

While carrying out short-term policy adjustments to ensure the stability of demand, we must also promote the upgrading of consumption and explore new

[1] The five priority tasks are: cutting overcapacity, reducing excess inventory, deleveraging, lowering costs, and strengthening areas of weakness.

economic growth points, guided by new development concepts. The potential driving forces for China's future economic development, such as 5G, new energy vehicles, energy saving and environment protection, improvement of living conditions and urbanization, will promote the expansion of demand and economic growth. In particular, 5G infrastructure investment will boost innovation and development of the new economy, such as the Internet of Things and AI.

Finally, it is crucial to further reform the market-based interest rate and RMB exchange rate regime, and to improve the efficiency of financial resources allocation and financial regulation. Financial institutions must improve their internal piloting system, and enhance pricing capability and risk management. We will continue to improve benchmark interest rates of the market and the yield curve of treasury bonds, and to refine the market-oriented interest rate regime. We are working to establish an interest rate corridor, improve interest rate management, and reinforce the transmission of policy interest rate to the financial market and real economy. We will continue to enhance exchange rate marketization, improve the market-based managed floating exchange rate regime with reference to a basket of currencies, strengthen the market-determined exchange rate, enhance the two-way floating elasticity of RMB exchange rate, and keep the RMB exchange rate at a reasonable and balanced level. In line with the aim to ensure that finance serves the real economy, we will continue to provide exchange rate risk management for import and export enterprises. We will steadily promote RMB capital account convertibility, optimize cross-border RMB policy framework and infrastructure, and attach importance to development, reform and risk prevention, while taking into account the impact of international changes on capital flows and improving macro-prudential policies on cross-border capital flows.

(3) **We should treat the challenges of external shocks as opportunities, and accelerate reform to improve property rights protection, state-owned capital management, corporate governance, income distribution and social security.**
(4) **We need to return to a multilateral framework to resolve trade friction.**

Given China's importance in the global economy and supply chain, shocks to the Chinese economy will dent global growth, especially growth in the East Asian region.

Since the global financial crisis that broke out in 2008, China's recovery has been crucial to lead the global economy back to normality. Most importantly, China has significantly increased domestic demand, which has reduced the current account surplus to a sustainable level. In 2017, net export contributed a mere 0.6% in our GDP growth. Even in the face of trade friction, we have announced sincere financial opening measures, including relaxing the restrictions on foreign ownership of financial institutions, and expanding their business scope in China. Most measures are under implementation, and the remaining ones will be in place by early 2020. China will adhere to the approach of pre-establishment national treatment and negative listing to level the playing field for foreign financial institutions.

Looking ahead, if we are to resolve trade friction we must maintain our commitment to a multilateral trade framework. No matter how imperfect the WTO might be, a multilateral solution is needed to fix and improve it. A unilateral approach that simply abandons the existing framework would certainly kill the public trust in and effectiveness of any future trade rules.

1.2 Estimation of China's Potential Output

Over the past 10 years, China's macroeconomic operation has shown a clear trend of change. Major macroeconomic indicators, such as economic growth, consumption, investment, and money supply, all showed a slowing trend. The average growth rate of real GDP dropped gradually, from 13% before the financial crisis to 6.6% in 2018. The average growth rate of total retail sales of consumer goods and fixed asset investment dropped from over 20% in 2008 to around 6 and 9% in 2018, and the M2 growth rate dropped from 16 to 8%, the lowest level in history. In general, a prolonged slowdown in an economy with broadly stable inflation usually results from a sustained decline in potential output growth. This raises a number of questions regarding China's current potential output trend. For example, what is the reason for the change in trend, and will the current trend continue for a long time? These issues are not only the focus of theoretical research, but also the key to future macro policy decisions. Existing theories and policy researches have put forward many different understandings, including the identification of economic periodicity and structural change, the reduction of technological growth space, the gradual fading of demographic dividend, and the continuation of the impact of financial crisis. However, on the whole, the existing discussion lacks sufficient quantitative analysis support, and some conclusions are inconsistent with the empirical facts.

For central banks, the measurement and estimation of potential output are particularly important. This is because the potential output not only reflects the medium and long-term supply capacity of the economy, but is also one of the core objectives of monetary policy. The corresponding output gap is directly included in the monetary policy decision-making rules, affecting the specific operation of monetary policy. Therefore, under the current economic environment, it is of great theoretical and practical significance to estimate China's potential output effectively and to analyze the influences of different factors on the potential output so as to predict the long-term trend.

In the sub-sections that follow, we first give a brief overview of the current mainstream methods for estimating potential output and compare their characteristics and applicability. Then, we estimate the potential output of China from 1993 to 2018 through four methods, namely production function method, state space model, macroeconometric model and DSGE model, from the perspective of monetary policy decision-making. Next, we analyze and forecast the causes and trends of potential output changes. Finally, we present the main conclusions and corresponding policy implications.

1.2.1 *Comparison and Analysis of Potential Output Measurement Methods*

"Potential output" refers to the level of total output that can be achieved under the condition that capital, labor and other factors of production are fully utilized. It can also be understood as "the level that can be achieved without triggering inflation for a period of time" (Okun 1962). Potential output describes not only the long-term growth path of the economy, but also the ideal state of macroeconomic operation without the influence of nominal stickiness, and reflects the long-term effective supply capacity of the economy. Potential output is often considered alongside concepts such as total factor productivity (TFP), which reflects the part of real output growth that cannot be explained by factor input, and is the core index to measure and evaluate the overall technical progress, as well as an important basis for estimating potential output. Although these concepts show an ideal state within the theoretical framework, in recent years they have moved from pure theoretical definition to the foreground of policy practice, and gradually become an important reference benchmark for macro policy decisions. By measuring potential output, policy-making departments are able to judge the trend and cycle of macroeconomic operation, reduce friction through policy adjustment, and achieve long-term sustainable economic growth.

Unfortunately, both potential output and total factor productivity are unobservable state variables that cannot be obtained directly but can only be estimated by different methods or models. In theory and in practice, a variety of ways or methods are used to estimate the potential output, and experience shows that results differ according to the estimation method or model structure applied. For that reason, and because no single method can obtain long-term robust estimation results, in practice different methods or combinations of methods are chosen according to the research objectives. While all estimation methods share the core idea of identifying and separating the cycle and trend components in the total output, they differ in terms of the dependent information set and information extraction methods, and according to method characteristics with different dimensions.

1.2.1.1 Univariate and Multivariate Estimation

Broadly speaking, the methods used to estimate potential output can be divided into univariate and multivariate estimation. The univariate methods in time series use the information of only a single variable to identify its own trend and periodic components. Those used in potential output estimation include, for example, HP filter (Hodrick and Prescott 1997), PC filter (Benes and N'Diaye 2004; Laxton et al. 1998), NB decomposition (Beveridge and Nelson 1981), and CF filter (Christiano and Fitzgerald 1999). The main idea is to achieve the separation of variable trend and periodic components by pursuing the minimization of loss function under certain assumptions. The empirical results show that the univariate filtering method is usually sensitive to the hypothesis conditions; the univariate HP filter method in particular is sensitive to the endpoint value of the sequence, and involves difficulties with regard to prediction and factor analysis. In addition, different settings of potential output and gap change lead to significantly different estimation results. In practical applications, univariate filtering is usually combined with the production function method to estimate the trend component of factor input.

Compared with univariate analysis, multivariate methods make better use of information and achieve more stable estimation results. Information related to output gap or periodic fluctuation is used to help identify the periodic components in output changes and realize the separation of cycle and trend. Methods include multivariable PC filter, PC filter that extends Phillips Curve (Gali and Monacelli 2005), PC filter that extends Okun's law, PC filter including capital utilization rate, VAR model, and multivariable structure state space model. Most of these methods are semi-structured models. Compared with single-variable methods such as HP filtering and NB decomposition, these methods have stronger explanatory power to data and more flexibility in model setting, which has become the conventional way for most central banks to estimate potential output and total factor productivity. The Federal Reserve's supply-side model and the Bank of England's aggregate supply and output gap models all take this form.

1.2.1.2 Estimation Methods

The potential output can be estimated by, for example, the production function method, state space model, macroeconometric model, or dynamic stochastic general equilibrium model (DSGE).

I. *Production function method*

The "growth accounting framework" adopted by the US Congressional Budget Office (CBO) is a typical method for estimating potential output based on production functions and accounting relationships (Shackleton 2018). The production function approach first applies the "index method" to calculate the input of factors and the corresponding output elasticity coefficient under the established production function form, and obtains the estimated value of total factor productivity. Next, it takes the employment gap or other variables that can reflect the change of economic cycle as the cycle index, successively removes the cyclical components contained in total factor productivity, labor participation rate, working hours and factor output elasticity, and gets the corresponding trend part of each variable, namely the potential level of related variables. Finally, capital service, potential labor input, potential TFP and other factors are substituted into the production function to calculate the final potential output. The advantage of this method is that it is less subject to short-term fluctuations and more focused on long-term supply capacity.

II. *State space model*

The state space model used in potential output estimation is usually a semi-structured model. Semi-structured design is not only conducive to extracting other information for cycle and trend identification, but also more convenient for segmentation of different industries. A representative example is the Federal Reserve's supply model (Roberts 2014).

III. *Estimation based on macroscopic model*

In addition to the production function method, estimating potential output based on macroeconomic models has become mainstream practice, especially for central banks in developed economies. Both DSGE and large macroeconometric models can realize joint estimation and overall consideration of potential output and TFP estimation. In the macro model, the description of total factor productivity and potential output is more detailed, and the identification of trend and fluctuation is more accurate, which is very conducive to monetary policy analysis. In COMPASS, the core DSGE model of the Bank of England, and FRB/US, the macroeconometric model of the Federal Reserve, technical progress not only contains trend and cycle components, but also can be subdivided into neutral, proprietary investment and labor enhancement, which facilitates more detailed analysis for different purposes.

1.2.1.3 Types of Estimation Framework

With regard to the different types of framework employed, the potential output can be estimated by local equilibrium analysis or under the general equilibrium framework. The production function method is a typical local equilibrium estimation method. Estimation methods that absorb financial information and employment information, such as PC filtering that extends Phillips Curve, PC filtering that extends Okun's law, and PC filtering that includes capital utilization rate, are all local equilibrium methods. The large macroeconometric model, DSGE model and partial state space model (Laubach and Williams 2003, 2016) are mainly estimates under the general equilibrium framework.

1.2.1.4 Selection of Estimation Method

In terms of objectives, different macro policies focus on different aspects of potential output, and the estimation methods and measurement methods adopted differ accordingly. The main purpose of the financial sector (such as the CBO and OBR) when looking at potential output is to analyze the trend changes in the economy, to assess the sustainability of the national fiscal balance and to determine the medium- and long-term impact of various shocks and policy changes on the national fiscal balance. Therefore, estimates of potential output carried out by the financial sector usually require long-term (usually more than 10 years) forecasts. Financial sector estimates of potential output must include multiple sectors and industries, with the possibility to conduct separate estimates in different sectors and industries. This sector also pays more attention to the influence brought by the trend change of factor input. Central banks focus on potential output not only to understand the economy's long-term trends, but also to further calculate the output gap. Output gap is the core element of monetary policy decision-making, which will directly affect policy operation. Consequently, central banks tend to focus more on short-term changes in potential output, particularly on inflation and employment. Monetary policy decisions usually require that the following conditions are satisfied: first, the measurement frequency should be high (usually quarterly), which is convenient for timely monitoring and analysis; second, the estimation should use segmented market data, in order to be able to explain market changes; third, the potential output should have the ability to analyze the impact of finance, and to predict potential economic changes.

Each of the many methods for estimating potential output comes with its own advantages and disadvantages. With regard to structure, the production method and state space model are relatively simple, with fewer introduced factors and more flexibility in use. The structural system of the macroeconometric and DSGE models is complex, while the degree of integration of the model is strong. In terms of data conditions, the production method is closely related to economic accounting data, and the calculation results are relatively stable under sufficient data conditions. The state space method usually has few observed variables, but the estimation results are greatly affected by the model structure. Macroeconometric models are usually larger in scale and involve more equations and variables. The DSGE model is similar to the state space model, but due to its stronger structure, it requires higher consistency between variables and data statistics standards. With regard to estimation method, the production method involves less estimation, and partial potential factor input estimation involves piecewise logarithmic linear regression. State space and DSGE models usually employ GMM or Bayes estimation techniques, and some parameters can also be calibrated. Macroeconometric models, especially large models, are difficult to estimate, so calibration and joint estimation are usually adopted.

In general, it is difficult for any single method to obtain long-term robust estimation results. Therefore, different methods are selected according to different research objectives. In policy practice, governments and central banks usually estimate potential output in a variety of different ways based on the characteristics of their economies.

1.2.2 Comprehensive Method Design of Potential Output Measurement in China

Based on the above analysis, in this chapter we empirically estimate China's potential output using four separate methods: the production function method, state space model, econometric model and DSGE model.

1.2.2.1 Data and Variables

The observed variables involved in the estimation process comprise real GDP, real interest rate, inflation rate, import price and real estate price inflation rate, savings growth, policy uncertainty, stock market volatility, output gap, M2 growth rate, working-age population, and labor remuneration. The DSGE model and state space model involve 14 random shocks. The real GDP is the annualized level after quarterly adjustment, and the logarithm is taken to remove the mean. The real rate is the average yield on the 10-year Treasury minus the average inflation over the next four quarters. The inflation rate is based on the price index, which is set in 2010. The change of import price and real estate price is the year-on-year growth rate of import price index and real estate price index respectively of 70 large and medium-sized cities. The growth of savings includes the year-on-year growth of fixed deposit, current deposit and personal deposit of enterprises. The remaining variables will be specified in subsequent estimation methods. All variables are quarterly data from 1993 to 2018.

1.2.2.2 Estimation Based on the Production Function Method

Formally, we have chosen to synthesize capital, labor, and technological progress to produce potential output in the form of the corvinglass (C-D) production function with constant returns to scale. The estimation of potential output by the production method has higher requirements with regard to the selection of input factors, so the estimation of input factors should start from the nature of service. In line with the "index method" recommended by the OECD, we do not classify capital and labor input by assets or sectors, but directly construct capital input index and labor input index to measure capital and labor input and other factors. Technological progress and labor output elasticity are calculated by residual method and labor remuneration and total income data respectively.[2] Specifically, the TFP growth rate is first defined as:

$$d\log A_t = d\log QGDP_t - (1-\alpha_t) \times d\log IL_t - \alpha_t d\log(IK_t)$$

[2]It should be noted that in the process of factor input estimation, the final results will be influenced by which components are eliminated from periodic fluctuations and how periodic components are removed.

where, $d\log A_t$, $d\log QGDP_t$, $d\log IL_t$, and $d\log IK_t$ are the logarithmic differences of total factor productivity TFP, real GDP, and labor and capital input indexes respectively. IL_t and IK_t are respectively labor and capital input indexes converted from 2010 data. α_t is the elasticity coefficient of capital output, which is directly calculated by the added value in the table of input and output. That is, $\alpha_t = 1 - WS_t / SGDP_t$ by definition, WS_t is workers' compensation, $SGDP_t$ is real GDP after deducting statistical errors and taxes. On that basis, α_t and TFP are further filtered by HP to obtain potential TFP_t^* and α_t^*.

Next, based on the obtained TFP_t^*, the potential output can be further calculated:

$$\log QGDP_t^* = \log A_t^* + (1 - \alpha_t^*) \times \log IL_t^* + \alpha_t^* \log IK_t + c$$

where, $\log QGDP_t^*$, $\log A_t^*$, $\log IL_t^*$, and α_t^* represent the logarithmic potential output, the TFP trend, the potential labor input, and the stable capital output elasticity, respectively.

In addition, in production method estimation, the number of population or labor force is not equal to the labor input in the measurement of potential output. In the empirical process, we usually estimate the potential labor supply from the working-age population (15–64 years old). The first step is to obtain the total potential labor supply through labor participation rate and the number of working-age population. Next, the actual employment size in the labor supply is estimated by the unemployment rate and the potential labor supply. Finally, by applying the working hours index, the actual number of employed people is converted into the actual total labor input. It can be seen that the whole process, from the number of working-age population to the final total amount of actual labor input, involves many links and variables, such as working-age population, labor participation rate, employment rate and working hours. Therefore, changes in population size and population structure are not the same as changes in total labor input, which is why some estimates regard slower growth of labor force or population as the main driving force of potential output decline. Based on the above model, the potential output estimated by the production method can be obtained.

1.2.2.3 Estimation Based on the Macroeconometric Model

Similar to the production method, we introduce the C-D production function into the existing macroeconometric model[3] to estimate the potential output. In order to better describe the change of total factor productivity, factors such as the number of working population, working hours and education hours are introduced into the model to internalize the change of TFP trend. Meanwhile, the output elasticity corresponding to different factors is estimated by the potential output equation, the TFP trend

[3]The macroeconometric model used in this paper is the quarterly macroeconometric model of the People's Bank of China, developed and maintained by the research bureau of the People's Bank of China in 2014.

equation and the Phillips Curve. The correlation equation of potential output is as follows:

I. *Potential output equation*

$$\log QGDP_t^* = 0.4 * \log(LS_t * AVHR_t) + 0.2 * \log(EDU_t/POPW_t) + 0.5 * \log(K_t) + Trend_t + \varepsilon_t^{YHAT}$$

Output gap is defined as:

$$GAP_t = 100 * \log(\sum QGDP_i / \sum QGDP_i^*)$$

where, LS_t is the number of working people, $AVHR_t$ is the average number of working hours per week, EDU_t is the number of school hours, $POPW_t$ is the number of working-age people, K_t is the capital stock, $Trend_t$ is the trend or potential TFP_t^* of total factor productivity.

II. *TFP trend equation*

$$\begin{aligned} Trend_t &= 0.0016 Bloan_t + 0.0012 Mgdp_t + 0.026 * \log(RD_t) + 0.02 * GDPREL_t \\ &\quad + Exog_t * TRP_t + \varepsilon_t^{Trend} \end{aligned}$$

where, $Bloan_t$ is the proportion of bank loan in total credit, $Mgdp_t$ is the proportion of total import in GDP, RD_t is the government r&d investment, $GDPREL_t$ is the per capita GDP ratio of China and the US, reflecting the impact of "catch-up" factors, $Exog_t$ and TRP_t are exogenous technological progress and time trend variables respectively.

III. *Phillips Curve*

$$d\log PI_t = -1.18 + \sum_{i=1}^{4} (\alpha_i \cdot d\log PI_{t-i}) + 0.002 * \frac{1}{4}\sum_{i=0}^{3} GAP_{t-i} - 0.22 * ECM_t + \varepsilon_t^{PI}$$

where, PI_t is the core price index. Here, CPI excluding food and energy is selected. ECM_t is the cointegration term, which describes the long-term determinants of prices, comprising mainly labor cost and non-labor cost. Formal satisfaction is as follows:

$$\log PI_t = 0.25 \cdot \log(NL\cos t_t) + 0.75 \cdot \log(L\cos t_t)$$

where, $NL\cos t_t$ and $L\cos t_t$ are non-labor cost and labor cost respectively. Based on the above equation, China's potential output from 1993 to 2018 can be estimated.

1.2.2.4 Estimation Based on the State Space Model

The state space model is commonly used to estimate the potential output. Most studies take the "supply-side" (SS) model setting and related estimates of the Fed (2003, 2015) FRB/US as the benchmark, and compare the estimated results of different countries. Here, we use the FRB SS model to estimate China's potential output.

I. *Model specification*

Similar to the SS model, Phillips Curve under the NK framework is used to depict the relationship between output gap and inflation rate. In order to better depict the characteristics of China's inflation changes in recent years, the Phillips Curve is modified and supplemented by introducing the inflation rate of import price and the inflation rate of real estate price. This modification ensures that the model takes account of the impact of the real estate price and the price of imported products on the overall inflation rate and improves the fitting effect. The extended Phillips Curve satisfies the following form:

$$\pi_t = \sum_{j=1}^{8} b_j \pi_{t-j} + b_y \tilde{y}_{t-1} + b_m \pi_{t-1}^m + b_o \pi_t^{HP} + \varepsilon_{\pi,t}$$

where, y_t is the total output, y_t^* is the potential output, $\tilde{y}_t$ is the output gap, $\tilde{y}_t = 100 * (y_t - y_t^*)$. π_t is the inflation rate, π_t^m and π_t^{HP} are the growth rates of import price index and real estate price index respectively.

The potential output is a random trend process, whose changes meet the following settings:

$$y_t^* = y_{t-1}^* + g_{t-1} + \varepsilon_{y^*,t}$$

$$g_t = g_{t-1} + \varepsilon_{g,t}$$

where, g_t is the potential output trend term, subject to the first-order unit root process. In addition to the core equation, the output gap estimated by the production method is introduced into the model as an observation variable, and the observation error is introduced into the output gap equation. The specific form is:

$$\tilde{y}_{GAP,t} = \tilde{y}_t + \mu_t + \varepsilon_{pbc,t}$$

$$\mu_t = \rho_\mu \mu_{t-1} + \varepsilon_{\mu,t}$$

$\tilde{y}_{GAP,t}$ is the output gap estimated by the production method GAP_t, and μ_t is the observation error. The changes of import price inflation rate and real estate price inflation rate follow the n-order autoregression process:

$$\pi_t^m = \sum_{i=1}^{n} \rho_i^m \pi_{t-i}^m + \varepsilon_{m\pi,t}$$

$$\pi_t^{HP} = \sum_{i=1}^{n} \rho_i^{HP} \pi_{t-i}^{HP} + \varepsilon_{HP,t}$$

All random impacts ε_t involved in the model are Gaussian white noise processes with iid.

II. *Parameter calibration and estimation results*

In the state space model, the prior distribution and initial value setting of most parameters mainly refer to the related researches of Laubach and Williams (2003, 2016) and Pescatori and Turunen (2016. It should be emphasized that the changes of import price inflation rate and real estate price inflation rate may be unstable to some extent. In the specific estimation process, we have made trade-offs of lag terms of different orders. By employing China's data from 1993 to 2018, the potential output trend under the state space model can be estimated.

1.2.2.5 Estimation Based on the DSGE Model

In order to depict the trend characteristics of China's rapid economic growth, we take Justiniano et al.'s (2011) DSGE model (JPT) with different trends as the basis, and use Chinese data for estimation after appropriate expansion.

In terms of mechanism, the JPT model contains a neoclassical growth process based on a NK model. Final products are divided into three categories: general consumer goods, investment goods, and capital goods, which are produced in three different sectors. Enterprises invest capital and labor to produce intermediate and final products. The final products can be used by consumers as consumer goods or by investment products manufacturers as input factors. The obtained investment goods will be further used as input factors by capital goods manufacturers and eventually form capital. The production process of intermediate products involves neutral technological progress, that of investment goods is affected by the progress of investment proprietary technology, while the capital formation process is mainly determined by the efficiency and capacity of capital formation. The main equations are as follows:

I. Intermediate production

Production technology: $Y_t = \eta_t (A_t^{1-\alpha} K_t^{\alpha} L_t^{1-\alpha})$.

Where, Y_t is output, K_t and L_t are capital and labor input, and η_t is neutral technological progress, satisfying $\log \eta_t = \rho_\eta \log \eta_{t-1} + \varepsilon_{\eta,t}$. A_t is labor-intensive technological progress. Let $z_t = \Delta \log A_t$ and z_t follow a smooth AR (1) process, satisfying $z_t = (1 - \rho_z)\gamma_z + \rho_z z_{t-1} + \varepsilon_{z,t}$.

II. Production of investment goods

In a perfectly competitive market for investment goods, manufacturers of investment goods purchase intermediate products and produce investment goods, and the production process meets the following requirements:

$$Max\{P_{It}I_t - P_tY_t^I\}, s.t\ I_t = \xi_tY_t^I.$$

Where, I_t is the output of investment goods, Y_t^I is the input of capital goods producers' intermediate products, and P_{It} and P_t are the prices of investment goods and consumer goods respectively. ξ_t refers to the progress of investment in proprietary technology (IST), which reflects the technical progress level of the production department of investment goods. The change satisfies $\upsilon_t = \Delta \log \xi_t$, and υ_t obeys $\upsilon_t = (1-\rho_\upsilon)\gamma_\upsilon + \rho_\upsilon\upsilon_{t-1} + \varepsilon_{\upsilon,t}$.

III. *Capital goods production*

Similarly, in the perfectly competitive capital goods production market, capital goods producers buy investment goods, convert them into capital and supply them to residents. The capital production process is:

$$i_t = \mu_t\left(1 - S\left(\frac{I_t}{I_{t-1}}\right)\right)I_t$$

where, i_t is the new capital formation and S is the adjustment cost of investment (Christinao et al. 2005). We assume that in the steady-state situation, the adjustment cost is 0, that is, $S = S'$. μ_t is capital formation efficiency shock (MEI), which describes the efficiency in the process where investment goods are installed and converted into capital that can be applied. Suppose it follows the following procedure: $\log \mu_t = \rho_\mu \log \mu_{t-1} + \varepsilon_{\mu,t}$.

IV. *Capital accumulation*

The capital accumulation equation satisfies:

$$\overline{K}_t = (1-\delta)\overline{K}_{t-1} + \mu_t\xi_t(1-S_t)\tilde{I}_t$$

where, $\overline{K}_t$ is the capital stock, μ_t is the capital formation efficiency shock, and S_t is the investment adjustment cost. It can be seen that the process of capital accumulation is affected by the impact of capital formation efficiency and investment proprietary technology progress. In addition, the model contains the impact of conventional monetary and fiscal policy shocks, price and wage plus shocks, and inter-temporal preferences of residents. Based on such a DSGE model, China's potential output growth rate from 1993 to 2018 can be obtained.

1.2.3 China's Potential Output and Output Gap (1993–2029)

1.2.3.1 Estimation Results

Figure 1.1 displays the estimated results of China's potential output through four methods: production function method, state space model, macroeconometric model and DSGE model.

As can be seen from the figure, with all four methods the overall trend of potential output is relatively similar, showing a phased characteristic. Due to the relatively simple structure of the production method and state space model, there are few introduced factors, and the estimation results are relatively smooth. The econometric model and DSGE model results are characterized by conspicuous short-term fluctuations, due to the complex structure of the models and many uncertain factors. Furthermore, all four models show that since the 2008 international financial crisis, the average growth rate of China's potential output has followed a continuous downward trend. Although the results of some methods show that the growth rate has stabilized, the trend is still weak.

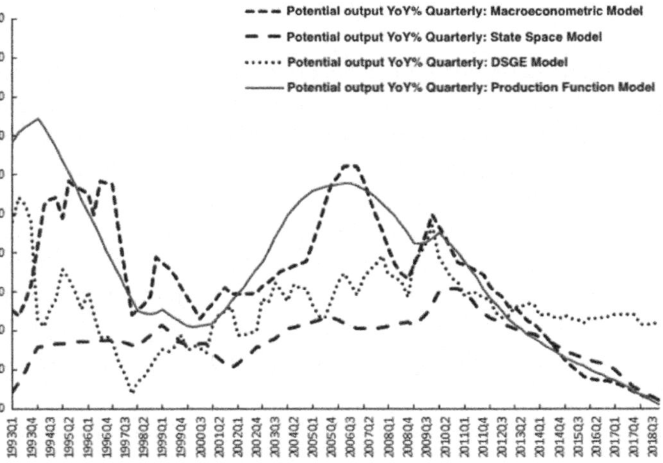

Fig. 1.1 Potential output trends estimated by different models

1.2.3.2 Weighted Average Analysis (1993–2018)

Next, by combining the estimation results of the above four methods, the average quarterly growth rate of China's potential output from 1993 to 2018 is obtained by weighted average (see Fig. 1.2).

I. *The overall trend and variation trend of potential output*

The estimates suggest that potential output growth averaged 9.4% between 1993 and 2018, slightly below the average 9.5% of real GDP. The average trend growth rate of total factor productivity (TFP) is 3.6%, and the average contribution rate to potential output is about 38.3%. For the year 2018, the annual growth rate of potential output is 6.4%, the output gap is about 0.2%, the TFP trend growth rate is 1.85%, and the contribution rate to potential output is about 30%. The trend growth rates of potential output and real GDP, output gap and total factor productivity in 1993–2018 are shown in Fig. 1.2.

On the whole, the trend change of China's potential output growth rate shows relatively clear periodic characteristics. This change is closely related to such factors as institutional reform, structural change, policy adjustment and the impact of the international financial crisis. The development trend of potential output is shown in Table 1.1.

Before the 2008 international financial crisis, the average growth rate of potential output was 10.4%. From 1993 to 1998, China's potential output declined year by year, from 11.5% in 1993 to about 8.4% in 1998, with an average annual growth rate of 10.9%. During this period the growth of potential output was slowed because, although there was a sharp increase in the scale of investment in the Chinese economy, this coincided with a decline in efficiency and the impact of the 1997 Asian financial crisis. From 1999 to 2007, the growth rate of potential output gradually picked up, with an average annual growth rate of 10.4%. Especially after China's accession to the WTO in 2001, with China's deepening integration into the global economic system there have been significant improvements to its management level and capital

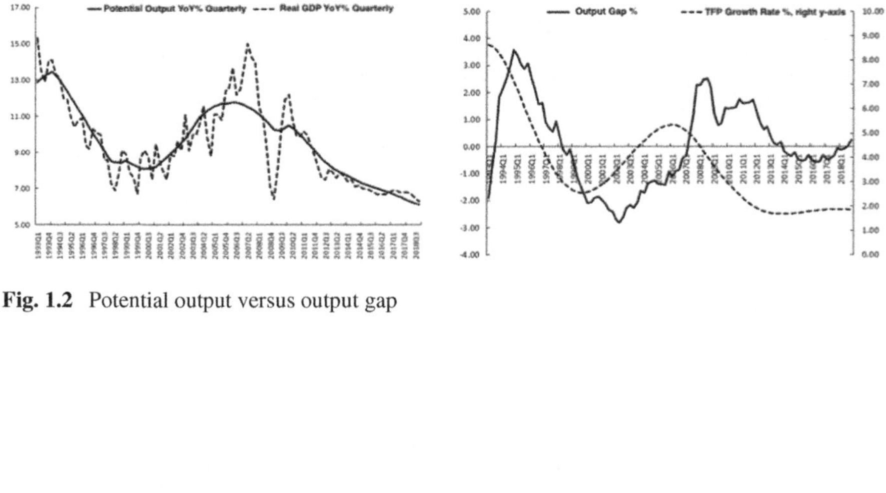

Fig. 1.2 Potential output versus output gap

Table 1.1 Growth rate of potential output and its drivers (It should be noted that because capital share α varies over time, boosting the aggregate does not equal potential output growth.)

									Units: %
	Average annual growth rate							To predict	
	1993–1998	1999–2007	2008–2012	2013–2018	Before the crisis of 2008	Post the 2008 crisis	Overall average from 1993 to 2018	2019–2024	2025–2029
Real GDP growth rate	11.3	10.1	9.7	7.3	10.6	8.1	9.5	5.6	4.6
Growth rate of potential output	10.9	10.4	10.3	7.1	10.4	8.2	9.4	5.5	4.6
Growth rate of labor input	1.1	0.8	0.4	0.3	0.9	0.3	0.6	0.2	0.1
Growth rate of capital input	11.4	12.1	14.2	10.9	11.6	12.0	11.7	7.5	5.8
TFP trend growth	5.5	4.3	2.8	1.9	4.7	2.1	3.6	1.9	2.3
Factors of potential output pull									
Labor input	0.6	0.4	0.2	0.1	0.5	0.1	0.3	0.1	0.1
Capital investment	4.9	5.6	6.9	5.2	5.3	5.9	5.6	3.5	2.6
TFP trend	5.6	4.1	2.8	1.8	4.7	2.3	3.7	1.8	2.1
Total factor pulling	11.0	10.1	9.9	7.1	10.4	8.3	9.5	5.4	4.8

utilization efficiency, and to the driving capacity of unit capital input to potential output.

After the 2008 crisis, the growth rate of potential output declined significantly. From 2008 to 2012, the annual growth rate was 10.3%. With the outbreak of the international financial crisis in 2008 and the profound adjustment of the world economy, China's economy faced continuous downward pressure. Supported by loose policies, the growth rate of potential output fluctuated downward, falling as low as around 8.3% in 2012. Since 2013, China's economy has shifted from one driven by factors to one driven by innovation. Coupled with the delayed impact of supply-side structural reform and other policies, the trend of potential output decline has slowed down. The average growth rate dropped gradually from 7.8% in 2013 to around 6.4% in 2018. Overall, the decline in potential output over the past decade has been pronounced.

II. *Analysis of potential output variation factors*

i. Overall change in potential output

Overall, from 1993 to 2018 capital input contributed 58.3% on average to potential output growth, labor input contributed 3.4%, and total factor productivity contributed 38.3% on average. Looking at different stages, the impact of capital input on potential output growth continued to increase. Before the 2008 financial crisis, China's potential output grew at an average rate of about 10.4%. The average contribution rate of real capital was about 50.8%, labor input was 4.4%, and TFP was 44.9%. After the financial crisis, the average growth rate of potential output decreased to 8.2%, and the average contribution rates of capital, labor and TFP were 71.1%, 1.8% and 27.1% respectively (see Fig. 1.3).

These results indicate that after the crisis, a great deal of attention was paid to the aggregation problem; TFP dropped sharply as a result of relying on high input; inefficient return sectors were increasing leverage, and the potential output growth rate was decreasing. Reversing this trend must rely on supply-side structural reform.

ii. Analysis of effective capital input decline

According to the capital accumulation equation, the change of capital stock is affected by the impact of capital formation efficiency, investment proprietary technology progress, and investment adjustment cost. The progress of investment proprietary technology (IST) is the technological innovation speed of the investment product production department. Different from neutral technological progress, the progress of investment proprietary technology is a trend impact process including unit root, which has a strong impact on capital formation and economic growth. Capital formation efficiency (MEI) reflects the ability of investment goods to form capital goods and be used in production. Although the efficiency of capital formation is a horizontal

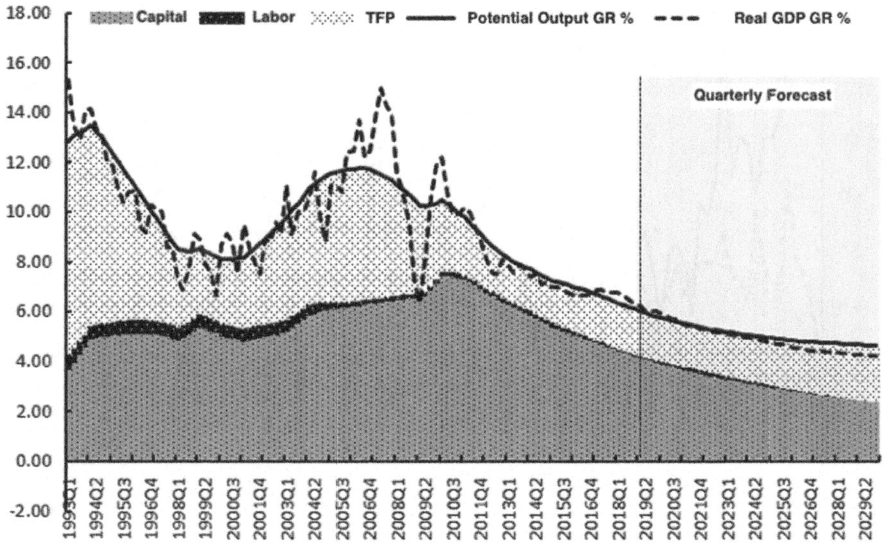

Fig. 1.3 Potential output and factor pull situation

impact, according to the DSGE estimation its impact is more persistent[4] and has a greater effect on the change of capital input.

According to the estimation and simulation results of the DSGE model (see Fig. 1.4), since 2011, China's capital formation efficiency and the progress of investment in proprietary technologies have both decreased significantly. In particular, the decline in capital formation has been larger, and of longer duration. The successive declines suggest that property investment grew rapidly between 2011 and 2013 as the government expanded infrastructure investment to cushion the impact of the financial crisis. Investment in infrastructure and real estate has a significant crowding out effect on other investment, especially manufacturing investment, and has resulted in a decline in the efficiency of capital formation and a slowdown in the growth of overall technological progress. From 2016 to 2018, although the growth of investment in real estate and infrastructure was restrained to some extent, the recovery of investment in manufacturing industry was slow, as seen especially in the sluggish growth of investment in private enterprises, small and micro enterprises and other small and medium-sized enterprises, which was not sufficient to become the main driving force of the economy.

In addition, the cost of investment adjustment reflects how difficult it is to adjust the investment structure. Generally speaking, the greater the change in investment growth rate, the higher the cost of investment adjustment will be, and the slower the growth of capital input. According to the DSGE model, the cost of China's capital adjustment has risen significantly in recent years.

[4]The autoregression coefficient of capital formation efficiency shock is $\rho_\mu = 0.91$.

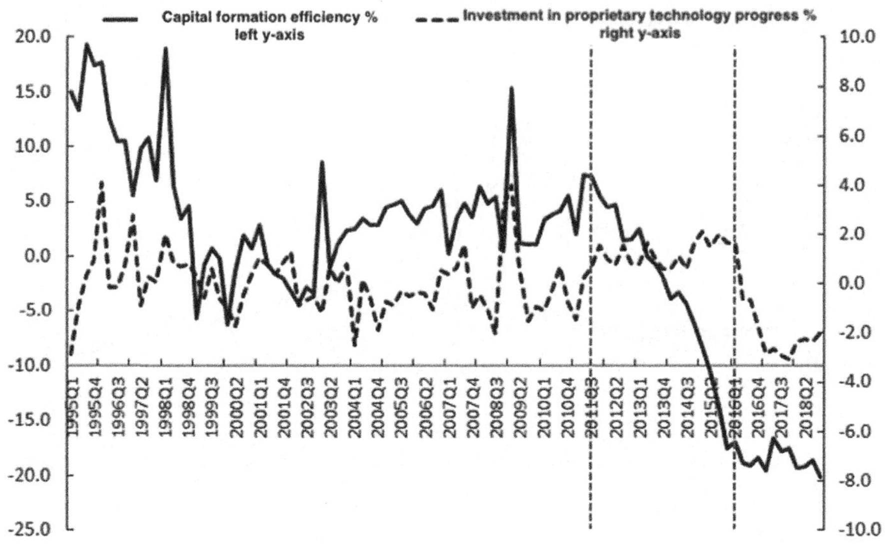

Fig. 1.4 Capital formation efficiency and investment in proprietary technology progress

iii. Change in effective labor input

According to the estimation results using the production method, the change of labor input in China is small and the contribution rate to the potential output growth is not high. Since the 2008 crisis, the low contribution rate of labor input to potential output has further exacerbated the downward trend of potential output (see Fig. 1.3). According to CBO estimates, the average contribution of effective labor input to potential output in the United States from 1950 to 2017 was 26%; it reached the lowest point in 2005, at over 5%, and since then it has been stable at around 5 to 6%, far higher than the average in China.

Meanwhile, the horizontal decomposition of the growth rate of labor input shows that the wage and price sticky shock before the crisis in 2008 accounted for nearly 50% of the growth rate of effective labor input, while the capital formation efficiency shock after the crisis mainly affected the growth rate of labor, and its explanatory power also exceeded 50%. From the decomposition of the fluctuation of labor input, it is clear that the capital formation efficiency and government expenditure have strong influence on effective labor in the short term. In the long run, wage stickiness, capital formation efficiency and investment proprietary technology progress have a great impact on the fluctuation of labor input (see Table 1.2). It can be seen that the decrease of capital formation efficiency and the change of investment proprietary technology have significant impact not just on capital input, but also on the change of effective labor input.

In addition, the effect of wage stickiness on labor input cannot be ignored. This further indicates that China's wage fluctuation is inelastic and the labor market search matching cost and adjustment cost are relatively high. Owing to these factors,

Table 1.2 Fluctuation decomposition of changes in labor input

Units: %

Labor input	Impact								
	Labor enhancement technique	Demand shock	Monetary policy shock	Wage sticky shock	MEI shock	Government spending	Price viscous shock	IST shock	Neutral technical shock
1st period	3.36	8.93	3.23	8.39	29.99	39.06	1.11	1.00	4.94
4th period	4.78	2.85	3.19	30.45	35.91	13.91	4.21	3.46	1.24
8th period	4.58	1.97	2.21	41.11	30.09	9.14	4.87	5.09	0.93
20th period	5.71	1.69	1.90	41.44	26.48	8.25	4.26	9.46	0.81

China's overall advantage in human resources has not been effectively played and fully utilized, while the prominent structural contradiction between labor market and labor supply and demand may be the main reason for the low contribution of labor input.

1.2.3.3 Trend Forecast of Potential Output (2019–2029)

According to the trend change of potential output and related factors, and under the condition that the macro policy environment remains basically stable, we forecast the trend of potential output and of related factors in the next 10 years according to the four models. In addition, we use weighted average to obtain the forecast of potential output and total factor productivity growth from 2019 to 2029 (Table 1.1 and Fig. 1.5).

The results show that without promoting supply-side structural reform, China's potential output growth will slow down in the next 10 years and gradually stabilize in the range of 4.8–5.1%, while maintaining the current economic structure and exogenous population trends. This highlights the necessity of supply-side structural reform. Only by promoting economic transformation and high-quality development can we reverse the downward trend of potential output growth.

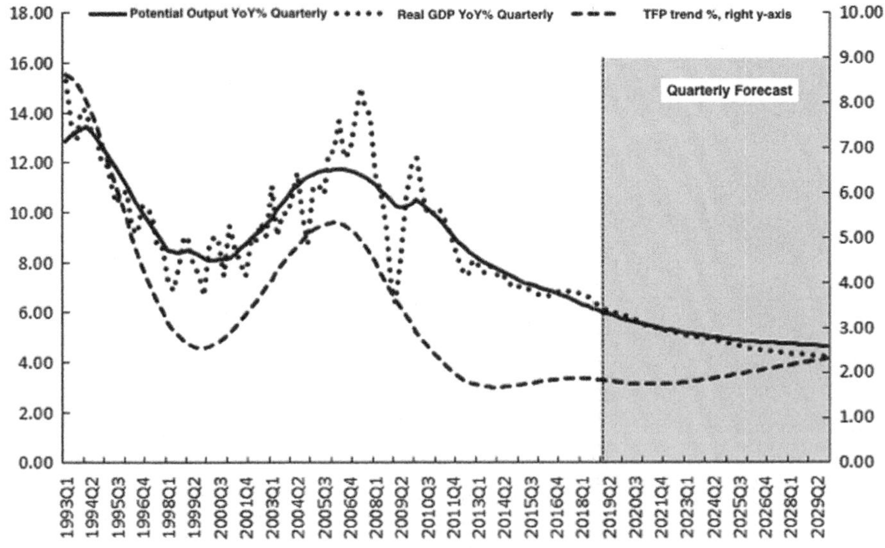

Fig. 1.5 Forecast of potential output and TFP growth trend in 2019–2029

1.2.4 Trends and Policy Recommendations for China's Potential Output

Based on the above analysis, four main conclusions can be drawn. First, from 1993 to 2018, China's potential output shows a trend of gradual slowdown, with an average growth rate of 9.4%. In more detail, the average growth rate of total factor productivity is 3.6%, that of capital input is 11.7%, labor input has an average growth rate of 0.6%, and the average contribution rate to the growth rate of potential output are 38.3%, 58.3% and 3.4% respectively. Second, in recent years, the slowdown of potential output growth is mainly caused by the failure of high investment to form effective capital, which leads to the continuous decline of the pulling force of effective capital input on potential output. However, the slow progress of investment in proprietary technology, the rising cost of investment adjustment, and the rapid decline of capital formation efficiency are the deep-seated reasons for the insufficient effective capital input and the slowdown of potential output. This is also the theoretical basis of supply-side structural reform. Third, the high cost of labor market search and the mismatch between supply and demand structure result in a low contribution rate of labor growth. China's population advantage is not fully utilized or effectively exerted, which has further aggravated the slowdown of potential output growth in recent years. Finally, if supply-side structural reform is not promoted, the average growth rate of China's potential output will continue to slow down in the next 5–10 years and will gradually stabilize in the range of 4.8 to 5.1%. Compared with developed economies, China still has a lot of room for potential output growth, especially in terms of labor input. High-quality economic development inevitably requires the promotion of supply-side structural reform, so as to improve the potential output growth rate by increasing TFP.

Therefore, we offer the following policy suggestions: First, more attention should be paid to improving the quality of investment and optimizing the investment structure in order to balance the short-term demand with the medium- and long-term reform goals. Second, the labor market and the quality of labor should be improved, the cost of searching and matching of employment subject should be reduced, the invalid supply should be reduced, and the contribution rate of labor input should be increased. Third, we need to strengthen institutional building, further promote supply-side structural reform, and boost total factor productivity. Fourth, in the face of potential output trend changes, monetary policy should pay attention to the identification of economic trend changes and cyclical fluctuations, maintain strategic focus, and improve the accuracy of macro policy response.

1.3 China's Economy Has Moved from High-Speed Growth to High-Quality Growth

As was pointed out in the report to the 19th national congress of the Chinese government, we are now in a new normal, and need to adopt a new concept of development. In line with Xi Jinping's economic theory of socialism with Chinese characteristics for a new era, we need to shift from high-speed growth to high-quality growth. To better understand this theory, it is necessary to grasp the background of the new normal, new development concept, and supply-side reform.

1.3.1 Background–New Normal, New Development Concept, Supply-Side Structural Reform

China's rapid economic growth depends on exports and investment. At the beginning of the twenty-first century, China launched its capital marketization reform, joined the WTO and began a process of urbanization. After 2007, as the subprime crisis triggered the global financial crisis, problems appeared in the external environment. In 2008, China launched a four trillion yuan (US$586 billion) economic stimulus package. After 2010, according to the calculation of Cai Fang, vice-president of the Chinese Academy of Social Sciences (CASS), China's demographic dividend disappeared and the economy reached the Lewis turning point. In 2013, China wanted to withdraw the stimulus launched in 2008, but due to the economic downturn, it entered a new round of stimulus. In the process, China's investment efficiency declined, and total factor productivity fell from around 4% to about 1%. One reason for this was the deterioration of the external economic environment, although that did start to improve from the end of 2015. Another was that, with the disappearance of the demographic dividend as China passed the Lewis turning point, it faced a new problem of aging population. In addition, the economy entered a transition period of total factor productivity decline. Responding to this situation, on December 10, 2013, in a speech delivered at the central economic work conference, Xi Jinping first proposed the "new normal." Then, on November 10, 2015, at the 11th meeting of the central leading group on financial and economics, he introduced the concept of supply-side structural reform. As a result, China has started to put into practice new development concepts to drive the next round of economic development.

1.3.2 Reform is a Combination of Bottom-Up and Top-Down

As we move from high growth to high-quality growth, we cannot dismiss everything that has gone before. Economic reform must be both bottom-up and top-down. Rather than focusing simply on finance, it is crucial to recognize the need for fiscal and tax reform, without which it will be impossible for China to achieve the two centenary goals. Moreover, we need to ensure that we are not satisfied with temporary solutions to problems, but instead identify and tackle the root causes. Just as, in the case of environmental protection, relevant departments should enforce laws strictly and not just make surprise inspections when there is serious pollution, so the reform of fiscal and tax systems requires the establishment of a system that not only arouses the enthusiasm of local governments, but also can be successful in the context of a unified big market. China is a large and diverse country; problems vary from place to place, and we cannot solve them all according to a single standard. For example, with regard to pension reform, we need to recognize that living standards and costs vary from place to place. In northwest China, a person needs only 1,000 yuan a year to maintain a basic living standard, far less than in Beijing or Shanghai. Therefore, the benchmark for reform should be determined according to the local situation, and not one universal standard. The discussion should start from the reality, not from the book.

In the early days of China's reform and opening up, the central government had a tight budget and left it up to local governments to explore new practices. The household contract responsibility system was a bottom-up innovation introduced by Xiaogang village in Anhui province. However, owing to the mishandling of relations between the central and local governments, many local initiatives have not received sufficient support. If this situation is not addressed, the result will be chaos; yet if the government does step in, it could lead to the death of local initiatives. At the current stage of development we need to give full play to the initiative of local governments, while also establishing a unified market; only with these conditions in place will China be able to shift from high-speed growth to high-quality growth. Take the development of the three northeastern provinces as an example. At present, we have implemented a balance of land allocation and subsidy. In places with developed manufacturing industries, such as the Pearl River Delta and the Yangtze River Delta, the land around cities is increasingly polluted, and is no longer suitable for agricultural production. Consequently, although there is a large amount of farmland around Beijing, Shanghai and other big cities, these lands are not actually used for agricultural production. Yet while capital and labor are now market-based, land is still controlled by plans. Because the supposedly "agricultural" land around big cities cannot be used for development, the real estate and land supply problems continue to worsen. If we were to establish a national unified land market of dynamic balance, to offset cultivated land used for other purposes, then through a system of market transactions land use could be optimized according to local conditions: land in the eastern region could be used for urbanization, while that in the northeast could be reserved for agricultural production. We must give full play to the comparative advantages of the three northeastern provinces, which are not state-owned enterprises but fertile farmland. In other words, we should solve the competition between regions through unified market thinking. The alternative, simply raising taxes on the rich and then transferring payments to the poor through the financial sector, does not allow the market to play a decisive role.

To take another example, after the events of July 2009, Xinjiang stood in urgent need of development. However, we need to consider carefully what might be the best way to achieve this. Xinjiang's biggest advantage is energy. If a national carbon quota market were to be established and Xinjiang was to develop clean energy, its carbon quota could be sold and the development problem solved through marketization. The national development and reform commission is also pushing for a national carbon trading market, but the plan has not yet been fully unveiled. In fact, it is perfectly possible to solve other problems through the market, not necessarily through the hand of the government.

In conclusion, China's shift from high-speed growth to high-quality growth must encompass two crucial features. On the one hand, we need to take full advantage of China's unified market, which has been reflected in many aspects, such as high-speed rail and online shopping. On the other hand, China's regional gap is very large. Therefore, we must facilitate and support regional initiatives and give full play to regions' comparative advantages on the basis of the single market.

1.3.3 Modernization of the National Governance System is Key to the Transformation from High-Speed Economic Growth to High-Quality Growth

The transition from high growth to high-quality growth is happening in an open economy. At the heart of the transition is, first and foremost, capital. Capital comprises two aspects: FDI and private investment. As emphasized in the report to the 19th national congress, China must develop a multi-tiered capital market. Currently, China's financial market contains too much fake capital; that is, debt. As Adam Smith pointed out more than 300 years ago, spending your own money is most efficient. If China is to attract capital, and especially high-quality capital, it must ensure institutional confidence. We need to improve our institutions and our entire economic system through reform and opening up. In particular, as emphasized recently, we need to protect private entrepreneurs and private capital, so as to ensure a macro-stable investment environment. After capital, the second crucial factor is talent. If we continue to destroy the environment to develop our economy, we risk being unable to attract the talent we need. Therefore, we require a new development philosophy to understand the transition from high growth to high-quality growth.

Recently, there has been a great deal of discussion about the US tax cut, and how China might respond. In nominal terms, America's tax burden has fallen from 35 to 20% or 21%. China's is now only 25%, which is not very high. On the other hand, some have argued that the burden on Chinese companies is heavy, and as Cao Dewang[5] has pointed out, utilities such as water and electricity, which are not supplied

[5]Cao Dewang is the Chairman of Fuyao Glass Industry Group Co., Ltd. The Fuyao Group, founded in 1987 in Fuzhou, China, is a large multinational company specializing in the manufacture of automobile safety glass and industrial technical glass.

by state-owned enterprises, are expensive. Moreover, China's land is monopolized, and the factor market is severely distorted, leading to high land costs. This is why the central economic work conference has called for deepening reform in key areas. By reforming water, electricity and gas, and establishing long-term mechanisms in the real estate sector, we can reduce the burden on enterprises. Without such reforms, tax cuts alone will not solve the real problem.

To understand development in an open environment, I would like to turn to another topic. Each year, the World Bank releases a report about doing business in 190 countries. In 2008, China ranked 86 for ease of doing business, improving only marginally to 78 in both 2016 and 2017. In 2012, China was ranked as low as 99. According to the report released on October 31st, 2018, China had leapt to 48th place, an indication of the dramatic improvements to its business environment over the past year, and of the remarkable success of the reform and opening up of its financial industry.

As reported one of a former deputy director of the state administration of taxation, the financial sector accounts for a high proportion of GDP, and does not serve SMEs, it is difficult and expensive for SMEs to obtain financing. In my view finance is a mirror image of the real economy, and many distortions in the real economy are reflected in finance. In recent years the disappearance of the demographic dividend, deterioration of the environment, and excessive investment have resulted in a decline in the total factor productivity and a drop in the potential growth rate, yet the government continues to pursue rapid growth. In this situation, it is inevitable that people will chase money, and this supply of funds will stimulate the real estate and infrastructure sectors, leading to rising prices and higher profits for the financial sector, with a consequent increase in its share of GDP. At the same time, as local governments, state-owned enterprises and the real estate industry all go after capital, this inevitably has a crowding out effect on small and medium-sized enterprises and the private economy. To solve this problem, GDP targets must be watered down and financial institutions allowed to set market prices based on costs and risks. While the government can take certain steps to ease the situation, such as setting up guarantee companies to guarantee loans to small and medium-sized enterprises, in general the problem of difficult and expensive financing for SMEs should be solved by the market. The key lies in the reports of the 18th and 19th national congresses of the Chinese government, which call for "letting the market play a decisive role" and "letting the government play a better role."

China's financial industry has made some achievements, but there remain serious problems. Comprehensive management and the contradiction between the separate industry supervision, financial industry development and supervision confuse. Each sector has its own self-interest and lacks the big picture, resulting in fragmented bond markets, and different regulatory standards and regulatory arbitrage. Financial enterprises, like general industrial and commercial enterprises, should follow a process of birth, aging, illness and death, but there is not yet any smooth exit mechanism for China's financial institutions. For example, Hainan Development Bank has been bankrupt for more than 20 years, but the absence of an exit mechanism means that the liquidation team still has access to loans from the central bank, which poses great moral hazard. To strengthen supervision and regulatory accountability, we must first ensure the authenticity of capital. Moreover, we must ensure that supervision is conducted properly and in full, and strictly in accordance with the regulatory rules. It should also be borne in mind that there is a great deal of difference between monopoly and competition. At present, there is a problem with regard to regulatory competition in financial regulation, where the China Deposit Insurance Corporation has no right to punish. If there is competition with regulatory authorities, the regulatory effectiveness will be greatly strengthened. Here, the key problem is how to implement the regulatory rules.

In the years ahead, deleveraging will become an increasingly important issue. Adding leverage is a long-term process, and deleveraging should be gradual. From the perspective of the financial market, after the announcement of the measures on capital management, the funds did not flow to the standard market (bond market, inter-bank market), but to the non-standard market, which shows that financial institutions are still increasing leverage. Because the non-standard market does not need to extract the corresponding capital and provisions, its continued prosperity shows that the financial industry has not taken the initiative to deleverage. Deleveraging in the real economy is easier to solve. For example, some infrastructure projects will be stopped, local government assets will not expand, debt will not expand, or assets will be sold to repay debt. State-owned enterprises can solve some problems through mixed reform and debt-for-equity swap. How the financial industry deleverages has a lot to do with the incentive mechanism of financial institutions and corporate governance. Lack of clarity in corporate governance is the reason why financial institutions are not actively deleveraging. The incentive mechanism of financial institutions is still profit-oriented, with no consideration of capital constraints or the principle of prudent operation. The fact that many problems of banks have been discovered not by regulators and shareholders, but by the national audit office and central leading group for inspection work, shows that there are failings in the corporate governance of banks, confusion as to who are the ultimate investors, and no clear distinction between supervision and development.

The key to transformation from high-speed growth to high-quality growth is to modernize China's governance system and capacity. This is reflected in various aspects, including the above mentioned relationship between central finance and local finance, reform of regulatory system and corporate governance of financial institutions. If we are to achieve the two centenary goals identified in the report to the 19th national congress of the Chinese government, we have a long way to go and a lot of work to do.

1.3.4 Development to High Quality Depends on Institutional Competition

To achieve the transition from high-speed growth to high-quality development, the core task is to modernize national governance. As noted previously, the rapid growth of China's economy and its shift from high-speed growth to high-quality development have been achieved in an open environment, where capital and talent are crucial factors. As such, these factors should be guaranteed by the system.

It is important to stress that "capital" is not the same as "fund." For a long time after the reform and opening up, the lack of financial capital did indeed cause problems for China's economy. We have solved the problem of financing development mainly by introducing FDI, holding down wages to curb consumption, and reducing the gap between workers and peasants. But China is not short of capital per se. Rather, it is short of capital that can really take risks. Since the reform and opening up, China's economic and financial system is actually conducive to the expansion of scale, the input of factors and the promotion of GDP growth. On the one hand, with regard to GDP, when looking to develop the economy local government starts by conceiving a project, then sets up the financing platform. Rather than relying on its own capital, it usually turns to government recessive guarantee bonds or loan financing. Yet regardless of financing guarantees, the industrial fund, or the government service to buy, the real situation is that local governments are amassing debt. In the absence of capital constraints, efficiency will not improve. On the other hand, Chinese financial enterprises do not follow a profit-centered modern corporate governance model. If a financial institution fails to lend money to state-owned enterprises and local financing platforms, this will have little impact on the immediate interests of managers. Conversely, if loans to private enterprises go wrong, they may be held accountable for the transfer of profits. However, in the enterprise with perfect corporate governance, the management layer must be responsible for the interests of shareholders, and the enterprise behavior should be conducted around profit. Due to the lack of capital that can bear risks in a real sense, there is still a gap in the corporate governance of financial enterprises, which leads to the problem of rigid payment. Without an effective risk sharing mechanism, the financial market is bound to expand blindly due to increasing leverage.

A qualified and highly skilled workforce is the second crucial factor, and is the key to competitiveness. General Secretary Xi Jinping has got to the root of the problem. Indeed, three of the strategies put forward in the 19th national congress's report is actually related to human resources, namely the strategy to rejuvenate the country through science and education, the strategy to strengthen the country through human resources, and the strategy of innovation-driven development. Attracting and developing talent are not primarily about infrastructure hardware, but more about public service software such as education, health care, housing, social security and the rule of law. In recent years, the development of Chinese universities has focused on size rather than quality, which has led more and more Chinese to send their children abroad for education. However, foreign education is a short-term way to train talents for China. In the long run, it is necessary to reform our education system to better adapt to the needs of moving from high-speed growth to high-quality development. In addition, entrepreneurship is closely related to talent. Following the 19th national congress of the Chinese government, we have taken a number of important measures, including emphasizing the protection of private capital and bringing new cases against private entrepreneurs to trial. This will create a stable environment for entrepreneurs to develop and create an atmosphere conducive to attracting talents and encouraging entrepreneurship.

The key to the transition from high-speed growth to high-quality development and international competition is institutional competition. Under open conditions, both capital and talents are mobile, and only by truly improving the system and mechanism can we better attract and maintain these crucial components so as to remain invincible in international competition.

In summary, to move from high-speed growth to high-quality development, China needs to modernize its governance. The socialist market economy is conducive to achieving common prosperity, avoiding polarization, paying more attention to medium- and long-term development strategies, and promoting coordinated social development. The key to building confidence in the four areas is to improve our systems and mechanisms, better attract capital and talents, and allow full play to the strengths of our system.

Chapter 2
Transformation of China's National Governance Framework

2.1 Modernization of China's National Governance System

Since the 18th national congress of the Chinese government, with comrade Xi Jinping at its core, has been observing the general trend, identifying the overall situation and taking practical action to manage China's continuing economic development. The steps taken range from proposing the "new normal" of economic development and promoting a new development concept, to deepening supply-side structural reform and overseeing the transition from high-speed economic growth to high-quality development. Xi Jinping's *Thought on Socialism with Chinese Characteristics for a New Era* is not only the theoretical crystallization of China's economic development over the past five years, but also the guiding ideology for China's economic work in the new era.

Finance, the lifeblood of the modern economy and the link connecting its various sectors, is a crucial component of modern governance. The financial theory of socialism with Chinese characteristics should be placed within the overall framework of thought on the socialist economy with Chinese characteristics in the new era. We should take serving the real economy as both starting point and goal, meet the demand for high-quality development, follow the new development philosophy, better leverage our role in modernizing China's governance system and capacity, deepen the reform of the financial system, and provide strong support for the two-step strategy. To do our financial work well in the new era and current stage of development, reform is the key. We must uphold both the socialist system and the reform direction of the socialist market economy. To do so, we must strengthen the ability of financial services to serve the real economy, while respecting the general rules of financial market development. In addition to solving the problems in domestic economic and financial operation, we must also fully recognize the decisive role of institutional competition in the context of economic and financial globalization. At the same time, we need to have top-level design and maintain a unified national market. We should also encourage pilot projects at the grassroots level. While the

Z. Xu, *Keep Reforming: China's Strategic Economic Transformation*,
https://doi.org/10.1007/978-981-15-8006-2_2

successful experience of China's reform and opening-up offers a valuable basis for future development, we should also draw lessons from previous reform. In order to solve the problems associated with the early stage of reform, such as lack of top-level design, excessive reliance on short-term administrative measures, and low tolerance for "trial and error," we need to deepen the reform in terms of improving the system and mechanism, establishing a sound long-term mechanism, and forming a favorable reform atmosphere.

2.1.1 Finance Serves the Real Economy

The report to the 19th congress of the Chinese government pointed out that "Socialism with Chinese characteristics has entered a new era. The principal contradiction facing Chinese society has evolved. What we now face is the contradiction between unbalanced and inadequate development and the people's ever-growing needs for a better life." Furthermore, "China's economy has been transitioning from a phase of rapid growth to a stage of high-quality development." Therefore, "We must put quality first and give priority to performance. We should pursue supply-side structural reform as our main task, and work hard for better quality, higher efficiency, and more robust drivers of economic growth through reform." In this context, finance takes serving the real economy as its fundamental starting point and foothold, and the adaptive transformation of China's financial system to the new stage of development is an inevitable requirement for high-quality development.

During the stage of rapid economic growth, financial services for the real economy focused mainly on "scale" and "quantity." At that time, the main contradiction in the financial field was between the demand for economic growth and the limited capital stock. Therefore, the main tasks for the finance sector were to mobilize savings, encourage capital accumulation, and promote economic growth. From an academic perspective, traditional western economics assumes that the three major mechanisms of financial effect on economic growth are all based on scale. First, Gurley and Shaw (1955) proposed that financial institutions use information advantages to reduce transaction costs, avoid liquidity risks and individual risks, and promote the transformation of idle social savings into productive capital, thus expanding the scale of capital formation. Second, according to Goldsmith, financial institutions can accumulate capital more efficiently by reducing information acquisition and supervision costs, optimizing resource allocation, and allocating savings to high-yield investment projects. Finally, McKinnon and Shaw pointed out that financial development could boost savings rates and promote economic growth. Chinese financial research also considers the overall contradiction and emphasizes the total balance, so as to make the supply of capital better serve capital demand. This is exemplified in the "comprehensive balance of fiscal credit" proposed by Huang Da. From the perspective of policy practice, we should recognize the importance of the "scale effect" of financial promotion of economic growth, give proper weight to the scale indicators of financial services, such as M2 and aggregate financing, and set annual targets for these indicators as an important measure of the financial services real economy. In our report on the work of the government, we set annual targets for M2 growth and credit growth, and dual targets for the growth rate of M2 and of social financing scale in 2016 and 2017. From 2007 to 2017, the annual growth rate of M2 was 15.3%, and the annual growth rate of aggregate financing was 17.7%.

As the economy has entered the phase of high quality development, the main contradiction in the financial field has also changed, to that between the demand for financial services for high-quality economic development and the shortage of effective financial supply. This reflects an imbalance in the supply structure, whereby capital is generally abundant, but there is little capital available to take risks effectively. Short-term investment is greater than long-term investment. While the amount of social financing is not insignificant, there is no efficient mechanism to guide the flow of capital effectively. Capital tends to favor large enterprises and large projects, crowding out the financing of small and medium-sized enterprises. Therefore, in line with the transition of economic development from scale expansion to transformation of quality, efficiency, and power, financial development should shift the focus from "scale" to "quality," and the financial function should be expanded from the traditional "mobilization of savings, facilitating transactions, and resource allocation" to "corporate governance, information disclosure, and risk management."

From the perspective of academic development, according to the theory of "financial deepening" put forward by McKinnon and Shaw, there are three levels of financial deepening. The first is financial growth, that is, the expansion of financial scale. The second level is the gradual optimization of financial products and institutions. At the third and final level, the gradual improvement of the financial market (price) mechanism enables the optimal allocation of financial resources. According to the theory of "financial function" (Levine 1997; Merton et al. 1992), in the early stage, financial function was mainly embodied in mobilizing savings, facilitating transactions, and resource allocation. As economic development raised new demands on the financial system, its functions expanded to include corporate governance, information disclosure, and risk management. These expanding financial functions further promoted economic growth, thus forming a virtuous circle of economic and financial development. From the perspective of policy practice, the 2018 government work report has lowered the quantitative growth targets of GDP, M2, and aggregate financing, such that "the main expected target for this year's development is to increase GDP by around 6.5%." Furthermore, while the 2017 government work report stated the intention to "strive for better results in actual work," that text does not appear in the 2018 report. We will maintain an appropriate increase in the broad money supply (M2), credit and social financing.

To ensure high quality development, finance should pay close attention to capital flow. In the early stage of economic development, the allocation of financial resources was typically characterized by loose aggregate and extensive structure, and more funds were flowing into capital intensive industries such as infrastructure and real estate, or even industries with excess production capacity. As the economy enters the stage of high-quality development, and the proportion taken up by the service industry increases, technological progress and total factor productivity have become important driving forces for economic growth. The allocation of financial resources should be gradually transformed into a stable aggregate and optimized structure, and the attention to capital flow and capital allocation efficiency should be further enhanced. According to the "optimal financial structure theory" proposed and demonstrated by Justin Yifu Lin (2009), only when the structure of the financial system matches the optimal industrial structure of the real economy can the function of the financial system be effectively exerted and the development of the real economy promoted. This raises a number of questions: With the continuous deepening of supply-side structural reform, does China's financial system structure match the economic structure in terms of its transformation and upgrading? In an increasingly rich and complex financial system, where does money go? Is the money flowing into the real economy? Have the financing needs of "small and micro," "agriculture, rural areas," and other weak links in society and private enterprises been effectively met? Will green credit be enough to support green economy development? Has the proportion of direct financing in the real economy increased? In the current transitional stage of promoting high-quality economic growth, it is worth paying more attention to these economic structure changes and to the evolution of the financial system in response to them.

High-quality development requires that monetary policy be stable and neutral, and that the shift from quantitative to price-based regulation be accelerated. From the perspective of monetary policy orientation, in the stage of high-quality development we should not only prevent aggregate demand from falling too fast in the short term, but also ensure that central bank liquidity provision does not solidify structural distortions or push up debt and leverage levels. Deleveraging is a futile exercise, while money must be subject to proper controls. Only a sound monetary policy can create an appropriate environment for supply-side structural reform and high-quality development. Only by downplaying quantity indicators such as M2 and aggregate financing can we truly downplay GDP growth targets and focus on quality instead of scale. With regard to monetary policy, there are currently problems and challenges in China's financial market, such as the micro-subject of supply and demand, the financial supervision system, and the development of the financial market. In the process of transition to price control, the monetary policy will still have to depend on quantity control to some extent. At the same time, we should be strengthening macroprudential policy, to ensure smooth development of, for example, financial stability and output prices. However, it should be fully recognized that excessive reliance on quantitative regulation will reduce the efficiency of interest rate transmission and the effect of monetary policy regulation (Ma Jun and Wang Honglin 2014). In order to meet the policy requirements of high-quality economic development, it is necessary to vigorously promote the development of the financial market and to accelerate the transformation of monetary policy to price-oriented regulation.

To serve the real economy, we must develop financial markets to support innovative development. In recent decades, there has been a global trend whereby "scientific and technological innovation begins with technology and becomes through capital." In traditional competitive industries, the technology is stable and investors can easily get real information and reach consensus. A financial intermediary verifies that the enterprise information is correct, so the financial intermediary is superior to the capital market. However, in scientific and technological innovation industries and a few natural monopoly industries, the production technology is subject to sudden change, and there are big differences among investors. For many investors it is necessary to verify the enterprise information multiple times, so the capital market is better than financial intermediaries. Recent economic studies have pointed out that equity financing is the most important external financing method for enterprise research and development (Brown et al. 2012). Hsu et al. (2013) conducted an empirical analysis based on 31-year data of 23 economies and found that for technology-intensive industries that rely on external financing, the more developed the equity financing of a country is, the more likely it is to promote the development of industrial innovation, while the boom of bank credit inhibits industrial innovation. On the other hand, with regard to the development and improvement of existing technology, indirect financing is more suitable. Consequently, while economies in which indirect finance is dominant, such as Germany and France, focus mainly on mature enterprise technology and technology improvement, the US, where equity finance plays a bigger role, has produced more new technology innovation enterprises (Hirsch-Kreinsen 2011). In recent years, China's financial system has not been short of money, but it has lacked financial capital. Rigid payment, open stock real debt and other problems distort the financial market, and capital cannot be effectively allocated to a large number of truly innovative small and medium enterprises (SMEs). Only when the financial market forms a relatively complete capital investment mechanism and supporting intermediary service system, will it be able to accelerate the transformation of scientific and technological innovation achievements into real productive forces, and promote scientific and technological innovation and entrepreneurship enterprises from scratch, from small to large, thus enhancing economic vitality and forming a new economic growth point.

In order to balance the relationship between innovation and regulation, an effective system of inclusive finance is needed. Based on a combination of government guidance and market leadership, China's inclusive finance has made remarkable achievements in terms of account penetration, savings penetration, micro-payments, and credit. A system of multi-tiered and wide-coverage inclusive financial institutions and products is already in place. In recent years, we have made the use of digital technology the focus of our policy to promote the development of inclusive finance. Under the initiative and promotion of the Chinese government, the G20 Hangzhou Summit adopted the G20 high-level principles on digital financial inclusion. In future we will need to give priority to solving the financial problem of the digital divide; resolutely combat illegal activities carried out under the cloak of inclusive finance; strengthen big data in the context of data security and privacy protection; establish a consumer protection system under responsible management; strengthen the construction of the basic regulatory system, including making up for the current shortage of supervision; balance good innovation with regulation; and guide development of the inclusive finance specification. At the same time, to promote the development of inclusive finance and financial poverty alleviation, we should ensure the sustainable development of finance and ensure that inclusive finance does not assume other financial functions.

In recent years, the design of some reform plans in the field of financial inclusion practice has been unscientific and unreasonable, with multiple conflicting objectives and vague focus. Moreover, administrative restraining measures have led to regulatory arbitrage, so that the implementation effect of reform has been quite different from the original intention. For example, to meet the goal of strengthening financial services for small and micro businesses, financial institutions are required not only to increase the supply of credit to those businesses, but also to prevent and control risks, prevent the rise of non-performing assets, and keep interest rates low. These three major requirements can hardly be met at the same time. Under such constraints, financial institutions have very little incentive to provide credit to small and micro enterprises. Consequently, a large part of the so-called "low interest" credit for small and micro businesses has actually flowed to local government financing platforms and the real estate market in the name of policy support. Meanwhile, the main obstacle to financing for small and micro enterprises is the availability of finance. To increase their access to finance, it is necessary to increase the tolerance of risk and the loan interest rate risk premium. Of course, the government can directly subsidize small and micro enterprises.

China must also develop green finance. By internalizing the externalities of ecological and environmental impacts through market-oriented means, we will be able to achieve the goal of reducing polluting economic activities. In guidelines issued in 2016, China sketched the top-level design of its green financial policy framework. From a policy perspective, it is a prerequisite to clarify "green" standards, a key to promote sustainable development and to explore green financial innovation, a method to combine top-level design with grassroots exploration, and a bottom line to effectively prevent risks. In the next step, we need to encourage green credit, green bonds, and the innovation and development of green financial products; support the development of carbon financial market products, for example through promoting industry environmental risk stress tests and risk quantitative tools for green investment and financing; encourage and support the conditional place through the professional green guarantee mechanism; set up a green development fund, and move more social capital to invest in green industry. In addition, we should develop a green index and related products, promote a mandatory green insurance system, and establish a mandatory environmental information disclosure system. The establishment of a unified national carbon quota trading market should also be explored. Under such a market framework, some regions, such as Xinjiang, will be able to develop clean energy and carbon sink industries, transfer carbon quota through a unified carbon quota trading market, and obtain funds for economic development through marketization.

2.1.2 *The Financial System and Its Functions Should Be Embedded in the Modernization of the National Governance System*

2.1.2.1 In the Context of Economic and Financial Globalization, International Competition is Essentially Institutional Competition

In an environment of economic and financial globalization and increasing openness, the mobility of capital and labor has been greatly increased. Countries with better systems and mechanisms can better attract capital and talents, realize the accumulation of production factors, and seize competitive advantages. The competitiveness of the system is embodied in vitality, efficiency, and resilience. Here, vitality means that the initiative of the micro-subject can be mobilized and exerted to the maximum extent; efficiency means that social resources can be allocated scientifically and reasonably, while resilience is the ability to withstand shocks and to self-repair. At present, many countries are pushing for structural reform. Whoever is more successful in reform and has a more competitive system will stand out in the future international competition.

Finance is the lifeblood of the real economy, and to a large extent the competitiveness of the financial system determines the competitiveness of the economic system. As an important part of the national governance system, financial governance should include a number of aspects: First of all, the market-oriented interest rate system plays a decisive role in the allocation of resources, and the market-oriented interest rate can be "released, formed and adjusted." The exchange rate should be fully flexible, effectively maintaining the balance of international payments and the independence of monetary policy. Second, a multi-level financial market system featuring uniform rules, transparent information, breadth, and depth, can effectively meet diversified demands for investment, financing, and risk management. Third, financial institutions should have sound corporate governance and internal risk control mechanisms. Fourth, the financial regulation and control system should be professional, robust, effective, and suitable for the development of a modern market economy under the conditions of opening up, while keeping to the bottom line that no systemic financial risks will occur.

Finance and the real economy mirror each other. The prominent problems and challenges existing in China's real economy, such as zombie enterprises, high leverage, local government debt, and real estate price bubbles, have developed due to the accumulation and exposure of long-term internal contradictions in the economic operation; at the same time, they explain the failure of the financial system to fully perform its functions in the national governance system. We should adhere to a problem-oriented approach and give full play to the role of financial governance in addressing the "grey rhino" problem in key areas of China, so as to serve the transformation of the real economy and the improvement of total factor productivity and competitiveness. To give better play to financial management in the national governance system, it will be necessary to consider and manage the relationships between the government and the market, between finance and banking, between deleveraging and improving corporate governance, between financial risk prevention and governance mechanism improvement, and between an aging population, pension sustainability, and the asset markets.

2.1.2.2 The Relationship Between Government and Market

In recent years, China's economic development has entered a new normal, with structural problems such as overcapacity and high leverage ratio becoming increasingly apparent. These phenomena are due to China's long reliance on Keynesian economic policies. In the hope of stimulating growth through positive macro-control, the government used incremental expansion rather than market resources allocation to absorb the inventory contradiction, which hindered the process of independent market clearing and created certain structural contradictions. In the wake of the 2008 global financial crisis, China launched a four trillion yuan investment stimulus program, which led to a global recovery. Nevertheless, over-reliance on aggregate demand management to maintain macroeconomic stability destroys the market mechanism in terms of information, motivation, resource allocation, and income distribution, while it also hinders the government from playing a better role in compensating for market failures. The overall result is slow progress in institutional building and a growing number of structural problems.

First, the high leverage ratio is a comprehensive reflection of the structural contradiction intensified by excessive stimulus. In China, the leverage ratio has been rising rapidly. In particular, the leverage ratio of non-financial enterprises is a serious problem, and the risks are concentrated in local government financing platforms and state-owned enterprises. The financial sector is also seeing an increase in leverage ratio, which carries hidden risks. The problem of leverage ratio is closely related to the long-term development of short-term stimulus policies. In an environment of excessive pursuit of GDP, state-owned enterprises and local government financing platforms blindly expand the scale of assets and fail to replenish capital in time. In some cases, fundraising projects that promise a fixed payout, and are therefore effectively debt, are actually classified as equity. All of these behaviors, along with a tendency to overdraw on government credit, contribute to the rising leverage ratio.

Second, zombie enterprises are the inevitable result of lax regulation and weak macro-regulation. The term "zombie enterprises" was first used in the context of Japan's long stagnation, where banks continued to provide financial support for highly inefficient and debt-ridden enterprises (zombie enterprises), thus creating the conditions for the "lost decade" of the Japanese economy (Hoshi and Kashyap 2004; Ahearne and Shinada 2005; Jaskowski 2015). Lax monetary policy and financial regulation are important factors in the formation and survival of zombie enterprises. Under the condition of low interest rates, banks can offer more favorable terms, making it easier for highly indebted enterprises to pay interest, and masking the fact that their business conditions are deteriorating. Meanwhile, banks engage in "zombie lending," offering "blood transfusion" loans to enterprises in the full knowledge that those businesses do not have the ability to repay, while hoping to delay the exposure of non-performing assets through continued loans.

In recent years, the concept of zombie enterprises has been introduced into the research and analysis of China's overcapacity industries. Such enterprises are rigid and "undead," which is the direct cause of continuous overcapacity, difficult market clearing, and reduced economic vitality (He Fan 2016). Tan Yuyan et al. (2017) point out that zombie enterprises are crowding out other enterprises, especially private enterprises, which may be an important reason behind the weakness of private investment in recent years.

Furthermore, just as the enterprise sector has not cleared the market, neither has the financial sector. Hainan Development Bank, which went bankrupt in 1998, has yet to complete bankruptcy liquidation, and the asset gap is still growing. This shows that the financial institutions market withdrawal mechanism has not yet been fully established, and there is still a reliance on administrative intervention and controls. Moreover, the main body of financial ecology "evolution" natural rules have not yet been fully formed. Consequently, there remain weaknesses with regard to the market clearing of the financial system and the corporate governance of financial institutions, which together have a detrimental impact on the financial system efficiency. Now that the deposit insurance system has been established, it is necessary to explore the establishment of a market exit mechanism for financial institutions: in an efficient financial system, only the fittest should survive. We must also strengthen external constraints on corporate governance of financial institutions, and promote their prudent and sound operation.

Third, excessive use of stimulus policies solidifies structural contradictions, while also creating problems such as reduced efficiency and a widening of the gap between rich and poor. Stimulus policies have a strong impact on the expansion of investment in state-owned enterprises, while private investment is more about "crowding out" rather than "crowding in." As a result, there is an obvious mismatch between the rate of return on investment and the growth rate of investment, which reduces the efficiency of resource allocation. Another consequence of the overuse of stimulus policies is the rise in asset prices, which further widens the gap between rich and poor, a phenomenon that is clearly incompatible with the goal of building a moderately prosperous society in all respects. According to the 2015 Report on the Development of Chinese People's Livelihood, published by the Chinese Social Science Survey Center of Peking University, in 2012 the Gini coefficient of net household wealth in China reached 0.73, with the top 1% of households owning more than one third of the country's wealth, while the bottom 25% owned only about 1% of the total wealth.

2.1.2.3 The Relationship Between Fiscal and Financial

The institutional arrangement of the relationship between fiscal matters, managed by the Ministry of Finance, and financial matters, regulated by the central bank, is at the core of the modern economic system. As China is still in the transition period of perfecting the socialist market economy, there remains an imbalance between the two, as shown in the following:

First, the increasing role of government in resource allocation is closely linked with the transfer of fiscal responsibility. The financing mode of local governments in China has changed from "land finance + platform loan" mode to "land finance + hidden liability" mode. By means of Public Private Partnership (PPP) project financing, made up of private equity and real debt, government guidance fund and special construction fund, among others, restrictions on the financing functions of local financing platforms are avoided. Local government debt risks are rising and highly opaque, and fiscal risks may be directly converted into financial risks. By the end of 2017, China's outstanding local government debt stood at 16.47 trillion yuan; adding in the 13.48 trillion yuan of central government bonds, the outstanding government debt stood at 29.95 trillion yuan, and the government debt ratio (debt balance divided by GDP) was 36.2%. Local governments use financial means to intervene in the allocation of financial resources, and induce financial institutions to increase financial support for local economic construction by means of financial deposits, financial subsidies, and incentives for the appointment and removal of senior executives. Furthermore, the fiscal responsibility of the central government has been transferred. In the process of divesting non-performing assets from state-owned commercial banks in 1997, borrowing from financial asset management companies in 1999, and recapitalizing financial enterprises such as securities companies since 2003, the central bank has provided a large amount of re-loans for financial stability and financial reform, thus shouldering responsibilities that should have been assumed by the government.

Second, from the policy perspective, there are still many conflicts between fiscal policy and monetary policy. In short, where fiscal policy is absent, monetary policy is forced to fill the gap. Monetary policy is best suited to aggregate control policy, focusing on short-term aggregate demand adjustment. On the other hand, economic structural adjustment should be the domain of fiscal policy, albeit supplemented by monetary policy. However, in China, due to the lagging behind in terms of change of government function, there remains a serious shortage of inputs into the "three farming" (agriculture, rural areas and farmers) sector, as well as in education, health care, social security, independent innovation, energy conservation and emissions reduction, and ecological protection. In all of those areas there are problems in terms of pension deficits, and gaps in funding. As a result, monetary policy has to shoulder some of the structural adjustment function, which in turn impacts the overall effect of macroeconomic regulation and control. In these circumstances the issuance of Treasury bonds and deadlines considers only the fiscal function; it is intended to respond to the fiscal deficit, to balance the budget, and reduce the distribution cost. Meanwhile, the Treasury's financial properties, its operation in financial markets, and the important role of monetary policy, where bond yields serve as a means of benchmark pricing, are ignored. Consequently, there is very little room for the financial markets to function properly.

Third, at the regulatory level, the Ministry of Finance acts as both owner and manager of state-owned financial assets. In the current state-owned financial assets management system, the primary identity of the Ministry of Finance (MoF) should be that of state-owned investor and shareholder. As such, the MoF should participate in the corporate governance of financial institutions to maintain and increase the value of state-owned assets. However, Ministry officials regard themselves as public managers, and the "principal-agent" relationship of state-owned financial assets is actually an administrative relationship between the superior and the subordinate, which is prone to the conflict and confusion associated with identity positioning.

To overcome the institutional root causes of fiscal and financial imbalances, it is necessary to take the following steps. First of all, we need to draw a clear line between the government and the market, and promote fiscal and financial integration. In this way, we will enable the market to play a decisive role in the allocation of resources and give better play to the role of the government. The government should avoid direct intervention in economic activities, reduce the crowding out of the private sector, leave the dominant power of resource allocation to the market, and create conditions for the market to better play its role in resource allocation. To promote the transformation of construction finance to public finance, it is essential that finance should not participate directly in economic construction and market activities, but should concentrate instead on the provision of necessary public goods and services for maintaining the market. We should actively restrict fiscal and other government economic activities in a broad sense, expand the space for the cultivation and development of the market, increase the flow of social financing to enterprises and individuals, transfer investment opportunities and risks to the market, and enable market participants to find new economic growth points through decentralized decision-making, trial and error, and innovation. Secondly, we should rationally define the boundaries of, and strengthen coordination between, fiscal policies and monetary policies, and form a synergy of policies. Monetary policy focuses on short-term aggregate demand adjustment to maintain price stability and economic aggregate balance, and to provide an appropriate monetary and financial environment for supply-side structural reform. Fiscal policy should focus more on economic restructuring, play a supporting role in targeted regulation, and serve the medium- and long-term economic development strategy. To further straighten out the relationship between the MoF and the central bank, government bond issuance should fully consider the impact on the financial market and its role. We should strengthen the management of the financial budget, while also improving its accuracy and refinement, and reduce disturbance to the liquidity management of the banking system caused by financial deposit fluctuation and Treasury cash management. We will move faster to improve the independent financial budgeting system and accounting standards to meet the performance needs of the central bank and its business development, establish and improve mechanisms for the central bank to set aside reserves, write off losses and replenish capital, and implement the legal provision whereby the central finance of the People's Bank of China makes up financial losses. Finally, we will clarify the boundary between financial shareholders' responsibilities and financial supervision. The Ministry of Finance, as the state-owned investor, should act according to its status as shareholder, and realize the maintenance and appreciation of state-owned assets by improving the corporate governance of financial institutions.

2.1.2.4 The Relationship Between Deleveraging and Improving Corporate Governance

China's macro leverage ratio is too high, a fact that is reflected in the high debt ratio of non-financial enterprises, especially local government financing vehicles and state-owned enterprises, which are actually hidden liabilities of the government. The high leverage of state-owned enterprises is closely related to the imperfections in their corporate governance. Although most enterprises now implement a governance framework of "three meetings and one layer" (general meeting of shareholders, board of directors, board of supervisors, and senior management), there are still clear deficiencies in the content and quality of corporate governance. The first is the absence of representatives of state-owned investors. Under the complicated authorization system, although the state or government (MoF) objectively exists as the major shareholder, the dual principal-agent mechanism of government in the enterprise management means that it is difficult for the same people to provide both supervision and balance. Consequently, the rights of state-owned shareholders lack effective protection. Meanwhile, the rights of minority shareholders are also ignored. Small and medium-sized shareholders lack the right to speak, and their enthusiasm for corporate governance is not high. In the context of "the same shares with the same rights," the rights and interests of small shareholders cannot be implemented, thus reducing the role of the shareholders' meeting and the board of directors, and the operation management and decision-making are not complete market behaviors. The second major deficiency is the lack of effective checks and balances mechanisms. In some enterprises the "three meetings" do not enjoy equal status; instead, the chairman is dominant, and the division of responsibilities implied in the "three meetings, one layer" structure has been lost. Moreover, the establishment of the board of directors and the board of supervisors, which combines the characteristics of the corporate governance structure of the Anglo-American law system and the continental law system, objectively limits the supervision function of the latter due to the absence of such responsibilities as auditing. Finally, information disclosure is inadequate. In the practice of corporate governance in China, in some enterprises information on major business matters, such as compensation, risk management status, corporate governance, and annual major events, is not disclosed fully or effectively, or in a timely manner. Furthermore, the external constraint force is too weak.

The backward state-owned capital management model is the fundamental obstacle preventing the establishment in China of effective corporate governance and a modern enterprise system. Many government departments and regulators still have a relatively poor understanding of the institutional framework of corporate governance, which focuses more on how to manage enterprises and how to use the power of government to help them become bigger and stronger. Departments of state-owned assets and financial regulators each develop their own principles according to their respective interests, engaging in departmental ownership and "feudal" supervision. Lacking top-level design and system considerations, the enterprise remains fully controlled by the industry authorities, i.e., the relevant government department. Therefore, it is not surprising that the government and enterprises remain intertwined, that development and supervision functions are not separate, and that operation behavior and resource allocation violate market principles. A typical phenomenon is the confusion between capital and assets. The managers and related management departments of state-owned enterprises misinterpret state-owned capital as assets belonging to the state-owned enterprises, ignoring the true meaning of state-owned capital as "net assets," after the deduction of liabilities. They understand the statement "enlarge state-owned enterprises" as being equivalent to "enlarge the assets of state-owned enterprises," ignoring the capital supplement, which eventually leads to high leverage.

In recent years, China has introduced market-oriented debt-for-equity swaps, with the aim of exploring ways to improve corporate governance through the financial markets. According to Zhou (1999), debt-equity swaps are a means used by commercial banks to preserve their assets when problems arise with normal commercial bank loans. Regular loan recovery methods involve a great deal of work, and may incur large losses, especially the "last resort" of bankruptcy liquidation. At first glance, debt-equity swaps can reduce the financial cost to the enterprise and help it to avoid bankruptcy, while at the same time preserving the commercial bank assets directly. However, while in theory this practice is intended to realize the improvement of corporate governance and operating performance, which should work to the advantage of both the debtor and the creditors, in practice, China's market-oriented debt-for-equity swap deviates from that essential idea, and does not play a full role in improving corporate governance. First of all, many enterprises adopt debt-equity swap to reduce financial costs rather than improve corporate governance. Some of these are actually high-quality enterprises; however, owing to the high leverage ratio and lack of ways to supplement capital, they use this method to adjust accounting books and reduce financial costs. In other cases, the enterprise is indeed difficult to operate, with insufficient solvency and an urgent need to improve corporate governance and operational performance; for these enterprises choosing "debt-equity swap" removes the threat of bankruptcy. Since there is no pressure of bankruptcy and liquidation, neither the enterprises nor the banks are sufficiently motivated to improve corporate governance and operation, and there is obvious moral hazard. Second, in some cases of debt-equity swap, shareholders and banks agree to hold stock for a certain period of time after the repurchase, and attach a higher rate of return. Nominally, this is equity, but in fact, it is still the creditor's right of fixed income, which belongs to the local adjustment of accounting statements, and the property of enterprise assets held by the banks has not changed substantially. As a result, banks remain "out of the loop" in corporate governance, neither sending directors nor participating in day-to-day operations, but simply waiting for the equity to wind down. This is the opposite of the original intention of debt-equity swap through bank shareholding, to improve corporate governance and enhance corporate profitability.

To thoroughly improve the corporate governance of state-owned enterprises, we must give full play to the role of financial governance. Always bearing in mind

China's unique characteristics and situation, we should strengthen the shareholding of financial institutions, encourage employee shareholding, explore the mode of holding companies, strengthen the leadership role of the party through the "two-tier structure," and implement market-oriented incentive and restraint mechanisms.

First, given the reality of indirect financing in China, the most feasible option in the short term is to strengthen the shareholding of financial institutions. Indeed, such shareholding, including by banks after debt-equity swap, and by the social security fund after the transfer of state-owned assets, is currently the only way to effectively supplement the capital of state-owned enterprises, strengthen the internal checks and balances, and improve corporate governance. With regard to the demand for supplementary capital, the role of financial institutions is difficult to replace. Private equity and other theoretically more suitable debt-equity swap investors cannot provide such large amounts of capital, and also carry with them the problems of non-standard and imperfect development. Hence, enterprises still need financial support from banks and insurance to deleverage and replenish capital. Moreover, with regard to the need to improve corporate governance, financial institutions can play a positive role by providing checks and balances. An important reason for the imperfect corporate governance of state-owned enterprises is that, while there are many administrative interventions, there are insufficient checks and balances. Financial institutions, as independent operating entities, have the subjective motivation to improve management and recover assets, and have relatively strong bargaining power and game ability, which can balance administrative intervention to a certain extent and fully reflect the voice of stakeholders in the decision-making of the "three meetings and one layer." In order to achieve the goal of improving corporate governance, banks, insurance, and other financial institutions must learn from the practice of industrial investment funds and select qualified professionals through market-based incentive and restraint mechanisms, instead of simply participating directly.

The problem of financial institutions holding stock ownership is due to the inappropriate choice of financial model. In international practice, the relationship between financial institutions and enterprises tends to follow one of three main financial models, namely the distance (arm's length), or "Anglo-Saxon" model, represented by the United States; the control guide (control oriented) model of Japan and South Korea; and the Rhine model represented by Germany, which falls somewhere between the distance and control models. Under the Japanese system, although there are restrictions on the proportion of enterprises directly held by banks, large banks can hold equity indirectly through the smaller banks controlled by them, thus breaking through the regulatory restrictions. Furthermore, because of their core position in the consortium, they enjoy strong control over the entity enterprises under that consortium. German banks, on the other hand, are limited to a certain proportion of capital, but play an important role in the board of supervisors, thus exerting influence on enterprises.

China's current financial model does not correspond exactly to any of the three models mentioned above. In the 1990s, China favored the Japan-Korea model. When Japan's bubble economy burst, China decided that the model could not work, and instead turned to the Anglo-Saxon model. However, due to half-hearted operation, the capital market was not developed according to that model. Ultimately, the development of the financial system requires a model, which should then be adhered to. It may be that the Anglo-Saxon model is the best choice for China. Nevertheless, given China's current situation, that model cannot be achieved overnight. The need to reduce leverage and recapitalize companies may mean that China must keep some aspects of the Japan-Korea model and the Rhine model, which allow banks to hold appropriate shares and play an active role as shareholder. Restrictions on bank-owned companies could be based on prudential regulation, with bank holdings linked to capital, as in the case of Germany's requirement that banks hold no more than 15% of a bank's capital in a single company. The total equity held by the bank in the enterprise shall not exceed 60% of the bank's capital.

Second, we should explore employee shareholding plans. Employees are important stakeholders of the enterprise, and also an important participant in corporate governance. The guidelines of the Chinese leadership Central Committee and the State Council on deepening the reform of state-owned enterprises clearly require "Strengthening internal supervision… We will improve the system of democratic management of enterprises in the form of workers' congresses, and strengthen democratic oversight by employees." Employee stock ownership is an important means to further protect the rights and interests of employees in enterprises and strengthen their participation in enterprise management, which is conducive to providing incentives, attracting and retaining talents, and improving the core competitiveness of enterprises. Drawing on the lessons learnt from previous attempts, we should allow employees to buy and hold shares in the enterprise in real money rather than through direct distribution. We should also explore stock option incentives, and improve the relevant accounting system, while preventing insider trading and price manipulation through lock-ups and trading restrictions.

Third, it will be worthwhile to explore the holding company model to improve the corporate governance of state-owned enterprises. The "State-owned Assets Supervision and Administration Commission (SASAC) + administration of state-owned enterprise" two-tier management structure should be replaced with a "SASAC + holding company (state-owned capital investment operating company) + state-owned enterprises" three-tier management structure. The introduction of holding companies conforms to the requirement to promote the reform of state-owned enterprises with the reform of state-owned capital, where the government only manages state-owned assets as the investor. This reform will further clarify the ownership of state capital and the functional positioning of relevant government agencies represented by SASAC. It will effectively eliminate government intervention and even the direct determination of the behavior of state-owned enterprises, such as the reduction of work enthusiasm and the low efficiency of process management. It will be conducive to the establishment of a modern–enterprise system for state-owned enterprises to ensure the separation of government administration from enterprise management.

In the field of state-owned financial capital management, Central Huijin Investment, established in 2003, provides an example of the three-tier structure of state council–financial holding company (Huijin Investment)–state-owned financial institution" three-tier structure. According to this model, a financial holding company is set up to manage state-owned financial assets according to the principles of marketization, legalization, and specialization. The biggest advantage of this model is that it can completely cut off the administrative connection between state-owned financial capital and governmental functional institutions; it ends the relationship of subordination to government, and government administrative intervention. The state-owned financial assets holding company exercises the function of investor and can guarantee the "personified" owner representative, which plays a positive role in solving the problem of investor incentive and constraint, and in strengthening the supervision and assessment of agent. However, after the China Investment Corporation (CIC) was set up in September 2007, Huijin became a wholly-owned subsidiary of CIC. Originally stripping the functions of the government institutions concerned investors try to the stagnation of the basic functions of reform, the management pattern once again return to the functions of the government agency intervention daily activities on the old way of financial assets, on the other hand, the CIC itself unable to completely on behalf of the national state-owned financial institutions with Huijin Investment shareholders completely isolated between functions, thus in the international market, its develop business of investment also is often read too much into profit and loss situation.

We should correctly understand the relationship between insisting on public ownership playing a leading role, and the holding company model. At present, the state-owned capital management refers to "state ownership" as "national ownership," which is the realization form of public ownership in the era of planned economy, but not the only realization form of public ownership. The 15th national congress of the Chinese government broke through the traditional theory that socialist public ownership has only two forms: state-owned and collective. The holding company model is intended to explore "social ownership" or "fund (social security fund) ownership" as forms of public ownership. As Huang Fanzhang (2005) pointed out, the public (or "the whole people") has at least three channels (or mechanisms) through which they may implement their wishes and interests with regard to state-owned enterprises (or enterprises owned by the whole people). They may do so first as workers, through the government's policies and plans and through the business decisions of enterprise principals. This is known as workers' sovereignty. Secondly, they can exercise "consumer sovereignty" through their own purchases in the market. Finally, by acting as investors, either directly through securities or indirectly through the "fund," they can exercise "investor sovereignty." If the government's policies or plans, or corporate decisions, go against the will and interests of the public and workers' sovereignty is weakened, the public can then use "consumer sovereignty" and "investor sovereignty" for feedback and restriction. The holding company model strengthens the public "investor sovereignty," which can better implement and realize the ownership of the whole people than is possible through state ownership.

Fourth, by implementing a "two-tier arrangement," we can strengthen the leadership by the party, while also achieving improved corporate governance. First, the state-owned capital investor status and the board of directors combined. The party represents the majority stake in the decision of the board of directors of the dominant, not only the ownership of the implementation of the state-owned enterprises, to protect the interests of the state assets investor, realize the investor control, at the same time, the tube cadre, national strategic goals and interests, usufruct and distribution, rewards and punishments, discipline, external coordination together, similar to the past "people, goods, content" integrated management, avoid micromanaging, "a pole". At the same time, we should wholeheartedly implement the principle of "one share, one right," properly handle the relationship between supporting non-public ownership and encouraging private and foreign investment, improve transparency regarding the decision-making process of major business operations, and protect the right of minority shareholders to participate in the company's decision-making and benefit distribution. Second, the establishment of the company's operating level and for grassroots cadres, employees of the party committee. We should give full play to the political core role of party organizations, including their control over ideological and beliefs education, organizational security, disciplinary inspection, personnel qualification examinations, and the protection of workers' interests. Such a double-layer arrangement not only conforms to the modern enterprise corporate governance structure, but also gives the board of directors and the operation level of the party organization a hierarchical role.

2.1.2.5 The Relationship Between Financial Risk Prevention and Governance Mechanism Improvement

China's financial risks are generally controllable, but the hidden dangers of financial risks are prominent in some key areas, behind which lies the construction of financial governance mechanism.

The first major risk is local government debt. Although China's local government debt risks are generally controllable, local government financing platforms and some state-owned enterprises have implicit guarantees, and some liabilities of state-owned enterprises actually constitute hidden liabilities of local governments. By the end of 2017, the asset-liability ratio of China's industrial enterprises above a certain size had fallen to 55.5%, the lowest since public data began to be available. However, the asset-liability ratio of state-owned enterprises remained stable at around 65%, largely due to the fact that state-owned enterprises were slower to deleverage, indicating the persistence of hidden debt pressure on local governments. With the hardening of financing constraints for local governments, their financing needs still need to be released in an orderly manner, "open the front door", in order to realize the orderly liquidation of risks.

The fundamental way to solve the problem of local government debt is to straighten out the fiscal and tax relations between the central and local governments, and to establish a local government financing market constraint mechanism. First, we need to regularize the financial relations between central and local governments, stabilize local governments' financial resources and power, cultivate the main types of local taxes, and promote the trial reform of real estate taxes. The second step will be to establish a system that allows each level of government the corresponding authority over finance, budget, taxation, and debt. Governments at all levels should have relatively independent and self-balancing finances, we should relax the central government's administrative constraints on debt quotas, and give play to the restrictive role of local people's congresses. Local people's congresses will decide independently on the amount, duration, and interest rate of bond issuance, increase the amount of debt local governments can borrow, and open up the "front door" for local governments to regulate their financing. We will improve the governance system, make debt information more transparent, and give greater play to the role of the financial market as a constraint. The third step is to explore the establishment of a local government bankruptcy mechanism, which should represent an important part of the modern financial system. Here, it is important to note that government bankruptcy refers to financial bankruptcy, not the bankruptcy of government functions. The government will continue to provide services and guarantees for public security, education, medical care, old-age care, and other public services. After bankruptcy, local governments must restore fiscal sustainability by reining in spending and raising revenue to improve deficits and pay down debt. To prevent moral hazard, the central government will not rescue bankrupt local governments unconditionally. If local governments accept central government assistance, they must sacrifice their autonomy. The financial market should play an important role in debt supervision. Investors will bear the losses caused by the bankruptcy of local governments, forming a positive incentive for investors to actively identify the financing capacity and credit rating of those governments. To force local governments to standardize the operation and management of financial affairs, improve transparency, and give full play to the restrictive role of the market, we will strengthen accountability; include performance indicators for financial management in the assessment, selection, and appointment of officials; and implement the requirements of the national financial work conference on "strictly controlling the increase in local government debt, holding local governments accountable for their debts for life."

In addition, we should work to attract private capital to participate in monopolistic industries by granting it the same shares and rights. In fact, local governments hold a lot of high-quality assets, but where there is no bankruptcy constraint they are not willing to use them to discount or finance, and instead continue to pursue the old business management philosophy. We will streamline administration and delegate power, and allow private capital to participate in monopolistic industries. At present, the market access barrier of some monopolized industries in China is still difficult to break through. Even if an opening is made in some areas, there remain "glass doors," "swing doors," and "revolving doors" behind them. We should promptly formulate plans, policies, and measures to substantially relax market access in electricity, telecommunications, transportation, oil, natural gas, and municipal public utilities, and promulgate specific measures to support nongovernmental capital in developing such services as old-age care, health, homemaking, education, training, culture, and education. Meanwhile, we will implement more inclusive fiscal, tax, and industrial policies, create a level playing field, innovate the cooperation mechanism between monopolized industries and private capital, avoid the unfair cooperation mode that allows investors to provide money, but denies them a voice, and strive to share the same shares and the same rights. Such a model will not only provide financing and financial resources to local governments, but will also optimize the allocation of resources and improve total factor productivity.

The second risk is the household sector leverage. Leverage in China's household sector is rising fast and may be undervalued. In 2017, the leverage ratio of China's household sector was 55.1%, 4 percentage points higher than the previous year. Considering that residents generally raise down payments through borrowing and use Internet finance, such as Ant Cash Now, Tencent Microcredit, JD Finance, and other products, the leverage ratio of Chinese residents may be even higher.

Much of the household sector debt is borrowed to meet housing demand, and the rapid increase in household leverage also reflects significant distortions in China's property market. At present, the first- and second-tier cities are strictly regulated, while the third- and fourth-tier cities have relatively relaxed policies. The contradiction between supply and demand in the first- and second-tier cities is not directly reflected in the price, but is reflected in the aspects of shrinking quantity, price stability, postponing the online sign, price distortion, and empty and high inventory. The housing reform and monetary compensation in third-tier and fourth-tier cities have reduced inventory, leading to high market heat, which could also lead to blind optimism. Indeed, residents' capital is flowing to the property market in third- and fourth-tier cities, which is another way to reflect the bubble.

Therefore, we should improve the long-term mechanism of the healthy development of the real estate market. In this regard, the priority is to establish a unified national land equivalent market for urban and rural areas. This is the only way to maintain the red line of 1.8 billion mu of arable land, realize market-oriented supply of land, enhance supply elasticity, adapt to urbanization and regional development, and improve land use efficiency. To realize such land marketization, we should further reform and improve the land bidding, auction and listing system. We should also pilot real estate tax reform. The National People's Congress (NPC) should authorize some cities and regions to carry out such reform in accordance with the principles of broad tax base, low tax rate, affordability, including stock, gradual implementation, and compatible incentives. At the same time, local governments should be encouraged to explore long-term real estate mechanisms suitable for local areas.

2.1.2.6 The Relationship Between Aging Population, Pension Sustainability and Capital Market

China's aging population is a major challenge to the sustainable development of pensions. At the end of 2019, China's working-age population was 896.4 million, accounting for 64.0%. The positive effect of the relaxation of the birth policy on the new population is not significant, and the trend of fertility intention and decline in total fertility rate may prove irreversible with the rise in income level. In this context, how to effectively guide pension savings and long-term investment in order to provide residents with strong pension security, is the key to the sustainable development of pensions.

In recent years, flaws in China's pension system have been exposed. First of all, nominally, China adopts the partial fully funded mode of "Basic Old-Age Insurance Scheme for Enterprise Employees (BOISEE);" however, personal accounts are empty accounts, and funds have been diverted to the current "pay-as-you-go" pension system, which is not sustainable in the context of aging population and declining proportion of working population. In practice, the two accounts have been commingled, whereas the funds in individual accounts are utilized to fund deficits in the social pooling accounts. Martin Feldstein (2005), a professor at Harvard University, argues that the pay-as-you-go system not only fails to meet the challenge of aging population, but also "crowds out" individual savings, reducing investment and output. Second, China's pension system is fragmented. The three-pillar pension system, corresponding to the government's mandatory public pension plans, supplementary corporate pension plans, and voluntary individual savings and pension insurance plans, has a fund distribution of 79%, 19% and 9% respectively. Consequently, there is excessive pressure on Pillar I, the social security fund. In 2016, the distribution of pension Pillars I, II and III in the United States was 22%, 39% and 39%. Third, the scope of pension investment is limited, and the important role in guiding the investment of funds and allocation of resources is not fully played. In the past, pension investment policies pursued "safety" to an excessive extent, and given the limited variety of investment, the returns were very meagre. Historically, China's social insurance fund balance was limited to bank deposits and the purchase of Treasury bonds, such that the annual rate of return is only about 3%. In comparison, from 2007 to 2017, the cumulative yield of real estate was as high as 766%, gold yielded 106%, the CSI 300 Index[1] 97%, the corporate bond index 78%, and the Shanghai 50 index 58%. Low returns discourage savers from investing in pensions and encourage short-term speculation in property. Fourth, with regard to the social polling accounts, payment of positive incentives is insufficient. Social polling accounts filling the gap with surplus will dampen the enthusiasm for pension payment in surplus provinces, and reduce the motivation of deficit provinces to make up for the gap, thus creating a negative incentive for non-payment or for paying less, while also enjoying a pension.

Perfect pension system reform should take into account that pension has a dual nature, closely related to both social security and financial intermediaries. As such, the reform should attach importance to the long-term investment and financing function of the capital market. It must achieve profitability of funds, improve the attraction of the pension, while also promoting capital market development and the improvement of corporate governance. To achieve this, the following steps should be taken:

First, it is necessary to fully fund individual accounts. From pay-as-you-go to fund accumulation, we should make account property rights clearer, and realize the positive incentive of "pay more and get more." By doing so we will emphasize individual

[1]The CSI 300 Index is a free-float weighted index that consists of 300 A-share stocks listed on the Shanghai or Shenzhen Stock Exchanges.

pension responsibility and realize the positive interaction between individual pension responsibility and income. Second, we will turn short-term household savings into long-term money, develop direct financing markets, and effectively support deleveraging. It is estimated that, by 2020, China's GDP will reach 100 trillion yuan and household financial assets will reach 200 trillion yuan. According to the structure of household balance sheets, 30% of household financial assets will be used for retirement, with a capital scale of about 60 trillion yuan. Pillar III of the balance of personal accounts retained 40 trillion yuan. If given to a professional institution, and assuming 20% were allocated in the equity financing market, the fund would be about 8 trillion yuan. As long as it is allocated scientifically, comprehensively, and prudently in equity financing, "long-term used money" can be formed, and the matching of long money in pension fund and equity financing period of enterprises is an important driving force for corporate deleveraging. We will also develop institutional investors and enhance the stability of the financial market. For a long time, the large number of retail investors, high volatility, and hype in China's capital market have weakened its attractiveness and ability to serve the real economy. Institutional investors have advantages of information and scale, and their investment decision-making is more professional and scientific. Their behaviors are closer to the "rational economic man" in the efficient market hypothesis. The improvement of their market status will be conducive to the healthy and stable development of financial markets. We should also vigorously develop Pillars II and III, and resolve the current weak points.

Second, we should allocate state capital to supplement the social security fund. Here, the aim is to repay the pension deficits of the social security system transition. China's Basic Old-Age Insurance Scheme for Enterprise Employees (BOISEE), established in 1997, combined "social pooling accounts" and "individual pension accounts." Because the government did not bear the cost of transformation to fill the gap caused by the elderly who did not pay fees, it is now necessary to draw on state-owned capital to supplement social security and make up the shortfall. Furthermore, the social security fund holds shares in state-owned enterprises and exercises the responsibility of investors. It can explore a new form of public ownership that is owned by the fund on behalf of "the whole people," and improve the corporate governance of state-owned enterprises. As a market subject with independent operation, the pension fund can exercise the duties of shareholders relatively independently, avoid the intervention of administrative departments, avoid the separation of government and enterprise and of government and capital, and completely transform the problem of administrative management replacing corporate governance. At the same time, pension managers take the maximization of shareholders' interests as the main goal, which is conducive to state-owned enterprises adhering firmly to the direction of market-oriented operation, thus ensuring the preservation and appreciation of state-owned capital.

Third, we will continue to implement local pooling and improve the portability of pensions. In the short term, although the national pooling can enhance the capacity to adjust the surplus and shortage of funds to deal with the pension income and expenditure gap in regions with a serious aging population, in the long term, the moral hazard problem is prominent, which is not conducive to the long-term sustainability of the pension system. Referring to international experience, it is better to continue to implement local pooling and improve the portability of pensions. The same residents in more employment after retirement, its overall account annuities treatment "provincial annuities pay cost and calculate every block treatment, concentration", both can improve the flexibility of the Labour market cross-regional employment, and to improve the enthusiasm of the people taking part in the social security system, expand coverage for social security, and improve the social safety net. Within the framework of central basic requirements and principles, provincial governments are responsible for the design of individual account systems, including transfer rules. In fact, in the era of Internet big data, China's payment system has reached an advanced level, and is fully equipped with the technical conditions of segmented calculation, collection, and distribution.

Fourth, pension investment operations must implement functional supervision. In accordance with the principle of "equal supervision for similar businesses," uniform access rules should be established for pension investment operators as soon as possible. To maintain the safety of pension investments, the participation of pension investment operation institutions in capital market activities should be supervised by the China Securities Regulatory Commission.

2.1.3 The Construction of a Modern Financial System Should Follow the General Rules of Financial Market Development

All countries, regardless of their stage of development, have faced problems and challenges in their development process. The fact that China's financial system started late gives China the opportunity to learn from international experience. In order to make full use of this advantage, we should thoroughly summarize and grasp the objective law of financial development, clarify the goal and path of modern financial system construction, and avoid detours.

2.1.3.1 Correct Understanding of the Comprehensive Operation Trend of the Financial Industry

In recent years, China has been promoting reform of financial supervision, in order to build a system suitable for the development trend of comprehensive operation. In November 2015, in the Note on the Proposal of the Chinese government Central Committee on Formulating the 13th Five-Year Plan for National Economic and Social Development, General Secretary Xi Jinping stated that "in recent years, the development of China's financial industry has been markedly accelerated… In particular, there is a clear trend of comprehensive operation, posing a major challenge to the current separate industry supervision system… We should adhere to the direction of market-oriented reform, accelerate the establishment of a powerful and effective modern financial regulatory framework that conforms to the characteristics of modern finance and coordinates supervision as a whole, and stick to the bottom line that no systemic risk will occur."

First, comprehensive management is not only an inevitable trend of economic globalization, but also a necessary requirement of financial liberalization and market-oriented development. In all major developed economies, the direction of development is towards comprehensive financial operations. In 1999, the United States abolished the Glass-Steagall Act, which restricted comprehensive financial operation, and passed the Financial Services Modernization Act. In 1986, the UK enacted the Financial Services Act, which greatly reduced financial regulation and encouraged comprehensive financial operations. Following the recent international financial crisis, the United States issued the "Volcker Rules," while the United Kingdom adopted the "Fence Rules," and the European Union issued the Karenin Report. In each case the aim was to improve the regulatory rules and risk prevention mechanism of comprehensive operation, rather than to overturn the overall pattern of comprehensive operation of the financial industry. Indeed, comprehensive management of the financial industry has become an internal demand of the real economy and financial development. With regard to the real economy, in a context of economic globalization the financial service needs of enterprises are increasingly integrated and diversified; they include diversified financing channels, personalized risk management tools, and convenient payment and transaction means. These needs can only be provided through the integrated operation of financial institutions to provide "one-stop" services. As for financial development, given the global trend towards financial disintermediation, comprehensive operation allows the financial industry to improve its competitiveness by effectively connecting and integrating various financial markets and formats, and by maximizing synergies.

Second, comprehensive management itself will not magnify risks. Rather, it is the maladaptation of supervision that is the source of risks. In fact, comprehensive management is conducive to the dispersal and reduction of risks. It allows financial institutions to "put eggs into multiple baskets" through business diversification, which brings synergy into play and realizes high efficiency with low risk. However, it also increases the management costs for cross-industry operations of banks, securities, and insurance, and faces the constraint of scarcity of cross-industry professionals. Since the 1980s, the development of science and technology has greatly improved the efficiency of financial activities, enlarged the benefits of business collaboration, and reduced the management costs of cross-industry operations, thus promoting comprehensive operation as an irreversible development trend of the financial industry. This presents challenges to the system of separate supervision. Under this system, the supervision institutions perform their own duties, and the lack of cross-industry financial supervision professionals means that it is difficult to achieve integrated supervision that corresponds to integrated operation. Furthermore, the root of the risk behind the subprime crisis was not comprehensive management, but the backward fragmented supervision. Some US commercial banks (such as Washington Mutual) experienced difficulties because of non-performing loans in traditional banking, not because of cross-border securities operations. Investment banks such as Bear Stearns and Lehman Brothers actually engaged in very little commercial banking, and the risks stemmed from their main securities businesses. One important cause of the crisis was the regulation prohibiting interest payment on demand deposits, which had led to a situation in which shadow banks such as money market funds stepped in to replace bank demand deposits. The rapid expansion of this practice bred potential risks. As Bernanke (2016) pointed out in *Courage to Act*, mixed operation is not the problem; rather, in the US the real problem is fragmented and separated supervision. This point echoes Geithner's (2015) argument set out in *Stress Test: Reflections on Financial Crises*, that "the separated supervision system in the United States is full of loopholes and competition of various forces, as well as subtle intrigues, but no one is responsible for the stability of the whole system."

Third, it is impossible to eliminate risks by restricting comprehensive operation. Indeed, such a restriction will only generate new risks. Restricting comprehensive operation reflects a typical misunderstanding of the relationship between access and supervision. It is impossible to eliminate risks by restricting business access. Financial institutions may choose higher risks in any business they engage in. Supervision should focus on how to reduce risk motivation rather than on setting up market barriers. In 1933, the United States introduced the Glass Steagall Act to restrict the diversification of American financial institutions; however, subsequent events proved that this was based on a wrong understanding of the lessons of the Great Depression. Rather than bringing security to the American banking industry, it increased the risk due to the long-term constraints placed on its business. The crisis of the Savings and Loan Association in the 1980s was second only to the Great Depression and the financial crisis. On the surface it appeared that the crisis was caused by the contraction of interest rate spread under the background of interest rate marketization, which led to an increase in risk appetite and excessive involvement in real estate. However, another important background at that time was that facing the impact of the massive diversion of savings by monetary funds and the fact that securities companies were operating lending businesses, the savings and loan institutions, as the banking institutions most restricted by segregation, were unable to provide comprehensive services to customers to mitigate the impact of interest rate spread contraction, and eventually followed an irreversible path of high-risk real estate financing. In fact, in the decades after the implementation of the Glass-Steagall Act, the US financial industry was not peaceful. Almost every 20–30 years, there was a systemic crisis in the banking industry. In 1984, the number of bank failures reached a new peak. Furthermore, separated operation also suppressed the international competitiveness of the US banking industry, so that in the 1970s and 1980s the major international banks were concentrated in Japan and Germany. It was in this context that the US finally abolished the Glass-Steagall Act in 1999 and replaced it with the Financial Services Modernization Act.

2.1.3.2 The Central Bank and Financial Supervision Cannot Be Separated

In the 1990s, there was a trend of separation between the central bank and financial supervision. From the perspective of academic theory, this trend was mainly influenced by the effective market hypothesis, and the idea of the central bank's single target and single tool (inflation targeting system). From the perspective of the principle of system design, the main consideration was the moral hazard whereby the combination of monetary policy (lender of last resort) and supervision may lead to the deregulation of the central bank. In terms of policy practice, in economies that implement the inflation targeting system, the central bank "institutionally" only undertakes the monetary policy function and anchors the inflation target. However, the international financial crisis in 2008 severely damaged the theoretical basis of the efficient market hypothesis and the central bank's single target system. It is not enough for the central bank to focus only on inflation and ignore financial stability. With the introduction of the concept of macro-prudential management into financial supervision, financial stability has once again become one of the central bank's core objectives, and its core role in macro-prudential management and systematic risk prevention has gradually been established.

The central bank's role in monetary regulation cannot be separated from the coordination and cooperation of financial supervision policies. From the perspective of modern money creation theory, the central bank's money supply is outside money, while the money created within the financial system is inside money. The monetary regulation goals are to be achieved by influencing inside money through outside money, while the supervision policy is characterized by strong authority and fast transmission, directly affects the financial institutions, and has the power to trigger the sharp adjustment of inside money, determining the effectiveness of monetary policy transmission to a large extent. Even if the central bank can regulate and control the outside money, without effective supervision it cannot control where the outside money is invested and how efficient it is, nor can it guarantee the financial support for the real economy.

Furthermore, the central bank needs to obtain related financial supervision information to perform its financial stability function. Minsky divided financing into three categories: hedging, speculation, and Ponzi scheme. Hedge finance relies on the expected cash income of the financing subject to repay the interest and principal. In speculative finance the expected cash income of the financing subject can only cover interest, but is not sufficient to cover the principal, so must rely on borrowing new to return the old. A Ponzi scheme is one in which the cash flow of the financing subject can cover nothing, and assets must be sold, or liabilities continuously increased. In order to maintain financial stability, the central bank will naturally assume the function of lender of last resort, and must therefore have the ability to guide social financing to form a structure dominated by hedge finance both legally and administratively. This ability will inevitably be based on the central bank's understanding of various types of financing in the financial system and the regulatory information of related risks.

In addition, the central bank's function as the lender of last resort requires the coordination of financial supervision policies to carry out crisis relief. The liquidity relief function of the lender of last resort has given the central bank an important position as the last line of defense for crisis relief. With regard to this role, Bagehot's Rule has been an important guideline for central banks to provide liquidity assistance since the nineteenth century. Because the problem financial institutions are a small minority, and the vast majority of banks in the financial system are still sound, central banks have neither the responsibility nor the need to provide free assistance to the troubled banks. Therefore, the rule requires central banks to take prompt and decisive actions in times of liquidity crisis to prevent the spread of systemic risks, and at the same time to abide by the principle of providing liquidity support to banks with liquidity difficulties rather than financial difficulties to prevent moral hazard. Institutions with liquidity difficulties should provide high-quality collateral and charge punitive high-interest rates. If the central bank does not participate in the prior and in-process supervision, and the regulatory information cannot be effectively shared, it is difficult for the central bank to grasp the asset status of a bank clearly, which impairs its ability to make accurate rescue decisions and reduces the efficiency of the rescue. In this situation, the implementation of rescue can be seen as a blood transfusion to an already insolvent financial institution. Here, the central bank's function as the lender of last resort has been simplified into a payment box, a situation that carries serious moral hazard.

2.1.3.3 The Supervision System Must Be Incentive Compatible

It is important that the goal of supervision is clear, and that the contradiction between development and supervision is properly handled. As pointed out by Holmstrom and Milgrom (1991), when faced with multiple task objectives, agents have the incentive to invest all their efforts in tasks where performance is easily observed while reducing or forgoing efforts on other tasks. In China, financial supervisors often directly assume the development function. Encouraged by the dual goals of supervision and development, supervisors will naturally focus on the development goals where achievements are more easily observed, while ignoring those where achievements are less obvious.

In addition, it is crucial that the right and responsibility of supervision should be equal. Economic research has long realized that supervision is not an abstract concept, but a sum of human behavior. Supervisors may deviate from the public interest goal due to the consideration of personal interests, leading to regulatory failure. One example is the imbalance of supply and demand in financial supervision. Financial supervision is a public good, but supervisors would not provide it without cost and hesitation in accordance with the public interest. Another example is the existence of rent-seeking. As long as the government intervenes in the allocation of resources through supervision, there will be rent-seeking in the private sector, which will reduce the efficiency of resource allocation. Furthermore, the influence of interest groups can lead to the capture of financial supervision, and the deviation of regulatory action from the public interest. An incentive-compatible supervision system will restrain supervisors' impulse to deviate from the public interest; through reasonable supervision division, strict accountability and punishment, salary, and other positive incentives, it will unify the supervisors' behavior with the overall goal of financial supervision.

With regard to the division of supervision, the incentive theory points out that as a result of the balance between the professionalization of supervision and the economy of supervision scope, the overall goals of financial supervision are divided and entrusted to several supervisors. Any mismatch between right and responsibility in the division of work will lead to a serious incentive distortion. Power without responsibility often leads to abuses of power, while responsibility without power cannot achieve the supervision objectives. From the perspective of the prior, in-process, and post-event management of financial risk, the central bank undertakes crisis rescue as the lender of last resort, and deposit insurance as a risk disposal platform. If it is separated from the prior and in-process daily supervision, not only will the crisis rescue and risk disposal be inefficient due to information asymmetry, but also, because the daily supervisors will not have to bear the rescue cost completely, this removes a disincentive to moral hazard. Therefore, under the divided work of incentive-compatible supervision, crisis rescuers and risk disposers often assume daily supervision functions.

For example, when deposit insurance was first established, it was mainly used as a "payment box," responsible only for paying depositors after the event. However, after being tested by real financial risks, the pure "payment box" model proved unsuccessful; it bore the responsibility to pay out after the event, but did not have the power of supervision in advance. Such a clear mismatch between rights and responsibilities makes it difficult to prevent regulatory tolerance and moral hazard, which leads to high disposal costs and the inability to prevent and resolve financial risks effectively. Looking to the international development trend, the deposit insurance system model gradually converged with a "risk minimization" model with symmetrical rights and responsibilities. In this system, deposit insurance can implement a risk-based differential rate, to promote fair competition and build positive incentives. There is also an early correction function, with the right to inspect and intervene in the problem banks. Before a bank becomes insolvent, it should take measures as early as possible to realize the "early detection and early disposal" of financial risks.

From the perspective of accountability mechanism, the fact that financial supervisors do not fully bear the costs of crisis and risk exposure caused by supervision failures means that supervision incentives are insufficient, and supervision efforts are below the optimal level. Moreover, even if there are clear laws and regulations, supervisors may not abide by the law. The function of the accountability mechanism is to punish supervisors based on supervision errors and strengthen their supervision incentives. For example, the collapse of Australia's HIH Insurance Group in 2001 was considered to be a serious regulatory failure on the part of the Australian Prudential Regulation Authority (APRA) and may have the benefit of political contributions. The Australian government set up a royal investigation committee to investigate, and many supervisors were held accountable and dismissed.

Supervision policies should also be open and transparent. According to Dewatripont and Tirole (1994), who introduced the theory of incomplete contract into financial supervision, because supervisors are vulnerable to the influence of political forces and may be captured by supervision, they may deviate from the goal of public interest; therefore, it is important that the discretion of supervision should match the independence of supervisors. Supervisors who have strong independence and can internalize public interests into their own goals can be given more powers of contingent supervision. On the other hand, for supervisors with weak independence, who are subject to greater influence from political pressure and interest groups, we should adopt a rule-based supervision system, reduce the contingent decision-making, and increase policy transparency. In fact, the latter case is the theoretical basis of international supervision rules such as the Basel Accord. The realization of incentive compatibility through transparent supervision rules is embodied in every stage of financial supervision development. For example, Bagehot's Rule explicitly requires that the liquidity support of the lender of last resort must be based on qualified collateral and punitive interest rate. Micro-prudential supervision requires financial institutions to match their total risk (total assets) with their risk tolerance (equity capital) through a clear capital adequacy ratio. Macro-prudential supervision imposes higher supervision requirements on systemically important financial institutions, requiring the conclusion of a "living will" to raise supervision constraints based on the implicit protection of "too big to fail".

2.1.3.4 A Modern Financial System Requires a Developed Financial Market

A modern financial system must feature a developed financial market. In China, the financial market has developed rapidly, in line with the improvement of residents' income and accumulation of wealth. Given China's status as the second-largest economy and a developing country that is increasingly close to the center of the world stage, we should fully understand the importance of financial markets to China's current and future development. First of all, the construction of a modern financial market system is essential for the high-quality development of the financial system. Compared with indirect financing by banks, financial markets have comparative advantages in improving corporate governance, enhancing information disclosure, and strengthening risk management. Financial markets establish strong external constraints through higher information disclosure requirements and transparency, and establish more effective internal incentives through a clear separation of ownership and management rights. At the same time, the development of financial markets can effectively promote the market-oriented development of other factor markets through the market-oriented allocation of capital factors. Second, a modern financial market system is necessary in order to implement the new development concept of "innovation, coordination, green, openness, and sharing." Innovative development is strongly supported by developed financial markets. Only by forming a relatively complete capital investment mechanism and a corresponding intermediary service system in the financial market, can we accelerate the transformation of scientific and technological innovation achievements into real productivity, and promote scientific and technological innovation start-ups to grow in both quantity and scale, thus forming a new economic growth point from nothing. Third, a modern financial market system is an important prerequisite for "deleveraging." In order to reduce the debt rate from the root, we must improve the long-term mechanism of transforming savings into equity investment. The key is to develop the financial market and replenish the capital of the real economy by vigorously developing equity financing. Fourth, a modern financial market system is an inevitable requirement for monetary policy to shift from quantitative control to price control. Monetary policy transmission with price control as the core is based on financial markets. Reasonable pricing in financial markets and the close correlation between markets can realize linkage and transmission of capital prices, which is an important prerequisite for monetary policy to shift to price-based control. Fifth, building a modern financial market system is a crucial step towards opening up the financial industry to the outside world. Historical experience shows that such openness will speed up the exposure of existing defects in the financial market. Only when the financial market itself is strong can the positive effects brought about by the expansion of opening, such as welfare improvement, efficiency improvement, and competitiveness improvement, be fully realized. Sixth, a flexible RMB exchange rate requires a foreign exchange market with breadth and depth. The flexible exchange rate is an important guarantee to resist external shocks effectively and maintain the autonomy of domestic monetary policy. The key lies in the depth and breadth of the market. Finally, the promotion of the RMB's international status also requires the rapid development of financial markets. Developed financial markets can meet the diversified needs of overseas residents to hold RMB assets, which will greatly enhance the attractiveness of RMB and promote the development of the currency's valuation and settlement function in trade and investment.

However, currently, there remain clear defects in the development of China's financial market. First of all, China's market is still subject to segmentation. The money market exists not only in the inter-bank market but also in the exchange market. Corporate credit bonds, short-term financing bonds, and medium-term bills, corporate bonds, and corporate bonds have the same functional attributes but are subject to different management systems due to different management subjects. Some supervision authorities have launched a so-called "financing tool" pilot similar to corporate credit bonds to build their own over-the-counter bond (type bonds) market. It should be recognized that modern financial markets are closely related to each other. The lack of overall coordination will not only affect market efficiency, but also create supervision gaps and supervision arbitrage, resulting in hidden financial risks. The distortion of a single market may often reflect problems in other markets. The second major defect is distorted pricing. In recent years, with the significant progress in relevant reforms, capital prices such as interest rates and exchange rates have played an increasingly important role in financial markets. However, the pricing mechanism in the financial market is still distorted. As a result of administrative intervention by local governments, the issue price of local bonds cannot properly reflect risks and liquidity. Tax preference causes government bonds to crowd out other bonds, pushing up the pricing of credit bonds. Relevant tax policies constrain the trading and liquidity of government bonds, which means that the yield rate of government bonds cannot easily become the benchmark for market pricing. The main body of the market deviates from the principle of market-oriented operation, and the distortion of behavior leads to the deviation of capital price from market supply and demand. Rigid payment leads to multiple de facto risk-free interest rates in the market, pushing up the expected return rate of risky assets.

With the promotion of reform of the financial supervision system, the further opening of the financial industry to the outside world, the introduction of new regulations on capital management, and other supervision policies, the market segmentation and pricing distortions in China's financial market are gradually being eliminated. Moreover, the entire structure of China's financial market will undergo major changes. Shadow banks will gradually disappear, while new disintermediation methods such as asset securitization and money market funds will emerge. In an environment of massive change, financial supervision and monetary policies should be well prepared for the challenges to come. Therefore, the newly constructed modern financial system must comprise multiple levels, and have unified rules, transparent information, depth, and breadth. Such a system will be conducive to proper handling of the relationship between the government and the market, between Treasury and finance, between deleveraging and improving corporate governance, between the prevention of financial risks and the improvement of governance mechanisms and, with an aging population, between the sustainability of pensions and the capital market. Taking these requirements as a guideline, we can outline and expand the key points to promote the overall deepening of financial reform.

2.2 Fiscal Relations Between Central and Local Governments

2.2.1 The Influence of Central-Local Fiscal Relations on Economic Fluctuation

The fiscal relations between the central and local governments are at the core of all national fiscal and tax systems, and this is especially true for a large economy like China. In particular, China's economic growth has long been driven by investment, and as local governments are important investment subjects, changes in their behavior will have an important impact on investment growth. In recent years, although the contribution of consumption to growth has been increasing, the impact of investment growth on growth volatility has also increased. This is because investment is much more volatile than consumption; furthermore, the contribution of export has changed from positive to negative, which has left a huge gap. In terms of investment structure, with the continuous decline of manufacturing investment, infrastructure and real estate investment, which are closely related to central-local fiscal relations, have become a decisive factor for the marginal fluctuation of investment and even the whole economic growth rate. They will also have an important impact on the evolution of fiscal, financial, and even the whole systemic risk.

2.2.1.1 As Local Government Financing Channels Tighten, Real Economy "Deleveraging" Will Bring Downward Pressure on the Economy

In May 2017, the Ministry of Finance issued the Notice on Further Regulating the Borrowing-based Financing Activities of Local Governments (No. 50 [2017] of the Ministry of Finance) and the Notice on Resolutely Curbing the Illegal Financing of the Local Governments in the Name of Government Procurement of Services (No. 87 [2017] of the Ministry of Finance). These two documents are the continuation and enhancement of a series of measures taken in recent years to prevent and defuse the risks of local government debt. The policy covers all illegal financing activities, such as platform financing, guarantees, PPP, government investment funds/industry funds, and government procurement of services. It blocks completely any possibility of forming contingent local government debt by illegal or disguised financing guarantee. In 2014, the Opinions of the State Council on Strengthening the Administration of Local Government Debts (No. 43 [2014] of the State Council) stripped local financing platforms of their financing functions and prohibited borrowing-based financing of local governments through financing platforms. In 2015, the new Budget Law began to allow provincial governments to issue bonds, with the size of issuance subject to central government approval. However, due to the limited amount of local government bonds under budget management, the expenditure needs of local governments for "steady growth" cannot be met. Therefore, it is impossible to fully implement the Opinions of the State Council (document No. 43) and the new Budget Law. To make up for the funding gap, local governments have to circumvent the restrictions on the financing functions of local financing platforms by means of PPP project financing, policy bank financing support, government guidance fund, and special construction fund.

At present, the global economy has not yet fully recovered from the impact of the 2008 international financial crisis, nor has China made a complete transition from the investment-driven growth model. Under the background of great downward pressure on economic growth, local government competition in terms of attracting business and investment and infrastructure investment is important to support the engine of economic operation; it is also an important pillar of counter cyclical macroeconomic policy. Without local government autonomy in matters of borrowing, and with the absence of legal channels of financing, simply blocking disguised forms of local government debt will only add to economic difficulties, rather than defusing financial risks. It may contribute to the creation of new risks, and trigger systemic risk. Therefore, we must strike a balance between the goals of stable growth and risk prevention (deleveraging). Measures to prevent local government debt risks should not be taken without thorough consideration of potential unintended consequences; in particular, central government should take care not to make heavy-handed interventions that might kill off local initiatives. Under the current circumstances, if we strengthen fiscal and financial supervision at the same time, and rush to deleverage the government departments, financial sector, and household sector, this could cause unnecessary fluctuations in the real economy. In the real estate sector, where fiscal, financial, and residential leverage ratios are closely related, the expansion and contraction of fiscal credit is key to government investment (infrastructure investment), and at the same time, is important support for financial and real estate credit expansion. It is a decisive factor in short-term economic fluctuations.

Historically, China's failure to straighten out the fiscal relations between central and local governments has repeatedly led local government behaviors into a vicious circle, where if the central government did step in, it might lead to the death of local initiatives, and yet if the central government did not step in, local initiatives could develop unchecked, with potentially chaotic results. In the period of planned economy, China's financial management was unified by the central government, and local governments basically had no financial autonomy. In the early stage of reform and opening up, under the fiscal contract system local governments' financial autonomy was increased, and cases of local governments concealing revenue and eroding central tax revenues occurred in great number, leading to the continuous decline of the "two proportions" (the proportion of fiscal revenue in GDP and the proportion of central government revenue in total fiscal revenue). Improper competition between local governments also occurred from time to time, for example, through the setting up of barriers to one another, competing for tax bases, or by local governments using preferential policy depressions to attract foreign investment in an excessive way.

In 1994, reform of the tax distribution system aimed to centralize fiscal power and increase the "two proportions." Under the terms of the reform, major turnover taxes such as value-added tax and consumption tax were to be collected by the central government. Article 28 of the 1995 Budget Law stipulates that "local governments shall not have deficits and shall not issue local government bonds," thus limiting their borrowing power. The fiscal capacity of local governments was greatly weakened, and the central government's macro-control capacity ability to prevent the economy from overheating was strengthened, which led to the successful "soft landing" of the economy in 1997. However, from 1998 to 2002, hit by the impact of the Asian financial crisis and weakened local financial resources, China's economy experienced a difficult period.

The tax distribution reform did not take away the right of local governments to use the proceeds from the transfer of land. With the housing system reform in 1998 and the development of the real estate market, and the implementation of the "Bid Invitation, Auction, and Listing" system for land in 2004, local governments found new sources of revenue and increased their dependence on land finance in the name of "City Operation." In order to cope with the impact of the 2008 international financial crisis, local governments have made increasing use of financing platforms to borrow off-budget, with land finance as the leverage fulcrum. Because there are currently no unified normative management measures for the debt of financing platforms, this has led to the rapid expansion of opaque implicit local government debt. It is estimated that the scale of local government debt reached 40% of GDP in 2015.

2.2.1.2 The Current Consolidation Approach Will Lead to the Financialization of Fiscal Risks

In countries with sound budget management systems, there is a strict boundary between government debt and non-government debt. However, government credit guarantees and backstop expectations are often implicit in the debt of local government financing vehicles. Such debts are quasi-government debts, in the opaque zone between government and non-government debts. Given the lack of a clear boundary between the government and the market, and between fiscal and financial matters, the writing off of some implicit debts by various regulatory documents issued by the Ministry of Finance only separated the debt repayment liability from the financial department, and did not help resolve risks. In fact, before the straightening out of central-local fiscal relations, and in the absence of stable and reliable financing resources for local governments, the rational choice for local government to solve its financial balance contradiction is still to enlarge GDP. Local governments do not actually stop borrowing in disguised form because the financial departments at higher levels do not bear the responsibility of debt repayment, or tighten supervision. On the contrary, in recent years, although the non-performing loans of financing platforms and the default risk of city investment bonds have declined, the debts have simply shifted from on balance sheet to off balance sheet, from loans to inter-bank investment, and to the so-called "equity and fund." The overall risk and the difficulty of supervision have not necessarily been reduced. Various financial risks with more hidden forms, more complex channels, and requiring more difficult supervision, cannot be ignored. In recent years, both the explosive growth of platform debt and the chaos in new violations have highlighted the importance and urgency of speeding up the institutional process of straightening out central-local fiscal relations and providing local governments with stable sources of revenue. Otherwise, simply relying on administrative orders to implement the Budget Law will only clear the liability of debt repayment in the form of law, and the actual risk will increase due to various non-standardized and disguised borrowing.

2.2.1.3 The Current Rectification Measures Do not Fully Take into Account Regional Differences

The recent measures to regulate and manage local government debt were based on an assumption that "one-size-fits-all," and therefore do not reflect the differences in economic development level and debt capacity among different regions. In some regions, debt risks are already evident; in others, there is still room to increase leverage. The latter can continue to play a positive role in stabilizing growth. At the deeper level of institutional mechanism, the reason why government departments tend to increase leverage, and why deleveraging is "embarrassing" and inconsistent with actual local fiscal risks, is related to the current fiscal system, in which the central government centralizes administrative power and financial resources, and local governments lack fiscal independence.

2.2.1.4 Policy Suggestions on Balancing "Steady Growth" and "Deleveraging"

Debt and growth are twin phenomena. In order to achieve a dynamic balance between steady growth and deleveraging, it is necessary to reform the fiscal relations between the central and local governments and improve the local government debt framework. To do so, we should begin by improving the performance evaluation system, diluting GDP growth targets, and guiding local governments in the right way. Then, it will be necessary to reform the debt management framework of local governments. More specifically, local governments should have the space to take initiative, while at the same time facing a hard constraint mechanism to prevent them from acting arbitrarily. We need to build a system that allows correspondent authority of finance, budget, taxation and debt to each level of government, so that governments at all levels are fiscally independent and self-balancing. We should also relax the central government's administrative constraints on the amount of debt, raise the limit on the amount of local government borrowing, and completely open the channels of standardized borrowing for local government, so as to avoid central government intervention that inhibits local initiatives. At the same time, we should ensure that there is an effective restraint mechanism so as to prevent the unrestrained and chaotic pursuit of local initiatives. Relevant measures could include improving the governance system, improving the transparency of debt information, and giving full play to the restraint role of financial markets. We should employ the binding role of local people's congresses, which will independently decide the amount, duration, and interest rate of the bonds. In addition, we should establish a bankruptcy system for local governments to impose hard constraints on their budget management. "Government bankruptcy" refers only to fiscal bankruptcy, rather than the bankruptcy of government functions. Here I am proposing a bankruptcy system that would be a constraint on local governments, not a punishment for residents, under which the basic public services enjoyed by the general public would not be significantly affected. Looking to the international experience, there have been more than 40 bankruptcies of local governments in the United States since 1980. As a result of the bankruptcy of the government of Orange County, California, in 1994, the government laid off 2,000 civil servants to save money on wages, but still needed to provide general public services. In fact, considering the role of local government as the main provider of public services, then regardless of whether the bankruptcy law is explicitly implemented, the benefits of solvency buffer and even debt exemption from restructuring opportunities will be greater than the costs, such as interruption of public financing channels and damage to reputation. For example, Article 903 of Chapter 9 of the United States Bankruptcy Code, "Reservation of the Power of State Government to Manage Local Government," makes clear that this chapter does not restrict or weaken the state government's power to manage local governments within or subordinate to the state in terms of political or governmental activities (including the cost of these activities), either through legislation or through other means.

We should also learn from the beneficial practices of fiscal federalism. By speeding up the rationalization of fiscal relations between the central and local governments, we will improve both the efficiency of fiscal fund allocation and the institutional guarantee to reduce fiscal and financial risks. Fiscal federalism is the mainstream mode in all major economies, in both federal and unitary states, and local finance has a certain level of independence. For China, an economy in transition and with different situations in different regions, it is particularly important that local governments should have some degree of independence. In particular, administrative powers as to whether and how property tax should be imposed, should be dominated by local governments and not necessarily planned by the central government, based on considerations of externality, information complexity, and incentive compatibility.

Finally, we need to strengthen coordination of fiscal and financial policies. This is important both for steady growth and for deleveraging. In the current situation, if fiscal deleveraging is accompanied by financial deleveraging, this may lead to a dilemma for monetary policy. Failure to ease liquidity could cause further tightening of the overall financial environment and harm the real economy, while easing liquidity will accumulate risks to a greater extent. In fact, in the context of increasing debt-oriented and financialized government financing, changes in the financial market have already had a direct impact on fiscal financing conditions, and risk transfer between fiscal financing and finance can easily occur. Basically, the fiscal and the financial are bound together for good or ill. We need to strengthen policy coordination and overall planning from the standpoint of preventing and controlling systemic risks.

2.2.2 *Improve the Financing Mechanism of Urbanization Construction*

Coordinated urbanization is a major strategic choice for China to achieve modernization, and represents the greatest potential for domestic demand over the next 20 years. At present, China's urbanization construction faces problems of non-standardized and unsustainable financing, which not only creates a bottleneck blocking further promotion of urbanization, but also hides certain financial risks. Finding the right way to provide standardized, stable, and sustainable financial support for urbanization is a major task. To this end, we should consider both domestic and foreign experience, adopt a combination of property tax and municipal bonds, use the future proceeds of urbanization construction to make up for the current gap in construction funding, and form a positive incentive to establish a sustainable financing mechanism for urbanization.

2.2.2.1 A Sustainable Financing Mechanism is Urgently Needed to Promote Urbanization

Urbanization is an integral part and a fundamental policy of modernization. It is the driving force of China's economic and social development and of the expansion of domestic demand. In the past 20 years, China's urbanization rate has grown rapidly, with an average annual increase of 1.2%. In 2011, the urbanization rate exceeded 50%. However, compared with the average level of 80% in developed countries and regions, the overall level of China's urbanization is still low, and there remains huge development potential. According to some predictions, by 2030 China's urbanization rate will have risen to 65–70%, and the urban population will have increased by about 300 million. This would reflect a growth in urbanization rate of about one percentage point per year, and the relocation of more than 10 million people from rural to urban areas every year. Given that the Chinese government Central Committee and the State Council have made clear plans to further promote urbanization, it is clear that China's urbanization is set to enter a new stage of rapid development.

Solving the problem of funding security is crucial to advancing China's urbanization. Compared with the situation in developed countries, China's construction funding gap is particularly prominent. This is because the process of urbanization is also a process of popularizing basic public services, which requires a large amount of investment in infrastructure, public utilities, and public services. Hence, solving the problem of capital security is crucial to the effective promotion of urbanization. Developed countries in Europe and America do not face such a stark funding gap, mainly because their process of urbanization took place relatively slowly, over one to two hundred years. It has therefore rarely been necessary to put large sums of money at one time into city construction. Meanwhile, the city governments of developed countries with mature financial systems have accumulated considerable wealth, and are able to fund urban construction and maintenance mainly through revenue. In contrast, China is in a stage of rapid development, and needs to invest large amounts of municipal construction funds in a relatively short period of time, while local governments have relatively weak financial resources. In other words, China's urbanization will face severe shortage of construction funds at present and in the future.

2.2.2.2 Problems and Risks in China's Current Financing Approach for Urbanization

For a long time, China's local governments have not had the financial power to match their administrative power, and this has exacerbated the financial pressure on urbanization. The reform of tax distribution in 1994 took fiscal power away from local governments, but did not remove their administrative responsibilities. Hence, while local governments, especially city governments, undertake a large amount of urban infrastructure, public utilities, and public service construction, they do not have the power to set special taxes to finance those activities, and most of the local taxes they do control are relatively small, sporadic, and unstable. Faced with a large gap in construction funding, they are restricted by the Budget Law and cannot borrow money directly.

To raise funds for construction, China's local governments rely on three main channels of financing. The first is income from land transfer. According to China's current laws and regulations, land transfer revenues are collected and managed by city and county governments and can be put into local treasuries. Therefore, under great financial pressure, many local governments adopt the mode of "land finance," supplementing their financial strength with land transfer revenue to support urbanization construction. The second channel comprises project financing arrangements mainly based on bank loans, including financing by local government financing platforms. Because China's Budget Law prohibits local governments from issuing bonds, city governments must use existing revenue to meet municipal investment needs. In the gap that developed between the relevant legal restrictions on borrowing and the actual demand for construction funds, local financing platforms emerged and developed rapidly, offering a means by which local governments could borrow money from banks, although not directly. Some financing platforms have the right to collect fees and cash flow for specific projects in the future, or to manage the price of relevant public services, such as municipal water supply and toll road pricing. In essence, this is a reliance on future income to finance municipal construction in the present. The third channel comprises other revenues. In order to increase revenue under financial pressure, local governments use various fees and off-budget income, resulting in many fiscal revenue and expenditure activities in the gray zone.

In practice, local governments raise funds to invest in urbanization construction through the above three channels, either through choice, or because of lack of any alternative. However, these channels have problems in terms of standardization and transparency, stability and sustainability, and hiding financial risks. For example, many local financing platforms have low transparency and a lack of clarity in terms of capital flow and internal management, making it difficult to form effective constraints and supervision over local government financing behaviors. At present, many local governments still use a variety of charging items, with unclear collection basis and different collection standards. Moreover, many of them are off-budget and are not standardized. With regard to the lack of stability and sustainability, the existing system does not stipulate that land transfer income must be used for urbanization construction; rather, that income is often included in the fiscal ledger "big account" for overall planned use. At the same time, the income scale is often influenced by land supply and demand and macro-control policies, and is therefore not a stable source of funds for urbanization construction. In addition, income from land transfer is usually collected from land rent for the next 40–70 years. The new Property Law stipulates that land use rights are automatically renewed upon expiration, but it is not clear whether local governments are allowed to continue collecting land use fees at that time; in other words, land transfer payments may be one-off and unsustainable. With regard to fiscal and financial risks, the local financing platforms causing concern are those that are implicitly guaranteed by local governments, but are not included in the unified management of local government debt and fiscal budget. This is likely to induce moral hazard, lead to excessive debt, and hide risks by obscuring the real debt base amount and the solvency of local governments. Meanwhile, as the liabilities of these platforms are mainly concentrated in bank loans, once default occurs the fiscal risks will spread to become financial risks. In view of this, the State Council promptly deployed the Ministry of Finance to take the lead in strengthening classified management and regulation of local government debt. It is therefore foreseeable that the financing intensity of local government financing platforms will be much lower than in the past. Finally, it should also be noted that the replacement of taxes by fees, and an overemphasis on fees while neglecting taxes, caused by gray income, will seriously erode the tax base and destroy the normal market economic environment.

Based on the above practical situation, we can ask, and answer, the following two questions: First of all, can we adopt the pay-as-you-go approach, and not use future money to support China's urbanization? In other words, can local governments do without borrowing? From the perspective of necessity, China is in a stage of rapid urbanization, which determines the existence of current large-scale and centralized demand for construction funds. At present, the fiscal accumulation and fiscal revenue of local governments are very limited, and are not sufficient to fully fund current urbanization construction. From the perspective of rationality, the improvement of urban infrastructure and public facilities, as well as the enhancement of public service capacity, will bring about the improvement of future value of the city; that is, the benefits of current urbanization construction investment will be reflected in the future. Therefore, it is reasonable for the city government to borrow future funds to support current urbanization construction; that is, to use those future benefits for current construction. From the perspective of feasibility, government debt must eventually be repaid by future tax revenue. Therefore, in the long run, government debt is equivalent to tax revenue. When current tax revenue is insufficient, government debt can be used to solve the problem of "time difference." In the current situation of insufficient external demand, China's high savings rate has remained around 50% for a long time, providing favorable conditions for local government borrowing. At the same time, the problem of financing platforms also indicates that a normative and transparent restraint mechanism should be established for local government borrowing, to avoid potential risks such as excessive borrowing.

Second, can we use a single income, and not comprehensive income such as tax revenue, to repay the local government urbanization debt? Due to a lack of fiscal and tax system arrangements to match urbanization construction, local governments have to rely on land finance under huge financial pressure, creating a situation in which land transfer income is the main or even single source of income for urbanization construction. Some local governments rely excessively on land finance, squeezing out land like toothpaste from a tube, which leads to high land price and a consequent adverse impact on all links of urban construction and social development. This practice affects the coordinated development of urbanization and the service industry.

High land prices will lead to high investment costs in public facilities, high housing prices, and high start-up costs in urban service industry. For example, in the case of laid-off workers, if the rental and sale prices of houses are too high, it will be difficult for them to start small businesses or find new jobs in this way, which will affect the development of the service industry and employment growth. Furthermore, excessive reliance on land finance inhibits the healthy development of the real estate market. This is because local governments are motivated to push up land prices in order to increase revenue, which will further reinforce the expectation of rising real estate prices and increase the difficulty of regulating the real estate market. Finally, reliance on land finance will also affect the integration of farmers into cities and towns, and further affect the urbanization process. Urbanization is a process not only of expanding urban land area, but also of farmers becoming citizens. At present, China's urbanization is more about the urbanization of land than the urbanization of population. 240 million farmers have not yet integrated into the cities. In addition to the restrictions of the household registration system, the high housing price also raises the threshold for farmers to live and work in cities and towns, making it difficult for them to live and work in peace and contentment. Some Latin American and Southeast Asian countries have not properly handled the industrial and employment problems in the process of urbanization, leading to urban slums and other social problems. If urbanization construction relies exclusively on the single income of land transfer, it will not only impair the standardization, stability, and sustainability of financing sources, but also adversely affect the development of related industries and employment, the coordinated development within cities and between urban and rural areas, and even the whole urbanization process. The only sustainable and fundamental solution is to perfect the relevant fiscal and tax system arrangements, giving local governments power of taxation (mainly property tax) correspondent to the authority over urbanization construction, and supporting further urbanization construction through property tax revenue, user fees (such as highways, water projects), and other comprehensive income. In the short term, local governments must rely on comprehensive income such as land income, fee collection, and other fiscal income, and in the future, they can rely on comprehensive income, mainly of property tax.

2.2.2.3 Financing Urbanization Construction: The International Experience

I. *The city governments have balanced financial and administrative power, and enjoy independent tax and debt issuing power*

Looking to the international experience, local governments, especially city governments, play a leading role in urban planning and construction. That role is matched by their strong autonomy in fiscal and tax legislation, and ability to provide effective financial support for urbanization construction. For example, the state and local governments in the United States have their own fiscal revenue and expenditure scope;

in particular, the city governments have independent tax power and debt issuance power. Tax power provides the city government with a stable and sustainable source of fiscal revenue, forming the basic guarantee to support the urbanization construction. At the same time, the city government can independently decide whether to issue municipal bonds to make up for any shortfall of current tax revenue.

II. *The financing gap of urbanization construction is solved mainly through municipal bond financing*

Internationally, the main way of financing urban government debt is through the issuance of municipal bonds through the capital market. Municipal bonds originated in the United States in the 1920s, and were gradually adopted in other developed countries and regions, such as Japan and Europe, after the 1970s. Today, developing countries such as India and Indonesia have also begun to issue municipal bonds to finance urban construction. Municipal bonds generally fall into two categories: general obligation bonds and revenue bonds. General obligation bonds are issued by the city government, with property tax and other tax revenues as an important source of repayment. Revenue bonds are issued for specific infrastructure projects and are repaid through the proceeds from the paid use of these facilities.

In addition to controlling the debt level of local governments reasonably through the balance of financial budget and the restriction of financial revenue and expenditure, municipal bonds can also establish positive incentive market constraints on borrowing by coordinating with institutional arrangements such as credit rating, information disclosure, market pricing, investor suitability, and external supervision. The advantages are embodied in three aspects. First, the use of municipal bonds is conducive to enhancing the transparency of city governments' debt situation and regulating their financing behaviors. The unified issuance of bonds, unified use, and unified repayment by city governments can curb all kinds of government financing behaviors that are non-transparent, non-standardized, unclear in terms of responsibilities and rights, and not subject to budgetary supervision, and can also provide long-term stable and sustainable sources of municipal construction funds. Second, this form of funding is helpful to strengthen the internal and external constraints on the debt behavior of city governments, and to encourage them to improve local financial ecology and pay debts on schedule. As the main body responsible for the promotion of urban construction, the city government issues municipal bonds in its own name. Under a series of hard indicators and market constraint mechanism, the debt risk can be effectively identified and priced. In this overall way, excessive debt of the city government can be restrained and the local financial ecology can be improved. It can also help to solve the problem whereby new officers ignore the promises made by their predecessors. Third, the use of municipal bonds is conducive to diversifying risks in the banking system and maintaining stability in the financial system. If the city government finances by borrowing, the debt is often mainly concentrated in the bank system. In the case of default, fiscal risks can be transferred to the banking system. Municipal bonds can enable more non-bank financial institutions and all kinds of investors to participate in the investment, strengthen the supervision and constraint on the city government, and effectively reduce the risk concentrated in the banking system.

III. *Property tax revenue: An important source of funding for municipal bond repayment*

In the international practice, the main repayment sources of municipal bonds are user fees, property taxes and other special taxes, and general fiscal revenue. Where public products tend to be used by only a few or selected people, the problem of funding source can be solved by charging users. This is mainly applicable to project revenue bonds, such as the expressway charging used to repay municipal bonds issued for financing construction of the expressway. If public products have more public features and it is difficult to realize user payment, the problem of funding source can be solved by relying more on property tax and general fiscal revenue, which corresponds to general liability debt in municipal bonds.

The use of property tax in urbanization has its own advantages. Tax is generally divided into purpose tax and general tax. The former is clearly targeted, and can only be used for a specific expenditure project; the latter includes taxes such as income tax and value added tax, and can be used for various fiscal expenditure items. To support urbanization construction by property tax revenue has an inherent rationality. The rise in value of land and real estate is due to enhanced location advantage, which is supported by the city government's public spending; hence the proceeds from the transfer of land, and the property taxes (mainly real estate tax) collected by the government should be used for the special purpose of supporting urbanization construction. The United States, Britain, Australia and many other countries take property tax as the main tax of local government revenue and an important source of funds to repay municipal bonds. International experience also shows that the level of property tax revenue is correlated with the level of urbanization, and there is a positive feedback incentive mechanism between them. By strengthening urban construction and improving the local public environment, the government can promote the appreciation of property, thus creating a richer source of property tax, even making it the major tax of the local government, further enhancing the solvency of the local government and promoting the development of urban construction.

Overall, international experience shows that the combination of municipal bonds and property tax is a reasonable and effective way to solve the financing problem of urbanization, and one that is widely used. By issuing municipal bonds, the current municipal construction expenditure can be supported with future income to improve the level of urbanization. At the same time, the property appreciation premium brought by municipal construction is recovered by property tax revenue, which serves as an important source of municipal bond repayment and realizes the efficient spread of the financial burden over time.

2.2.2.4 Reform of Institutional Mechanisms and Establishment of a Sustainable Financing Mechanism for Urbanization

Comparing the international experience with China's situation, we can find that the problems regarding China's urbanization construction financing are concentrated in two main aspects: First, the support of the current fiscal and taxation system for urbanization construction is not clear, and local governments are not empowered to set up a special purpose tax; coupled with the fact that city councils have very limited financial resources, this means that their current revenue is not sufficient to meet the needs of the municipal investment. Second, due to the restrictions of the Budget Law, local governments are not allowed to borrow directly and use future earnings for municipal construction in the current period.

The solution to the problem is to translate future earnings of urbanization construction to the current period, spread the financial burden across the timeline and pay it back gradually; this will require the reform of institutional mechanisms and a combination of property tax and municipal bonds. At the same time we should form a positive incentive mechanism whereby the improvement of municipal construction level and the increase of property tax revenue promote each other and create a virtuous cycle. Specifically, the following four measures can be taken to promote the establishment of a sustainable urbanization financing mechanism.

First, we should amend the Budget Law to empower city governments to issue municipal bonds. There are many levels of local government in China, but urbanization construction is mainly carried out directly by city governments, including governments of provincial capitals, prefecture-level cities, and relatively big counties. By contrast, provincial governments have less responsibility and burden in this regard. At present, the revision of the Budget Law should be taken as an opportunity to promote the unification of local governments' administrative power and financial power under the premise of guarding against risks and ensuring the overall balance of revenue and expenditure, and to empower city governments to issue municipal bonds conditionally according to the actual situation. In fact, China's bond market does have the necessary conditions for the introduction of municipal bonds. The total amount of bonds under custody in the bond market exceeded 25 trillion yuan, and the annual trading volume exceeded 200 trillion yuan. The variety of different bonds is constantly increasing, the market restraint mechanism has been initially established, and the awareness of institutional investors' assumption of risks is generally established. In recent years, China's Ministry of Finance has issued bonds on behalf of local governments, and Shanghai and other local governments have issued bonds on their own. Some urban construction investment bonds are somewhat similar to municipal bonds.

Second, we should improve the fiscal and tax system and establish property tax. Although real estate tax has been piloted in Shanghai and Chongqing, there is currently no real property tax in China. In order to establish stable, standard, and sustainable sources of urbanization funds and ensure the smooth issuance of municipal bonds, the existing real estate tax should be perfected or a new property tax established. As far as possible, there should be room for flexibility in terms of tax base, tax rate, and reduction and exemption policies. This will make it more reasonable for local governments to match their administrative and financial power, and should realize a virtuous circle among urbanization construction level, property tax revenue, and municipal bond payment ability. It will also conform to the principle of "who invests, who gains, and who is responsible."

Third, urban construction investment bonds should be transformed to provide a standard source of funds for urbanization. Under the circumstances that the Budget Law has not been modified, project income bonds with clear repayment sources can be used as a breaking point. A considerable number of urban construction investment bonds in China have the characteristics of quasi-municipal bonds, but lack relevant institutional norms. Standardized transformation of urban construction investment bonds should make it clear that the income bonds of municipal bonds are those that raise money for utilities and pay mainly from user fees. Furthermore, we must insist on the principle of comprehensive consideration and market constraints, and integrate the management of income bonds and debt repayment arrangements into the unified management of local government debt and fiscal budget.

Fourth, we should actively explore multiple ways to raise funds to support urbanization. According to the 12th Five-Year Plan, market access will be relaxed and private capital will be encouraged to enter basic industries, infrastructure, municipal public welfare programs, social undertakings, and financial services. The capital demand for urbanization construction is large, the construction and recovery cycle is long, and the government's investment pressure is too great. It is suggested that China should learn from international experience and explore diversified ways to raise funds, such as using the PPP model and involving the private sector in providing public goods and services, as well as asset securitization of local financing vehicles.

2.2.2.5 Issues for Consideration

I. *The effectiveness of fiscal restraint mechanism and the problem of "new officers ignore their predecessors' promises"*

Under the current Budget Law, local governments are not allowed to engage in debt financing. This financial constraint mechanism does not meet the actual demand, and its constraint capacity is decreasing. It has already been broken through to some extent by disguised approaches and hidden risks. The basic intention of strict fiscal discipline in the current Budget Law is good. The European sovereign debt crisis and the US "fiscal cliff" exposed by the financial crisis show the importance of strict public fiscal discipline. However, it is important to ensure that fiscal discipline is realistic and thus can be strictly observed. Under real fiscal pressure, if there is no reasonable financing channel, then even if the local government is strictly prohibited from borrowing, it will try to circumvent the restrictions through various means. Such disguised borrowing is often opaque and irregular, and is not only risky, but also weakens the effectiveness of fiscal discipline. The past county and township debt problems and the recent excessive debt problems of local financing vehicles all reflect this contradiction.

By explicitly empowering the city government to issue municipal bonds we will give full play to the role of market restraint mechanisms. As long as we continue to monitor the total debt level of local governments and thoroughly evaluate the local financial ecology, this will not only ensure the financial support for the construction of urbanization, but also form a relatively effective fiscal constraint mechanism for local governments.

First, the key to preventing local government debt risks lies in properly controlling the overall level of local government debt. By controlling the source of fiscal balance and linking local government debt to fiscal revenue, we can effectively control the scale of government debt and prevent excessive debt by stipulating the ratio of total government debt to assets, debt ratio or debt repayment ratio.

Second, the introduction of municipal bonds can make full use of the financial market restraint mechanism to strengthen local government debt management. The basic functions of financial markets are risk assessment and price discovery. Through the constraint mechanism of the financial market, municipal bonds issued by different cities can present different prices in the market, reflecting different ratings and credit levels, as well as different risks and solvency. If disclosures and ratings indicate that the government's fiscal conditions are too weak or it is over-indebted, investors will raise price requirements, reduce investment, or even stop buying the bonds it issues. This approach will not only help investors to judge risks and make decisions, but will also restrict the financing behavior and fund use efficiency of the city government. Of course, the effectiveness of such a constraint mechanism depends largely on the degree of market perfection, including whether rating companies are independent and whether the rating work is transparent. In addition, the fact that local residents constitute the main body of municipal bond investment can enhance the constraints on the city governments' debt behavior. Since urbanization construction is conducive to improving the quality of basic public services, local residents have an incentive to buy municipal bonds. Moreover, local residents have a better understanding of whether the use of local municipal bond funds is reasonable and efficient, and about the level of solvency. If the funds are not used properly or the debt is excessive, local residents can report this directly to the local government and even stop buying the bonds, a fact that is conducive to the accurate pricing of municipal bonds and forms an effective restriction on government debt.

Third, the evaluation of local financial ecology is also conducive to further strengthening the constraints on local government debt behavior, especially the problem of new officers ignoring the promises made by their predecessors. After the People's Bank of China put forward the concept of financial ecology in 2003, the Chinese Academy of Social Sciences organized an independent and fair evaluation on regional financial ecology, and achieved good results. Poor local financial ecology will affect local capital inflow. In the absence of financial ecological assessment, local governments borrow from banks without external supervision and constraints. Once the leading group members of local governments are changed, it will be much more difficult for banks to recover loans; indeed, the banks may end up with nothing. The issuance of municipal bonds, coupled with financial ecological assessment, will bind local governments. Once municipal bonds are issued, the current government will assume repayment obligations for the sake of maintaining its own credit, regardless of whether the previous government made the right decision. It will not dare to repudiate a debt easily, since if it does so its rating will immediately be lowered, which will affect the evaluation of local financial ecology. Thus, municipal bonds will form an effective constraint mechanism for the local governments' debt issuance behavior.

II. *Mutual matching of property tax and municipal bonds*

Through the combination of property tax and municipal bonds, we can realize the spreading out of the financial burden on the timeline in the process of urbanization. It is important to note that only when the two are used together can we form a more efficient translation with good constraint mechanism. We cannot achieve this by any single measure. If property tax is imposed without municipal bonds, the current funding gap cannot be made up. Although in the long run, the scale of property tax will continue to grow with the development of China's urbanization, this will be a gradual process, and property tax will be insufficient to collect the revenue needed to meet the current municipal construction fund demand. If municipal bonds are used without real estate tax, investors will question the stable and predictable source of municipal bond repayment. This will affect their investment confidence, so that municipal bonds may not be issued or the financing cost will be very high.

There may be concerns as to whether property tax, which is now on only a small scale, will grow into an important source of revenue to support urbanization in the future. It should be noted that, under the current system of one-off collection of land transfer fees, the government will face the dilemma of financial exhaustion caused by less and less land for sale. Unlike land transfer fees, property tax is levied on the basis of the market value of the property and there is no danger of interruption. Moreover, as mentioned above, there is a positive feedback mechanism between the collection of property tax and the construction of urbanization. By strengthening urban construction, the government can promote the appreciation of property, create a richer source of property tax, and the income can be used to further improve the local public environment. It will be necessary to conduct an in-depth study on the relationship and transformation between land transfer system and property tax, so as to fundamentally solve the problem that local governments rely too much on land finance and affect the healthy development of the real estate market.

III. *Risk prevention and resolution of existing local government financing vehicles*

If the new financing mechanism of municipal bonds and property tax can be established in the very near future, this will not only provide better financial support for accelerating urbanization development, but will also help solve the current risks of local government financing vehicles. Projects that rely entirely on user fees can be retained because they are financially sustainable, with a self-cycle of current investment and future repayment of principal and interest. Other projects that do not have this feature should be adjusted and designed so that they can be transformed into a combination tool that relies mainly on municipal bonds and property tax repayment, and at the same time receives the support of city finance and the support and constraint of the financial market. Under such a combined mechanism, the quality of financial assets invested in urbanization construction and risk control will be better guaranteed, and there will be obvious improvement to the current risks of local government financing vehicles and their way out.

2.3 Local Financial Management Autonomy

In recent years, the implicit liabilities of local governments in China have grown rapidly, far exceeding the explicit liabilities. Financing vehicles and city investment bonds are the main forms of local governments' implicit liabilities. They are often counted as corporate sector debt, which makes it difficult to judge accurately the leverage risk of all sectors in China. These problems are related to the unsound financial relationship between different levels of government and the unclear boundary between fiscal and financial responsibilities in China. Looking to the international experience, major economies have relatively complete incentive and constraint institutional frameworks for local financial management. Self-discipline by local governments, legal and administrative constraints by the central (or federal) government, and financial market constraints can work together. For a small number of local governments, there are also relatively reasonable risk management and responsibility sharing mechanisms. Compared with the experience of major economies, the incentive and restraint mechanism of China's local financial management is still far from perfect, and needs to be improved.

2.3.1 Incentive and Restraint System Framework of Local Financial Management

2.3.1.1 Fiscal Management System with Local Autonomy

In most large economies, in both federal and unitary government systems, the usual mode is a hierarchical inter-governmental fiscal system that allows local autonomy. In this fiscal management system, each level of government has correspondent authority of finance, budget, and taxation, where its fiscal power matches its administrative power. This minimizes the intervention of the central government in the fiscal management of local governments.

Federalism itself is formed by the transfer of power by local governments, which have greater autonomy. For example, the federal, state and local governments of the

United States independently exercise their respective budgetary powers and independently prepare, approve, and execute budgets at their own levels. It is a system of self-reliance, self-balance and self-management. Similarly, Germany implements a fiscal system of federal, state and local level management, in which each level of government has its own budget and is responsible to its own parliament. As another example, when the Brazilian Constitution was amended in 1983, Brazil increased the transfer payments from the federal government to local governments and expanded the state tax base. The share of disposable fiscal revenue of state governments continued to rise. In 1988, Brazil's new Constitution stipulated that state and municipal governments should have greater autonomy in terms of fiscal revenue and expenditure.

The unitary state grants local fiscal autonomy through the authorization of the central government. For example, the French Socialist government's decentralization reform of 1982 gave more administrative and financial powers to local elected officials. In March 2003, a constitutional amendment further enriched the right of local autonomy, recognized the legislative power and financial autonomy of territorial units, and enhanced the independence of local finance. Since 1949, Japan has taken a number of steps to promote decentralization reform and enhance local financial resources and financial autonomy, for example through the Decentralization Promotion Act (1995), the Comprehensive Decentralization Act (1999), and Reform of the Intergovernmental Finance System (2006).

2.3.1.2 Stakeholders' Role in the Health of Local Finance

The sound and effective operation of economy and finance by local governments benefits local residents, local government employees, and elected officials. Residents benefit from increased job opportunities; from excellent education, health, public security, and other local public services; and from lower costs of public services such as pension and medical care, and the tax burden, so as to avoid transferring the current debt burden to future generations. The benefits for government employees are tied to the state of local finance. Finally, with ample local financial support, public officials benefit from the fact that jobs are more stable, with no risk of layoffs due to government spending cuts; salaries rise in line with the economic development; and pension, medical insurance, and other benefits are guaranteed. In addition, elected officials face the political constraints of the electoral system and must be accountable to the people. The health of the fiscal and economic system is ultimately reflected in the ballot, and directly affects whether elected officials can obtain government positions.

Conversely, if state and local government finances are not functioning well, there will be adverse impacts for residents and ordinary public employees. First of all, the quantity and quality of local public services will be affected. For example, in 2013 the US city of Detroit filed for bankruptcy. As a result, municipal construction shrank and public services were stretched thin. The number of police officers was cut by 40%, making it the least safe city in America. At the same time, the tax burden increased. At the time of the city's bankruptcy, more than 200,000 people were drawing pensions and healthcare benefits, 40% of the government's revenue had to be used to pay for retirement benefits or interest payments, and public employees' pensions alone used up all property tax revenues. The city had to raise revenue through higher taxes and new taxes; it became the most heavily taxed city in Michigan, which accelerated the exodus of the middle class and worsened its revenue position. As the cost of public services rose and the quality of public services declined, Detroit's residents had to move to other areas, leaving only 700,000 of its original 1.7 million residents. Losses for government employees included pay restrictions, layoffs, and pension losses. Before the city's financial bankruptcy, employees of Detroit's municipal government could retire after 25 years of service and receive $30,000 a year in pension and health insurance. Financial ruin decimated retirement benefits and eliminated health insurance. To take another case, after the outbreak of the sovereign debt crisis in Greece in 2009, the Greek government announced cuts in government spending and the number of public servants, and implemented a series of fiscal austerity measures including freezing the recruitment of public sector employees and reducing civil service pay. Given that the interests of local residents, government employees, and elected officials are all tied to the quality of local financial management, it is clear that the budget review of fiscal operation and major projects is crucial, and should be very strict.

2.3.1.3 Central Aid Often Comes at the Expense of Local Autonomy

Many countries have responded to poor local financial management by setting up bankruptcy mechanisms for local governments. Government bankruptcy refers to the fiscal bankruptcy of the government, not the bankruptcy of government functions. Anarchy is not allowed. Bankrupt governments bear the burden of maintaining a minimum level of public services for urban residents, while at the same time improving the condition of deficit and debt deterioration and restoring fiscal balance through various means to control expenditure and increase revenue. In order to prevent moral hazard, the central government will not unconditionally rescue local governments after they go bankrupt. If local governments want higher levels of government to help them, they must sacrifice their autonomy. For example, when the city of Detroit went bankrupt, Kevin Earl, the emergency manager appointed by the state of Michigan to replace the elected mayor, temporarily stripped the city of its autonomy. When France's regional governments run out of money and default on their debts, the provincial governors who represent the President will take charge directly; the original local government and local council are dissolved. Debts owned by the former local government are paid by the central government, then after the election of a new local government and parliament, new fiscal plans (including, for example, tax increases and spending cuts) are drawn up to gradually repay the original debts and the debt repayment funds advanced by the central government. In Japan, local governments can seek fiscal reconstruction according to the Act on Special Measures for the Reconstruction and Revitalization. However, by doing so they become bankrupt and are deprived of their autonomy, so that their budgets have to be approved by the central government.

2.3.2 Central Government Restraint of Local Government Financial Management

Under the principle of local autonomy, the central or federal government usually does not interfere in the daily financial management decisions of local governments, and in principle does not undertake the responsibility of rescuing local governments. However, the practice of various countries shows that the central government is not completely immune to local financial crises, so central governments in different countries pay varying degrees of attention to the local financial situation and supervise local debts.

2.3.2.1 Relationship Between Rescue Responsibility and Extent of Supervision

German law does not explicitly stipulate the federal government's obligation to guarantee the debts of local governments, but Germany's constitutional court has ruled that the states should abide by the "principle of fidelity," which allows the federal government and other states to bail out a state if it is unable to pay its debts. To some extent, therefore, German municipal bonds are implicitly guaranteed by the government. Before 2009, the Ministry of Finance only provided "window guidance" (oral intervention) on local government bond issuance, with weak binding force. Since June 2009, Germany has implemented the "Debt Brake," which formally limits the size of local government bond issuance. Bond issuance conditions have been tightened.

Before the local financial crisis in Brazil, the federal government had relatively weak binding power over local financial management, and it did not exert effective control over the financial behavior of local governments. After the second oil crisis in 1979, local governments encouraged public enterprises to borrow from foreign markets, regardless of their ability to pay. In 1989, 1993 and 1996, Brazil experienced local government debt crises, all of which were bailed out by the federal government. In the process of provided this assistance, Brazil's federal government began to impose a series of financial constraints on local governments. In the second bailout, the federal government ruled that states that defaulted would not be allowed to raise new debt, and amended the Constitution to allow the federal government to deduct funds for local debts from central transfer payments to local governments. In the third crisis, the federal government worked together with the state governments to formulate the Incentive Plan to Promote Restructuring and Fiscal Adjustment of State Governments. For states with weak fiscal restructuring, the federal government would stop providing transfer payments or would even confiscate their tax revenues to pay off debts.

2.3.2.2 Relationship Between the Investor Structure of Local Bonds and the Extent of Central Government Intervention in Local Debt Management

US municipal bonds are the only category in the bond market to be held primarily by individuals, with individual ownership at about 40%. The reason is that individual income taxes make up a large portion of US tax revenue, and the income from individual investments in municipal bonds is usually tax-free. This individual-based investor structure means that the smooth issuance of municipal bonds depends on market acceptance, and the federal government does not need to intervene too much. At first, most of Japan's local government bonds were purchased by state-owned financial institutions controlled by the central government. The allocation of financial resources was similar to fiscal transfer payments, so the central government had strict debt management over local governments. Before 2005, local governments in Japan had to get the approval of the autonomous minister (now the Minister of General Affairs) to issue bonds, so as to prevent the local government debt from ballooning; ensure the healthy operation of local finance; prevent excessive inclination of funds to rich regions and ensure reasonable allocation of funds; and coordinate the allocation of financial resources among central government, local governments, and the private sector. As the financing of Japan's local debts shifted from government funds to private funds, the management by central government gradually decreased. Since 2006, the Japanese government has stopped using this approval system, instead highlighting the autonomy of local governments in issuing bonds, and strengthening the binding role of local councils.

2.3.2.3 Central Government Legislation and Regulation to Restrict Local Financial Operations

Brazil's Fiscal Responsibility Law (FRL) and its supporting laws have established a general framework of three-level government in fiscal and debt budgeting and implementation and reporting systems, and formulated highly operational quantitative indicators to regulate local government debt. For example, Brazil's local governments must report their revenues to the federal government every year and must report on government debt every four months. Local governments must not borrow more than their capital budgets, and the debt ratios of state governments must be less than 200%, while those of municipal governments must be less than 120%. If local governments fail to fulfill their obligations under the FRL, those responsible will be dismissed from their positions, banned from working in the public sector, fined, or even prosecuted. At the same time, the central bank has imposed some restrictions on commercial bank lending to the public sector. Local government debt shall not exceed 45% of a bank's net assets. Banks are prohibited from lending to states that borrow illegally, break the deficit limit, or fail to federal government or any other bank. In addition, Brazil has mandatory disclosure of information, and all lending transactions by local governments must be registered in the national information system, or be considered illegal. The information system is open and transparent, connected, and accessible to all banks. The system runs automatically and cannot be manually adjusted.

2.3.2.4 Central Government Agencies to Monitor Local Financial Operations

Before France passed its decentralization reform in 1982, local governments needed special permission from the central government to issue municipal bonds. Since 1982, local governments have been able to issue municipal bonds independently, without central government approval. Meanwhile, the central government closely monitors the financial operation and debt situation of local governments through the administrative and judicial systems. With regard to administrative supervision by the Ministry of Finance and its accredited institutions, in August 2001, France set up a Debt Management Center under the Ministry of Finance to monitor the assets and liabilities of governments at all levels on a daily basis, and ensure that governments at all levels can repay their debts in a timely manner. Accredited agencies supervise and inspect the financial operation and liabilities of the local governments and, if problems are found, they advise the local government and report to the superior financial department. This kind of timely supervision has ensured the benign state of local government debt and financial operation and greatly reduced the occurrence of local financial bankruptcy and insolvency. With regard to judicial supervision, the court of auditors is an independent state institution authorized by the national assembly and the highest judicial organ to check the use of government funds. Its main tasks are to assist parliament and the government in supervising the implementation of financial laws and regulations, and to examine the accounts of central and local government departments, schools, hospitals, and other public utilities. The court of auditors has set up a budgetary discipline tribunal to hear cases of financial and economic discipline violations by leaders of state organs and public utilities at all levels.

2.3.3 Financial Market Restraint on Local Financial Management

2.3.3.1 Financial Markets Can Provide Whole-Process and All-Dimensional Constraints

In both federalist nations, such as America, Brazil, and Germany, and unitary states, such as France and Japan, local governments can issue local government bonds (municipal bonds) directly and autonomously. Independent issuance of bonds not only expands local government financing channels and increases residents' financial investment channels, but also plays a role in restricting local financial management through market mechanisms such as credit rating, price volatility, and mortgage liquidity. The US municipal bond market has a large scale and is a model of financial market constraints. For example, with regard to information disclosure, the United States has the most complete government balance sheet preparation and disclosure of any country in the world. At both federal and local government level, there are relatively detailed accounting standards. The role of credit rating is also important. Local bond underwriters should hire credit rating agencies to rate the bonds and upgrade the bonds through the insurance operations of bond insurance agencies or banks. In addition, with regard to the bond insurance mechanism, more than half of the US local government bonds are insured, which greatly improves their security and the trading activity of the secondary market, and enhances the liquidity of the bonds. Practice shows that these measures have controlled risks well in the United States, and have laid a foundation whereby issuers can obtain the funds needed for development, while investors can obtain reasonable investment returns.

In the bond market, if a local government leaves a bad credit record, such as a default, it will be punished by rising financing costs or even market bans. As a member of the European Union and a country that uses the Euro, Greece can be seen as a regional government in Europe. In 2009, three major global credit ratings successively downgraded Greece's sovereign credit rating. On December 7, 2009, Standard and Poor's warned that Greece's sovereign debt rating would be cut one notch from A−. On December 8, Fitch cut Greece's sovereign debt rating to BBB+ . On December 21 Greece's debt problems began to turn into a debt crisis, as the spread on 10-year government bonds rose to 264 basis points.

2.3.3.2 Bond Markets Are More Binding and Risk-Averse Than Credit Markets

Bond market discipline has three advantages over bank lending. First of all, investors of the bond market are more diversified, which reduces risk concentration. Second, the bond market is more transparent. There is timely disclosure of risk factors, with no delay or accumulation into a "grey rhino" or "black swan." Third, bond market participants are very sensitive to the yield rate, and the signal transmission of capital price is smooth. When the financial situation of local governments changes, bond prices are more sensitive to risk factors, which can better restrict the financial management behavior of local governments. The German experience shows that the shift from indirect to direct financing has strengthened the constraint of financial markets on local government debt. Before 1991, local governments in Germany raised money mainly from banks. Germany has about 2,000 banks, of which the majority are regional banks such as local government-funded credit cooperatives (about 1,200) and savings banks (about 450), so it is hard for banks to turn down government funding applications. Weak financial market discipline has had a negative impact on fiscal soundness, and fiscal and bank "bundling" can also transmit risk between each other. Since 1991, through the establishment of the local government bond market, Germany has formed market-oriented constraint on government borrowing. The openness and marketization of financing costs have prompted local governments to consolidate their finance and limit excessive debt growth.

2.3.3.3 Financial Market Conditions Affect the Binding Force of Credit Ratings

Although the issuance of Japanese local government bonds has a long history and a large scale, for a long time there was no proper credit rating of Japanese local government bonds, which meant that the market could not fulfill its role as a constraint on those bonds. There were three main reasons for this situation. First, the approval system concentrated excessive risks on the central government, which led to a lack of demand for credit rating on the part of both local bond issuers and investors. Second, the excessive transfer payment meant that regional differences in the solvency of local governments were too small for the credit rating agencies to conduct rating on that basis. Third, there had been no default of local debt repayment in Japan since the 1950s, which further reduced the need for credit rating of local debt. However, with the long-term stagnation of the economy, the financial conditions of Japanese governments at all levels deteriorated significantly. The reform of the fiscal investment and financing system and transfer payment system led to a rapid widening of differences in the solvency of different regions. Given these changes to the market environment, the market demand for the credit rating of local government bonds greatly increased. In order to adapt to this change, in 1999 the famous Japanese credit rating agency, "R&I", began to conduct credit rating on 28 local autonomous bodies that issued local bonds publicly. The credit rating of Japanese local government bonds mainly focuses on: (1) the regional economic strength and its trend, which can lead to increase or decrease of tax revenue; (2) the balance between the debt scale and the debt repayment funds of the issuer; (3) the financial situation and structure of revenues and expenditures of local governments (including transfer payments), and (4) financial operation capacity and debt repayment willingness of local governments.

2.3.4 The Gap Between China's Local Fiscal Incentive and Restraint Mechanism and Those of the Major Countries, and Suggestions for Improvement

2.3.4.1 The Space for Exploration of Local Autonomy in Fiscal Management

Legally, in a unitary state, the central government has unlimited liability for the debts of local governments. In order to strictly enforce financial and economic discipline, the fiscal boundaries between the central government and local governments should be clearly distinguished, and thorough fiscal decentralization should be implemented. Each level of political power should have correspondent administrative power, financial power, property rights, and creditor's rights. Since there is no local autonomy in China, leading cadres are actually appointed by higher levels, and there is no incentive mechanism for local officials to be "accountable to the people." This makes it difficult for people's congresses at the same level to have a substantive binding effect on budget deliberations; it is also difficult to restrain local governments by means of higher levels' takeover of local autonomy. If we can establish a system of local autonomy in fiscal management, we will have a legal basis whereby each local government is responsible for its own actions, which will help to prevent and defuse local debt risks.

2.3.4.2 Expand the Power of Local Governments to Issue Bonds Independently

China's financial market is dominated by indirect financing and state-owned financial institutions. As was once the case in Japan, the financing of local governments is dominated by bank credit, so it is difficult for the financial market to exert a restrictive effect on local governments, and it has to rely on the central government to intervene in local financial management. Although the new Budget Law, which came into effect in 2015, allows local governments to issue bonds on their own, they still face a strict central approval system. The power to issue bonds is limited to provincial governments, while the main users of such funds are urban governments. Furthermore, compared with the huge stock of local debts and annual financing needs, the annual quota of local government bonds approved by the budget is too small, forming a seller's market, and investors lack choice. Moreover, from the perspective of market investors, because approval authority lies with the central government, the central government has joint and several liabilities for local debts. This creates an expectation of central rescue and "rigid payment," which makes it more difficult to take the risks of local debts seriously, and inhibits the operation of market constraint. According to the 2017 National Conference on Financial Work, "we should give priority to the development of direct financing, and form a multi-level capital market system with complete financing functions, solid basic systems, effective market supervision, and effective protection of investors' legitimate rights and interests." In this regard, expanding the autonomy of local governments to issue bonds will be a breakthrough. The power to issue bonds should be delegated to municipalities and county-level governments that spend money directly, so that the entities that borrow, use money, and repay debts remain the same. Central government control over the amount of local government bonds that can be issued should be removed. The issuance scale of local government bonds should be expanded, and questions of whether they can be issued, and at what price, should be screened and decided by the financial market. There is no need to worry about the disorderly issuance of local government bonds.

2.3.4.3 Improve the Match Between Local Government Revenue and Spending

The reliance on transfer payments will lead to soft budget constraints on local governments and the expectation of a central government backstop. The experience of Japan shows that only by reforming the transfer payment system and improving the identification of local government debt risk can the financial market give an effective credit rating based on local governments' actual financial situation. Therefore, it is necessary to improve the match between local governments' income and expenditure, reform the transfer payment system, reduce the dependence of local governments on the central transfer payment, and truly reflect the local fiscal balance and debt risk. China is a vast country with large differences in resource status and level of economic and social development among different regions. It will take a long time to gradually narrow these differences in wages, pensions, medical benefits, and other aspects. At present, it is neither fair nor sustainable to overemphasize the equalization among regions and let the rich regions support the poor. In fact, free movement of people and free circulation of goods are the most basic conditions for the market mechanism to promote equal access to basic public services. In these aspects, China still lags far behind developed countries. The key measures, therefore, are to break down local protections, preserve the domestic single market, and explicitly prohibit any act that hinders the single market. We should end the household registration system and promote free movement of labor in the single market, for example, by increasing the proportion of pension contributions to personal accounts and making pension accounts more portable.

2.3.4.4 Explore Local Financial Bankruptcy and Accountability Systems

In the absence of a local government bankruptcy system, risks cannot be locally segregated. Consequently, whatever the origins of a payments crisis, the ultimate debtor will be the central government. For China, under pressure from local debt, the greatest significance of establishing a local government financial bankruptcy mechanism lies in clarifying the hierarchical model of government decision-making responsibility, and bringing the accountability model back to "who borrows, who pays." When governments at all levels borrow to finance development, they must set the development goal based on the availability of financial resources. This tailoring of development goals to what financial resources allow can help promote sustainable urbanization. At the same time, we need to improve the system for selecting officials, hold local officials accountable for life, and effectively constrain the financial operations of local governments. Officials in China often move from region to region and from department to department, and are constantly subject to the constraints of organizational and disciplinary authorities. In accordance with the requirements of the National Conference on Financial Work on "strictly controlling the increase of local government debt, holding local governments accountable for their debts for life and checking their liabilities backwards," the inclusion of financial management performance indicators in the assessment, selection, and appointment of cadres will effectively control local government debt.

To explore the bankruptcy system for local governments, China needs to clearly delineate the responsibilities of governments at all levels when their fiscal revenues and expenditures go wrong. Ordinary people should not bear the cost of financial ruin, but they will suffer from the loss of welfare due to lack of money for local infrastructure, utilities, and public services. Financial bankruptcy is not a government bankruptcy; public security, education, medical care, pensions, and other public services should be guaranteed. Local governments themselves should bear the losses and strengthen accountability. Decision-makers should be held accountable for life, and ordinary public officials should also bear certain losses in terms of salary and pension benefits. Furthermore, the financial market should play a role in the distribution of benefits and responsibilities for local government bankruptcies and financial restructuring. First, we should not blindly believe in the rigid payment capacity of local governments, but should identify the transparency of their information so as to promote the formation of a good atmosphere in which local governments can promote fiscal reform and improve the transparency of the whole fiscal operation and management. Second, we should identify the financing capacity and risk credit rating of local governments, and treat differently the financing needs of different local governments, so as to achieve a balance between preventing risks and stabilizing growth. Third, investors should bear the losses of local government financial bankruptcy and the role of market restraint should be given full play. Despite the issuance of the Opinions of the State Council on Strengthening the Administration of Local Government Debts (No. 43 [2014] of the State Council), and the subsequent repeated insistence by the central government on the principle of not bailing out local government debt, it is hard to turn market expectations around. It takes a specific case in which local state-owned enterprises and governments are allowed to fail, as happened in Detroit, for investors to really believe in the central government's determination to block the implicit guarantee.

2.4 Measures to Eliminate Leverage

In recent years, China's debt leverage has attracted a great deal of attention, especially with regard to the high leverage of non-financial enterprises. Among the non-financial enterprises, the leverage ratios of state-owned enterprises and overcapacity industries are relatively high, while those of the residential and government sectors have also increased. However, the increase in the leverage ratio of the financial industry, and its potential risks, have received relatively little attention.

From the macro point of view, high leverage is the result of the government's excessive stimulation of the economy under the background of a decline in the potential economic growth rate. From the micro perspective, weak corporate governance, inadequate monitoring and regulation, and soft budget constraints are the main reasons for the high leverage of enterprises, local governments, and financial institutions.

Therefore, while monetary policy remains stable and neutral, the goal of economic growth should be downplayed. In terms of micro policy, strengthening corporate governance, standardizing the financial and tax relationship between the central and local governments, optimizing financial supervision, and improving the incentive and restraint mechanism are effective measures for deleveraging, with the potential to fundamentally and effectively resolve the debt risk of high leverage. In order to promote the deleveraging of the financial industry in an orderly way, we should not only avoid the risk of debt-deflation caused by violent deleveraging and table shrink, but also use macro policies, monitoring, and regulation to maintain the pressure on financial institutions to deleverage.

2.4.1 Leverage Ratio in China

In recent years, the problem of the leverage ratio in China has aroused widespread concern. Although there are differences in data caliber, the rapid growth of leverage ratio, and the increasing debt burden have become the consensus of all sectors of society.

From a macro perspective, China's overall leverage ratio is not high, but it is rising relatively fast. By the second quarter of 2016, the leverage ratio of China's real economy sector (government + non-financial enterprises + residents) was 254.9%, which was around the middle level among 42 sample countries counted by the BIS (Bank for International Settlements), far lower than the 281.4% of developed economies in the same period, and only slightly higher than the average level of all samples and of G20 countries, by 7.6% and 7.7%, respectively. However, the overall leverage ratio of China has risen rapidly, from 148.3% in 2008 to 254.8% in 2015, which is higher than the overall leverage ratio of all samples, emerging economies, and the United States.

China's leverage problem is mainly concentrated in the non-financial enterprise sector. Especially since 2008, with the expansion of the credit scale the leverage ratio of the non-financial sector has increased significantly, from 98.6% in 2008 to 170.8% in 2015. At present, China stands fourth in the total sample, after 343.3% in Luxembourg, 267.2% in Ireland, and 213.8% in Hong Kong, China. However, these three economies are all world-famous offshore financial centers, with high leverage ratios, and therefore cannot be used as a comparable reference frame.

The leverage ratio of government departments is generally stable, but the debt risk of local governments cannot be ignored. Since 2008, the leverage ratio of the government sector has grown steadily, from 31.6 to 44.4% in 2015. In 2015, the leverage ratio of the Chinese government sector was only higher than that of 15 economies such as Hong Kong and Luxembourg.

It is worth noting that local government debt and potential risks have been a constant focus of attention, both at home and abroad. According to the results of the last local government debt audit in 2014, as of December 31, 2014, the balance of local government debt was 24 trillion yuan, including 15.4 trillion yuan of local government debt with repayment responsibility and 8.6 trillion yuan of local government contingent debt. However, these are only the explicit debts. When taking into account the problems of urban investment debts, various other implicit debts, and the fact that the financing platform borrows as a state-owned enterprise, the government debt ratio is likely to exceed the government debt warning line of 60%. Especially in recent years, some local governments have been keen to set up various kinds of special funds, guiding funds, PPP (cooperation between government and social capital) with equity investment on the surface, debt investment in the essence, and the multi-level nesting and docking of bank financing, and funds like trust, continuing to increase the leverage.

Meanwhile, the leverage ratio of the financial industry requires far more attention than it currently receives. In recent years, with the development of China's financial industry there have emerged diverse financial tools, financial products, and financial formats, and the shadow banks in the financial industry are expanding. At the same time, some financial institutions are borrowing short and lending long, and constantly increasing leverage in the financial market, resulting in the rapid rise of leverage in the financial industry. Although there are no very accurate data to show the financial leverage situation and risk level in China, relevant signs indicate that the leverage rate of the financial industry is rising rapidly, and the implied risk is greater than that of non-financial enterprises.

2.4.2 *The Relationship Between Leverage Ratio and Financial Risk*

Although the level of leverage was once regarded as an early warning indicator of systemic crisis, studies at home and abroad show that the relationship between leverage and the threshold of financial crisis has not been determined. In fact, it is the rising rate of leverage, rather than the level of leverage, that is more closely related to crisis. We need to be highly vigilant about the rapid rise of leverage in the short term.

In 2013 Nomura Securities proposed the famous "5–30" rule, which states that in the five years before a crisis, the proportion of credit to GDP will generally rise by more than 30%. Reinhart and Rogoff (2011) argue that soaring debt in the real economy sector is often the prelude to banking crisis, and the rapid rise of public debt is closely related to sovereign debt crisis.

In terms of domestic research, an econometric study of 41 economies including China found that if a country's leverage ratio increases from 5 to 10% annually, the average annual economic growth will drop by about 0.4 of a percentage point, and the probability of a systemic crisis will jump from 12 to 40% (Song Li, Niu Muhong et al. 2016). If the average annual change in the leverage ratio of the residential sector increases from 3 to 5%, the probability of a real estate crisis will increase by 8.6 percentage points, while a rise in the leverage ratio of the government sector from 5 to 10% will increase the probability of a debt crisis by 20%. If the average annual change in the leverage ratio of enterprises increases from 5 to 10%, the probability of a credit crisis and a stock market crisis will increase by 16.1 percentage points and 9.5 percentage points, respectively.

Furthermore, with regard to the relationship between leverage ratio and economic growth, the risk of adding leverage varies greatly across different leverage ratio levels and different economic cycle stages. At present, China's macro leverage ratio has exceeded the inflection point that is conducive to economic growth, and the marginal income of adding leverage continues to decline, while the marginal risk increases. In recent years, the overall social leverage ratio and the rapid rise of M2/GDP mainly reflect the decline of economic efficiency rather than the deepening of financial reform. Meanwhile, the expansion of asset bubbles in real estate and other industries also increases the risk that inflation will be systematically underestimated.

As mentioned just above, China's macro leverage ratio has exceeded the inflection point of leverage conducive to economic growth, and the incremental debt needed to increase unit GDP has been expanding. According to the data of the People's Bank of China, from 2011 to 2015, China's marginal leverage ratio (incremental debt/incremental GDP) rose from 158.7 to 406%, and the stock leverage ratio rose from 180 to 234%. The rising speed of the marginal leverage ratio exceeded that of the stock leverage ratio, indicating that the debt expansion speed was faster than the output expansion speed; that is, with every 1% new debt, the acceleration of the leverage ratio would be faster than 1%.

In fact, with the changes in factor endowment and external economic environment, China's economy is undergoing the transformation of speed shift and power conversion. On the one hand, the effect of monetary and credit expansion on the economy has gradually weakened, and the return on investment in the real economy has been declining. From 2007 to 2015, the amount of capital investment required per unit of GDP increased from 3.5 to 6.7. On the other hand, a large amount of liquidity is flooding the financial market and the real estate market, and the asset bubble will further intensify the financial de-materialization and strengthen the fragility of the financial system. The above two aspects come down to one point; that is, on the margin, the return of continuing to add leverage is lower than the risk.

Finally, the problem of leverage in the financial industry can all too easily be ignored, yet the high leverage in that industry is closely related to financial risk and financial crisis. In general, losses in the market can be recovered and adjusted by the market itself. However, if the leverage ratio is too high, market losses will hit the economy and the financial system badly.

Since the outbreak of the international financial crisis in 2008, the US financial industry has gone through an obvious process of deleveraging. Although the losses of subprime loans themselves were not great, about 650 billion US dollars, the impact was much bigger, due to the high leverage ratio of financial institutions. In 2015, China's stock market experienced a continuous spiral slump. Many investors made highly leveraged investments through HOMS, a fully managed financial investment cloud platform. It was the highly leveraged investments that caused the stampede in the financial market and the subsequent slump.

2.4.3 Two Major Deleveraging Strategies

2.4.3.1 Grasp the Essence of Deleveraging, Address Both Symptoms and Root Causes, and Strive to Implement the Strategy to Solve the Root Cause of Rapid Increase of Leverage Ratio

There has been much discussion about deleveraging strategies. It has been argued that the leverage ratio of residents is not high at present; in addition, according to one school of thought, the leverage ratio of non-financial enterprises can be reduced through the development of real estate; another view holds that the stock can be deleveraged through debt-to-equity swap.

The above suggestions are optional measures in the short and medium term, which can alleviate some urgent needs. However, in the long term, these measures fail to grasp the essence of the problem: why does the leverage ratio of non-financial enterprises rise rapidly in the short term? If the essential contradiction is not solved, although leverage replacement and stock deleveraging can alleviate the financial risks of enterprises, the chronic disease will still exist and the symptoms will recur.

We should realize that if a country's economic and financial system is healthy, the leverage ratio will not expand indefinitely. In the case of the subprime mortgage crisis in the United States, there were also problems in corporate governance and inadequate supervision. Risks had steadily accumulated at the micro-level and eventually led to crisis at the macro level.

From experience, neither leverage replacement nor debt-to-equity swap can fundamentally solve the problem of deleveraging, whether through market-oriented means or administrative means. If there is no solution to the governance of state-owned enterprises, and if the soft fiscal and taxation constraints of local governments cannot inhibit their drive to expand their debts recklessly, then debt reduction at any stage and deleveraging by any means cannot solve the problem. Just as when a tumor is removed but the cause of the disease has not been eradicated, the problem will remain and grow again.

2.4.3.2 Grasp the Rhythm and Make Overall Plans for Deleveraging

We should stabilize the market expectation of macro and regulatory policies, deleverage in an orderly fashion, and prevent the risk of "debt-deflation" caused by policy superposition from inducing systemic risk. We should maintain strategic focus, and continue to use macro policies and supervision to put pressure on financial institutions to deleverage, and to prevent moral hazard.

The central government set deleveraging as an important element of the "three deleveraging, one reduction, one compensation," which has become a major task of supply-side structural reform. Especially since the 2016 Central Economic Working Conference, with the implementation of steady and neutral monetary policy, the increasingly tight financial supervision policy and, particularly, the gradual implementation of the unified supervision of asset management products, it is bound to change the financial industry to a large extent in recent years business form of market and financial institutions.

Overall, the gradual decline in the leverage ratio of financial institutions and non-financial enterprises is a high probability event. Of course, the policy trend is good, but in terms of strategy we still need to pay attention to the coordination of all aspects, the pace of promotion, and orderly deleveraging. Violent deleveraging should be avoided, and certain deleveraging pressure should be exerted on financial institutions to prevent moral hazard.

First, we must realize that the decline in leverage ratio is a relatively slow process. As the saying goes, "diseases come on horseback, but go away on foot," and the institutional problems with high leverage will not be solved overnight. For example, the corporate governance and soft budget constraints of state-owned enterprises and financial institutions, from Huishan Dairy to Shandong's serial debt risk cases, all illustrate that although the corporate governance of Chinese enterprises and financial institutions is relatively complete in form, there are still differences in spirit, and a real incentive and constraint mechanism has yet to be established.

It should also be noted that the high leverage ratio is closely related to the under-development of direct financing under the high savings rate. With regard to reducing the savings rate, the author's research on "Public Finance and High Saving Tendency of China's National Income" indicates that the unconstrained investment behavior of broad public sectors such as state-owned enterprises and government departments is difficult to change in the short term. (On the other hand, the establishment of public finance is also a slow process.) China's high savings rate is structurally characterized by a rising savings rate in the public sector (government + state-owned enterprises) and a relatively stable savings rate in the private sector (residents + private enterprises). The rising savings rate in the public sector is basically the result of the government's enthusiasm for increasing investment and ensuring growth while ignoring people's livelihood, public services, and public products. Furthermore, the development of equity financing is not a short-term competitive achievement.

Moreover, if the coordination among different departments is not smooth and policies overlap, this may lead to debt-deflation risks and further induce systemic risks. The debt-deflation theory proposed by Fisher (1933) comprehensively outlines the evolution of the debt-deflation interaction in a typical economic cycle. Starting from the process of large-scale deleveraging or scale reduction, once these policies lead to a sharp drop in asset prices, which will induce a drop in money supply and deflation, the balance sheet of enterprises may further deteriorate (real debt rises), which will lead to further asset selling by enterprises, thus forming a vicious circle of debt-deflation.

In China's current deleveraging process, if the combined effect of diverse policies causes overexertion, the rate of debt will be likely to reduce faster than the rate of leverage, while the economic growth rate may decline due to credit contraction, i.e., $\Delta\text{debt}\downarrow > \Delta\text{leverage ratio}\downarrow \rightarrow \Delta\text{GDP}\downarrow$. Because of the fragility of the financial system, this may lead to risk exposure for financial markets and financial institutions.

In conclusion, deleveraging requires a process. It is necessary not only to avoid the risk of debt liquidity and asset bubbles caused by an excessive increase in leverage ratio but also to grasp the pace of deleveraging, to prevent the damage to economic growth caused by excessive compression of credit and investment, and to guard against the risk of debt-deflation caused by deleveraging and scale reduction. Before the reform of the financial supervision system, it is necessary to coordinate the promulgation of macro policies and financial supervision measures under the leadership of the Chinese government Central Committee and the State Council, to maintain strategic concentration on the fluctuation of the financial market, to ensure that there is no systematic financial risk, to deleverage in an orderly manner, and to exert pressure on financial institutions to urge them to take the initiative to deleverage (Figs. 2.1, 2.2, 2.3 and 2.4).

2.4.4 Measures to Address Both the Symptoms and the Root Causes

2.4.4.1 Weaken the GDP Growth Target, Maintain a Stable and Neutral Monetary Policy, and Encourage the Market Main Body to Actively Deleverage

Over-stimulated short-term macro-economic policies are harmful and carry no benefits, creating a macro-environment of high leverage. Under the condition that the potential economic growth rate has declined, if the economy is excessively stimulated this will inevitably aggravate the overcapacity and solidify the distortion of the economic structure.

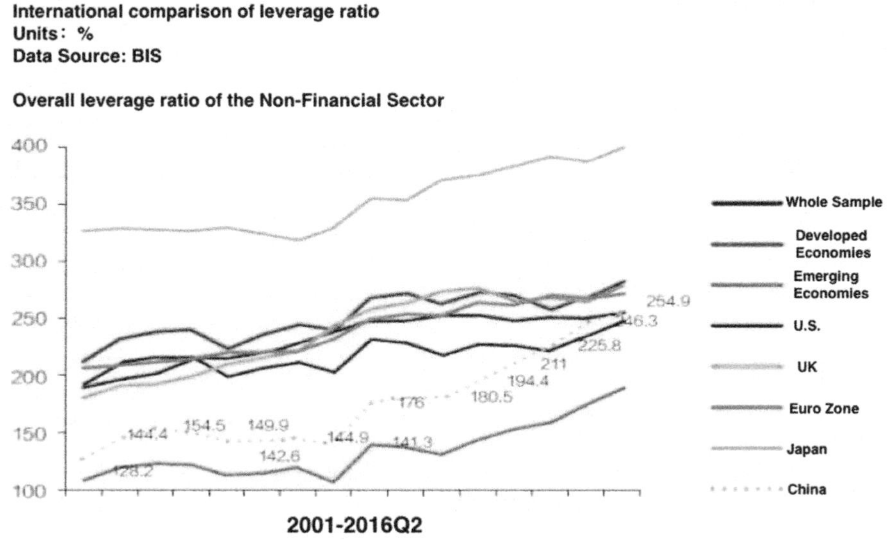

Fig. 2.1 Overall leverage ratio of the non-financial sector from 2001 to 2016

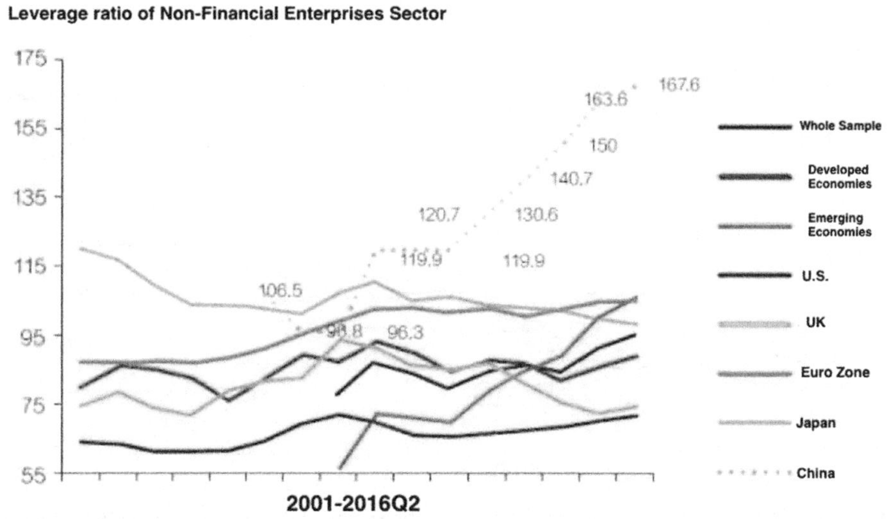

Fig. 2.2 Leverage ratio of non-financial enterprises sector from 2001 to 2016

China has controlled and restricted the issuance of bonds by local governments through the Budget Law and the Opinions of the State Council on Strengthening the Management of Local Government Debt (Document No. 43). Nevertheless, restrictions have eased somewhat in recent years. Local governments pursue economic growth through a series of measures such as government industry funds, government

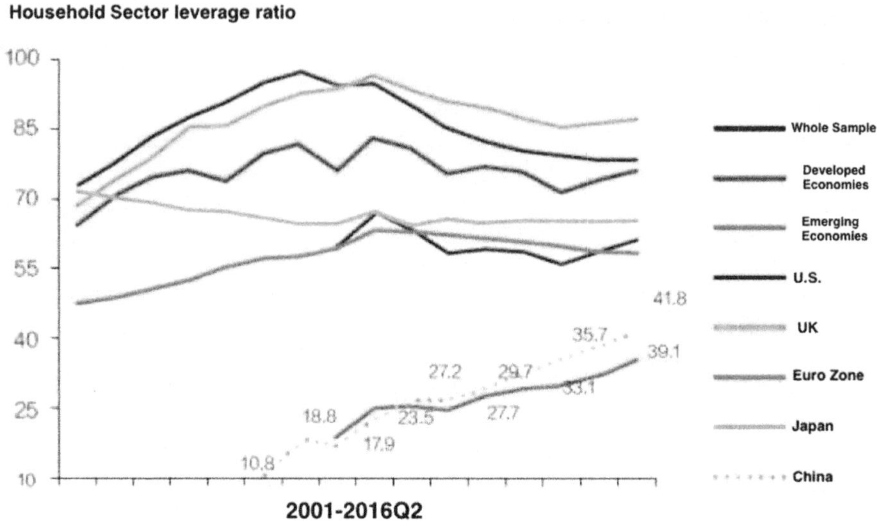

Fig. 2.3 Household sector leverage ratio from 2001 to 2016

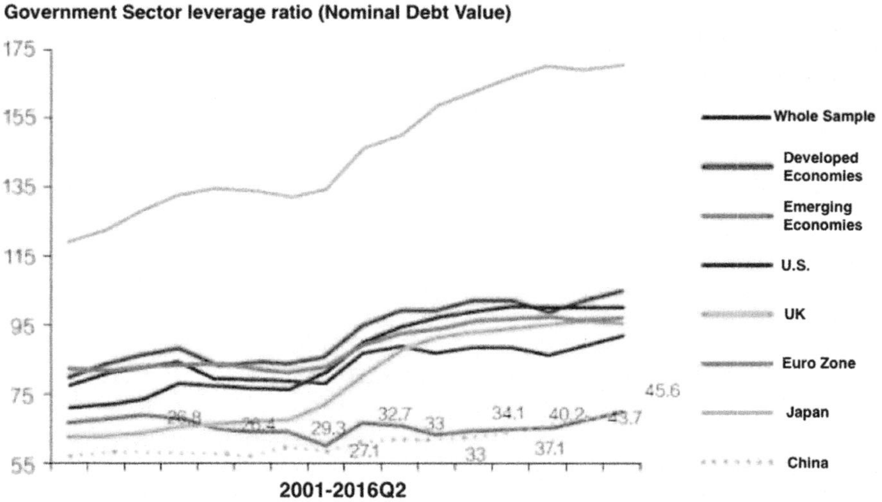

Fig. 2.4 2001–2016 government sector leverage ratio (nominal debt value). *Source* BIS; Data up to 2016Q2

special funds, government guide funds, and PPP, all methods that have equity investment on the surface, but debt investment in the essence. Under the condition of low investment returns, this will inevitably lead to an increase in the leverage ratio of local governments, and will promote an increase in the leverage ratio of the whole society. Clearly, therefore, the soft constraint of fiscal and taxation relations between the central and local governments requires reform.

At the same time, weak financial macro-regulation is an important external environment for the rise of the leverage ratio. Financial supervision contests monetary regulation. Based on its huge and direct influence on financial institutions, the supervision department consciously or unconsciously goes beyond the scope of supervision, taking financial development as its main business and financial supervision as a sideline, resulting in a rapid rise in the leverage ratio of the financial industry itself. However, macro-economic regulation is implemented by different departments. The subjectivity and autonomy of monetary policy are not enough, and the total monetary gate is difficult to control. As a result, the asset scale of China's financial system has expanded rapidly in recent years, and bubbles such as stock and real estate markets have accumulated and burst repeatedly.

At present, in order to curb the rise of the overall social leverage ratio, especially that of non-financial enterprises, the implementation of a stable and neutral monetary policy is the first choice for short-term countermeasures. In the context of a decline in the potential growth rate of the economy, the rapid growth of debt means that the proportion of debt flowing to unproductive or inefficient sectors is increasing. Although the stock of debt can be restructured gradually, if shadow banks continue to expand rapidly in the short term, the risk of a sudden interruption of the credit cycle will continue to increase. Therefore, we should keep the monetary policy steady and neutral, and promote the reasonable growth of monetary credit.

Meanwhile, we should realize that China's high leverage ratio is mainly due to deep structural problems in the social economy. We need to clarify the priorities of multiple targets and dilute the GDP growth target. Monetary policy should be more stable and neutral, and fiscal policy should be more effective. While safeguarding the macro environment for deleveraging, we should also promote more structural reforms and encourage non-financial enterprises, local governments, and financial institutions to take the initiative to deleverage.

2.4.4.2 Straighten Out the Financial Relationship Between Central and Local Government, Establish an Incentive Compatibility Mechanism for Local Government Financial Revenue and Expenditure, and Harden the Financial Constraints of Local Government

In 2016, the reform of the division of tax revenue between the central and local governments, and the division of administrative and expenditure responsibilities between the central and local governments, were officially launched. Under the full implementation of the project to replace business tax with value-added tax, the business tax will cease to be the main local tax. Although the pilot phase of this project adopted the "labeling" method to classify all this income as local income, this was a transitional arrangement that will not affect the local financial resources after the reform is completed. The correct reform direction is still to increase the central administrative power and expenditure responsibility. In the future, the contradiction between local governments' lack of main taxes and the mismatch between their administrative power and financial resources may be further highlighted.

An important successful experience of China's reform is to fully mobilize the enthusiasm of both the central and local authorities. By mobilizing the local initiative, we can stimulate its reform momentum. Therefore, we should consider granting the local government the power of tax administration, strengthening the construction of the local government public service capacity, granting local government the financial power and resources commensurate with its responsibilities, and getting rid of the dependence on land finance. In terms of policy, we should thoroughly study the implementation path of property tax, comprehensively reform resource tax, accelerate the reform of consumption tax, cultivate local main taxes, and enhance the ability of local independent development. At the same time, we should give full play to the role of local people's congresses and form hard constraints on local debts.

2.4.4.3 Solve the Core Problem of Corporate Governance

In 2001, China's economy was in a state of deflation. My investigations into the level of available funds showed that both state-owned and collective enterprises lacked funds, while private enterprises did not. Private enterprises indicated that when the economic situation was uncertain, investment was tantamount to excessive risk-taking, so they relied entirely on their own funds to invest, thus reducing leverage rather than borrowing money and adding leverage.

From the perspective of enterprises, the current administrative management mode of state-owned enterprises remains largely unchanged. State-owned enterprises have low asset efficiency and lack vitality. They have a strong impulse to pursue asset scale and increase leverage. This is an important reason why the overall solvency of the enterprise sector is declining, the leverage ratio is continuously rising, and credit risk is increasing.

In addition, under the background of increased risk of corporate default, the rise of the leverage ratio in the corporate sector cannot be separated from the cooperation of financial institutions. Some financial institutions have imperfect corporate governance, and soft budget constraints. Consequently, high returns become personal bonuses, losses become the responsibility of the government, moral risks are particularly prominent, and the willingness and ability to manage and prevent risks are insufficient.

For example, while investigating a rural credit union in a poor area, I had the following conversation with the director.

Me: Could the rural credit cooperative be privatized?

Director of Rural Credit Cooperative: It can't be privatized. If it is privatized, there will be no financial institutions to serve the "three rural issues."

Me: Does the rural credit cooperative make profits?

Director: We have no profits.

Me: Is there any private lending?

Director: Yes.
Me: Do they make money?
Director: Of course.
Me: Are you willing to contract the rural credit cooperative?
Director: Yes, I'm willing to.
Me: Will you make money?
Director: Of course, I will.
Me: If you contract this rural credit cooperative, how will you manage it well?
Director: I will take measures to control various costs such as wages and promote product innovation.

This conversation shows the importance of corporate governance. When commercial financial institutions become bigger and stronger, they tend to focus only on their own development without considering the rise of risks. The fundamental reason is that the corporate governance problem has not been effectively solved. Therefore, further reforms are needed to improve the incentive-compatible corporate governance structure of state-owned enterprises and financial institutions and to strengthen financial constraints. We should strengthen the bankruptcy and liquidation mechanism for state-owned enterprises, from simply doing large-scale operations to improving their competitiveness in strategic areas of key sectors and making longer-term inter-period arrangements.

2.4.4.4 Promote the Reform of Financial Supervision

The problem of China's financial system lies in the fact that there is comprehensive management but separate supervision. If the supervision and development of the financial industry cannot be separated, the problem of authenticity of capital will not be solved. Because regulators are keen to encourage regulated institutions to expand their territory, this will inevitably lead to inadequate supervision, the spread of shadow banks, and a rise in the leverage ratio of the financial sector.

More importantly, when the governance of financial institutions is not perfect, and financial supervision is not in place, the financial safety net relies excessively on the central bank. The role of the central bank in stabilizing finance has been simplified to that of a "payment box;" that is, the central bank participates in the rescue, but not in daily supervision. This asymmetry of right and responsibility will inevitably lead to time-consuming and inefficient rescue and disposal. The bottom-up approach of "spending money to buy stability" will often cost more.

Therefore, we should strengthen macro-prudential financial management, and strengthen and improve the functions of the central bank, so as to prevent systemic financial risks. We should strengthen functional supervision and comprehensive supervision to achieve full coverage of risk supervision. We should also strengthen the independence and autonomy of the central bank's monetary policy under the leadership of the Chinese government Central Committee and the State Council, reduce interference from other departments, implement a stable and neutral monetary policy, and create a suitable monetary and financial environment for economic growth and supply-side structural reform.

It is important to realize that financial security has been reformed, not guaranteed. Many financial institutions carry out high leverage investment arbitrage in the financial market. When the financial market is tight, all kinds of unexpected events may cause large market shocks. Overemphasis on market stability may force the central bank to put money into the market. In this system pattern, which has clear moral hazard characteristics, the insufficient overall capital level will inevitably lead to an expansion in the asset scale of the shadow banks, which will in turn result in a higher leverage ratio and higher potential risk.

Historically, China's governance strategies have all focused on debt risk disposal, while ignoring the construction of system and constraint mechanism. This inevitably aggravates the problems of rigid payment and moral risk, and leads to the repeated growth of financial risks. Only by introducing a market exit mechanism for financial institutions and by straightening out the distortion of financial resources allocation caused by government credit supporting bank credit, can we really solve the problem of rigid payment.

2.5 Market Clearing

Since the reform and opening up, China's market economy system has gradually been established, and the scope and extent of the government's direct participation in economic activities have been reduced. The allocation of resources is now basically determined by the market, and the macro-regulation framework can ensure the basic stability of the macro-economy. However, since the global financial crisis in 2008, although China's "four trillion economic stimulus plan" is conducive to short-term economic stability, the increasing role of government in economic activities means that the development trend of the relationship between the government and the market has largely been reversed. In the post-crisis period, the normalization tendency of Keynesian crisis response policies has evolved into a macro-policy that is systematic, loose, and soft: stimulus policies that emphasize aggregate demand management in real economic regulation, rigid payment, and market assistance in financial market management have forced currency issuance; structural contradictions have become increasingly serious; and structural reforms have been subject to repeated delays.

When the central government made the judgment that economic development had entered a new normal, the traditional economic growth mode could no longer be considered sustainable. Since then, leverage ratio has risen rapidly in a short period, and macroeconomic efficiency has dropped sharply. From the perspective of economic history, the decline in economic efficiency, the prominent structural factors, and the dilemma of macro-economic policies in promoting growth and preventing risks (controlling leverage) are actually the consequences of the long-term implementation of Keynesian stimulus policies. The only way out of the current dilemma is to thoroughly reflect on the consequences of the structural contradictions brought about by those policies. While controlling the total amount of money, we should firmly and continuously push forward the structural reform on the supply side, so as to truly let the market play a decisive role in the allocation of resources and realize structural adjustment through market clearing.

2.5.1 Market Clearing and Demand Management

Whether the market can be cleared independently and what role the government should play in that process have been core topics throughout the history of economic thought. Since the publication of Adam Smith's *The Wealth of Nations*, different schools of economics have given different answers based on their beliefs about the spontaneous power of the market, and have proposed different assumptions about relevant systems. At various times, disputes have arisen between the plan and the market, and between Keynes and Hayek. Modern economics often regards the issue of whether the market can be cleared independently as the key assumption in theoretical models and policy discussions. From the perspective of analytical technology, the question with regard to market clearing is whether the price can be adjusted flexibly to make the supply and demand balance automatically. From the perspective of deep mechanism, the question refers to whether the relevant productivity (manufacturers' production activities include, for example, technical equipment), consumption behavior, and even relevant systems can be adjusted flexibly. Finally, from the perspective of institutional reform, the question refers to the extent to which government can create the necessary institutional conditions to ensure the effective operation of the market mechanism.

With regard to the question of whether the market can make sufficient adjustments spontaneously and finally realize market clearing, in the history of economic theory we can find three main schools of economic thought: classical and neoclassical non-intervention propositions based on liberalism and market belief; Keynesian government intervention based on "animal spirits" and demand management; and the western supply school and China's supply-side structural reform policy, both of which focus on structural reform. These theories are explained in more detail in Table 2.1.

One school, based on liberalism, insists that the market can be cleared independently and therefore opposes government intervention. According to liberalism and neoclassical economics, the market has the function of self-regulation. When the market is hit, wages and prices can be flexibly adjusted in the short term to make the market self-clearing. In the long term, wages and prices will guide the allocation of resources to realize the maximization of social welfare; hence the government, as the "night watchman" of the market (system), should not interfere with the market operation in general. Monetarism, represented by the American economist Friedman, inherited the concepts of neoclassical economics, further emphasized the inherent automatic stability of the market, and pointed out that changes in the money

Table 2.1 Three schools of economic theory

Three schools	Main idea	Theoretical basis	Policy orientation	China's practice
Classicalism and neoclassicism	Based on liberalism and market belief, it advocates *non-intervention*	Adhere to the principle that the market can be cleared independently, wages and prices will guide resource allocation and reset, with self-regulation function	The government is the "night watchman" of the market. "Inflation is ultimately a monetary phenomenon" (government policies are the root cause of undesirable disturbances); under the "rational expectation" of the economic subject, any government intervention policy will be cancelled out by the reasonable expectation of the public. Economy is a spontaneous process. The deviation between market interest rate and equilibrium interest rate is the cause of economic fluctuation. Therefore, artificial monetary and credit expansion should be avoided to depress market interest rate. Otherwise, resources will be further misallocated, preventing the economy from readjusting to equilibrium state	In the early stage of reform and opening up, it was adopted to *cultivate the market mechanism*

(continued)

Table 2.1 (continued)

Three schools	Main idea	Theoretical basis	Policy orientation	China's practice
Keynesianism	Advocates government intervention	Because of "animal spirits," price stickiness, information asymmetry, incomplete competition, etc., the market cannot be cleared independently	When the investment expectation deteriorates, the government needs to reduce interest rates to stimulate effective demand, so as to achieve balanced economic growth. It advocates that the government should reverse the cycle of regulation, and control and reduce the unemployment rate through deficit finance	Since 2008, more active macro-regulation has been implemented to stimulate growth and the contradiction in stock has been digested through incremental expansion
Supply-side school	Focus on supply-side reform	Believe in the spontaneous adjustment and the self-clearing of the market, and adjust the government's behavior	The supply-side structural reforms focus on removing factors that hinder the effective operation of the market, and on restricting the government's administrative intervention in economic activities, and governmental economic activities, so as to make room for the private economy and create conditions for the market mechanism and market micro-subjects to operate better	After the central government put forward its strategic judgment on the new normal of the economy, it initiated structural reforms on the supply side to strengthen the decisive role of the market in the allocation of resources

supply are the fundamental and dominant causes of changes in economic activities and price levels. "Inflation is ultimately a monetary phenomenon;" that is to say, government policies are the root cause of undesirable disturbances. On the other hand, the Rational Expectation School holds that under the "rational expectation" of the economic subject, any government intervention policy will be offset by the reasonable expectation of the public, so any government intervention policy of any nature will be invalid, and the automatic adjustment of the market economy should be adopted to maintain economic stability.

In contrast to liberalism, Keynesianism advocates government intervention. According to this school of economic thought, in the short term, due to the stickiness of price and wage adjustment, "animal spirits," herding effect, and other factors, the market cannot be cleared by its own strength alone. In the case of weak aggregate demand the government must actively intervene in order to achieve the maximization of social welfare. In Keynes' analysis of the continuous economic recession and high unemployment during the Great Depression, he points out that the market supply and demand do not automatically balance, that there may be insufficient effective demand, and that total demand may often be less than total supply. Therefore, in periods of economic depression, the government should intervene to make up for the deficiency of effective demand through expansionary economic policies. The School of Neo-Classical Synthesis, represented by Samuelson, continues and develops Keynes' economic thought and policy propositions, advocating that macro policies should "go against the wind" and reduce the unemployment rate through deficit finance. New Keynesianism (NK), represented by Stiglitz, provides the basis for Keynesian intervention thought from aspects such us menu cost, price stickiness, incomplete competition, and information asymmetry.

With regard to the academic history, Keynes' (1936) macroeconomics is closely related to the monetary quantity theory of the New Cambridge School's cash balance theory (Pigou 1917). Its main origin can be found in the natural interest rate theory of Wicksell (1898), the founder of the Swedish School, itself related to the Austrian School. Based on the capital theory of Böhm-Bawerk (1884), Wicksell held that the deviation between the market interest rate and natural interest rate is the root of economic fluctuation. Under the condition of full employment, investments deviating from equilibrium would face losses and eventually be cleared out of the market. Based on Wicksell's thought, Myrdal (1939) gave a complete definition of natural interest rate: first, the natural interest rate is the interest rate consistent with the rate of return on physical capital or productivity; second, the natural interest rate is the interest rate that can make the capital supply and demand (savings and investment) consistent; third, the natural interest rate is the interest rate that keeps prices neutral (neither rising nor falling). Keynes (1930) pointed out that since savings and investment as equilibrium conditions (afterward) must be equal, the theory of loanable funds in classical economics does not distinguish between the money market and the product market. Later, Keynes (1936) proposed liquidity preference theory, turning the understanding of the natural interest rate to the first meaning. When income increases, income growth will be faster than consumption growth due to diminishing marginal propensity to consume. However, when investment expectations deteriorate (increased investment caused by savings leads to a decline in the marginal efficiency of capital), market interest rates cannot fall sufficiently, due to speculative money demand and liquidity preference. Thus, the investment cannot completely make up the savings gap, and savings cannot be fully converted into the investment, resulting in insufficient effective demand. Therefore, the government is required to reduce interest rates to stimulate demand to achieve balanced economic growth.

While they shared with Keynes a common origin in Wicksell (1898), Austrian economists such as Hayek developed quite different theories and policy suggestions. Based on the Menger-Böhm-Bawerk analysis method, Mises had close academic ties with Wicksell, creatively extended the Austrian School, which focuses on subjective value analysis of marginal utility to the monetary problem, combining currency with micro-theory. He argued that the upsurge of the economic cycle is mainly due to a temporary mismatch of resources caused by low-interest rates. Hayek (1935) further expanded Mises' analysis of economic cycles, dividing production into the production of final consumer goods and various intermediate products under the circuitous mode of production. The more intermediate products are produced (i.e. circuitous production is more complicated), the more capital and money are required, and the time preference rate is more likely to deviate from market interest rate, thus causing economic fluctuations. If there is no artificial monetary credit expansion and interest rate change, the change of time preference rate will make the interest rate change spontaneously; the circuitous production process will also be adjusted spontaneously to ensure the economic equilibrium, and the economy will not fluctuate. From Mises' and Hayek's theories on economic fluctuation and cycle, it can be found that time preference determines the supply of savings (i.e. capital); the circuitous production process determines the demand for capital; and the interest rate at which the supply and demand of borrowing capital are consistent (savings and investment are equal) is also the equilibrium interest rate of the economy. As long as the monetary interest rate is equal to the equilibrium interest rate, the impact of interest rate on prices is neutral, which is consistent with the second meaning of Wicksell's natural interest rate. Based on the subjective utility marginal analysis method and belief in classical economics, the Austrian School argues that the economy is a spontaneous process, and the deviation between the market interest rate and equilibrium interest rate is the cause of economic fluctuation. Therefore, artificial monetary and credit expansion should be avoided to depress the market interest rate. Otherwise, resources will be further mismatched and hinder economic readjustment to the equilibrium state.

In the 1930s, Hayek's famous debate with Keynes ended temporarily with the victory of Keynes (1936). After World War II, western countries implemented traditional Keynesian policies with government intervention in demand management, and for a long time their macro-economies achieved steady and sustained growth. However, behind the prosperity was the structural contradiction that had been generally ignored. Until the emergence of stagflation after the oil crisis in the 1970s, Keynesianism was at a loss. Against the background of the rise of supply economics, Reagan and Thatcher implemented a series of economic reform policies, including tax cuts, privatization, and welfare cuts, aimed at limiting government intervention and restoring market vitality. The change of economic thought and policies finally led the western world out of stagflation and back to economic growth. The key to supply economics and its economic policies lies in the firm belief in the spontaneous adjustment of the market and the market's self-clearing. It focuses on removing the factors that hinder the effective operation of the market through supply-side structural reforms, and on restricting the government's administrative intervention in economic activities, and governmental economic activities, to create space for private economy and conditions for the better operation of the market mechanism and market micro-subjects. Although this is different from the meaning of China's current supply-side structural reform, focusing on the supply-side to promote structural reform and strengthening the decisive role of the market in the allocation of resources are common to both, and are also the main characteristics that distinguish this approach from traditional Keynesian demand management policies.

2.5.2 *Rethinking Keynesianism*

In recent years, China's economic development has entered a new normal, as structural contradictions such as overcapacity and high leverage ratio become increasingly prominent. These phenomena are not unique to China's economic development, but are the general consequences of the long-term implementation of Keynesian economic policies. They stem from the excessive superstition of Keynesianism: hoping to stimulate growth through positive macro-regulation and to digest the contradictions in stock through incremental expansion.

After the global financial crisis that broke out in 2008, China introduced a "four-trillion economic stimulus plan" and took the lead in the global recovery. Repeated use of stimulus policies and the normalization of unconventional policies are conducive to short-term economic stability; however, not only do they not solve the problem, they may actually worsen the inherent contradictions in the economic structure. The long-term over-reliance on aggregate demand management to maintain the macro stability undermines the basic functions of market mechanisms in the fields of information transmission, incentive formation, resource allocation, and income distribution, while also creating a need for government to play a more effective role in making up for market failures and improving the efficiency of market allocation of resources. The slow progress in institutional mechanism construction and the accumulation of structural contradictions have forced us to face up to the importance and urgency of the long-delayed supply-side structural reform, until we approach the limit of the logic of "incremental reform."

First of all, the high leverage ratio is a comprehensive reflection of the structural contradictions intensified by the excessive stimulus policy. While the overall leverage ratio is not high, the rate of increase is relatively fast. In fact, the level of leverage ratio has little to do with the economic crisis, while the rate of increase is closely related to it. It should also be noted that the non-financial enterprise sector has an outstanding leverage ratio and concentrated risks, while the leverage ratio of the financial industry is rising and has potential risks.

From the perspective of monetary policy, since China relies mainly on indirect financing through bank credit, monetary expansion is first manifested in the balance sheets of real economic sectors in the form of debt expansion. Therefore, stimulating growth with loose monetary policy will inevitably come at the expense of a rising leverage ratio. From the perspective of fiscal policy, the expansion of government expenditure dominated by investment is directly reflected in the high savings rate of the public sector, and debt to other sectors is formed through the debt-dominated financing system to push up the leverage ratio. Therefore, fiscal stimulus will inevitably have side effects that lead to an increase of leverage ratio.

Another inevitable consequence of loose supervision and weak macro-regulation is the phenomenon of "zombie enterprises." Originating from the research on the long-term stagnation of Japan's economic growth, in recent years the concept of "zombie enterprises" has been introduced into the research and analysis of overcapacity industries in China. Such enterprises are frozen but not dead, and idle but not expelled from the market, and are therefore directly responsible for the continuous overcapacity and the difficulty in clearing the market. In 2016, the Central Economic Work Conference pointed out that to eliminate production capacity, "we must 'seize the bull by the horns,' and deal with 'zombie enterprises.'".

The loose monetary policy is an important condition for zombie enterprises to develop and continue to exist. Where banks are able to provide preferential interest rates, highly indebted enterprises can pay interest more easily. Loose financial supervision allows banks to engage in "zombie lending," while the desire to cover up bad debt losses leads directly to the existence of zombie enterprises. Indeed, behind the large number of zombie enterprises is not only the lack of clearing in the product market, but also the lack of clearing in the financial market. Under the condition that zombie enterprises are frozen but not dead, and idle but not expelled, monetary easing actually transfuses "blood" to zombie enterprises first, creating a crowding-out effect on the investment and production of normal enterprises, and blocking the conversion of momentum from old growth to new.

Finally, excessive stimulus policies not only solidify the structural contradiction, but also bring about the problems of decreasing efficiency and a widening of the gap between rich and poor. Our series of policies aimed at stabilizing growth mainly mobilize state-owned investment, while the proportion of private investment keeps declining, but the return on investment follows an opposite trend. In 2016, the fixed asset investment of state-owned and state-controlled enterprises and private enterprises were 21.3 trillion yuan and 18.8 trillion yuan, respectively, the former being more than the latter. In the same period, the total profits of state-owned and state-controlled enterprises and private enterprises were 1.2 trillion yuan and 2.4 trillion yuan, respectively, the former being only half of the latter. In the pattern of obvious mismatch between the rate of return on investment and the growth rate of investment, it is inevitable that the faster the investment growth is stimulated, the faster the efficiency decreases.

Another consequence of the excessive stimulus policy is the rise in asset prices, which further widens the gap between rich and poor, and thus runs counter to the goal of achieving a well-off society in all aspects. According to the Report on China's

People's Livelihood Development 2014, published by the China Social Science Survey Center of Peking University, the degree of property inequality in China is rising rapidly. In 2012, the Gini coefficient of the net property of Chinese households reached 0.73, with the top 1% of households occupying more than 1/3 of the country's property and the bottom 25% owning only about 1% of the total property.

2.5.3 Supply-Side Structural Reform

Facing the prominent contradictions in China's economic operation, the Third Plenary Session of the 18th Chinese government Central Committee stated that to further clarify the boundary between the government and the market, we should "make the market play a decisive role in the allocation of resources and better play the role of the government," unswervingly push forward the structural reform on the supply side, give full play to the decisive role of the market, reform and perfect the market-oriented macro-regulation system, and realize structural adjustment through market-clearing while controlling the total amount of money.

The central government has already taken significant steps in the supply-side structural reform of "cutting overcapacity, reducing excess inventory, deleveraging, lowering costs, and strengthening areas of weakness." Indeed, these measures have made remarkable progress in solving the structural problems. China's economic restructuring shows obvious signs of improvement, laying a good foundation for the market to play a decisive role in the allocation of resources. In 2016, China's final consumption expenditure contributed 64.6% to economic growth, an increase of 4.7 percentage points over 2015. The added value of the service industry continues to grow faster than that of industry. In 2016, the added value of tertiary industry accounted for 51.6% of GDP, exceeding 50% for two consecutive years. In 2016, the proportion of general trade exports was 53.8%, and the trade pattern structure was optimized. At the same time, innovation played an increasingly important role in economic development, and the proportion of Chinese patent applications in the world total was rising rapidly. Energy conservation and consumption reduction had achieved remarkable results. Energy consumption per unit of GDP in 2016 decreased by 5.0% compared with 2015. The proportion of clean energy consumption, such as hydropower, wind power, nuclear power, and natural gas, increased by 1.6% compared with 2015. Also, the number of newly-established enterprises reached a record high, and there was no problem with the total employment.

2.5.3.1 To Push Forward the Supply-Side Structural Reform, We Should Maintain Our Strategic Focus

In order to cut overcapacity, we should start with the disposal of zombie enterprises and resolutely eliminate backward production capacity. To reduce inventory, the key is to establish a long-term mechanism to promote the healthy development of the real estate market and to solve the problem of excessive inventory of real estate in third- and fourth-tier cities. With regard to deleveraging, under the premise of controlling the total leverage, we should take reducing the leverage ratio of enterprises as the top priority. The urgent tasks are to speed up the reform of state-owned enterprises and of the central and local fiscal and taxation systems, and to straighten out the price mechanism to effectively change the incentive mechanism. In order to reduce costs, efforts should be made to streamline administration and delegate power, bring down transaction costs, and put into effect the tax reduction effect of "replacing business tax with value-added tax." To strengthen weak links, we need to make up shortcomings not only in the development but also in the system. While seeking to "cut overcapacity, reduce inventory, deleverage financing, lower cost, and strengthen weak links" as a whole, we should not let the mechanical GDP growth target restrain the implementation of policy, and must ensure that the economic growth is not the most important goal; rather, the core is the social employment situation. Similarly, the exchange rate level itself is not that important; rather, the essential point is that the exchange rate mechanism should be flexible. If we do not seek truth from facts and take advantage of the circumstances, but instead mechanically and stubbornly adhere to dogma, we will only strengthen distortions, which will ultimately be reflected either in the real estate industry, excess capacity, and the financial market, or in exchange rate fluctuations and capital flows. The attitude of maintaining financial stability and preventing financial risks should also be changed. "Prevention of financial risks" is mainly to prevent systematic risks. If we pursue short-term and local stability to the exclusion of all other considerations, it is inevitable that we will make monetary policy excessively lax and, in fact, small risks will proliferate and eventually lead to a great crisis.

2.5.3.2 Prerequisites for Promoting Supply-Side Structural Reform and Preventing Systematic Financial Risks: Reform and Improve Macro-Regulation, Control the General Gate of Monetary Policy, Implement Stable and Neutral Monetary Policy, and Maintain the Basic Stability of the Total Amount of Liquidity

Given that soft budget constraints are common in enterprises and financial institutions in China's economic transition and that the macro-control framework system still has obvious planned economy characteristics, lax and soft macro-regulation policies often lead to further aggravation of structural problems, a consequence of the long-term implementation of Keynesian stimulus policies in transition countries. To promote the supply-side structural reform and let the market play a decisive role in resource allocation, we need to strengthen constraints from two aspects: the macro-regulation framework and the implementation of specific policies. First, we need to reform and improve the macro-regulation framework such that it has at the core indirect regulation, which can adapt to the decisive role of the market in resource allocation. The current macro-regulation system has distinct characteristics of a planned or transitional economy. The National Development and Reform Commission occupies the leading position in the "troika" macro-regulation framework. The macro-regulation is implemented through national economic development planning, industrial policies, investment policies, consumption policies, price policies, and micro-interventions policies, among which "investment planning often comes first, financial investment follows, and financial departments cooperate." Such a regulatory framework is conducive to the large-scale implementation of Keynesian stimulus policies but runs counter to the requirements of the allocation of market resources and the direction of market economy reform. The correct direction of macro-regulation framework reform is to truly implement the spirit of the Fifth Plenary Session of the 18th Chinese government Central Committee and the 13th Five-Year Plan. Specifically, we should "improve the policy system that focuses on fiscal and monetary policies, and coordinates industrial policies, regional policies, investment policies, consumption policies, and price policies to enhance the coordination of fiscal and monetary policies." We must also implement a stable and neutral monetary policy, control the overall monetary gate, and create a suitable monetary environment for structural reforms on the supply side.

For many years, under the guidance of the Keynesian stimulus concept and zero-risk absolute stability concept, China's monetary policy has been steady and slightly lax in implementation. The reasons for this include great downward pressure on the economy and large fluctuations in the financial market. From the perspective of economic structure and macro efficiency, blindly easing monetary policy can be likened to drinking poison to quench thirst. It cannot fundamentally solve structural contradictions, but may further distort and solidify structural problems. The issue of money to rescue financial products and stabilize financial markets under the goal of zero risks often leads to systemic financial risks and is the root of chaos in financial crises. Many cases of financial crisis show that the formation of systemic risks follows a very similar road map: continuous lax monetary policy is accompanied by the availability of credit, resulting in the excessive expansion of credit and the mutual stimulation of asset prices, thus triggering asset bubbles and financial crises.

2.5.3.3 Promote the Reform of Public Finance and Strengthen Local Government Restrictions

The construction and investment of China's fiscal policy has obvious color. Broad government economic activities, including local government financing platforms and state-owned enterprises, have been expanding in recent years. The experience of the past decade shows that the government's economic activities continue to overrun and expand. Although this is conducive to the short-term stability of the macro-economy, the severe structural contradictions and the decline in efficiency are already very serious. In order to further promote the structural reform on the supply side and let the market play a decisive role in the allocation of resources, it is necessary to transform the functions of the government according to the logic of the socialist market economy. The first task is to push forward more thorough public finance reform and promote the transformation of construction finance to public finance. The core of public finance is that, as far as possible, finance does not directly participate in economic construction and market activities, but mainly provides necessary public goods and public services to support the market. We should proactively restrict financial and other broad government economic activities, expand space for the cultivation and development of the market, make more social financing flow to enterprises and individuals, transfer investment opportunities and risks to the market, and make market participants find new economic growth points in the process of decentralized decision-making, trial and error, and innovation. The second task is to harden the soft budget constraints of local governments. We should change the local government's financial competition and GDP evaluation competition mechanism, abolish the dependence on land finance, and eliminate from the root the local government's impulse of investment, financing, and profit. We should cultivate the main types of local taxes, deeply study the implementation path of property tax, comprehensively reform the resource tax, accelerate the reform of consumption tax, strengthen the construction of local government public service capacity, and empower local governments with the financial rights and resources to match their responsibilities. We should also promote the financial transparency of local governments through securitization of local government debts and strengthened supervision. In addition to the approval of the people's congress at the corresponding level, the local government's liability limit and budget rules should also be subject to the supervision and examination of the government at the next higher level.

2.5.3.4 Relax the Market Access Requirements for Private Capital to Enter Monopoly Industries

Relaxing the access requirements for private capital is conducive not only to the capacity reduction of traditional industries and the development of new economy, but also to curbing the trend whereby private capital is moved away from domestic investment and towards foreign investment. Although the central government has issued a series of documents relevant to this issue, the barrier to market access of some monopoly industries is still insurmountable. The proportion of private investment in some infrastructure sectors ranges from below 5% to only 30% at most. Even where openings exist, there are still "glass doors," "swing doors," and "revolving doors" behind them. We should promptly formulate plans and policies to greatly relax market access in the fields of electricity, telecommunications, transportation, oil, natural gas, and municipal utilities; and implement specific measures to support private capital to enter service industries such as pensions, health, home economics, education training, and culture and education. At the same time, we also need to implement more inclusive fiscal and taxation policies and industrial policies, create a fair competitive environment, innovate the cooperation mechanism between monopoly industries and private capital, avoid the unequal cooperation mode that allows investors to provide money but does not allow them the right to speak, and achieve the same rights and shares according to law.

2.6 State-Owned Capital Management

The report of the 19th National Congress of the Chinese government clearly stated that "we should improve the management system of all kinds of state-owned assets; reform the authorized management system of state-owned capital; accelerate the optimization of the layout of state-owned economy, structural adjustment and strategic restructuring; promote the maintenance and appreciation of state-owned assets; promote the strengthening, optimization, and expansion of state-owned capital, and effectively prevent the loss of state-owned assets." In order to achieve this wide-ranging strategic goal, "we must focus on improving the property right system and market-oriented allocation of factors," take improving corporate governance as the core, accurately distinguish the concepts of "capital" and "assets," and make a systematic analysis from many perspectives, such as historical evolution, practical requirements, and path design.

From the perspective of the state-owned asset management system, state-owned capital corresponds to the concept of "capital" in economics, not the concept of "asset" in accounting. Only the "net assets" after deducting the liabilities of the state-owned enterprises belong to the state and are real "wealth." Due to confusion between the concepts of "capital" and "assets," and a large number of problems of soft debt constraint, there have arisen problems of a lack of distinction between shares and debts, and of investment that appears on the surface to be equity investment, but is in essence debt investment; as a result, much nominal state-owned capital is illusory. Moreover, due to large debts in the fields of medical care, pensions, and education, the actual state-owned capital is far below the book level. Under the condition of "strata title" of China's state-owned capital and the existence of "governance radius," it is necessary to clarify the property rights and responsibilities in the management framework, to establish an "entrust-agent" framework with compatible incentives, and to put in place a modern enterprise system by improving corporate governance. At the same time, we can use a "double-level arrangement" to strengthen both the Chinese government's leadership and the protection of shareholders' rights and interests.

2.6.1 The True Nature of State-Owned Capital

In terms of the structure of the balance sheet of an enterprise, i.e., Assets = Liabilities + Owner's Equity, state-owned capital is the "owner's equity," not the "assets." Even if it is a wholly state-owned enterprise, as long as the enterprise is in debt to the outside world, its legal person property is not all owned by the state, nor can it all be regarded as the wealth of the state. Only the net assets after deducting the debt can belong to the state and be the real "wealth." For a long time, we did not clearly distinguish these two concepts. However, the report of the 19th National Congress of the Chinese government stated the intention "to promote the maintenance and appreciation of state-owned assets, and to promote the strengthening, optimization, and expansion of state-owned capital." This not only makes a clear conceptual distinction, but also points out the general direction for the next step to improve all kinds of state-owned asset management systems.

With regard to the historical formation of state-owned capital, on the one hand it is a huge state-owned asset, while on the other the government has large debts in many areas, such as medical care, pensions, and education. Overall, therefore, the state-owned capital is far below the book level. Before 2003, due to the distorted accounting system, the cost of state-owned enterprises and the wages of employees were strictly limited. Many abnormally high book profits were artificially made, paid for by the low wages of employees and the debts in the fields of medical care, pensions, and housing. These book profits were used for investment, so the book state-owned equity did not reflect reality. The state-owned enterprises that have entered the market through the shareholding system reform have formed a large number of assets through the debt expansion of their invested subsidiaries and sub-subsidiaries, but their income should be used to repay the principal and interest of the debt first, and cannot simply be classified as state-owned assets. Therefore, the state-owned equity is far lower than the statistics, and is even in deficit.

Capital in a strict sense plays a major role: it is the basis for calculating and determining leverage ratio; it is the subject and provides the ability to bear risks; it has the ability to absorb losses and is the basis for liquidation and disposal sequence; and it acts as a measure of capital gains reflecting the company's performance. At present, the capital stock of many state-owned enterprises is formed by borrowing money. The specific manifestations include local governments or financial departments borrowing money and injecting capital, co-managing accounts, tax return, reuse of capital, and capital not absorbing losses. Special government debt, replacement debt, and special debt are also used as capital. In fact, there is a crucial difference between the phenomenon of investment that appears to be equity investment but is essentially debt investment, and "leveraged buyout." The latter is based on an open financial and contractual arrangement, which defines in advance the responsibilities and rights of the purchaser and creditors and the responsibilities, rights, and interests of the acquiree. The source of funds is transparent, and there is no private "drawer agreement." If a buyout is financed by using its own credit, a leveraged buyout will really bear the losses in case of problems. In contrast, the state-owned shares based on investment that only appears to be equity investment, but is in essence debt investment, are illusory. Financing depends on the income of the project to repay. Even if the project fails, losses will be borne not by the financial department and the local government, but by the financial institutions that provide the financing. Thus, the nature of a company established through investment that only appears to be based on equity, but is actually debt investment, has undergone fundamental changes, and the above-mentioned functions of capital itself cannot be brought into play.

The distinction between "capital" and "assets" also needs to emphasize the concept of "strata title" of state-owned capital. With the fiscal system of dividing revenue and expenditure between the central and local governments, the state-owned capital managed by the central government and the state-owned capital managed by the local government should be owned by different levels. According to the principle of "who contributes, owns," the governments at all levels should exercise the ownership of the state-owned capital and perform the responsibilities of investors. Even in the case of ownership by the whole people, such as the transfer of state-owned capital to replenish the social security fund and the conversion of collective land into state-owned land, the ultimate actual beneficiary will not be the whole people, which is still a concept of strata title. Therefore, in view of the reality of the stratification of the property rights of state-owned capital, it is necessary to clarify the property rights and responsibilities in the management framework and to establish an incentive-compatible "entrust-agent" framework.

2.6.2 The Key to State-Owned Assets Management Lies in "Governance" Rather Than "Management"

Another direct impact of confusing the concepts of "capital" and "assets" is that the work of the state-owned assets management department is still mainly to manage the enterprises, focusing on the comprehensive management of personnel, affairs, and assets, rather than to manage the capital owned by the country. For example, when the State-owned Assets Supervision and Administration Commission (SASAC) conducts performance appraisal, it takes the enterprise as the unit, and the appraisal object is mainly the income and profit of the enterprise, rather than taking the return on investment of state-owned capital as a whole; while in promoting the adjustment of industrial layout, this is mainly to be directly executed by enterprises rather than by capital operation.

The Third Plenary Session of the 14th Chinese government Central Committee emphasized that the direction of reform of state-owned enterprises is to be found in the modern enterprise system of "clear property rights, well-defined right and responsibility, separation of government administration from enterprise management, and scientific management." The Fourth Plenary Session of the 15th Central Committee introduced the concept of "corporate governance." However, at present, some government departments and regulatory agencies lack an understanding of the significance of establishing a modern enterprise system. To a large extent, they remain at a relatively low level of departmental jurisdiction and industry management. The policy focus is more on how to manage enterprises and how to use the power of government to promote enterprises to become bigger and stronger. Each administrative department formulates its own principles based on the interests of its own department; in effect, it is still engaged in departmental ownership, lacking top-level design and systematic consideration. This corresponds to the old path of the industry department being in charge of the overall management of the enterprise. Given the lack of division between government, capital, and enterprise and between the development and regulatory functions, and the violation of market-oriented principles in enterprise management behavior and resource allocation, such problems are hardly surprising.

In particular, because of the overlapping of the public management function and the investor function of government departments, and the conflict of multiple objectives of state-owned enterprises, there are contradictions and conflicts in the management of state-owned capital that are difficult to reconcile. As government departments perform both public management functions and investor functions, acting as both "referees" and "athletes" at the same time, it is difficult to build an effective firewall around the existing administrative system, making the "entrust-agent" relationship of state-owned capital more of an administrative superior-subordinate relationship. Multiple identities lead to multiple target requirements for state-owned enterprises, hindering the realization of preservation and appreciation of state-owned assets. That is, when exercising the function of public finance, the enterprise focuses mainly on social objectives, macro-regulation objectives, and public welfare objectives; in this role state-owned enterprises are regarded as tools for the government to implement macro-regulation and public management, which requires them to have certain responsibilities for social and economic stability. When exercising the function of the investor, the state-owned enterprise is regarded as the specific operator of the state-owned capital, with more emphasis on preserving and increasing the value of the state-owned assets and pursuing the maximization of the return on capital. Due to the lack of an effective firewall between the owner's function and the public management function, and given the multiple targets set by government departments, the state-owned enterprises often have to swing and balance between the profit target and the social target.

2.6.3 Establishing a Layered Management Model of State-Owned Capital

From the perspective of corporate governance, the field of operation of any manager or management organization will be restricted by the "governance radius." In practice in China, the SASAC manages a large number of state-owned enterprises, which are distributed among dozens of industries and hundreds of product sub-markets. If we continue to adhere to a unified management model with strong planned economy characteristics, adopt a two-tier management structure of "SASAC—state-owned enterprises" and issue specific guidance on enterprise development and business operation on an individual basis, the result may be that the more we manage, the worse the effect will be. The development of state-owned enterprises will deviate from the trend of marketization and will also lead to the loss of state-owned capital.

In this sense, breaking the traditional two-tier management structure of "SASAC—state-owned enterprises" and replacing it with the three-tier structure of "SASAC—holding company (state-owned capital investment and operation company)—state-owned enterprise" not only meets the requirements of driving the reform of state-owned enterprises with the reform of state-owned capital, but also fits well with the principle that the government only manages state-owned assets as a contributor. This will further clarify the ownership of state-owned capital and the functional orientation of relevant government agencies represented by SASAC, and can effectively eliminate problems such as low work enthusiasm and poor efficiency of process management caused by the interference of government will and interests, and even direct intervention, in the behavior of state-owned enterprises. Overall, this will be conducive to the establishment of a modern enterprise system in state-owned enterprises. In effect, the use of holding companies and other financial or quasi-financial intermediaries to establish a firewall between SASAC and state-owned enterprises will ensure the separation of government functions from enterprise management.

In the field of state-owned financial capital management, the establishment of Central Huijin Investment Ltd. in 2003 represented the implementation of the three-tier structure of "State Council—financial holding company (Huijin Company)—state-owned financial institutions." Here, the core idea is to set up a financial holding company to manage state-owned financial assets according to the principles of marketization, legalization, and professionalization. The greatest advantage of this model is that it can sever completely the administrative connection between the state-owned financial capital and the government's functional agencies, decouple them from the subordinate relationship, and block the administrative intervention from the government. The state-owned financial asset holding company can ensure the "personification" of the owner's representative when exercising the function of investor, which has a positive effect on solving the problems of investor's own incentive and restraint, and on strengthening the supervision and assessment of agents. However, since the founding of the CIC in September 2007, Huijin Company has become a wholly-owned subsidiary of it. The original reform attempt to divest the Ministry of Finance of the function of investor of state-owned financial capital has basically stalled, and the MoF has once again returned to the old path of interfering in the daily operation of financial assets. Moreover, the CIC has been criticized by the international market for its inability to completely isolate itself from Huijin's function as a shareholder of state-owned financial institutions on behalf of the state, and its own profit and loss in carrying out investment business has often been over-interpreted.

2.6.4 *Strengthening the Leadership by the Chinese government and the Protection of Shareholders' Rights and Interests Through a "Double-Level Arrangement"*

In the proposed "double-level arrangement", the first level will combine the identity of the investor of state-owned capital with the authority of the board of directors. The Chinese government can control the board resolution on behalf of the majority equity, which not only realizes the party's control over the ownership of state-owned enterprises, effectively protects the interests of state-owned investors, and improves the investor's control power, but also integrates the management of cadres, national strategic goals and interests, income rights and distribution, rewards and punishments, discipline, and external coordination, similar to the "comprehensive management of people, money, and things" that used to be said in the past, to prevent everything from going too far and everything from going to the end. At the same time, we should wholeheartedly implement the principle of "the same share and the same right;" handle the relationship between adhering to the public ownership as the main body and supporting the non-public ownership, encouraging private and foreign investment; improve the transparency in the major business decision-making process of enterprises; and protect the rights of small and medium-sized shareholders to participate in the company's decision-making and benefit distribution.

The second level of the two-tier arrangement will involve the establishment of the company's management level and party committees for grassroots cadres and employees. We should give full play to the political core role of the party organization, including improving the control power of ideals and beliefs education, organization guarantee, disciplinary inspection, personnel qualification examination, and employee benefit guarantee. Through the double-level arrangement, the management structure will not only conform to the corporate governance structure of modern enterprises, but will also differentiate the role of the board of directors and the party organization at the management level. The People's Bank of China has carried out a pilot project with this arrangement in its affiliated banknote printing and minting company, financial electronic companies, and gold coin companies, and has achieved positive results.

2.7 Pension Issues

China's pension contribution rate is too high, which damages the competitiveness of enterprises. Reducing the social security contribution rate is an important element in the task of "reducing costs." Historically, the main reason for the high contribution rate is that the current social security system was established only relatively recently, and so the people who are now elderly and drawing pensions did not contribute to it; furthermore, the government did not bear the cost of system transition. Following the implementation of the new system, the financial burden of the "deemed contribution" policy was transferred entirely to employees, making it difficult to lower the pension rate. The low welfare practice under the old system is an important source of huge state-owned assets, and it is therefore appropriate to use the transfer of state-owned capital to make up for the historical debts of pensions. At the end of 2017, the State Council issued the Implementation Plan for Transferring Some State-owned Capital to Enrich the Social Security Fund, under which state-owned capital would be used to replenish the social security fund according to the proportion of 10%. In future, the proportion of social security transferred from state-owned assets should be increased in line with the needs of the sustainable operation of the pension system. In addition, making real personal pension accounts and carrying out pension investment operations will be important countermeasures to enhance the financial sustainability of China's pension system. China's basic pension system adopts a defined benefits (DB)-type pay-as-you-go system, which is not suitable for the current situation of an aging population. In the future, China should shift to developing a defined contributions (DC)-type fund accumulation pension system and establishing real personal pension accounts, which will not only share the dividends of economic development in the form of long-term investment, but will also help develop direct financing markets and enhance the ability of institutional investors to stabilize financial markets.

Comparing the two pension management modes of national overall planning and local responsibility, under the real condition of unbalanced development among different regions the former will cause a moral hazard to the local government, while the latter places more emphasis on the responsibility and self-restraint of the local government, which is more conducive to maintaining the long-term sustainability of the pension system. Under the condition of "stratified ownership" of China's state-owned capital and the existence of "governance radius," a local social security system with overall planning will better facilitate the implementation of the policy of transferring state-owned capital to replenish social security funds. At present, China's payment system is highly developed, which provides a foundation for the establishment of a system of "decentralized responsibility of provinces, segmented payment of inter-provincial mobile employment, and accumulative pension payment in retirement areas." Local governments' responsibility for pension affairs will not affect the free flow of labor. In the future, no matter which department approves the establishment of pension investment and operation institutions, their investment activities in the capital market shall be subject to the unified supervision of the CSRC.

2.7.1 Excessive Pension Rates Affect the Competitiveness of Enterprises

In the years from 1986 to 2005, China's endowment insurance system underwent multiple reforms, eventually arriving at the current system. In the process of reform, the pension contribution rate has been continually increasing. The Interim Provisions on the Labor Contract System in State-owned Enterprises, promulgated in 1986, stipulated a total rate of 18% (15% for enterprise contributions); the Decision on Deepening the Reform of the Endowment Insurance System for Enterprise Employees, issued in 1995, increased the total rate to 26% (23% for enterprise contributions); while in 2005, the Decision of the State Council on Perfecting the Basic Endowment Insurance System for Enterprise Employees stipulated a total rate of 28% (20% for enterprise contributions). This contribution rate is amongst the highest in the world, much higher than that in most developed and major developing countries, and is out of proportion to China's population structure.

The high pension rate has become a "stumbling block" that hinders China's economic development. Enterprises face a dilemma: evasion is illegal, but if they contribute according to the regulations, the labor cost is too high. At a time when the supply of labor is declining, and the labor cost is rising sharply, lowering the pension rate will represent an important breakthrough to reduce the cost of enterprises. However, judging from the current situation, as the pension income and expenditure in many provinces have deteriorated, once the rate is lowered, the imbalance in the pension system will inevitably worsen, which presents another dilemma.

2.7.2 State-Owned Capital Should Be Allocated to Repay the Historical Debts of the Social Security System Transition

Historical and institutional factors have caused China to incur large social security and pension debts; the historical debt repayment mechanism of the basic endowment insurance system is missing; and the government has not repaid the cost of restructuring. China's social endowment insurance system was established relatively late, in 1997. Before that, enterprises and employees did not make contributions to the endowment insurance system. However, after entering the new system, these employees were treated as if they had already made contributions. In 1997, when the partial accumulation system of combining social pooling with personal accounts (unified accounting) was established, the government did not bear the cost of restructuring to make up for the gap caused by the missing contributions. Instead, according to the principle of fixed income based on support, enterprises and employees are responsible for the high pension rate. The working generation not only has to support the retired generation through intergenerational transfer, but also has to prepare for its own future, thus causing future generations to have to raise their contribution rate. In fact, even though the pension rate is excessive, the social pooling fund paid by the enterprise is still insufficient, the funds in the personal account are diverted to provide pensions for retirees, and the empty personal accounts constitute hidden debt. The operation of empty personal accounts means that the current so-called "unified accounting" endowment insurance system is actually a pay-as-you-go plan with a total rate of 28%.

Allocating state-owned capital to replenish the social security fund is the most reasonable solution. Before 1997, employees did not make pension insurance contributions, which actually made the cost of enterprises unreal, expanded the capital accumulation of state-owned enterprises, and formed huge state-owned capital. Only by allocating state-owned capital to enrich the social security fund and make up for the historical arrears of the pension due to deemed contributions, can the rate of social security contributions be reduced. In fact, in 2003, the Decision on Several Issues Concerning the Improvement of the Socialist Market Economic System, carried by the Third Plenary Session of the 16th Chinese government Central Committee, stated that various means should be adopted, including transferring part of the state-owned capital to enrich the social security fund according to law. In the Decision of the Third Plenary Session of the 18th Chinese government Central Committee, the reform task of "allocating some state-owned capital to enrich the social security fund and reduce the social insurance rate in due course" was once again put forward.

In the future, more efforts should be made to allocate state-owned capital to social security. According to the Implementation Plan of Transferring Part of State-owned Capital to Enrich the Social Security Fund, issued by the State Council in November 2017, the central and local state-owned and state-controlled large and medium-sized enterprises and financial institutions will be included in the scope of transfer, with the transfer proportion being 10% of the state-owned shares of enterprises. Stock dividends and operating income will be earmarked to make up for the gap in the basic pension insurance fund for employees of enterprises. In the past, some experts estimated that if the state-owned shares were allocated successfully, the pension contribution rate could be reduced by 3–5 percentage points. At present, the transfer has not been completed, and the pension contribution level has not been lowered. In the future, the pension contribution rate should be taken as an indicator of the effectiveness of the transfer of social security from state-owned assets, and the transfer ratio should be further increased.

2.7.3 Ensure the Individual Accounts Are Fully Funded

According to the payment model adopted, pension systems can be divided into defined benefits (DB) and defined contribution (DC). Under the DB-type plan, the retirement benefits of employees are determined first, and then the contribution level of each year is determined according to the pension to be paid in the future based on the actuarial principle. Under the DC-type plan, the contribution level is determined first, and the funds are included in the personal account and handed over to financial institutions for investment and operation. When employees retire, they will receive pensions according to the accumulated value of the personal account fund. The employees themselves will take all investment risks. China's pension system is a DB type, and pension payment is a rigid expenditure obligation for the government. Data from the Ministry of Human Resources and Social Security shows that the demand for public pension funds was 3.97 trillion yuan in 2015 and is expected to surge to 7.28 trillion yuan by 2025.

According to the financing model, the pension system can be divided into two types: pay-as-you-go and fully funded. China nominally adopts a partial accumulation model that "combines social pooling and personal accounts;" however, in reality, it is a pay-as-you-go system. Personal accounts are empty accounts, and funds have been misappropriated to pay current pensions, which is not sustainable in the context of the aging population. According to the China Pension Actuarial Report 2018–2022, compiled by the World Social Security Research Center of the Chinese Academy of Social Sciences, in 2018 one out of every five people across the country were not contributing to the basic endowment insurance of urban enterprises, and in 2022 the corresponding figure will be one out of every four people; in 2018, more than two payers were supporting one retiree, and in 2022, there will be fewer than two payers supporting one retiree.

In recent years, the focus of discussion about pension system reform has been on measures such as the transfer of state-owned assets income to social security, and delayed retirement. In the future, the pension security system should also focus on fully funding the personal pension account, making the property rights of the account clearer, and realizing the positive incentive of "more contributions, higher payments." The gradual realization of fully funding personal pension accounts means that the pension security system will change from a pay-as-you-go system to a fund accumulation system, and the treatment standard of pension security will change from the DB type to the DC type.

The DC-type pension plan of the development fund accumulation system has the policy effect of "hitting three birds with one stone." First, it emphasizes the responsibility of personal pensions and realizes good interaction between personal pension responsibility and income. Second, it turns the short-term savings of the family sector into "long-term money," develops the direct financing market, and effectively supports "deleveraging." We assume that the financial assets of households will reach 200 trillion yuan. According to the structure of the household balance sheet, 30% of the household assets will be used for pensions, with a capital scale of about 60 trillion yuan. The third pillar of personal accounts keeps about 40 trillion yuan. If it is handed over to a professional organization for operation, assuming that 20% is allocated to enter the equity financing market, the capital will be about 8 trillion yuan. As long as it is scientifically, comprehensively, and prudently allocated in equity financing, "long-term money" can be formed. Matching the long-term money of pension funds with the term equity financing of enterprises is an important driving force for enterprise departments to deleverage. Finally, this pension plan arrangement will develop institutional investors and enhance the stability of financial markets. For a long time, China's capital market has had many retail investors, great volatility, and a strongly speculative atmosphere, which has weakened the attraction of the capital market and its ability to serve the real economy. Institutional investors have the advantages of information and scale, a more professional and scientific investment decision-making mode, and behavior that is closer to that of the "rational economic man" in the effective market hypothesis. The improvement of their market position will help promote the healthy and stable development of financial markets.

2.7.4 Unbalanced Development in China

There are large regional differences in the income and expenditure of the pension system. The data show that there is a significant gap between provinces in the accumulated fund balance, and there is a trend of further differentiation. On the one hand, the scale of funds in eastern provinces with high accumulation, such as Guangdong and Beijing, continues to rise. The Annual Report on China's Social Insurance Development 2016, published by the Social Security Management Center of the Ministry of Human Resources and Social Security, shows that in 2016, the accumulated balance of pension funds for employees of urban enterprises in Guangdong Province was 725.8 billion yuan, accounting for 19.6% of the national total. Other areas with accumulated balances exceeding 100 billion yuan include Beijing, Jiangsu, Zhejiang, Shandong, Sichuan, Shanghai, Shanxi, and Anhui. These nine regions have a total balance of 2.61 trillion yuan, accounting for 70.6% of the total balance. On the other hand, the risk of depletion of the balance in some provinces in the northeast and northwest is increasing. The Annual Report on China's Social Insurance Development 2016 shows that in 2016, the number of provinces whose current income could not meet their pensions had increased to seven, namely Heilongjiang, Liaoning, Hebei, Jilin, Inner Mongolia, Hubei, and Qinghai. According to the China Pension Actuarial Report 2018–2022, published by the Academy of Social Sciences, the number of provinces that are unable to "make ends meet" in 2018–2022 is estimated to be 13 or 14.

In the short term, although national overall planning can enhance the ability to adjust the surplus and shortage of funds to cope with the pension income and expenditure gap in regions with a serious aging population, in the long term there is obvious moral hazard, which is not conducive to the sustainability of the pension system. For developed regions with surplus pension, if there is no incentive mechanism of "paying more and getting more," the enthusiasm for paying pension insurance will be dampened. For less developed regions, if it is expected that the responsibility for pension payment can be transferred to the central government, the number of pensioners will be increased in violation of regulations. In fact, some areas have already seen a sudden expansion in the scope of pension recipients. Comparatively speaking, the mode of local responsibility is more likely to respect the reality that levels of economic development differ among different regions. Furthermore, incentive compatibility between pension insurance contributions and retirement benefits is the arrangement most conducive to maintaining the long-term sustainability of the pension system.

2.7.5 Implement the Policy of Transferring State-Owned Capital to the Social Security Fund as Soon as Possible

From the perspective of the historical formation of state-owned capital, huge state-owned assets are the result of "low wage, low welfare, and high accumulation" of the older generation of workers. Before 2003, due to the distorted accounting system, the cost of state-owned enterprises and the wages of their employees were strictly limited. Many of the abnormally high book profits were artificially created, resulting from the low wages paid and the debts owed in fields such as medical care, pensions, and housing. These book profits were used for investment. Today, there is a consensus in China that in order to make up for the government's historical debts in these essential areas, we must find ways to allocate more social security funds from state-owned assets.

Transferring part of state-owned capital to social security will be conducive to improving the corporate governance structure of state-owned enterprises. Many cases show that more than 50% of the shares of state-owned enterprises are controlled by the central or local financial management departments, and there are major corporate governance defects, often leading to major losses of state-owned assets. In many industries with full market competition, using a large amount of public financial resources in the name of making state-owned enterprises bigger and stronger, but without paying attention to corporate governance, will only waste those resources. Conversely, if we focus on improving the corporate governance and relative holding of state-owned enterprises, we can achieve the strategic goal of enlarging and strengthening those enterprises while also freeing up more public financial resources for improving the livelihood of the people.

"Stratified ownership" of the state-owned capital management system determines that the local overall social security system is more conducive to the implementation of the policy of transferring state-owned capital to enrich the social security fund. Under the circumstance that China's central and local governments divide their revenue and expenditure, the state-owned capital managed by the central government and the state-owned capital managed by the local government should be owned by different levels. According to the principle of "who contributes, owns," the governments at all levels should exercise the ownership of the relevant state-owned capital and perform the responsibilities of investors. Even in the case of ownership by the whole people, for example the transfer of state-owned capital to replenish the social security fund, the ultimate actual beneficiary will not be the whole people, and is still a stratified concept. Under the condition of the "stratified ownership" of the state-owned capital and the existence of "governance radius," the implementation of the policy of transferring state-owned capital to replenish the social security fund requires a local coordinated social security system.

2.7.6 Improve the Portability of Pensions

China is a huge country. Many of its provinces have a higher population and larger land area than those of a medium-sized country. It is difficult to find international experience that provides a reasonable reference in the design of China's pension system. Therefore, we should give priority to independent design according to the situation of a large country with unbalanced development. If we wish to make international comparisons, we must look to the experience of big countries or associations of countries. For example, China can learn from the EU's practice of increasing the portability of pensions among its member states. In the unified market of the European Union, member countries can be regarded as local governments to some extent. Due to the huge differences in the living standards of member countries, it is unrealistic to establish a "unified" social security system. On the premise that each country formulates different endowment insurance policies according to its own situation, EU social security directives such as "Council Regulation (EC) No 1408/71" and "Council Regulation (EC) No 574/72" set out six provisions to enhance the portability of endowment insurance among member countries and ensure that the "individual behaviors" of member countries will not have a negative impact on the free flow of personnel in the region. In detail, these provisions are: (1) Temporary freezing of contributions: When the payer migrates from country A to country B, the previous endowment insurance records will be kept by country A, and his or her historical contributions in country A will not be transferred to country B or paid to him or her. This part of historical contributions will be temporarily "frozen" until he or she reaches the retirement age, and then issued to him or her according to the prescribed standards. (2) Separate payment: As long as the person concerned has been in a member country's pension plan for more than one year, the country should pay the pension to the person concerned when he or she retires. (3) Proportional payment: The amount of pension will be calculated on the basis of the time that the person concerned participated in the endowment insurance in the country. The longer he or she participates, the more pension he or she will receive. (4) Final takeover: The last member country in which the person concerned worked prior to retirement will be responsible for "taking over" the person's scattered (less than one year) endowment insurance period in each member country. (5) Cumulative calculation: If an EU citizen does not meet the requirements of a country for the time he or she has taken part in pension insurance, the time he or she has taken part in pension insurance in other member countries will also be counted. (6) Irrelevant residence: The eligibility for the pension has nothing to do with whether the payer lives in the paying country or the European Union or the European Economic Area. All pensions must be paid in full and on time, without deduction, modification, or default of any kind.

Learning from the practice of the European Union, China can continue to implement local pooling before realizing national pooling of basic pensions. When a resident retires after employment in many places, the pension benefits of his coordinated account shall be subject to "payment by sections and calculation by sections in each province, and centralized issuance of pension." This arrangement will improve both the flexibility of cross-regional employment in the labor market, and the enthusiasm of people to participate in the social security system, expand the coverage of social security, and improve the social security network. Regarding the transfer of personal accounts, within the framework of the basic requirements and principles of the central government, the provincial, local government is responsible for the design of the personal account system, including the transfer rules. In fact, in the era of Internet big data, China's payment system has reached the world's advanced level and fully meets the technical conditions of "calculate by sections, collective distribution."

2.7.7 Develop Pension Investment and Operations

The pressure on the income and expenditure of the endowment insurance fund is increasing, and the sustainable development of the endowment insurance system can be ensured only by increasing the sources of income and reducing expenditures. There are three main ways to increase the funding sources of the pension system: the first is to raise the payment standard, but this conflicts with the "cost reduction" policy; the second is the transfer of state-owned capital to the social security fund to expand strategic reserves, which involves many interest groups and takes a long time; the third, and most feasible, is to invest and operate the pension funds that have been collected to obtain investment income.

In the past, the pension investment policy was overly focused on the pursuit of safety, and was limited by too few investment types and very low returns. Meanwhile, the balance of China's social insurance funds could be purchased only from Treasury bonds and deposit banks, except for a certain period of payment, with an annual yield of only about 3%. In contrast, from 2007 to 2017, the cumulative rate of return on real estate was as high as 766%, the rate of return on gold was 106%, the rate of return on the Shanghai and Shenzhen 300 index was 97%, the rate of return on corporate bonds index was 78%, and the Shanghai 50 index rose by 58%. The case of misappropriation of social security funds in Shanghai in 2006 can be understood, to a certain extent, as an attempt by local governments to pursue higher returns on pension fund balances.

The pace of relaxing restrictions on pension investment is accelerating. In March 2012, Guangdong became the first pilot province for local pension investment to enter the market. Since then, the pilot has been gradually expanded. In August 2015, the State Council issued the Measures for the Administration of Investment in Basic Endowment Insurance Funds, which achieved a breakthrough in the investment policy of basic endowment insurance funds and officially allowed provinces to entrust the National Social Security Fund Council to manage their endowment funds. So far, nine provinces have signed entrustment investment contracts with the Social Security Fund Council, with the amount of entrustment investment reaching 430 billion yuan. In addition to the contracts signed by nine provinces, Tibet, Gansu,

Zhejiang, and Jiangsu also plan to entrust investment operations, which will increase the funds invested by about 150 billion yuan.

For pension investment and operation, the financial supervision system should work in cooperation with a due division of labor. Pension fund investment supervision develops in line with the pension fund policy. The first pillar of the basic endowment insurance funds did not have a market-oriented investment. The management of the endowment insurance funds was basically undertaken by the government finance department without financial supervision. With the development of a supplementary pension plan as the second pillar, the market-oriented investment of pension funds developed rapidly, and the supervision of pension fund investment came into being. In the third pillar of the personal pension plan, participation groups have been dispersed, investment targets have been diversified, and the requirements for pension fund investment supervision have been further raised. From a worldwide perspective, the supervision of pension funds has undergone a change from "institutional supervision" to "functional supervision." In order to maintain the consistency of financial supervision, the pension funds of South Korea, Australia, and Japan are under the unified supervision of financial supervision institutions. In South Korea the responsible body is the Financial Supervision Authority, in Japan it is the Financial Department, and in Australia the Prudential Supervision Authority. Under the separate supervision system of China's banking, securities, and insurance, unified rules should be established as soon as possible for institutional access in accordance with the principle that the same type of business shall be subject to the same supervision. The CSRC shall be responsible for the behavior supervision of pension investment and operation institutions participating in the capital market, so as to safeguard the safety of pension investment and operation and protect the rights of financial consumers.

Chapter 3
Transformation of China's Financial System

3.1 Reflections on the Financial Crisis

A decade has passed since the US subprime mortgage crisis triggered the global financial crisis. Faced with the consequences of light-touch and fragmented regulation guided by laissez-faire ideology, central banks have played a crucial role in crisis response. While the traditional view holds that the safe operation of all individual institutions is equal to overall financial security, and price stability can automatically achieve economic and financial stability, with the outbreak of the global financial crisis the international community had to completely abandon that interpretation.

In the aftermath of the crisis there has been a general shift toward super-central banking. There is now a consensus that central banks should strengthen macro-prudential management and play a greater role in dealing with systemic risk and financial regulation. Exploring the causes of the global financial crisis and summarizing the experience and lessons of other countries in dealing with the crisis are of vital significance to China's efforts to prevent and defuse financial risks, win the battle to avoid systemic financial risks, and better realize high-quality economic development in the new era.

3.1.1 The Causes of the Global Financial Crisis

Although a myriad of factors coincided to trigger this "once-in-a-century financial tsunami," the deep underlying fault line lay in the international institutional system. First of all, in a system of "regulatory competition" against a background of deregulation, the fragmented and divided supervision then in place was totally unsuitable for the general trend of comprehensive management. Since the 1980s, the Washington consensus advocating neoliberalism (Williamson, 1989) had become the mainstream trend of thought in many countries. As a result, the idea that "the least regulation is

Z. Xu, *Keep Reforming: China's Strategic Economic Transformation*,
https://doi.org/10.1007/978-981-15-8006-2_3

the best regulation" was widespread, and the rapid development of financial innovation blurred the boundaries of traditional financial industries, leading to "regulatory competition" and "regulatory capture" of different financial industries in different countries. The regulatory systems of various countries became more and more departmentalized and fragmented. In order to please the interest groups in their own sectors, attract potential regulatory objects, or expand the scope of regulation, regulators were competing to lower regulatory standards.

Second, under the "single instrument, single target" framework, central banks tended to separate their functions from financial supervision and therefore ignored asset bubbles and systemic risks. According to the traditional view, as long as the price stability can automatically achieve economic and financial stability, the central bank needs only to focus on the inflation target and adopt interest rate regulation; it should not consider the asset bubble, but only clean up after the bubble bursts (Greenspan, 2002). Before the financial crisis, this separation of regulatory functions from the central bank had become a trend among very many countries.

As a result, before the crisis, virtually no single institution adopted macro-prudential policies from the perspective of overall financial stability, or was truly responsible for systemic financial risks. Because central banks did not have enough regulatory information, they could not intervene effectively in advance or even carry out a timely rescue after the event. The core capital adequacy of systemically important institutions was generally insufficient, and there was a huge regulatory vacuum formed by cross-market, overlapping and complex financial products. The credit and leverage ratio rose rapidly, and the shadow banking system developed at a fast pace. Finally, with the outbreak of the subprime mortgage crisis in the United States, the situation developed into a global systemic financial crisis.

3.1.2 *Reflections on the Response to the Global Financial Crisis*

The main reason why this financial crisis was not as severe as the Great Depression is that central banks had learned from that earlier crash, and from the experience of crisis management after the Second World War, and gave full play to the function of lender of last resort.

I. Under the impact of the financial crisis, confidence is more important than gold. As lender of last resort the central bank is the "anchor" to maintain market confidence and financial stability.

When an economy is hit by systemic crisis and falls into recession, there is a run on the financial institutions, the liquidity of the financial market dries up rapidly, and the function of the financial system is seriously damaged. There is a golden 24-h period for crisis response, and the more decisive and timely the rescue, the better the policy effect will be.

First, with regard to the decision-making process, the central bank crisis relief decisions are smoother. Although governments may try to break through the traditional policy of non-intervention by providing institutional guarantees, implementing nationalization, or replacing the market with government credit to support market confidence, the many institutional and procedural obstacles to national decision-making mean that these measures cannot be carried out in a timely manner, so there is a lag in crisis response. For example, on September 28, 2008, the US Congress rejected the $700 billion rescue bill of the Bush administration, and the financial market deteriorated rapidly. As the lender of last resort, the central bank has traditional liquidity tools and is able to conduct policy innovation flexibly, and the decision-making process is smoother. It has a natural advantage in crisis relief (Fischer, 2016).

Second, from the perspective of policy means, central bank rescue tools are more flexible and diverse. For example, as the subprime crisis deteriorated, the Federal Reserve was able to use the discount window to provide liquidity support to financial institutions, to innovate policy tools to assist different market participants, to coordinate market financial institutions, and thus successfully eliminate the market panic (Domanski et al., 2014). The Fed also created a variety of tools to assist non-Fed members and government-backed institutions. Even as the crisis worsened, the Fed bought up large amounts of corporate commercial paper to boost market liquidity and ease tight credit conditions.

Third, with regard to the size of the rescue, the central bank has more room. Because of budget caps, fiscal policy space is very limited. Since the crisis, the United States, Britain and the European Union have spent more than $1 trillion of public funds to rescue the financial system, but this sum is far lower than the $1.73 trillion of assets bought by the Federal Reserve during the crisis and the first round of quantitative easing.

I. Taking the lead from the central bank to dispose of problematic financial institutions in accordance with market-based principles is crucial to timely and effective resolution of financial risks.

As outlined above, the central bank has clear advantages over micro regulators and other financial departments in terms of decision-making process, policy means and rescue scale. Consequently, when the financial market is in turmoil, market participants naturally turn to the central bank as the cornerstone of financial market stability.

In addressing a situation of financial crisis it is important first to give full play to the leading role of the central bank and try to defuse financial risks through the market system itself. In the resolution of the bankruptcy of LTCM in 1998, the Federal Reserve did not use funds to rescue the company, but took the lead of Merrill Lynch and 15 other market institutions to jointly take over LTCM, effectively resolving the financial market risks. After the subprime mortgage crisis in 2007, the Federal Reserve adopted similar measures, mainly relying on market adjustment and traditional liquidity means to stabilize financial markets, and providing bridge loans and coordinating the acquisition of Bear Stearns and Merrill Lynch by JPMorgan Chase and Bank of America.

Second, the central bank should provide liquidity assistance to financial institutions with systemically important problems in accordance with Bagehot's law. In the wake of the collapse of Lehman Brothers, the Fed tried to lead market forces to defuse the risks, but failed to do so because of the rapid deterioration in financial markets following the government takeover of Fannie and Freddie. It was in view of the lessons learned from the failure of Lehman Brothers that the Federal Reserve, after comprehensive assessment, considered AIG to be of global systemic importance, and therefore adhered to the Bagehot rule of lender of last resort by providing unlimited liquidity support to that corporation, thus successfully preventing the spread of systemic risk. The difference in the treatment of Lehman Brothers and AIG was mainly due to the difference in the Federal Reserve's understanding of their systemic importance.

Third, it is necessary to deal effectively with the regional small and medium-sized institutions. In the US, this is done mainly through the FDIC orderly bankruptcy liquidation. Since 2007, the FDIC has dealt with more than 530 regional problem institutions. Because deposit insurance effectively protects most depositors, institutions are small and do not cause large-scale runs or systemic risks.

I. The central bank has to participate in daily supervision. After the crisis, major economies generally strengthened the financial supervision responsibilities of the central bank, creating a super central bank.

When the central bank performs the function of lender of last resort to rescue troubled institutions, it needs to judge the liquidity and systemic risk status of troubled institutions accurately and in a timely manner so as to take corresponding rescue measures. The Bank of England failed to rescue Northern Rock in time because it lacked first-hand regulatory information. Similarly, due to the lack of a central counterparty clearing mechanism, the Fed did not have complete access to Lehman Brothers' financial market trading information; as a result, it failed to realize that Lehman's failure would have a systemic impact on the market. By contrast, the London Clearing House (LCH) introduced a central counterparty clearing mechanism, which promptly disposed of $9tn of open positions, including Lehman, without causing losses to other market players or to LCH.

In view of the above, in the years after the global financial crisis there has formed a new and important consensus that the central bank should be responsible for the overall supervision of systemically important financial institutions, the overall supervision of important financial infrastructure, and the overall statistics of the financial industry. Therefore, while strengthening financial supervision, all countries have turned to the super-central bank model, giving the central bank a more important role in financial supervision and the prevention of systemic financial risks. The UK has re-entrusted the Bank of England with prudential supervision, and has made the central bank fully responsible for monetary policy, macro-prudential and micro-supervision. In the US the Federal Reserve has become a "super-regulator," explicitly charged with macro-prudential supervision to maintain financial stability. The European Union has established a macro-prudential management system framework led by the central bank, which is responsible for both micro-prudential and macro-prudential functions and directly supervises systemically important financial institutions.

II. Crisis relief should maintain financial security and prevent moral hazard in a balance. It should not only keep the bottom line of risks, but also strengthen market discipline.

Major central banks in the United States, Europe and other countries require good and sufficient collateral from each other when they bail out troubled institutions. Perfect collateral arrangement plays an important role in ensuring the safety of central bank funds and unimpeded monetary transmission channels (Bindseil, 2014).

Furthermore, adjustment of the deposit insurance amount must guard against moral hazard. During the crisis all countries raised deposit insurance quotas, but the increases were modest and limited rather than full insurance, which effectively strengthened market discipline while resolving systemic risks (Anginer et al., 2014).

In addition, according to the principle of incentive compatibility, corporate governance should be at the core of the equity transformation of problem financial institutions. While rescuing troubled financial institutions, governments all over the world have diluted the original equity of those institutions to improve their corporate governance and strengthen the constraints of capital risk taking.

Finally, in order to avoid undermining market discipline and causing new moral hazard, governments should withdraw or transfer the assets of troubled institutions to central banks. After the global financial crisis, massive government guarantees and nationalizations put huge strain on national finances. As financial markets stabilized, governments withdrew or handed the assets over to central banks.

III. Countries must be alert to the side effects of unconventional monetary policies and the financialization of fiscal risks, and further enhance the central bank's policy autonomy.

With limited fiscal space, countries rely on central bank bailouts and unconventional monetary policies to stimulate economic recovery. However, expansionary monetary policy alone cannot solve the deep problems of economic development. Without profound structural reform, unconventional monetary policies have limited marginal effects, and the long-term effect of promoting output prices is not ideal (Borio and Zabia, 2016). After the crisis, a large amount of money flowed not into the real economy, but into capital markets such as real estate and stocks. This is an important reason why, in many countries, economic recovery has been slow, but the housing price and stock market have long returned to pre-crisis levels.

A further potential problem is that the central bank undertakes too many policy objectives, and the monetization of fiscal deficit damages the autonomy of monetary policy. Quantitative easing and low interest rate policies are more conducive to fiscal low-cost financing, which is actually the monetization of fiscal deficit and the transfer of fiscal risks to the financial sector (Bayoumi et al., 2014). The excessive reliance of fiscal policy on monetary policy and the proposal to strengthen policy coordination make it more difficult to exit unconventional monetary policy, which also damages the autonomy of monetary policy (Powell, 2014).

3.1.3 The Implications of the Global Financial Crisis

The global financial crisis demonstrated that the security of all individual institutions is not equal to overall financial security, that there may be a synthetic fallacy, and that price stability is not a sufficient condition for economic and financial stability. The central bank should strengthen macro-prudential policies and play a bigger role in the response to systemic risks and financial supervision, so as to effectively prevent and defuse financial risks and keep the bottom line of avoiding systemic financial risks.

The financial management system has always developed dynamically in a balance between preventing risks and encouraging innovation. Although an excessively laissez-faire approach to financial supervision was an important cause of the crisis, strict financial repression is not an effective means to ensure financial security. Since the 1980s, the financial industry has changed markedly. For example, the rapid development of financial transactions technology has led to a decline in the status of traditional banking, asset pricing theory has grown in prominence, the financial markets (especially the bond and derivatives markets) have increased, the relationship between the various financial markets have become more and more close, and economic and financial globalization have brought countries together into a globally integrated financial system. Financial industry comprehensive management needs to adapt to the financial innovation that is taking place in this context of economic globalization, and to meet the demand for enterprise comprehensive financial services. the us and Europe to countries such as the financial industry comprehensive management is actually separated operation of financial industry in fact breakthrough limit after confirmation, even after the global financial crisis, the financial sector also should not also not be returned to the pattern of separate operation and supervised respectively. Indeed, the Volcker rule, which was eventually adopted in the US, has been heavily revised. Since the crisis the development of regulatory policies has been a balance between risk prevention and innovation.

Since the beginning of this century, China's financial industry has made a qualitative leap, which represents a key aspect of China's progress to become the world's second largest economy. It is no longer realistic to restore China's financial industry to the separate state of the period before the 1990s, nor can separate supervision effectively prevent and resolve systemic financial risks, let alone meet the needs of modern economic development under open conditions. Accurate diagnosis and treatment of the current financial chaos is conducive to the establishment of a modern financial system. A policy of "giving priority to insurance" and "taking separate measures" can only solidify the existing structural contradictions, resulting in the accumulation of risks. The greater the level of insurance, the greater the chaos and the greater the inability to adapt to the development and transformation of the modern economy. This in turn, may lead to moral hazard and new risks.

Sound monetary policy and macro-prudential policy are twin pillars, and the central bank and financial regulation cannot be separated. Since the crisis, many countries have taken a wider global view of financial risk, rather than a more restricted industry development view, and have adopted a central bank model aimed at limiting the impact of systemic crisis and maintaining overall stability. In China, the contradiction between separate supervision and comprehensive operation without effective supervision is the main reason for the prevalence of regulatory arbitrage and the accumulation of financial risks.

From the experience of Internet financial regulation in China, it is difficult to completely separate behavioral supervision from prudential supervision. When the central bank is responsible for controlling systemic risk, it should also coordinate prudential supervision and behavioral supervision. The fundamental way out is to establish a comprehensive financial supervision system dominated by the central bank, with "three overall plans" and effective coordination between prudential supervision and behavioral supervision. Should with matrix management ways to enrich the financial stability and development committee, strengthening the management of the people's bank of China in the macro-prudential and systemic financial risk prevention in the core position, strengthen business line across departments to coordinate, and the comprehensive use of resources, which can cost on the reform of small vibration and maximum achieve reform. At the same time, in the course of risk prevention and crisis response, we need to strengthen market discipline and give full play to the role of the deposit insurance system in orderly bankruptcy settlement of troubled institutions, breaking the peg, avoiding risk squeeze and defusing systemic financial risks.

The more resilient the economy, the more risk response means reserves, the lower the impact of financial crisis. The global crisis of 2008 was the first international financial crisis originating from mature developed economies since the collapse of the Bretton Woods system. Emerging economies were relatively less affected by the crisis and contributed much more than developed countries to world economic growth after the crisis, largely because they had learned the lessons of the Latin American debt crisis in the 1980s, the East Asian financial crisis in the 1990s and the emerging market currency crisis in the early 2000s (Kenc et al., 2016). Emerging economies have carried out very many beneficial explorations of macro-prudential policies (Upper, 2017) and attached great importance to the "original sin" problem of currency mismatches (Eichengreen et al.,). Gradually, they have overcome the fear of floating exchange rate and adopted a more flexible exchange rate arrangement (Silva, 2015). Before the outbreak of the global financial crisis, the economic fundamentals of emerging economies were generally better than those of developed economies, large precautionary foreign exchange reserves had been accumulated, and monetary and fiscal policies were more aggressive. All these factors played an important role in successfully defusing the impact of the crisis and ensuring rapid recovery (Didier et al., 2011).

The risks facing China today are largely due to incomplete progressive reform. We need to deepen the reform of making interest rates and exchange rates more market-based, while improving the twin pillars of monetary policy and macro-prudential regulation. We must also ensure that the market plays a truly decisive role in shaping the prices of financial factors, making the economy more resilient and better able to withstand the impact of crises.

Furthermore, while giving full play to institutional advantages, we must further improve institutions and mechanisms to provide a solid economic foundation for preventing and defusing financial risks. Whatever the decision-making system or policy concept, there are huge obstacles for developed economies to conduct crisis rescue and economic stimulus through fiscal means. It was not until the G20 Hangzhou Summit in 2016 that countries reached a consensus on increasing fiscal spending. It should be noted that China has incomparable advantages over developed economies in terms of decision-making mechanism and fiscal space for crisis response. Although China's stimulus package, the "four trillion yuan," is highly controversial, we cannot deny its significance in stabilizing confidence and promoting economic recovery.

We should also realize that only by comprehensively deepening reform can we effectively remove the institutional root causes behind risks and difficulties and maintain financial stability and security. The main reason for the controversy over the "four trillion yuan" is that China's institutions and mechanisms are not perfect, and there are shortcomings such as excessive adjustment, extensive means, inability to effectively identify projects, and difficulty in withdrawing from stimulus. This is also an important background for the rapid rise of macro leverage ratio and the gradual emergence of a shadow banking system and local debt problems since the crisis. Nevertheless, in recent years, against the background of the effective implementation of the central supply-side structural reform, not only has the long-standing problem of excessive growth of monetary debt been effectively controlled, and the rate of increase of macro leverage ratio been significantly reduced, but the overall economic development has gradually entered into a virtuous cycle of steady growth and significant improvement of the quality and efficiency structure.

These changes indicate that the Chinese economy is now in the high-quality development stage of rapid growth. Henceforth, the main thrust of policy should be on deepening the reform of supply side structural work and improving the quality and efficiency of economic development. In this way we can guard against and defuse financial risks to provide a solid economic foundation.

3.2 Prevention and Control of Systemic Risks

To achieve high-quality development, we must focus on preventing and defusing financial risks. Unless we achieve this, it will be difficult to complete the building of a moderately prosperous society in all respects, let alone pursue high-quality development. Preventing and defusing financial risks is the eternal theme of financial work, and concerns national security, overall development and the safety of people's property. At present, China has a solid foundation for preventing and controlling systemic financial risks.

Judging from the current situation, the rapid accumulation of financial risks has been curtailed, and potential risks for high-quality development have been brought under control. With the active yet prudent deleveraging and the in-depth progress of supply-side structural reform that have taken place in recent years, the momentum of China's rapid increase in leverage ratio and the rapid accumulation of potential risks have been checked. In 2017, the growth rate of China's macro leverage ratio slowed down significantly, rising by only 2.7% points over the whole year, with corporate and government leverage ratios both decreasing compared with the previous year. Meanwhile, the awareness of risk prevention in various aspects is being strengthened, and the market expectation of rigid payment and implicit guarantee is changing, thus creating favorable psychological conditions for the prevention and control of financial risks. On the whole, we have kept the bottom line of preventing systemic financial risks, and ensured that, in general, financial risks are under control. This has provided greater scope for us to continue to deepen reform and promote high-quality development.

In the long run, the Chinese economy is well positioned to prevent and control systemic financial risks and has a solid foundation for maintaining steady growth. China's economy is at a crucial stage of transforming its growth model, optimizing its economic structure and transforming its growth drivers. However, China's economy is large in size, and there is great potential for the development of a new type of urbanization, the service sector, and high-end manufacturing. There is also ample room for the upgrading of consumption. Hence the basic features of a resilient economy with potential for further growth remain unchanged. As China's economic reform continues to advance, supply side structural reform stage performance, and better to delegate deepening and innovation driven development strategy implementation, the excess capacity continue to dissolve, real estate stocks fell, the supply and demand gradually improve, to adapt to the consumer to upgrade the industry and strategic emerging industry rapid development, continue to optimize the economic structure. These positive changes in economic fundamentals provide a favorable macro environment for preventing the outbreak of systemic financial risks. Moreover, the overall control of financial risks provides a strong guarantee for the stable and healthy development of the economy.

However, we should also recognize that the financial sector is prone to frequent risks at present, and this situation will continue in the coming period. China's economy is undergoing profound transformation, and the rapid growth is taking place against a backdrop of some institutional and structural contradictions. Financial reform is at a crucial stage, in which financial operations are subject to risk-sensitive periods and seasons. As such we must attach great importance to financial risks and take positive and effective measures to prevent and resolve them properly.

First, we need to win the battle to prevent and defuse financial risks and create a stable macroeconomic environment for high-quality development. Finance and real economy are mirror images of each other. At present, China's micro and partial financial risk exposure is a necessary pain in the process of high-quality development, and financial risk is a direct reflection in the financial field of structural contradictions in the real economy. It will be impossible to resolve the structural institutional contradictions behind financial risks overnight. Instead we must adhere to the centralized and unified leadership of the Party in accordance with the requirements for high-quality development, complete the work to prevent and defuse financial risks, stick to the bottom line of thinking, and seek improvement in stability. We need to have a clear grasp of the main contradictions and give priority to tackling those that cause systemic risk and may affect social stability and economic problems. In the process of structural deleveraging, we need to increase our tolerance for normal and non-systematic risk exposures that meet the requirements of high-quality development. We need to take good care of the liquidity sluice gates and refrain from flooding them. We will work quickly to improve weaknesses in the regulatory system, effectively control macro leverage ratios and risks in key areas, actively defuse risks in shadow banking, properly handle risks in various financial institutions, and comprehensively clean up and rectify the financial order. For some individual risk events, directional blasting can be carried out. Overall we need to be active and prudent to strengthen market constraints, release pressure ahead of time, and broaden policy space for high-quality development.

Second, we need to comprehensively deepen reform to ensure that financial risks are under control, and provide long-term impetus for high-quality development. Only by comprehensively deepening reform can we keep the bottom line of avoiding systemic financial risks and provide a long-term guarantee for high-quality development. First, should be about the financial and real economy, finance and real estate and the financial system internal achieve the goal of a virtuous cycle, three effective coordination, mix, continuously enhance the ability of financial services entity economy, actively build the real economy, science and technology innovation, modern financial industry system, the coordinated development of human resources. Then, in order to deal with external shocks such as the possible increase of economic and trade frictions, we need to build momentum for reform so as to stabilize investor expectations, prevent cross-infection of financial risks and provide institutional guarantees for high-quality development. We must deepen reform to effectively control the macro leverage ratio, improve the adaptability of the financial structure, comprehensively strengthen the development of rigid constraint systems, and effectively prevent and control systemic risks. Finally, in the process of deleveraging, we need to put in place a macro-control policy system that adapts to high-quality development. Against the background of effectively preventing and defusing financial risks, we should have a good grasp of the direction and intensity of policy regulation. We should not only use monetary policies to maintain a stable and neutral monetary environment, but also give play to the role of fiscal policies to optimize the leverage structure, so as to compensate for the shortcomings of high-quality development.

3.3 Incremental Financial Openness

According to this year's government work report, "orderly opening of bank card clearing and other markets, liberalization of restrictions on the business scope of foreign insurance brokerage companies, relaxation or elimination of restrictions on foreign ownership in banks, securities, fund management, futures and financial asset management companies, and unification of market access standards for Chinese and foreign banks." The further opening of the financial industry to the outside world reflects China's determination to deepen the reform and opening up. The fact that there remain certain negative views toward this project, sometimes expressed as skepticism or even conspiracy theories, and a tendency to overestimate the risk of opening to the outside world and underestimate the benefit, is a sign of a lack of confidence.

In fact, the reform and opening up has not brought systemic negative impact to China's financial industry; rather, it has promoted the development of the whole financial system and the improvement of international competitiveness. The main difficulties we face now are to do not with excessive opening up, but with insufficient opening up, insufficient competitiveness of the financial sector and excessive financial restraint. This is exactly the crux of many problems in China's financial sector reform and development. Indeed, the opening up of China's financial sector is not a one-off step. Rather, it is a steady and orderly opening under the premise of improving macro-prudential management, strengthening financial supervision and enhancing financial market transparency. Next, in line with the work plans of the Chinese government central committee and the state council, we need to strengthen our confidence in the four areas, actively promote the opening up of the financial sector, further enhance the international competitiveness of the financial system, and raise the reform and development of the financial sector to a new level in the new era.

3.3.1 Opening to the Outside World

Reform and opening up complement and reinforce each other. Reform inevitably requires opening up, and opening up inevitably requires reform. There are two levels of opening up. The first is to bring in foreign institutions or for domestic institutions to "go global." The second is to develop the domestic financial market in accordance with the relevant rules, and respect and adapt to the rules and practices of the international market. This is opening up at a higher level.

China's financial industry has achieved significant development and progress in a short period of time, largely due to the promotion of domestic reform by opening to the outside world. The 40-year reform and opening up of the financial industry has been a process of realizing the progress and prosperity of the whole industry by opening to the outside world, introducing competition, and optimizing the allocation of resources. It has improved the competitiveness and robustness of financial institutions and fundamentally reduced financial risks. It has not only helped to attract capital, but has also promoted the reform of financial enterprise property rights and corporate governance structure. When the Asian financial crisis broke out, China's large state-owned commercial banks improved their competitiveness and robustness by decisively introducing external strategic investors, financial restructuring, and stock market reform and listing.

The opening up has also promoted the structural optimization of the financial market and product innovation, and significantly improved the efficiency of serving the real economy. All types of non-residents can borrow in the interbank market. The stock market introduced qualified foreign investors (QFII) to the bond market in 2002, and gradually expanded to renminbi QFII (RQFII), Shanghai-Hong Kong Stock Connect and Shenzhen-Hong Kong Stock Connect. The inter-bank bond market has been fully opened to qualified foreign investors, and there are no quota restrictions on the entry of foreign or domestic institutions. The offshore market is expanding in size and geography. The convertibility of RMB under capital accounts has been advanced in an orderly manner.

We have also promoted the building of the financial system and institutions, and increased China's voice in international affairs. Since the reform and opening up, especially since the 18th national congress of the Chinese government, China's monetary policy and financial regulatory system have been in line with international standards based on China's national conditions. China has also explored the construction of a macro-prudential policy framework, and established a deposit insurance system. We will comprehensively deepen market-oriented reform of interest rates and exchange rates, further enhance the decisive role of the market in allocating resources, and improve the efficiency of the allocation of domestic and foreign resources. The RMB has been added to the International Monetary Fund's Special Drawing Rights basket, and China's participation in international economic and financial governance has been enhanced.

3.3.2 The Current Main Problem is Insufficient Openness Rather Than Excessive Openness

Compared with the rest of the world, the degree of opening up of China's financial sector does not match China's status as a great power and international influence. As the world's second largest economy and largest exporter, China's financial openness ranks far behind major developed economies, and in recent years has even been surpassed by many developing countries. Even horizontal comparisons between different industries have left the financial sector relatively open. Foreign financial institutions' market share in China is generally low. Even the most open bond market is far from being wide and deep enough.

These shortcomings can be traced to a number of institutional factors, which will be the key areas for reform in the coming period. Perhaps most notably, the corporate governance structure of financial institutions is not perfect. Corporate governance structure in recent years, Chinese financial institutions the essence, shaped like a heavy form light and god away from problems, form the "three a" useless internal checks and balances mechanism, information disclosure yan wide implementation of rules and regulations, incentive constraint does not reach the designated position, big shareholder control, management control and external intervention, the serious problem of modern enterprise system target distance there is a big gap.

In addition, market innovation lacks momentum, and product development and service capabilities are weak. In contrast to mature markets, where innovation is dominated by the market, China's financial market innovation mechanism is not flexible. As a result of high barriers to entry and a lack of innovation power, market development is still at a low level, and some financial products remain at the stage of preliminary imitation of similar foreign products, without consideration of Chinese consumer spending habits, cultural norms, or purchasing power.

Furthermore, the regulatory environment requires further improvement. The institutional environment of accounting, auditing, taxation, and law; and the institutional arrangement of financial market infrastructure, are not in line with international standards, which restricts the development of financial institutions and the financial market. China's application procedures for specific business qualifications and licenses for financial institutions are still not open and transparent. There remain gaps between China's accounting standards, choice of auditors, transparency of tax policies and perfection of the legal system on one hand, and international standards on the other.

3.3.3 The Current Problem is a Lack of "Four Confidences"[1]

In recent years, the process of promoting the opening up of the financial industry has attracted some negative views, even a variety of skepticism and conspiracy theories. Generally speaking, these erroneous views can be roughly divided into the following types:

The first category is the failure to correctly understand the dialectical relationship between financial industry opening to the outside world and financial security. Some people believe that the opening up of the financial industry will inevitably bring about a significant increase in financial risks, which will lead to financial insecurity and even financial crisis. There are also some fears that keeping the financial sector relatively open is more conducive to risk control and financial security. Some people even believe that China's success in resisting the Asian financial crisis and the recent

[1] Matters of Confidence is a state of mind which the history and the era have entrusted to us, it includes the confidence in the path, theory, system and culture of socialism with Chinese characteristics.

international financial crisis was due to the relatively closed and isolated nature of its financial sector. In fact, opening up itself is not the source of financial risks. On the contrary, opening up will help enhance the competitiveness of financial institutions, fundamentally prevent and defuse financial risks, and maintain national financial security and stability. Moreover, a closed financial sector is more likely to cause risk accumulation and threaten financial stability. A closed-door policy can reduce the efficiency of the financial sector and domestic competition ability, weaken the ability to cope with financial risk and financial crisis, and cause the loss of function of financial markets and inefficiency in financial resources allocation, thus having a serious negative impact on the entire economic and financial competitiveness in international trade.

The second category is a misunderstanding of the dialectical relationship between the advantages and disadvantages, and active and passive aspects, of China's financial industry opening up. The belief that opening up the financial sector will do more harm than good is not in line with the development law of China's financial industry. Some critics even advocate conspiracy theories, suggesting that openness is nothing more than a "speech trap" carefully constructed by western countries. In fact, promoting reform and development through opening up is not only an inherent requirement of the development of the financial industry, but also an inevitable choice to actively guard against and defuse systemic financial risks.

On the one hand, the financial industry itself is a competitive industry, which needs to improve its efficiency and vitality through full competition. To some extent, opening to the outside world means introducing new competitors and new competition mechanisms. Market competition will be more adequate and more conducive to the development of financial innovation and the effective allocation of financial resources. In contrast, lack of competition will lead to slack in the system, resulting in high leverage, low capital, non-performing loans and other phenomena, and a proneness to financial crisis. For developing countries, opening wider to the outside world can introduce advanced international management concepts, technologies and models, improve the efficiency of the financial system, and maintain financial stability.

On the other hand, promoting reform through opening up is an important means to effectively resolve deep-seated financial problems and ensure that there are no systemic financial risks. Integration into the global economic and financial system is also a process of participating in global competition, which itself faces certain market risks. In particular, closer contact with the international financial market will lead to more frequent flow of monetary capital and other financial factors, and greater impact from international financial market fluctuations. Therefore, we should face up to the existence of financial risks, and proper risk exposure is an important measure to effectively reduce systemic risks. In the process of opening wider to the outside world by participating in international market competition, China's financial industry will be encouraged to narrow the gap and improve its competitiveness, so as to improve the risk management level and crisis response and handling capacity of the entire financial system.

The third category mistakenly equates opening to the outside world with abandoning it. Some argue that too much openness in the financial sector will lead to a decline in China's macro-control capacity. Others view the relaxation or abolition of the foreign equity ratio of financial institutions as a curse, which may lead to not only the loss of national wealth, but even the overall loss of economic and financial control in extraordinary times. In fact, however, opening to the outside world does not mean abandoning it, but is a means of promoting domestic reform. In the process of opening to the outside world, China has constantly improved its macro-control capacity and promoted the modernization of its governance system and capacity from an institutional perspective.

Ever since the first stages of reform, China's financial market has reflected the characteristics of progressive reform exploration. With the advance of relevant supporting reforms, the financial market began to promote comprehensive and in-depth opening up. Similarly, restrictions on foreign ownership have been relaxed, although not fully, and regulation has not been overly lax. In recent years, requirements on related transactions, shareholders' qualifications, and macro-prudential requirements have been further enhanced. However, these changes are related to the current regulatory reform and are regulatory arrangements for all capital, whether foreign, private, or state capital, not just for foreign capital.

3.3.4 Adhering to the Opening Up of the Financial Sector is an Important Part of China's Reform and Opening Up

The Chinese government central committee and the state council attach great importance to the opening up of the financial sector. The report to the 19th national congress of the Chinese government emphasized that we need to promote a new pattern of all-round opening up, substantially ease market access, and expand the opening of the service sector to the outside world. General Secretary Xi Jinping stated at the fifth national financial work conference that we should actively yet prudently promote the opening up of the financial sector, and properly arrange the opening sequence. Expanding the opening up of the financial sector is not only a valuable experience that has contributed to China's sustained and healthy economic development over recent years, but also the basic principle that China will always adhere to in the future. In the next step, we should continue to promote reform and development by further opening up in a steady and orderly manner. We should make it clear that opening up the financial sector does not mean abandoning it, but is an important step towards improving macro-prudential management and strengthening financial supervision and transparency in the financial market, so as to form a sound pattern of domestic reform and opening up to the outside world.

First, we need to work out a timetable and roadmap for the opening up of the financial sector. In doing so we should be guided by three basic principles, namely competition, coordination, and the prevention of risk. In more detail, as a competitive industry, the financial industry should follow the principle of pre-establishment national treatment and negative list, while its opening up should be coordinated with the reform of the exchange rate formation mechanism and the process of capital account convertibility. Then, the degree of openness should be equal to the prevention of financial risks, and matched with the ability of financial supervision. In the future, we will follow these three principles and work together to further open up the financial sector, improve the RMB exchange rate regime and enhance the convertibility of the capital account. We will continue to ease market access and further relax restrictions on foreign ownership, business scope and shareholders' qualifications in accordance with the principle of treating domestic and foreign investors alike. We will continue to improve the mechanism for setting the RMB exchange rate, enrich the structure of investors in the foreign exchange market, and make the RMB exchange rate more flexible. We will also further open up the financial market, make the RMB more freely usable, and open up the capital account in an orderly manner.

Second, the structural problems in China's financial market should be gradually solved in the process of opening up. Compared with mature market economy countries, China's financial market still has significant structural problems. For example, the proportion of direct financing is too low, shadow banks squeeze bond markets, and the structure of the bond market itself requires improvement. Furthermore, there is a lack of equity financing, investors mainly retail, while the development of derivatives is not sufficient. In the future, by continuing to respect and adapt to the international market rules and practices and to the open and perfect financial regulatory framework, we will deepen the reform of the domestic financial market; realize direct and indirect financing, equity and debt financing, and basic products and derivatives; and achieve coordinated development. the construction form adapted to superpower status of open economy, full range, reasonable structure, service efficient, safe and sound, more inclusive and competitive, support the real economy, the sustainable development of modern financial market system.

Third, we will improve the macro-prudential management framework, establish a national security review system for foreign investment, and better ensure China's financial security. The fifth national financial work conference strengthened the responsibilities of the People's Bank of China with regard to macro-prudential management and systemic risk prevention. In the future, we should continue to improve the macro-prudential policy framework for external debt and cross-border capital flows, and further improve the risk management level under convertible conditions. In addition, we can follow the example of Europe and the United States, and while engaging in further opening up we can establish and improve the national security review system for foreign investment, so as to protect China's legitimate rights and national security interests.

Fourth, we will improve the internal and external institutional environment of the financial sector to create better conditions for the reform and opening up of that sector. We will improve the modern enterprise system, deepen the reform of corporate governance in financial institutions, clarify the boundaries and responsibilities of the three committees and one layer, strengthen internal incentives and constraints, and straighten out the management boundaries between government departments, regulatory agencies, and financial institutions. We will gradually shorten the negative list of the financial sector, replace access restrictions with prudential supervision, and encourage foreign investment to participate in the development of China's financial market, so as to enhance the international competitiveness of China's financial institutions. We will further strengthen the development of financial infrastructure to ensure the safe and efficient operation of the market and overall stability. We will accelerate the improvement of infrastructure for payment and settlement, and improve the financial system for financial enterprises. We will strengthen education and protection of financial investors, pay close attention to the protection of domestic investors' overseas investments, and explore ways to establish a protection system for foreign investors. We will strengthen weak links in the financial system, promote the development of accounting, auditing, tax, and legal systems, and build an open, inclusive and internationally compatible financial market.

3.4 Green Finance in China

China has entered a new era, in which the development of green finance is an important national strategy. In November 2012, the 18th national congress of the Chinese government placed ecological civilization construction at the strategic center of the overall layout of socialism with Chinese characteristics, with the grand goal of achieving "Beautiful China." In October 2015, the fifth plenary session of the 18th Chinese government central committee put forward five new development concepts, namely "innovation, coordination, green, open, and shared development." In the same year, the central committee of the Chinese government and the state council issued the general plan for system reform of ecological civilization and the outline of the 13th national five-year plan for 2016, both of which stated that China should "building a green financial system."

China is already playing an important leading role in promoting green finance in the international community. Under the initiative of China, in 2016 the G20 Hangzhou Summit issued a communique that included green finance for the first time, and on September 6 of that year, the G20 green finance team was formally established. The 2016 G20 green finance comprehensive report made clear the definition of green finance, its purpose and scope, discussed the challenges to green finance, and proposed seven policy options to promote the global development of green finance. These moves marked important steps toward a new global consensus to develop green finance. At the same time, China has vigorously promoted green finance in bilateral and multilateral cooperation. For example, China and the UK have jointly explored the content and methods of environmental information disclosure by commercial banks and asset management companies; China and the United States have established the Sino-US building energy conservation and green development fund, while China and Luxembourg released green bond indices at the same time.

Furthermore, green finance standards compiled by Chinese institutions have now been adopted by overseas trading institutions.

3.4.1 The Unique Background of China's Green Finance Development

A decade ago, when China was debating whether to join the Copenhagen Accord on carbon emission reduction, many people in China were persuaded by a "conspiracy theory" that this was a deliberate attempt by developed countries to include China in the system of limiting emission reduction so as to increase the cost of development and weaken competitiveness, thus hindering China's economic development. Today, people's understanding has changed. The serious levels of smog and other forms of pollution, depletion of resources, and other environmental problems have raised people's awareness that the one-sided pursuit of GDP and neglect of harmonious economic, social, and ecological development will eventually lead to unbalanced and unsustainable economic development. People from all walks of life are increasingly aware of the importance of sustainable development.

Indeed, with the rapid development of China's economy, environmental problems are becoming increasingly serious. Persistent smog, severe environmental pollution, and waste of resources now threaten China's sustainable development. Eighty-two percent of people in China drink from shallow wells and rivers, 75% of which are contaminated. More than 19% of the country's arable land is polluted to dangerous levels. The proportion of clean energy is only 15%, far lower than the level of 1/4 to 1/3 in developed countries (Ma Jun, 2018). In 2013, Tsinghua University professor Li Hongbin published the results of a study into the long-term effects of air pollution on life expectancy. Based on evidence of China's Huaihe River heating line, points out that long-term exposure to air pollution, the total suspended particulate matter every 100 μg/cubic meter, will shorten average life expectancy by 3 years. Based on the level of total suspended particulate matter in northern China, 500 million residents will lose an average of five years of life due to severe air pollution. Therefore, it is of high economic and social value to formulate and implement stronger air pollution control policies.

In future, we will develop green finance and make green industries a new source of economic growth. For a long time, China's economic development has been excessively driven by real estate and infrastructure construction, and this traditional growth model is not sustainable. In the search for new growth points, one clear direction is to promote green development. Through green transformation, we will break the path dependence on the traditional development model and gather new drivers for economic growth.

Research shows that green investment has a significant driving effect on national economic development. Therefore, the development of green finance can play a role in stabilizing growth while also adjusting the structure. It is estimated that in the field of energy conservation, the annual output value of the energy efficient technology and equipment market during the 13th five-year plan period can reach 700 billion yuan. In the field of sewage treatment, membrane technology alone can create a market size of 70 billion yuan. In addition, the green financial system can change the financing cost and availability of different types of projects, and guide social capital to gradually withdraw from industries with high pollution and energy consumption.

On August 15, 2005, Xi Jinping, then the party secretary of Zhejiang province, made a speech in which he stated that "Lucid waters and lush mountains are invaluable assets." This insight, based on Xi's personal experience in northern Shanxi, Fujian and Zhejiang provinces and on a long period of in-depth thought, brings together China's economic and scientific development in one unified concept, and points the way forward.

It should also be noted that China's concept of green finance has deep cultural roots. Traditional Chinese cultural philosophy emphasizes "harmony between man and nature" and stresses that "a gentleman makes money in right way." In recent decades, China's economic development has focused too much on the pursuit of GDP and neglected the harmonious development of economy, society, and natural environment, resulting in a series of problems regarding the environment, resources and food safety. This is contrary to our traditional cultural concepts.

3.4.2 Significant Features of China's Green Finance Development

Green finance development in western developed countries is mainly promoted by market intermediaries and non-governmental organizations. The economic development of those countries has followed a pattern of "pollution first, treatment later." However, this model hinders sustainable economic development. In the 1960s and 1970s, the Club of Rome addressed concerns and questions regarding the development mode in developed countries, discussing the relationship between human development prospects in terms of population, resources, food and ecological environment, and a series of fundamental problems. In 1972, a research report entitled "The Limits to Growth" noted that "the earth is already overburdened, the limits of human beings are facing growing challenges, all kinds of resources shortages and environmental pollution are threatening human survival."

Once developed countries had realized that economic development needs to follow a sustainable development path, some market intermediaries and NGOs began to explore the practice of green finance development from the bottom up. In 2003, ten banks, including Citibank, Barclays, ABN AMRO and WestLB, announced the equator principle. Subsequently, the principle of socially responsible investment and the concept of environmental, social and governance (ESG) factors became fashionable in the investment sector, so that gradually environmental factors were incorporated into investment decisions. Through the continuous promotion of market institutions and non-governmental organizations, the international community has gradually formed a consensus on the development of green finance. In December 2015, nearly 200 parties to the United Nations Framework Convention on Climate Change (UNFCC) reached agreement at the Paris Conference on Climate Change, making arrangements for post-2020 global action on climate change, thus marking the beginning of a green, low-carbon and sustainable transition of global economic activities. There are significant differences between China and western developed countries in their promotion of green finance and sustainable development; specifically, "top-down" government promotion is an important feature of China's green finance development. The Chinese government is the first ruling party in the world to take ecological progress as an action program, while China is the first country to make green development a national strategy. This fully reflects the features and advantages of the socialist system. Of course, while giving full play to the role of the government, it is necessary to combine this with the "bottom-up" exploration and practice at the grassroots level, and at the same time to form a consensus in the whole society.

3.4.3 Top-Level Design and Grassroots Exploration Should Be Organically Combined

The combination of "top-down" design and "bottom-up" grassroots exploration is an effective path to promote the development of China's green financial core. Against a background of green consensus and policy adjustment, the development of green finance can contribute to improvement of the ecological environment and realization of the internal requirement for sustainable development, and can help to meet the objective need for China's supply side structural reforms. The financing needs of green enterprises and green projects will form a huge market "blue ocean," attracting financial institutions to innovate a variety of products and services to adapt to business development, increasing consideration of environmental benefits in the process of business expansion, and taking the initiative to achieve green transformation.

3.4.4 The Top-Level Design and Institutional Arrangements of Green Finance Are Being Continuously Improved

In accordance with the overall scheme of reform of the ecological civilization system and the need to make much starker choices with graver potential consequences, in August 2016 the People's Bank of China and seven other ministries jointly issued the "guidance on building a green financial system." This document provides the definition of green finance, incentive mechanism, financial disclosure and green product development plan, and risk control measures. Green indicators are gradually being incorporated into financial policies, regulatory provisions, and relevant legal systems. In addition, the environmental impact assessment law, water pollution prevention and control action plan, and other laws, regulations, and policy documents issued by China in recent years have created a sound legal environment for the development of green finance.

3.4.5 *The Green Financial Market is Booming, and the Market Size and Product Structure Are Rapidly Improving*

Currently, green credit is undergoing healthy development in China. The scale of green credit is growing rapidly, with significant environmental benefits. According to data released by the China Banking Regulatory Commission (CBRC), the green credit scale of China's 21 major banking institutions increased from 5.2 trillion yuan at the end of 2013 to 8.22 trillion yuan at the end of June 2017. Furthermore, the development of China's green bond market is remarkable. This market is closely connected with the ESG investment concept, which advocates full consideration of environmental, social, and corporate governance factors in the investment decision-making process. China's first green bond, launched at the end of 2015, was widely recognized by the market. In a total of 49 issuers issued 1990 billion yuan of green bonds. These included 158 billion yuan of green financial bonds, ranking first in the world in terms of both total issuance and individual size. In 2017, China issued 250 billion yuan of green bonds, making it one of the world's largest issuers of labeled green bonds. Other important aspects of the development of China's green financial market include the orderly development of the carbon market, and the launch of the pilot reform of green finance regions, which has achieved effective results.

China's green finance development is in the forefront of global efforts in this area, and has been highly recognized by the international community. However, some doubts remain, for example as to whether China's green bonds really meet "green" standards. Only by addressing these questions can China ensure that it retains international recognition and continues to promote the healthy and sustainable development of green finance.

3.4.6 *Key Issues in the Development of Green Finance in China*

3.4.6.1 A Clear "Green" Standard is the Premise

In May 2017, the *Financial Times* reported that western developed countries questioned China's green bonds (Hornby, 2017). This claim raises the question of what constitutes a "green" standard. Key to the development of green finance standards are scientific support and public recognition. The core of green finance is to realize the allocation of capital elements, which has much in common with financial poverty alleviation, financial support for agriculture, and small rural support. In essence, it is a financial policy, which should aim at specific targets and service objects so as to ensure that funds can flow to green, energy-saving, and environment-friendly enterprises and projects.

In developing green finance, China has attached great importance to standards from the very beginning. In terms of green financial product standards, from 2012 to 2015 the former CBRC successively issued the green credit statistical system, key evaluation index of green credit implementation, energy efficiency credit guidelines, and other green credit policies, which clarified the standards, statistical caliber, and classification of green credit. The People's Bank of China (PBOC) and the national development and reform commission (NDRC) have issued a catalogue of green bond support projects and guidelines for issuing green bonds, and determined the standards that meet the scope of green projects. In addition, the PBOC, the Shanghai and Shenzhen stock exchanges (SSE) and the inter-bank market dealers' association (IBMA) have published standards on information disclosure of green bonds, requiring issuers to disclose the use of funds raised, project progress and environmental benefits achieved on an annual or semi-annual basis. In the development of green finance, we have always stressed that green finance is not a basket and cannot be filled with everything.

Building a scientific, unified and coordinated standard system of green finance is a systematic project, and people's understanding of green is also deepening. For example, "two high and left" enterprises are not necessarily non-green enterprises, since many of their green transformation projects should be considered as green projects. On the other hand, high-speed rail projects are not necessarily green projects, especially those in sparsely populated areas. At present, while the benchmark for green standards differs between departments, we are gradually forming a consensus through discussion. The PBOC is leading relevant departments to promote this crucial work.

In June 2017, the PBOC, the former CBRC, the China Securities Regulatory Commission, the former China Insurance Regulatory Commission, and the State Standards Commission jointly issued a development plan for the construction of the standardization system of the financial industry (2016–2020). This listed the "green finance standardization project" as one of five key projects for the standardization of the financial industry during the 13th five-year plan period. In January 2018, the Research Bureau of the PBOC established a working group to promote the formulation of green finance standards. In addition, the PBOC has discussed and promoted the establishment of an international standard system of green finance in international exchanges and cooperation on green finance. Recently, the PBOC has also been in discussions with the UK and the Hong Kong monetary authorities, among others, as to whether a unified standard can be used for green bonds to ensure the green nature of relevant projects.

3.4.7 *Improving the Business Sustainability of Green Finance is Key*

Green finance is not viable without business sustainability. Such business sustainability depends on several factors. First, it requires strict enforcement of environmental law, which is the necessary environment for the development of green finance. Second, only when fiscal and tax incentives and guidance policies are well implemented can they be conducive to the sustainable development of green finance. Third, we should cultivate the social responsibility and green investment consciousness of market entities such as market intermediaries. Only when more market entities invest in green projects can the cost and price of those projects be effectively reduced. Market players should adopt innovation to improve the rate of return of green projects, while at the same time, the price mechanism should be used to attract capital allocation. Specifically, it is reflected in two main aspects:

I. Adhere to market orientation
We need to give full play to the basic role of the market in allocating resources, increase the rate of return of green projects through institutional innovation, guide the allocation of financial resources to green areas of energy conservation and environmental protection, withdraw from polluting industries, promote green transformation and upgrading of the industrial structure, and serve the green development of the real economy. Furthermore, it is necessary to increase innovation in green financial products and services and in the green finance business model. We can do this through the price mechanism and the use of green credit, green bonds, green industry fund, compensation fund green guarantee, and green products and tools, by widely mobilizing various resources to provide green financial origin, and by promoting green financial sustainable development. Finally, we need to strengthen the social responsibility of market players and their awareness of green development.

II. Strengthen government guidance
We need to increase incentives and guidance for green development, including the establishment of a pool of green projects to link qualified green projects with funds; establish a green guarantee fund, improve the risk compensation mechanism, and improve the risk tolerance of investors; and provide financial support for green projects, especially those with a semi-public or public nature, for example through a financial interest discount, tax preference, and the establishment of a government green development fund. We should also use monetary policy tools such as central bank refinancing and rediscount, so as to reduce the financing cost of green projects.
At the same time as implementing the incentive measures outlined above, we will also strengthen the constraints on the development of non-green projects. For example, we will increase the requirements for environmental information disclosure, build a public platform for sharing environmental information, improve the construction of green financial infrastructure, and enhance market transparency. We will also clarify the legal responsibility for environmental

protection, strictly enforce the law on environmental protection, and achieve the internalization of environmental benefits of enterprises by increasing the cost of pollution projects and reducing the cost of green projects. In addition, we will improve green rating and certification, cultivate responsible green investors, and make more investors willing to buy and invest in green products and projects.

III. Focus on exploring green financial innovation

The financing needs of green projects are diverse and have multiple levels. Consequently, it is necessary to give full play to their subjective initiative, actively explore and innovate, and match and adapt financial products and services according to the specific needs of different projects. Pure public goods may be borne by financial funds or public funds, while projects with good returns that can be operated commercially should take full advantage of the supporting role of finance and provide corresponding financial products according to project requirements.

IV. Risk prevention is the bottom line

In essence, green finance is still finance, and risk prevention is the eternal theme. In developing green finance, China should firmly adhere to the principle of the bottom line of risks. The risk points of green finance focus on five main weaknesses: First, the definition standards of green projects are not uniform, and in some fields there is no complete consensus on what constitutes a green project. Second, information disclosure is not perfect, and certification and rating are not standardized. Third, at present it is possible for supposedly "green" funds to flow into non-green projects; consequently, it is necessary to strengthen the follow-up supervision and management of green funds. Fourth, green projects carry a risk of high leverage and high debt. Finally, it is necessary to guard against "greenwashing," "false green," and other risks.

3.4.8 Pilot Reform and Prospect of Green Finance Area

On June 14, 2017, the 176th executive meeting of the state council deliberated and adopted the overall plan of green finance reform. It was decided to implement innovation pilot zones in Zhejiang province, Guangdong province, Xinjiang Uygur autonomous region, Guizhou province, and Jiangxi province. Thus China's green finance entered a new stage of development, which combines "top-down" top-level design with "bottom-up" regional exploration. Over the past two years, the green finance pilot areas have engaged in much useful exploration and promotion of green development through financial innovation.

Currently, we are seeing the emergence of more and more innovation in green financial products and services. Examples include the establishment of a green financial franchise system, optimization of the green credit process, improvements to the pricing of credit products and innovation in green credit products, expansion of the scope of green credit collateral, and use of the capital market to broaden the financing channels of green industry. As we continue on this path we will fully implement environmental pollution liability insurance and vigorously innovate green insurance products. We will also explore green asset securitization.

China should also establish and improve incentive and restraint mechanisms to strengthen the business sustainability of green finance. This will include using monetary policy tools to support the development of green finance, effectively using refinancing, rediscount and other means to guide financial resources to green industry. We will also include green bonds and loans as qualified collateral of the central bank to promote green development. Special funds will be set up for the development of green finance, and financial institutions that effectively serve the transformation and upgrading of industries will receive financial awards and subsidies. We will also establish a green financial risk compensation mechanism to provide corresponding risk compensation for losses brought about by force majeure caused by financial institutions supporting green transformation development.

China is already making progress in building green financial infrastructure. This includes, for example, the construction of a green information disclosure mechanism to provide a better platform for financial institutions to price and identify risks of green financial products. We will strengthen the disclosure of green information, label green assets with "green labels," help financial institutions solve the problem of environmental information asymmetry, and provide a more accurate basis for pricing and risk control of green financial products and services. In doing so we will take the construction of a green project database as the starting point to promote the identification and rating of green projects.

We will also strengthen oversight and guard against risks. For example, we will include green finance in the macro-prudential assessment (MPA), guide financial institutions to prudently develop green finance business, establish regional self-discipline mechanisms of green finance industry to promote the standard development of green finance, explore innovation in regulatory mechanisms, promote the green transformation of financial institutions, establish a regulatory evaluation system for local green banks, and realize the automation, precision, normalization and visualization of green bank ratings and green operation monitoring. We will establish an early-warning mechanism for green financial risks, carry out credit risk monitoring and stress testing, and explore ways to prevent and defuse green financial risks.

In the next stage, the construction of the green finance pilot zone will be problem-oriented, market-oriented and more proactive. We will begin by exploring and improving the standard system of green finance. Then, we will optimize the construction of a green project library. The next steps will be to encourage corporate financial institutions to carry out environmental information disclosure, and to deepen institutional innovation in green finance. In addition, we need to further improve the system, form a synergy of effective work in green finance, strive for more institutional innovation, explore replicable and scalable experience and models for China's green finance development, enhance the ability of green finance to support the green transformation of the real economy, and promote China's sustainable economic development.

3.5 China's Inclusive Financial Development

Since the global financial crisis broke out in 2008, great changes have taken place in international economic and social development trends. From the earliest days of the Occupy Wall Street movement in the United States, both the US and Europe have seen increases in national populist sentiment, and rising protectionism. As inequalities between different social classes have widened, and globalization has gathered pace, so the desire to bring about common prosperity, within and between countries, has grown. As social differentiation and inequality within a country increase, inclusive financial also is mainly from the early poor countries' exclusive prescription, developed into the current every country attaches great importance to the general social and economic development policy, to strengthen the economic and social development of an inclusive, especially to promote employment, entrepreneurship to eliminate social poverty, promote the development of Shared and realize the fairness and justice is important, is paid attention to by the international community.

In working toward the goals of shared development and common prosperity, the Chinese government has always attached importance to inclusive finance. Over the years, it has implemented differentiated fiscal, monetary and regulatory policy, made available subsidized loans for the purposes of poverty alleviation, promoted the reform of rural credit cooperatives and the development of microfinance institutions, and guided financial institutions to set up the "three rural" financial division. These measures have achieved significant results. In particular, agriculture, rural areas and farming, and small micro enterprise financial services continue to improve, and technological innovation has accumulated much valuable experience.

At present and in the coming period, the development of inclusive finance faces new challenges and opportunities. From the perspective of the social development mission and potential demand for inclusive finance, there is still a long way to go. China has 800 million farmers, and more than 1,500 towns and villages with no financial resources. According to estimates by the World Bank, in 2014 some 2 billion adults worldwide still lacked access to the most basic financial services. Moreover, although China is taking a lead in the rapid development of science and technology, achieving more and better information processing technology and ways of low-cost expansion of financial services, there remain many unsolved problems, which require theoretical reflection and practical action.

3.5.1 Current Progress in the Development of Inclusive Finance in China

The Chinese government has always attached great importance to inclusive financial services in weak areas such as agriculture, rural areas, farming, and small and micro businesses. Looking back at the recent development of inclusive finance, especially in the last five years, the basic experience of China is the combination of "government guidance and market leadership." On the one hand, the government is strengthening the financial infrastructure construction, such as credit payment at the same time, also took some incentive policies and measures to guide the inclusive financial development, the comprehensive use of the difference in the reserve requirement ratio as the people's bank of China, support for small and poverty alleviation refinancing and rediscount monetary policy tools, such as tax and regulatory departments issued a series of fiscal and taxation awards and differentiated regulatory policy. Government support policies, on the other hand, cannot fit all, emphasize the inclusive finance marketization, the path of sustainable development, financial institutions and other market main body should play a leading role in the inclusive finance development, by promoting financial institutional reform in recent years, agricultural sustainable and financial institutions in the financial services a broad and deep coverage progress at the same time.

Thanks to the joint efforts of various parties, China's inclusive finance has achieved remarkable results in terms of account penetration, savings penetration, micro-payment and credit. First, an extensive and multi-tiered system of inclusive financial institutions and products has taken shape. The reform of rural credit cooperatives has continued to advance, and while legal persons remain stable in county areas, the efficiency of supporting agriculture and rural areas is constantly being improved. Large financial institutions have intensified their work in inclusive finance, and the financial business units of agriculture, rural areas, and farming are playing an increasingly important role in those areas. With the rise of e-commerce, banking, insurance, wealth management, and other kinds of financial institutions are using the new information technologies to provide fast, convenient retail payment; small deposit and withdrawal; microfinance and small insurance and other financial services; comprehensive, innovative financial products, and financial services. Second, basic account services such as payment and settlement now cover almost the whole population and all regions. According to a random sample of World Bank surveys, more than 79% of Chinese adults have bank accounts. By the end of 2016, 8.353 billion personal bank accounts had been opened and 6.125 billion bank cards were in use, with an average number of bank cards per citizen of 4.47. In rural areas, the number of card holders per capita was 2.8, and there were nearly 1 million rural withdrawal service centers, covering more than 500,000 administrative villages and more than 90% of the population. The scale of online payment and mobile payment is also growing rapidly. Third, the availability of financing support for the development of urban and rural credit systems has improved significantly. A total of 172 million rural households had credit files, and nearly 92.48 million rural households had access to bank loans, with a balance of 2.7 trillion yuan. Based on the rapid development of e-commerce and the application of big data credit investigation technology, the problem of "difficult and expensive financing" for small and micro enterprises has also been largely resolved.

The development of digital inclusive finance has great potential. Digital finance, which covers traditional finance digitization, mobile finance, emerging Internet finance, and other fields, has natural advantages in solving the traditional problem of inclusive finance, that is, the high risk and high cost of a small amount of agriculture-related financial services. In 2016, hangzhou summit of G20 leaders officially by the G20 inclusive financial senior principles, the inclusive financial development planning (2016–2020), "clearly put forward that" actively guide the inclusive financial service main body with the help of the Internet and other modern information technology means, reduce financial transaction costs, extension service radius, expand the inclusive scope and depth of the financial services. In recent years, China has witnessed the development of digital inclusive finance. From basic financial services such as deposit and transfer payments, to loan financing, insurance, investment, and other comprehensive financial services; from small scattered individual financial services to the whole industry chain of large credit; and from credit evaluation and customer acquisition to the backend in risk control management, digital technology has a crucial role to play in product development, business modelling and risk control. The penetration of such technology is deepening, expanding the prospects for application and the potential for development. Non-cash payment and data-driven business models enable financial institutions to more accurately identify and manage risks. At the same time, with the aid of the industrial chain and value chain, business circle, and logistics information system support, digital technology can effectively solve the traditional problems of high cost and high risk associated with small agricultural loans, and in combination with offline services will also be able to provide insurance, derivatives, and currency exchange combined services, among others.

3.5.2 China Faces New Tasks and Opportunities in Developing Inclusive Finance

The desire for common prosperity and the concept of shared development increase the need for the development of inclusive finance. In 2015, the fifth plenary session of the eighteenth central committee of the Chinese government presented a set of strategic objectives on the path toward realizing a well-off society in respects, and introduced a new development concept, namely shared development. Xi Jinping, general secretary of the fifth national financial work conference, once again stressed the need for the construction of a system of inclusive finance; and for strengthening the small micro enterprises, rural, and remote areas of financial services. According to the development strategy for agriculture, rural areas, and farming, and the poverty alleviation strategy, there are still 800 million rural residents in China, and more than 1,500 towns and villages with no financial support. Under the conditions of traditional technology and the current financial system, the problem of difficult and expensive financing for small and micro businesses has been eased by years of continuous policy efforts, but it has not been solved comprehensively and systematically. From the perspective of social and economic reform and development, as farmers become more prosperous owing to increased income or the receipt of land expropriation compensation, the demand for savings services will increase dramatically, agricultural industrialization such as leading enterprises and production base, and the formation of the industrial chain, small micro enterprises can trigger more comprehensive and efficient financial service demand, the improvement of rural infrastructure and rural land system reform, also for inclusive financial development has brought the new needs and new opportunities.

The low cost of digital finance and mobile Internet and the expansion of financial services by means of big data risk control provide an unprecedented opportunity for the thorough solution to traditional inclusive finance problems. China has built the world's largest 4G network, and mobile phone penetration rate has reached 95%, covering not just the urban population but also most of China's rural population. The Internet penetration rate has reached 51.7%, with 710 million users, where the global average penetration rate is only 3.1%, and the Asian average is 8.1%. mobile net silver size of more than 500 million households, on the whole, China's digital "hardware" of the development of the financial condition of obvious advantages, pratt & whitney financial has taken off in the leap type development stage. Further improvement is expected in financial services for agriculture, rural areas, farmers, and small and micro businesses, including deposit, loan, foreign exchange and financial management and investment. For example, in terms of supporting the transformation of agricultural industrial structure, we can point to the example of a grape farm in Hebei province, where banks have used digital technology to transform the credit sales relationship between enterprises in the industrial chain into a guarantee relationship, providing financial services with larger scale, more comprehensive means and products, and deeper involvement. Similar financial services can organize a large number of scattered individual farmers, more effectively introduce large capital, large production, large market and large circulation, and improve the level of agricultural industrialization and the quality of agricultural products supply. In the field of industrial restructuring and upgrading, relying on the "Internet + " model, financial services are being integrated into intelligent manufacturing, providing consumers with more personalized products and services with higher technical content. In addition to the huge financing needs of the new urbanization in infrastructure construction, with more new citizens China urgently needs to broaden the channels of financial management and investment. Against this background, with the help of the popularization and application of digital technology and the Internet, the channels used by financial institutions to gain customers will be greatly broadened, the cost of gaining customers will be greatly reduced, and the risk control will be real-time and accurate. Of course, to realize the full potential of financial technology and digital inclusion, good hardware is not enough. Good software is also needed, such as an innovation-friendly regulatory system with effective risk control.

3.5.3 Balance Innovation and Regulation

Neither the idea of inclusion nor digital technology will change the nature of finance. Whether Internet companies get involved in inclusive finance business, or traditional financial institutions use "Internet plus" to expand service radius, the finance industry will still be subject to traditional credit risk, liquidity risk and operational risk. In addition, as the introduction of digital technology gathers pace, financial risks are more concealed, and spread not only more rapidly but also over a wider and deeper range, thus increasing the systemic risks in the financial field and generating many risks related to technology and spread scope, such as system security, information disclosure, and investment fraud. While inclusive finance brings benefits for social and economic development, it also brings the chasing of capital. At the same time, many ordinary consumers have weak financial ability and self-protection awareness and the relevant regulation is characterized by gaps, weak links, and an inability to keep pace with the needs of the development of the situation. Consequently, there is a need to improve safety awareness among consumers, providers, and regulators. By taking action in this regard, we can guide the healthy development of inclusive finance.

We will begin by addressing the digital divide that digital inclusion may bring. Inclusive finance serves mainly disadvantaged groups, whose members tend to be characterized by low level of education, low income, older age, and poor understanding of digital technology. The essence of the so-called financial "digital divide" is that while technological progress brings benefits to the majority of people, it may have a negative impact on the interests of a minority of vulnerable groups due to their insufficient subjective ability to use digital technology. This is not only common in history, but also a natural law. We need to push forward the reform of financial institutions from the supply side and encourage them to develop Internet financial products and services targeted at vulnerable groups. We will focus on diversifying the forms of inclusive finance, combining online and offline activities, as well as traditional and digital finance. At the same time, the government should strengthen the education of ordinary consumers.

We will also resolutely crack down on illegal financial activities disguised as digital inclusive finance. Digital technology is neutral; while advanced technology may be used in promoting inclusive finance and even the development of the entire financial industry, it may also be used by criminals. Under the banner of inclusive finance and under the cloak of the Internet, swindlers offer financial products with false claims about the potential earnings. Consumers believe they are obtaining high interest rates, but in fact the crooks have "harvested" the principal. In the past two years, there have been many "runaway" events in the field of Internet finance. Local governments and relevant regulatory authorities should take decisive measures to effectively identify these fake financial products in accordance with the criminal law and relevant judicial interpretations, distinguish innovation from crime, "strike early, strike small, strike accurate," and punish illegal financial activities according to the law. We should standardize information disclosure of digital financial institutions, crack down on false and illegal publicity, implement proper management of investors, and emphasize that "sellers are responsible."

Against the background of big data, China will also strengthen data security and personal privacy protection. Currently, the rapid development of technology in a situation of insufficient data protection is leading to many serious cases of personal privacy information disclosure. There is an urgent need to promote the orderly development of the data market while ensuring respect for and security of the data subjects. In my view, in order to develop inclusive finance with digital finance, the first step is to guarantee the right of confidentiality of data subjects, the right to obtain, use, and control their information, and the right to allow or not allow others to know or use their personal information. In China, the legislature has explicitly required financial institutions to follow the principles of legality, legitimacy, and necessity in collecting information, and to assume the obligation of obtaining users' consent, explicitly collecting rules of use, and protecting data security. With the rapid development of intelligent finance, it is necessary to ensure that the final decision to grant or deprive consumers' rights is made by human beings rather than machines. To strengthen the rights to information main body of the portable and forgotten, the former index according to the main body can be accessible to the data in general electronic format from a service provider to another service provider, the latter index according to the main body has the right to require data controllers to remove certain information, limited data controller using data analysis of characteristics of automation.

It is also necessary to establish a consumer protection system for responsible investor suitability management. In view of the characteristics of the large number of "long tail" subjects of digital inclusive financial services, special attention should be paid to the protection of consumer rights and interests, and to the establishment of a consumer protection system of responsible investor suitability management. Financial products that are not suitable for ordinary investors should be sold online only in combination with offline investor suitability management. Under the environment of separate supervision, the centralized supervision departments of various digital financial formats should be responsible for establishing their own consumer complaint, acceptance, and disposal mechanisms, and for implementing service standards and regulations. The next step will be to actively explore a comprehensive consumer protection mechanism and establish a diversified financial consumption dispute resolution mechanism. We will mobilize all sectors of society to popularize digital financial literacy, improve public financial literacy, strengthen risk awareness and education, guide the establishment of the "buyer's own" investment concept, and build a long-term mechanism for financial consumer education.

Finally, we will strengthen the basic regulatory system and strengthen weak links in oversight. We need to speed up the improvement of effective basic regulatory systems and strengthen comprehensive, coordinated, and functional oversight of digital financial risks in terms of preventing liquidity risks, credit risks, and operational risks. At the same time, efforts should be made to enhance innovation in regulatory technology, to make full use of big data technology to enrich regulatory information, and to improve regulatory means and methods and the effectiveness of digital financial regulation.

The ultimate goal of technological progress and financial development is to promote social harmony and progress. Although many challenges remain, given the growing international consensus on fairness and sustainable development, inclusive finance offers an unprecedented opportunity to alleviate the income gap. It can create development opportunities and promote economic transformation, while also acting as an important force to promote social equity and justice. I believe that as long as we innovate "real" finance and manage financial risks under digital conditions, inclusive finance will have a "real" future.

3.6 Corporate Governance Dilemma

Corporate governance is at the core of the modern enterprise system. As emphasized by the third plenary session of the 14th Chinese government central committee, the modern enterprise system of "clear property rights, clear powers and responsibilities, separation of government administration from enterprise management, and scientific management" is the direction of state-owned enterprises reform. Subsequently, the fourth plenary session of the 15th central committee introduced the concept of "corporate governance." Over more than two decades of great effort, China's corporate governance reform achieved remarkable results. More recently, however, China's corporate governance practices have slipped backwards. especially with the 2003–2006 this period compared to the large state-owned commercial Banks reform of state-owned enterprises and financial institutions to corporate governance structure heavy form light nature, "shape and god from" problem is outstanding, the investor absence leads to the investor rights violations are widespread, central huijin company holding the potential of corporate governance mode, give full play to form has set up the "three meetings and one layer" (general meeting of shareholders, board of directors, board of supervisors, and senior management) useless internal checks and balances mechanism, information disclosure, wide implementation of rules and regulations, larger gap between the goal of modern enterprise system is to reform.

3.6.1 Corporate Governance in China Has Major Flaws

At present, the internationally authoritative normative document on corporate governance is the G20/OECD Corporate Governance Principles (hereinafter referred to as the Principles) approved by the G20 Antalya summit in November 2015. As a member of the G20, China has committed to the Principles, which means its corporate governance will be in line with international standards. According to the Principles and the current corporate governance practices in China, although the "hardware" aspects of corporate governance, namely the structure and procedures, have been basically formed in domestic enterprises, there are still significant defects in the "software" aspects of concept, personnel and execution.

3.6.2 The Absence of Owners and of State-Owned Shareholders' Rights

The primary goal of corporate governance is to solve the principal-agent problem that arises from the separation of enterprise ownership and management right. By providing appropriate incentives and constraints, it seeks to ensure that the board of directors and management act in accordance with the interests of the company and shareholders. This is why the Principles include "shareholders' rights, equal treatment of shareholders, and core ownership function." In China, there are two main problems. First, in many Chinese enterprises, especially state-owned enterprises, the biggest problem of corporate governance is the absence of owners and the absence of shareholders' rights. This creates a situation in which it is easy to form insider control. Under the complicated authorization system, although the state or government objectively exists as a major shareholder, it is difficult for the state to play the role of supervision and check and balance, so that the rights of state-owned shareholders lack effective protection. Moreover, when appointing the chairman of state-owned enterprises, government departments usually consider loyalty rather than corporate governance perspectives such as representing the interests of state-owned shareholders. Second, the rights of minority shareholders are ignored. Small and medium-sized shareholders have no voice, so lack enthusiasm to participate in corporate governance. Furthermore, the "same share and same right" cannot be implemented, which reduces the role of the shareholders' meeting and board of directors, and operation, management, and decision-making do not have the characteristics of complete market behaviors.

3.6.3 Lack of Effective Checks and Balances

The three elements outlined in the Principles, namely "the role of institutional investors, stock exchanges and other intermediaries in corporate governance," "the role of stakeholders in corporate governance," and "strengthening the responsibility of the board of directors," depend upon the formation of effective checks and balances in the corporate governance mechanism. The corporate governance framework should first ensure the "three committees and one layer" of checks and balances. Given the complexity of managing business affairs in a rapidly changing market, shareholders should not be expected to assume responsibility for managing specific business matters. Instead, the board of directors should take a more prominent position, with responsibility for formulating corporate strategies and major behavior plans; selecting, motivating, and replacing management teams when necessary; and strengthening effective supervision of the board of directors and the chairman. Management is responsible for day-to-day operations.

In China, there is currently a lack of effective checks and balances in corporate governance. First, the boundaries of the "three committees and one layer" are not clear; powers and responsibilities are not clear, and the internal checks and balances are virtual. On the surface, most enterprises have a complete "three will be a layer." In fact, however, the chairman of the "one long monopoly" phenomenon is prominent, the chairman, President (general manager), supervisors long become the DE facto one, two, three handles. Personnel rights, financial rights, risk decision-making rights and other core operating resources are all in the hands of the chairman. The management layer is "overhead," which brings a series of problems such as personal will supremacy, lack of awareness of rules, ineffective system construction, and weak basic management. Meanwhile, the board of supervisors is a virtual entity; it often ignores the obvious problems in corporate governance and business decision-making, lacks a sense of responsibility, and falls far short in terms of performing its duty.

Second, the core role of the board of directors is weak in China. In the absence of effective checks and balances, the board of directors is generally characterized by low efficiency in performing its duties, insufficient participation rate, and low enthusiasm in decision-making.

Third, in China there is no effective system of audit, nomination, and remuneration and appraisal committees. These committees under the board of directors represent important structures of corporate governance. A reasonable and effective professional committee can not only make up for inherent defects such as lack of professionalism of the board of directors and difficulty in performing daily supervision functions, but can also prevent the abuse of power, better play the role of independent directors, and achieve better internal checks and balances. For example, the audit committee is responsible for supervising internal and external audits, auditing the company's financial information and disclosure, and reviewing the company's internal control system, so as to ensure the independence and objectivity of the audit results, improve the transparency of the company's information, and effectively serve the decision-making of the board of directors. Meanwhile, the nomination committee has a key role in the selection and appointment of candidates for the roles of directors and managers. Based on the relevant selection criteria, the committee selects and reviews candidates, before making their recommendation to the board of directors. This system can effectively prevent insider control and ensure the independence of the board of directors. The remuneration and appraisal committee is responsible for reviewing the remuneration policies of directors and managers and assessing their performance, which can form an effective incentive mechanism and check and restrain the moral hazard of directors and executives. These scientific norms and effective checks and balances are absent in the practice of corporate governance in China. The professional committees of some corporate boards do not even draw up annual work plans. The strategy and development committee, capital planning committee, related transaction control committee, and remuneration and appraisal committee do not meet regularly as required. Because of this, "secret salary systems" and other practices that clearly violate corporate governance principles can be approved and put into effect by the board of directors.

Fourth, in Chinese enterprises there is no external check and balance mechanism of stakeholders. The third-party checks and balances represented by independent audit, capital constraints represented by bankruptcy liquidation, and supervision and restraint of internal staff are generally absent. Some enterprises regard employees as fighting tools and arbitrarily cut their salaries, which is clearly contrary to the basic requirements of protecting the rights and interests of stakeholders.

3.6.4 Inadequate Information Disclosure

Previous versions of the Principles have stressed the importance of "information disclosure and transparency." An effective corporate governance framework should ensure the timely and accurate disclosure of all major information of the company, including not only the financial and business performance, but also non-financial information and related transactions. In the practice of corporate governance in China, some enterprises fail to disclose timely, sufficient and effective information related to major business issues, such as salary, risk management status, corporate governance, and annual major issues. In addition, external constraints are weak. Some executives hold stakes in companies through various platforms, but do not disclose the exact source of the funds, hiding much of the important information that should be disclosed. Some companies also waive disclosure of specific compensation information for executives through the so-called "secret pay system."

3.6.5 The Institutional Roots of Corporate Governance Abuses in China

Government administrative intervention and "feudal" supervision are the fundamental reasons why effective corporate governance and a modern enterprise system cannot be established in China. Among some government departments and regulators in China, the understanding of corporate governance is still largely at the lower level of departmental jurisdiction and industrial management, and the policy focus is more on how to manage enterprises and how to use the power of the government to push enterprises to become bigger and stronger. Hardware-making department, financial regulators from their respective interests, develop their respective principles, this was actually doing department of ownership and the "feudal" regulation, the lack of top-level design and system considerations, walk the remains of the competent department of comprehensive pipe industry enterprises, the resulting assets, enterprise management, development and regulatory functions both principles of market economy, the behavior of enterprise management and the allocation of resources against disadvantages such as it is not surprising. Government departments and regulatory agencies interfere in corporate governance, most obviously by appointing executives directly through administrative means. In recent years, in the process of market access and risk management, the regulatory authorities have frequently appointed senior executives of financial institutions, which not only affects the regulatory independence, but also ignores the phenomenon of inadequate corporate governance of financial institutions.

Yet while corporate governance defects and institutional defects are common in China's state-owned enterprises and financial institutions, many of the contradictions and problems have been hidden by the rapid economic growth that has been taking place since 2003. As economic development enters the new normal, institutional, structural and long-term problems related to lagging corporate governance reform are coming to light. It is because of the imperfect corporate governance framework that some financial institutions are tempted to conduct extremely short-term business behaviors, such as "more water and more water;" blind pursuit of scale expansion and short-term profits; high leverage and excessive risk taking; and neglect of quality, risk, and long-term mechanism construction. In an environment where corporate governance checks and balances are absent, for many large state-owned companies their main business is not prominent, and core competitiveness is not strong; instead, they operate a large number of subsidiary businesses, youthful, make and management in capital operation, which can lead to sharp rises in corporate leverage, "zombie" companies, and excess capacity. Enterprises may engage in blind expansion and overseas investment, resulting in further structural contradictions and a deepening of the resources mismatch, some areas of potential risk to accelerate the agglomeration. In this situation, improving corporate governance will be the necessary breakthrough to accelerate structural transformation and maintain the sustained and healthy development of the national economy.

In view of the drawbacks and institutional defects of corporate governance in China, the holding company model represented by the Central Huijin Company offers an important opportunity to explore reform, improve corporate governance, and realize the transformation from "enterprise management" to "capital management," which has played a role in the early stage of the reform of state-owned commercial banks. However, its institutional arrangement also has certain defects, which restricts its ability to give full play to its positive role. The Central Huijin Company does not have the power to appoint and remove senior executives of state-owned commercial banks. In fact, it only partially assumes the power of state-owned investors. The constraints on senior management of banks are non-rigid and cannot fundamentally solve the problem of the absence of all state-owned capital owners. In addition, since the equity exchange of the Central Huijin Company in 2007, although it nominally holds the equity, it actually bears the debt. In fact, the state-owned equity of state-owned commercial banks is no longer real money, which further weakens the role of the state-owned investor of the Central Huijin Company.

3.6.6 Some Suggestions

In future, we should deepen reform of corporate governance, uphold public ownership as the main body, a variety of ownership economy common development of the basic economic system of the key areas, is the perfect modern enterprise system, deepen the state-owned capital management, maintain the market order and promote economic restructuring. The key steps will be to improve the management efficiency and guard against the accumulation of systemic risk.

Adhere to the top-level design, break up the division of departments, and accelerate the formulation and promulgation of unified corporate governance principles according to the Chinese model.

The G20/OECD Corporate Governance Principles were an important outcome of the G20 summit in Antalya in 2015. As a promoter of that summit, China should adhere to its commitment to "lead by example." We should draw on international experience, and break the existing pattern of separate, self-defined standards for various departments according to China's specific national conditions and corporate governance practices. We should accelerate the formulation and promulgation of unified corporate governance principles, and create a corporate governance model with Chinese characteristics.

3.6.7 Strengthen the Party's Leadership and Strengthen the Protection of Shareholders' Rights and Interests Through the "Two-Tier Arrangement"

Some people believe that strengthening the party's leadership and improving corporate governance are contradictory. However, this is a misunderstanding; in practice, the two can be harmonized in a "two-layer arrangement." The first layer comprises the state capital contributor and the authority of the board of directors. The party represents the majority stake in the decision of the board of directors of the dominant, not only the ownership of the implementation of the state-owned enterprises, to protect the state-owned capital, the investor interest, improve investor control, and put the party cadres, national strategic goals and interests, usufruct and distribution, rewards and punishments, discipline, external coordination together, similar to the past about "people, goods, content" integrated management, avoid micromanaging, "a pole". At the same time, we will earnestly implement the principle of "one share and one right," properly handle the relationship between upholding public ownership as the main body and supporting the non-public sector, while encouraging private capital and foreign investment; improve the transparency of major business decisions of enterprises, and protect the rights of small and medium-sized shareholders to participate in corporate decision-making and profit distribution. The second layer comprises the management level of the company and the party committee for grass-roots cadres and employees. This allows for the political core role of party organizations, including improving the control force in such aspects as education of ideals and beliefs, organizational security, discipline inspection, personnel qualification examination, and interest protection of employees. This two-tier arrangement not only conforms to the governance structure of modern enterprises, but also enhances the role of the board of directors and the party organization at the management level.

3.6.8 Improve Internal and External Checks and Balances

In order to strengthen internal checks and balances we will clarify the boundaries and responsibilities of "three associations and one layer," strengthen incentives and constraints, and avoid the bureaucratic structure of "one, two, three handles." The board of directors and senior management shall be supervised by the board of directors and senior management. The main responsibilities of the board of directors in formulating strategic planning, supervising the implementation and enhancing the core competitiveness shall be clarified, and the contents of the board of directors' operation and the directors' performance shall be strengthened. We will employ strict criteria in the selection of directors, enhance the professionalism and independence of independent directors, establish a sound system for independent directors to speak up, and punish those who violate regulations. We will also establish and improve the working system and mechanism of the professional committee, and give full play to the professional advisory function of the committee under the board of directors. We will strengthen the responsibilities of the board of supervisors, supervise the board of directors to establish the concept and development strategy of prudent operation, supervise the scientific nature and rationality of executive compensation plans, regularly report to the regulatory authorities, comprehensively evaluate the performance of directors, and require them to strengthen their performance in risk management and internal control. We will also establish a good corporate culture and value standards, strengthen the construction of incentive and restraint mechanisms, adjust assessment indicators so that they no longer focus on scale and short-term interests, reflect the long-term interests of the management and employees, strengthen the coverage of incentive policies on risks, and strengthen the accountability of responsibility subjects.

At the same time, we will give full play to the checks and balances of stakeholders. We will clarify the management boundary between government departments, regulatory agencies and enterprises, and prevent administrative departments from abusing their power to interfere in the management of micro subjects. The legal rights of stakeholders should be clearly defined in the corporate governance framework to improve the participation of employees in corporate governance. We will establish and improve an effective bankruptcy settlement framework and enforcement mechanism, further strengthen the principle of share capital loss absorption and bankruptcy enforcement, strengthen the role of creditors as external supervisors, and prevent evasion and cancellation of financial debts. The supervision department should return to the standard of supervision and strengthen the evaluation and supervision of the internal management, risk control, incentive, and constraint of the enterprise governance, while not interfering in the daily operation of the enterprise.

3.6.9 Improve the Information Disclosure System

First, we will improve the scope of information disclosure. This includes complete information about the company's financial and operating conditions, major shareholders and actual controllers, remuneration of board members and senior management, information about board members and their independence, related transactions, employees, and other stakeholders. Second, we will improve the quality of information disclosure. We will use high-quality accounting and disclosure standards to improve the relevance, reliability and comparability of reports, and employ independent, competent external auditors to provide quality audit services. We will also strengthen the construction of information communication channels, so that all parties concerned can obtain relevant information equally, in a timely manner and at low-cost. Finally, we will strengthen constraints.

Chapter 4
The Transformation of China's Monetary Policy Framework

4.1 China's Practical Experience in Sound Monetary Policy

In 1984, when the People's Bank of China (PBC) began formally to perform the functions of a central bank, it operated under the condition of extremely complex economic constraints and structural characteristics. Since then, the monetary policy authorities of China have broken through the ideological shackles, engaged proactively in exploration, and formed the policy system and theoretical basis of China's sound monetary policy according to China's real economic situation and the needs of macro-regulation. The global financial crisis has brought new challenges to the traditional monetary economics and the monetary policy of the central bank, demanding profound reflection among theorists and policymakers. This chapter makes an in-depth analysis of the practice and valuable experience of China's monetary policy since the crisis, providing a comprehensive assessment of recent developments in foreign macroeconomic theories, and of the new direction of the monetary policy framework, mode of monetary policy operation, and changes in monetary policy regulation strategies. Events have proved that the valuable experience accumulated in China's financial macro-regulation is consistent with the reflection of global central banks following the most recent international financial crisis. It is therefore worthwhile to summarize and clarify the lessons that have been learned. An in-depth understanding of the experience so far is of great theoretical and practical significance for China's monetary policy in the transformation under the new normal, and for the goal of boosting the supply-side structural reform.

4.1.1 China's Monetary Policy Framework

The development of economic theory and the policy practice of the central banks of various countries provide a very useful reference for China's monetary policy

Z. Xu, *Keep Reforming: China's Strategic Economic Transformation*,
https://doi.org/10.1007/978-981-15-8006-2_4

regulation. However, the mainstream economic theories are all based on the situation of developed countries, and the development of those theories is aimed mainly at solving new problems emerging in the developed countries. Given China's unique trajectory, from planned economy to market economy, from low-income country to upper-middle-income country, and from the edge of the world economy to global significance, foreign mainstream economic theories are not immediately relevant to China's reform and development and macro-regulation. If we simply follow the existing theories to guide China's policies, we will face the problem of trying to 'fit a square peg into a round hole.' In addressing the urgent need for China's economic development and macro-regulation, China's monetary policy authorities have broken through the shackles of the inherent planned economy. Now, they must hold their nerve and continue to avoid falling into the trap of relying solely on the foreign theories. This approach will require constant efforts devoted to policy exploration. Furthermore, in order to ensure the long-term sustainable and healthy development of economy and finance, while also achieving the final goals of monetary policy such as stability of output and price, the authorities must strive to solve the institutional obstacles and deep-seated contradictions in economic and financial development and monetary policy transmission.

Since 1984, when the PBC began formally to exercise its duties as a central bank, it has gradually realized the first major transformation of China's monetary policy regulatory framework. Through unremitting efforts and exploration, and the combined application of multiple monetary policy tools, it has steered a course from direct regulation to indirect regulation, and has gradually formed a quantitative monetary policy regulatory framework with broad money supply as the intermediate goal and price stability as the ultimate goal. At the same time, the degree of marketization of financial macro-regulation has gradually increased, and the role of the market in the allocation of financial resources has continuously improved. In considering the reform experience so far, we can draw the following lessons: First, in the selection of monetary policy objectives, we should emphasize the stability of prices while also taking other objectives into account. Second, we should reform and improve a series of monetary policy tools in accordance with the requirements of indirect regulation. Third, we should choose a regulation mode that combines quantity, price, and macro-prudential policies based on the needs of the development stage and national conditions. Fourth, we should always pay attention to the combination of short-term macro control and medium-to-long-term financial reform, focus on the "online repair" of the financial system, steadily promote the market-oriented reform of interest rates and exchange rates, and constantly improve the transmission mechanism of monetary policy. After years of development and practice, this monetary policy regulatory framework is becoming more and more mature. It not only stood the test of the Asian financial crisis at the end of the last century, but also played a positive role in coping with the recent global financial crisis. It has been proven effective through various domestic economic cycles, and has achieved good regulatory effect.

After emerging from the mire of "stagflation," since the mid-1980s major developed countries have been experiencing an era of "great moderation," characterized by high growth and stable inflation. The progress of monetary economic theory has contributed greatly to this. Under the condition of rational expectation, the "new neoclassical synthesis" (NNS), which takes as the micro-foundation real structural characteristics such as market friction and sticky prices, and carries out long-term dynamic general equilibrium analysis, has been widely recognized by academia and policy makers. Taking inflation as the primary target and (implicitly) adjusting only short-term (mainly overnight) interest rate tools under specific rules (Taylor's rule, Taylor 1993) has become the currency regulation mode commonly adopted by major central banks. However, the theory of monetary economics is always closely linked with policies, and develops with the accumulation of experience. In particular, under the impact of the "once-in-a-century financial tsunami," it has become clear that the original "mature" monetary economics theory suffers from major paradigm defects. After following that theory for many years, the monetary policy authorities in the mature economies were forced to conduct a large number of unprecedented and innovative policy experiments, thus prompting profound reflection in theoretical circles. To date, the international academic community and the central banks of major countries have made remarkable progress in macroeconomic theory, monetary policy framework, monetary policy operation mode, and monetary policy regulation strategies. From the perspective of theory and policy practice, there are differences among countries, but there are also many common problems.

Events have proved that the valuable experience accumulated by China's financial macro-regulation is consistent with the reflection of global central banks since the recent international financial crisis. It is therefore worthwhile to summarize that experience and suggest how further improvements might be made. In recent years, both the internal and external environments of China's economy have undergone distinct changes, and the constraints faced by the monetary policy have become more complex. At a time when China's monetary policy is in transition under the new normal, opportunities and challenges coexist. It is therefore of great theoretical and practical significance to track the latest developments in monetary and economic analysis theories and monetary policies of major countries since the global financial crisis, while also taking full advantage of the successful experience and institutional advantages of China's monetary policy.

4.1.2 The Development Trend of Macroeconomics and Monetary Policy Theory

Since its introduction by Keynes (1936), macroeconomic theory has been applied to policy practice. However, faced with the real problems of macro economy and monetary regulation, monetary authorities have been forced to adopt new and innovative policy, thus prompting academics and practitioners to reflect deeply on macroeconomic theory. Indeed, macroeconomic theory and monetary policy have been explored and tested in crisis after crisis, and continue to mature day by day. In the aftermath of the global financial crisis, macroeconomic theory has once again shown distinct Keynesian characteristics. Today, the main focus of macroeconomic theory research and development is on how best to introduce financial factors into the general equilibrium analysis framework of macroeconomics, how to describe the model structure more accurately, estimate the model parameters more precisely, and conduct economic analysis in combination with traditional econometric models.

4.1.2.1 The Return of Keynesianism

By introducing price stickiness and considering the general equilibrium method of total supply and total demand (IS-LM), Keynes (1936) broke through the perfect market hypothesis of classical economics and neoclassical economics. Instead, he suggested that the fluctuation of economic cycle could be explained by his Theory of Insufficiency of Effective Demand, which provided a theoretical basis for policies to intervene in the economy to smooth out economic fluctuation. This approach became the mainstream of macroeconomics after the Second World War. However, traditional Keynesianism tends to focus only on the macro-aggregate relationship, lacks the necessary micro-foundation, and does not consider the influence of micro-subject behavior and policy impact on micro-decision-making and incentive mechanisms. Moreover, it mainly focuses on short-term comparative static analysis, and adopts static or adaptive expectations to deal with long-term dynamic problems. These shortcomings are summarized in the Lucas Critique (Lucas 1976). There is a severe time inconsistency (Kydland and Prescott 1977) in the discretionary monetary policy guided by traditional Keynesianism, and countries finally fall into a painful stagflation dilemma. Driven by the monetarism represented by Friedman (1968) and the rational expectation school represented by Lucas (1976), the new classical economics, which advocates economic freedom, weakens the price stickiness and demand fluctuation of traditional Keynesianism, and instead emphasizes the micro-basis and rational expectation of macroeconomics. This approach replaced traditional Keynesianism as the mainstream of macroeconomic theory.

Friedman was an early advocate of neoclassical economics. The monetarist theory he promoted mainly adopted the partial equilibrium comparative static method and dealt with economic dynamic problems through the adaptive expectation method (Smithin 2003). However, in practice, since the 1970s the monetary quantity target system has proved ineffective for many countries, and monetarism has gradually faded out. It has become a consensus among economists that monetary economic analysis should adopt a structured method with micro-foundations, rational expectations, and general equilibrium characteristics (DeJong and Dave 2007; Liu 2016). The Real Business Cycle Theory (RBC) (Kydland and Prescott 1982) is based on the rational expectations of microeconomists under the assumption of a complete market. It can effectively overcome the Lucas Critique and theoretically explain the economic cyclical changes. Therefore, it is highly praised by many economists. However, under the complete market hypothesis, the RBC states that economic fluctuations are mainly caused by technological shocks and have nothing to do with finance. Moreover, the

RBC model does not include monetary policy, since there is no price stickiness hypothesis. In fact, under the condition of complete competition and full price elasticity, Cooley and Hansen (1989) show that according to the RBC approach, money can only affect nominal variables such as price, but not entity variables such as output, which also means that neoclassical macroeconomics cannot provide help for monetary policy decisions. Moreover, RBC holds that economic fluctuations are mainly driven by the supply side and have nothing to do with demand. If the price can be adjusted flexibly enough, then the fluctuation of economic output is the best response to the fluctuation of supply, and any attempt by monetary authorities to smooth out the economic fluctuation is redundant. The RBC model is not widely accepted by monetary authorities at present. Although other neoclassical macro models can also get short-term non-neutral monetary effects under specific conditions (Lucas 1972), and in recent years monetary policy analysis has been conducted under the DSGE framework by considering the role of the banking sector (Basu et al. 2012) under the complete market hypothesis, limitations of theoretical and policy analysis mean that neoclassical macroeconomics has not had a wide impact on policy formulation.

Because the efficient market hypothesis of the neoclassical macro theories represented by RBC is not completely consistent with the reality, the economic explanations offered by such theories are often not ideal. Meanwhile, New Keynesian (NK) economists have developed a large number of micro-based price stickiness models, such as menu cost and staggered price setting (Mankiw 2006). Since the 1990s, it has been more realistic to use the RBC method for reference and to introduce the incompletely competitive price stickiness NK model with a micro-basis, which has better explanatory power to the economy and can effectively implement policy evaluation. This approach has gradually gained favor from academia and central banks of various countries. The dynamic stochastic general equilibrium model (DSGE), which is widely used by central banks, is an extension of the original NK model combined with the specific situation of different countries. It should be pointed out that although the price stickiness of NK is the same as that of traditional Keynesianism, the modeling method under the condition of rational expectation is the same as that of neoclassical macroeconomics, which is totally different from that of traditional Keynesian neoclassical synthesis (Samuelson 1955); this explains why NK is also known as the new neoclassical synthesis (Goodfriend and King 1997). The NK model is closer to economic reality. It not only contains the core connotation of traditional Keynesian theory but also emphasizes the vital role of expectation management in the realization of optimal monetary policy. Consequently, the NK model has become the mainstream method of modern monetary economic analysis and central bank policy research in major countries. The successful performance of monetary policy with reference to the NK model during the period of "great moderation" has dramatically enhanced economists' confidence in achieving output and price stability through precise policy adjustment.

Since the global financial crisis, based on the lessons of the "great depression," countries have successfully avoided the rapid spread of crisis through large-scale stimulus policies, which is a typical anti-cyclical demand management operation of Keynesianism. In particular, although the economic deterioration in the early stage of the global financial crisis exceeded that of the great depression, due to timely and hefty expansionary demand management, the crisis led only to a "great recession," and did not develop into a depression (Furman 2014). At the same time, all countries are aware of the importance of fiscal policy, income distribution, social security and other policies. Especially during the current period, when the economy is in a continuous downturn and is likely to enter a long-term stagnation, the question of how to integrate structural issues such as financial stability, macro-policy coordination, the gap between rich and poor, and national policy coordination into the NK model is at the forefront of theoretical research.

4.1.2.2 New Developments in Macroeconomic Theory Since the Global Financial Crisis

I. Introducing the Financial Factor System into the DSGE Model Framework

The global financial crisis has shown that the traditional macro model generally underestimates the depth of crisis and the duration of recession; moreover, the systematic deviation is too optimistic, mainly due to the failure to include the financial system in the model analysis. Traditional macroeconomic analysis rarely discusses the impact of financial institutions and financial markets on monetary policy transmission and the real economy. The development of information economics in the 1970s made people realize the importance of information asymmetry to the effective operation of financial markets (Stiglitz and Weiss 1981). Many studies on economic crisis (including the "great depression") have shown that information asymmetry and financial friction will cause economic instability (Mishkin 1997). In particular, the global financial crisis has demonstrated that the relationship between financial institutions, financial markets, and the economy is more important than macroeconomists and central banks had previously thought, and the role of the financial system in the macro economy can no longer be ignored.

In fact, long before the outbreak of the global financial crisis, economists had realized that the traditional macro model has no defects in financial institutions. Specifically, by adhering to the traditional model, the fluctuation of credit can only be triggered by the demand fluctuation of the demand side, which is the enterprise. However, this is obviously inconsistent with the fact that during times of crisis, such as the "great depression" and the Japanese economic crisis, the financial institutions' own ability to supply credit is impaired, resulting in severe credit fluctuation and thus amplifying the crisis. Therefore, economists have tried to introduce financial factors into the traditional macro model, chiefly through the financial accelerator mechanism (Bernanke and Gertler 1986), the collateral constraint mechanism (Kiyotaki and Moore 1997), and by considering the production function of specific financial sectors (Goodfriend and McCallum 2007). While there are overlaps between these three methods, in terms of modeling ideas the core of each of them is to analyze the amplification effect of changes in credit supply (rather than credit demand) on economic fluctuations due to the friction of the financial system under the condition of asymmetric information. However, the mainstream macro models employed before the crisis did not fully recognize the critical role of finance, which is also one of the reasons why the subprime crisis was unexpected.

II. Providing More Accurate Descriptions of the Economic Structure

It should be noted that the DSGE model belongs to the structured method. This means that general equilibrium analysis based on a microscopic basis is prone to lead to model setting errors and can result in large deviation in the analysis. Therefore, in the development of the DSGE model method and macroeconomic analysis, the main goal is a more accurate description of the economic structure. In addition to the systematic introduction of financial factors, it also includes the introduction of multiple departments through the use of input–output information, re-examination of the relationship between economic trends and fluctuations, consideration of non-fundamental information shocks, introduction of heterogeneous micro-subjects, expansion of open conditions, and adjustment of inflation dynamics (Yellen 2016c).

4.1.2.3 Taking the Solid Theory Based on China's Reality as the Support, and Performing Well in Monetary Policy Regulation

I. China's Monetary Policy Experience in Transition

As early as 1991, when considering establishing a socialist market economy system with Chinese characteristics, Comrade Deng Xiaoping pointed out that finance is "the core of the modern economy… if we do a good job in finance, the whole thing will perform well." Following this logic, in macroeconomic analysis and policy regulation, monetary policy authorities and other macro-regulation departments all attach great importance to the role of the financial sector, especially banks. Although this is, to a large extent, to make up for the objective needs caused by the long-term absence of a modern financial sector during the planned economy period, recognition of the important role played by finance in policy practice is consistent with the theoretical progress since the global financial crisis, which has seen macroeconomic analysis pay more attention to financial factors. In fact, China's policy practice is ahead of the mainstream theory, as can be seen in examples such as "online repair" of problem financial institutions, development finance, green finance, and other policy practices during the crisis. Moreover, China's monetary policy has not adopted the "impossible trinity" angle solution for financial macro-regulation, but instead has explored and adopted the intermediate solution arrangement of limited opening of capital projects, managed floating exchange rate, and a certain degree of autonomy and independence of monetary policy, according to the reality of China's economy and finance. Although such arrangements increase the difficulty of expectation management and weaken the effectiveness of policy to a certain extent, they provide necessary and sufficient space for policy regulation and regulation among financial stability, market development, system reform, and economic growth. Such arrangements generally ensure stable economic development, while providing conditions conducive to accelerating the construction of related supporting facilities and fully grasping favorable opportunities to realize the goal of clean and floating reform. These monetary policy practices with Chinese characteristics will eventually enrich mainstream macroeconomic and monetary policy theories.

Of course, for the central bank in the world's largest newly developing transition economy, the real conditions for monetary regulation are more complicated. China's monetary policy should not only focus on controlling inflation, but also take into account the needs of transition development and financial reform. At the beginning of the reform and opening up, due to the asymptotic property of the system reform and market development, the government continued to use traditional planned economy tools and methods such as credit limit management to manage and regulate the economic operation. Since the 1990s, the economic and financial environment has changed significantly, raising new requirements for macro-regulation, as follows: First, with the deepening of the market-oriented reform, the ability and willingness of micro-subjects to make independent decisions have gradually increased, and the effect of traditional administrative and quantitative direct regulation has weakened, thus requiring a shift to market-oriented and price-oriented indirect regulation. Second, since the turn of the century, and especially following China's accession to the WTO, the opening up has entered a new stage. The persistent twin surplus in international payments and large amount of funds outstanding for foreign exchange have led to excess liquidity, so that an efficient hedging operation platform is needed to cope with inflation pressure. Third, since the international financial crisis, a consensus has been reached on the need to strengthen macro-prudential management. The implementation of regulatory requirements such as capital adequacy, liquidity and leverage ratio, and centralized liquidation of derivatives all require sufficient support from financial markets. In this context, the PBC and other relevant departments proactively take measures to promote the development of the financial market relying on the inter-bank market; to strengthen the construction of market infrastructure; and to improve the depth and breadth of the market. The practice shows that the inter-bank market (including the currency, bond, and foreign exchange market) has unique advantages in acting as a regulatory platform: First, its characteristics of facing institutional investors and over-the-counter markets are suitable for macro-management departments to carry out relevant regulatory work. Second, given its scale, the inter-bank market occupies an absolute dominant position. It is also the main platform for liquidity and investment and financing management of major financial institutions in China's financial system. It has strong ability to carry out policy operation and transmit policy guidance. Relying on the platform of the inter-bank market, the management departments actively carry out various macro-regulation operations that are routine and respond to the impact of the crisis. Entering the new century, the PBC has actively carried out open market operations in the inter-bank market, adjusted the market interest rate in a timely manner, and guided market expectations. In the absence of sufficient national bonds as hedging tools, it began issuing central bank bills in the inter-bank market in 2003. The annual issuance increased from 720 billion yuan in 2003 to 4.2 trillion yuan in 2009,[1] effectively offsetting excess liquidity and easing inflationary pressures.

In response to the once-in-a-hundred-year global financial crisis, the central bank was accurate in judgment and quick in action. After successfully coping with the immediate impact of the global financial crisis, it accelerated the marketization reform of interest rate and exchange rate along with the convertibility process of capital items. Thus, the two-way opening up of the financial industry has been further deepened, and the internationalization of RMB has been significantly improved. In the face of the new normal of "the three-period superimposed",[2] the central bank implements macro-prudential management, adjusts monetary and credit policies in a timely manner, and innovates and enriches the monetary policy toolbox. Monetary policy is generally stable and closely coordinated with other macro policies to effectively maintain the basic stability and healthy development of macro economy and finance. With the changes in international capital flows that have taken place in recent years, China's base money issuance channels have undergone fundamental changes. Furthermore, changes in the liquidity environment have led to certain fluctuations in the currency markets. In this regard, the PBC has launched a large number of liquidity innovation management tools, such as the Standing Lending Facility (SLF), Medium-term Lending Facility (MLF), and Pledged Supplementary Lending (PSL), to optimize the refinancing system and implement internal rating of financial institutions. On the basis of improving collateral tools of financial institutions, it also carries out the pledge and refinancing of credit assets and continually enriches the variety of open market operation terms, thus compensating for the lack of market liquidity and ensuring the stable development of the money market.

In general, China's monetary policy authorities shoulder multiple missions of reform, development, and macro-regulation. In the uncertain environment of economic structural change and under the condition of multiple equilibria in theory, the PBC has always realized the basic stability of prices while achieving rapid economic growth through flexible, moderate, and prudent monetary policies in limited policy space to meet the needs of the economic cycle and macro-regulation. Consequently, it was able to withstand the severe tests of the Asian financial crisis and the global financial crisis, and accumulated a great deal of valuable experience of financial regulation and mechanism construction in transition economies.

II. Establishing a Solid Theoretical Support According to China's Real Situation

China is now the second largest economy in the world, with a market economy system that is developing rapidly. Consequently, the role of macro-regulation is increasingly important. The Third Plenary Session of the 18th Central Committee

---

[1] In the whole year of 2009, a total of 4 trillion yuan of central bank bills were issued and the amount of repo operations reached 4.2 trillion yuan.

[2] This Chinese economic term means to deal with the slowdown in economic growth; make difficult structural adjustments; and absorb the effects of previous economic stimulus policies simultaneously.

of the Chinese government proposed that we should "improve the macro-regulation system and make the macro-regulation more prospective and targeted." The Fifth Plenary Session emphasized that we should "improve macro-regulation…, take precision regulation measures, implement anticipatory adjustment and fine-tuning in due time, and make it more targeted and precise," and put forward higher requirements for the theoretical research work of the central bank. The PBC attaches great importance to the supporting role of research in financial reform and monetary regulation, and Governor Zhou Xiaochuan has long advocated critical policy research as the main pillar of the bank. Over the past decade, the PBC research system has focused closely on the major strategic deployment by the central government and on the central works of the central bank. By building a new think tank platform, the China Financial Forum (CFF), it has strengthened the integration of resources with the academic field, financial institutions, and internal business departments, forming a distinctive "big research" pattern of the central bank. In recent years, the relevant results of macroeconomic theory research by the Central Bank of China have also been published in the form of working papers, thus strengthening exchanges with domestic and foreign theoretical circles on macroeconomic theory research with Chinese characteristics, and promoting the in-depth development and improvement of China's macroeconomic theory and monetary policy analysis.

PBC researchers began early to conduct macroeconomic model analysis, and were among the leaders in building the DSGE model and focusing on Chinese issues. As China faces more complex economic constraints and structural characteristics than many of the developed countries, researchers from the Central Bank of China realize that it is not appropriate simply to apply foreign models when conducting macro-theoretical research in the China context; rather, it is necessary to take into consideration China's unique institutional factors. For example, the DSGE model developed by the research bureau has been applied extensively according to the typical characteristics of China's economy and finance. Now adapted to include new financial sectors such as shadow banks, the feature of alternation of generations, and the land finance and real estate sectors, the model has been used in substantial theoretical and empirical research on such vital issues as the pension gap and its financial impact, fiscal limit calculation, the macro impact of bond swap and real estate policies, potential output, and sources of economic fluctuations. Nevertheless, researchers from the central bank recognized very early that although the DSGE model has essential advantages in research methods, it is also subject to certain defects in terms of robustness. The DSGE model is mainly used to simulate the effects of different policies. It is not robust in economic forecasting. In particular, the short-term forecasting effect is probably not as good as VAR and traditional econometric models.

In terms of development of the DSGE model, there are currently two main directions. One is a DSGE model that takes into account the factors of system transformation, while the other is the semi-structured DSGE-VAR model (Linde et al. 2016) in combination with the traditional econometric model. In fact, most central banks do not rely entirely on the DSGE model for decision-making, but also refer to the analysis results of VAR, traditional econometric models, and other models. For example, the Federal Reserve attaches great importance to the role of the FRB/US macroeconomic econometric model, established based on structural equations in monetary decision-making (Fischer 2016c). Researchers from the China's central bank have done extensive work on DSGE based on the typical characteristics of China's economy and finance, while establishing a new generation of large-scale macroeconomic models and continuously exploring other reliable macroeconomic analysis and prediction methods that fit China's reality.

In the process of China's economic and financial reform, the researchers of the central bank do not stick to the existing theories, but put forward many theoretical analyses and policy proposals that are conducive to promoting the financial reform in line with China's reality. For example, considering the fact that there are very many "intermediate states," they extend the classical "impossible trinity" theory, find out the intermediate system arrangement theory, and apply it to China's macro-theoretical analysis (Yi and Xian 2001). In terms of the sequence theory of financial reform that is prevalent internationally, the researchers consider China's reality and put forward policy proposals to promote China's interest rate, exchange rate, and the opening of capital projects in an overall and coordinated way (Sheng and Xi 2015).

4.1.3 Target Framework and Operation Mode of Monetary Policy

In the wake of the global financial crisis, and driven by the return of Keynesianism and the development of macroeconomic theories, many countries have adjusted their monetary policy theories and policy operational frameworks accordingly. First of all, while price stability is still an important objective of monetary policy, it is not a sufficient and necessary condition for economic stability. The inflation targeting regime that was the mainstream before the crisis is also under suspicion. Second, targeting the natural interest rate with the real interest rate should not be the whole operation of monetary policy. From the experience of monetary policy operation of major economies in recent years, under the condition of the liquidity trap interest rate policy is invalid, and quantity control is more important. Structural and differential monetary credit policy is also necessary and reasonable. Third, the change in price level is a comprehensive phenomenon, and there is no simple corresponding relationship with the currency supply. Fourth, monetary policy is subordinate to the countercyclical demand management policy system. It should be in line with the economic and financial situation, and should not stick to any mechanical policy rules.

4.1.3.1 New Direction of the Target Framework of Monetary Policy

I. Discussion on Inflation Targeting and Monetary Policy Target

Although there are many reasons for the "great moderation," inflation as (one of) the main objective(s) of monetary policy is crucial to the stable development of the economy. Especially since the 1990s, many countries (for example, New Zealand) have adopted inflation targeting, which is considered to be one of the most significant achievements of macroeconomic theory (Fischer 2016b). However, following the global financial crisis, under the condition of ultra-low (zero, negative) interest rates monetary policy cannot effectively stimulate economic growth, and once again attention has focused on the objectives of monetary policy. Economists have conducted in-depth analysis and discussion on the possible options of raising the target inflation level, nominal GDP targeting, price level targeting, or inflation targeting combined with macro-prudential policies (Williams 2016).

Inflation targeting belongs to the group of complex target rules (Svensson 2011). The corresponding Taylor's rule is a simple instrument rule for interest rate adjustment considering inflation and output gap (Taylor and Williams 2011); it remains robust under the condition of zero interest rate (Gust et al. 2015). Svensson (2012) also admitted that interest rate decisions in inflation-targeting countries such as Britain and Sweden mainly depend on conditional forecasts of current interest rates, and there are still difficulties in policy evaluation. In fact, monetary policy has shown an increasingly apparent tendency of discretion in recent years (Taylor 2014). In the face of an uncertain economic and financial environment, many inflation-targeting countries have not strictly followed the complicated target rules (Kahn and Palmer 2016). From 2001, the policy interest rates of major countries, including the United States, deviated from the normal level revealed by Taylor's rule (IMF 2008). In the view of many economists, this was an important reason behind the global financial crisis (Nikolsko-Rzhevsky et al. 2014). Low-interest rates encourage residents to increase consumption, and financial institutions tend to increase leverage and take more risks, thus strengthening the risk channel of monetary policy transmission (Gambacorta 2009). Therefore, once the financial market is basically stable, many economists, including Taylor (2015), strongly advocate the normalization of monetary policy. Of course, Bernanke also refuted, pointing out that the Federal Reserve will focus on many variables in practice, rather than just the output gap and inflation gap.

II. Adherence to Inflation as the Main Objective of Monetary Policy and Exploration of Monetary Policy Tool Rules and Monetary Policy Target Framework According to China's Reality

Compared with multi-objectives, the single objective of monetary policy is clear, concise, and easy to communicate, which helps to strengthen the independence of the central bank. However, the inflation targeting system, in which the inflation level is the sole target, has always been controversial. Relevant research shows that the improvement of monetary policy performance by inflation targeting is mainly achieved by enhancing policy transparency (Sims 2004), and that the policy effect of stabilizing output carries the cost of a certain amount of output loss (Goncalves and Carvalho 2009). Therefore, at present, most central banks still implement multi-objective monetary policies. In this regard, the Federal Reserve is a typical representative.

The reality of China's social economy and finance determines the multi-objective system of the central bank. During the period of China's economic transformation, the social and economic structure is in the process of adjustment, and the financial market is under continuous development. The constraints faced by the monetary policy authorities are complex. In addition to the legal goal of stabilizing the currency value and promoting economic growth, the monetary authorities also shoulder the annual goal of full employment, the balance of international payments, and the dynamic goal of promoting the reform and development of the financial industry (Zhou 2016). Of course, the objectives of monetary policies are not of equal importance, and the particular emphasis changes over time. Multiple objectives inevitably overlap and interfere with each other, and the response to this must be guided by discretion. Given the huge size of China's economy, it is clear that the external goal of the balance of payments should be subordinated to the internal goal (economic growth and price stability). There is a great overlap between the goal of full employment and the goal of economic growth, and promoting the development of the financial market also encourages the better functioning of financial services to the real economy. In the process of China's economic transformation, the realization of policy objectives such as employment, the balance of payments, and financial market stability is also an important prerequisite for price stability, which means the economic balance with zero output gap and the result of other policy objectives. Therefore, price stability is always one of the most important monetary policy objectives of China. Furthermore, price stability is relatively easy to quantify and evaluate, and thus easy to operate. Taking price stability as the main priority goal, we can achieve a similar effect to that of monetary quantity targeting, avoid the inconsistency of policy over time, and reflect the concept of monetary policy rules.

While making inflation one of the most important goals of monetary policy, we should also actively explore the specific forms of China's monetary policy operation. Similar to major developed countries, under the impact of financial innovation and financial disintermediation, the effectiveness of China's monetary quantity control is increasingly declining. In particular, with the completion of the market-oriented reform of interest rates, the necessity and urgency of transforming to an interest-based monetary price control mode are increasing (Zhang 2015). Influenced by the development of the financial market and the transmission mechanism of monetary policy, China has given up direct credit regulation and now adopts a mainly quantitative-based indirect monetary regulation mode (Zhou 2013). However, quantity control and price control are an interactive process. When quantity is not in a reasonable range, price transmission will encounter problems; similarly, regardless of the price factor, it will affect the efficiency of quantitative means. Therefore, at the beginning of the implementation of indirect monetary policy regulation, the PBC not only gave full play to the role of quantity control, but also attached great importance to the role of price control. It kept a clear understanding of the side effects of quantitative regulation, such as "one size fits all" and "sudden brake." While easing the control of deposit and loan interest rates, the PBC has proactively explored the market-oriented interest rate regulation mechanism and promoted the transformation of monetary policy to the price control mode by building basic systems such as the Shibor money market benchmark interest rate. In particular, after more than a decade of development, China's financial market has acquired sufficient breadth and depth, and has developed a more sensitive and effective market-oriented interest rate system and transmission mechanism. It can be said that since the deposit and loan interest rate regulation was basically abolished in 2015, China's interest rate marketization and monetary policy regulation have entered a new stage of deepening reform, in which establishing and perfecting an interest rate formation and regulation mechanism suitable for the market is at the core. This requires solid basic research on interest rate policy rules, strengthening the estimation of natural rates such as China's potential output and equilibrium real interest rate, and exploring interest rate policy rules that follow China's reality.

It is also important to note that in the process of China's economic transformation, some enterprises and financial institutions do not take maximizing profits as the ultimate goal of behavioral incentives, which are quite different from those of developed countries. The structure of the financial market is not perfect, information asymmetry is severe, and the importance of the monetary policy credit transmission channel, as a correction of traditional interest rate channel, is more prominent. Some microeconomic subjects are not sensitive enough to the change in interest rate, and enterprises and local governments also have the impulse to invest. When considering whether money supply, credit volume, or money price should be the main factors, we should pay attention to their volatility and controllability. Therefore, in the future, we should take careful note of changes in money supply, loans, and other liquidity, while gradually focusing on the regulation of money price. Drawing lessons from both the unconventional monetary policy experience of developed economies during the recent financial crisis, and the monetary policy practice of China's monetary policy authorities over the past 20 years, China's effective monetary policy should not stick blindly to any mechanical policy rules, but should carry out precise regulation according to the behavior characteristics of residents, enterprises, and commercial banks, as well as the condition of the financial market. Furthermore, adjustments should be adopted in line with changes in social economic structure and the system of the financial market.

In addition to inflation targeting, China's monetary policy objectives must also take into account employment and economic growth, the balance of payments and financial stability, and the changes in emphasis on different monetary policy objectives over time. According to Tinbergen's Rule, the number of policy tools or control variables must be at least equal to the number of target variables, and these policy tools must be independent of each other (linear independent). Therefore, as a short-term demand management policy, China's central bank should continually enrich monetary policy tools and improve the effectiveness of the monetary policy. This has been reflected in the practice of monetary policy in China in recent years. For example, due to the fact that the adjustment of reserves may cause balance-sheet effects with strong signal significance, and considering the liquidity conditions and the needs of economic structure transformation, the PBC uses more open market operation and innovative liquidity management tools to meet the liquidity requirements of different terms in the market, while appropriately increasing "precise" financial support for key areas and weak links. In the future, we should further explore and enrich the monetary policy theory that adapts to the Chinese policy objective with inflation as the core while also taking other objectives into account, and improve the monetary policy objective framework in line with China's reality.

4.1.3.2 New Mode of Monetary Policy Operation

I. Communication and Forward Guidance of the Central Bank
i. Expectation management and forward guidance

Driven by the "rational expectations revolution," central banks in various countries have realized the importance of policy communication and transparency to improve the effectiveness of monetary policy (Blinder et al. 2008). By expertly guiding market expectations, policy operations can achieve the desired goals much more easily. Monetary policy is also called "the art of expectation management" (Woodford 2003), and expectation effect plays an increasingly important role (Friedman and Kutter 2011). Following the global financial crisis, in order to stabilize the financial market and stimulate the economy, many countries have carried out large-scale quantitative easing, with policy interest rates falling to ultra-low levels, and therefore encountering the dilemma of zero lower bonds. In this process, central banks across the globe have not only strengthened their regular communication but also guided public expectations by commitments on the low-interest rate. Forward guidance has become an essential way for central banks to communicate and manage expectations (Carney 2013).

Although there is a great deal of research to show that forward guidance can effectively improve the transparency and effectiveness of monetary policies, guide public inflation expectations under the condition of zero interest rates, and contribute to economic stability (Ball et al. 2016), other studies have questioned its effectiveness (Kool and Thornton 2015). Because forward guidance continuously revises the future interest rate path, it is not a stable and reliable communication strategy. It may eventually limit the optimal monetary policy path and space of the central bank, incur the problem of time inconsistency, and damage the credibility and policy reliability of the central bank's monetary policy (Powell 2016). Therefore, Yellen (2016a, b), chairman of the Federal Reserve, has gradually reduced the dependence on forward guidance in practice and tends to rely on data dependency for decision-making.

ii. Communication mechanism of monetary policy, expectation management, and the effectiveness of monetary policy

The PBC has long recognized the importance of monetary policy communication. In 2019, it made clear proposals for carrying out inflation expectation management effectively. With regard to the practice of forward guidance in various countries after the global financial crisis, while a necessary consensus has been reached on the vital role of expectation management and communication, there remain many open issues worthy of discussion, including the degree of communication, the pertinence of communication, the technical basis of communication, and the optimal communication strategy. In recent years, a large number of empirical studies on China's monetary policy communication and expectation management have shown that while China's monetary policy transparency and communication are generally effective, there is still much room for improvement (Ma 2015). In the future, we should increase the frequency, clarity, accuracy, and consistency of information disclosure; explore various channels to express the central bank's judgments and policy intentions on economy and finance, and gradually institutionalize them in a regular way so as to improve the independence, authority, and market credibility of the central bank's monetary decision-making under the established institutional framework, and effectively improve the policy effect of monetary regulation.

It should be pointed out that although policy communication and transparency are very important, if we were to rely only on expected management without the support of other traditional means, we would be left with "a source without water and a wood without roots." The significant negative correlation between the amount of money liquidity and the interest rate price is the theoretical basis of the traditional interest rate regulation, such as the open market operation of the central bank. As Thornton (2004) pointed out, the expected effect and liquidity effect promote each other and jointly affect interest rate changes very early. Just as the forward guidance is intended to promote the policy effect of quantitative easing, unconventional liquidity measures also effectively promote the decline of interest rate level and enhance the effectiveness of expectation management (Klee et al. 2016). Therefore, the relationship between liquidity effect and expectation effect cannot be separated. This means that expectation management should be combined with traditional means such as liquidity management. In recent years, the PBC has further improved the central bank's interest rate regulation and transmission mechanism, strengthened the guidance of short-term policy interest rate through continuous 7-day repo rate, and provided liquidity through the normalization of the medium-term lending facility (MLF) such that it can perform its function as medium-term policy interest rate. To a large extent, the liquidity innovation management tools with different terms are designed to make up for the low transmission efficiency of short-term interest rate, medium- and long-term interest rate, and credit market interest rate in China's money market. In this regard, the latest empirical test shows that the central bank's 7-day repo rate and MLF interest rate, the two main operating interest rate products, have an overall upward transmission effect on the national debt interest rate and loan interest rate. This finding provides a useful direction for theoretical exploration on unblocking the transmission channel of interest rate in the transition economies.

II. Interest Rate Corridor Mechanism and Interest Rate Guidance of the Central Bank
i. Deposit and loan facilities and interest rate corridor mechanism

Because the adjustment of reserves has a severe impact on the money supply, and obtaining loan support from the central bank will damage the reputation of financial institutions (stigma effect), the role of required reserves and re-lending (rediscount) is increasingly weakened (Furfine 2003). Since the 1980s, the "three magic weapons" of the central bank have made great achievements only in open market operation. At the same time, the adoption of large value payment system has dramatically improved the operation of the financial market and efficiency of monetary transmission; consequently, many countries have improved the monetary operation process accordingly (Woodford 2001), and implemented deposit and loan facilities and interest rate corridor (or channel system). The central bank provides liquidity to financial institutions at a loan facility interest rate (usually higher than the target interest rate) to meet their required reserve or to clear account position requirements, or compensates financial institutions for excess reserve or clearing account deposits at a deposit facility interest rate (usually lower than the target interest rate). In this way, the market interest rate is automatically locked in the interest rate corridor, effectively stabilizing the liquidity and interest rate expectations of financial institutions (Whitesell 2006). This mode has gradually been adopted by many countries, particularly since the global financial crisis (Goodhart 2009). For example, in 2003, the Federal Reserve transformed the discount window into an automatic borrowing mechanism, setting the discount rate higher than the target interest rate of the federal funds (usually 50 basis points higher), to represent the upper limit of the money market interest rate (Furfine 2003). In 2006, the Federal Reserve was authorized by Congress to pay interest on the reserves of financial institutions in 2011. The global financial crisis accelerated this process, leading to the formation of a bilateral interest rate corridor mechanism in 2008. Japan paid interest on reserves after the global financial crisis, while emerging market countries such as India and Turkey also began to try interest rate corridor arrangements.

From the experience of various countries, it can be seen that by increasing the operating frequency of the open market, implementing bilateral interest rate corridors and a narrow interest rate corridor interval, applying interest compensation for deposit reserves and assessment of average reserve in lag periods, strengthening policy communication, and improving transparency, it is possible to reduce the deviation of the money market interest rate from the target level of the central bank and to make it more conducive to the interest rate guidance of the central bank (Bindseil and Jablecki 2011). At the same time, the interest rate corridor has an optimal moderate range, which can be larger under imperfect market conditions (the ECB's interest rate corridor range was initially 200 basis points, then dropped to 150 basis points).

The deposit facility interest rate should be lower than the target interest rate. Otherwise, the transaction cost premium quoted by the institution will not be effectively compensated, and the central bank will become the only provider of market liquidity, as illustrated by Australia's experience in expanding the interest rate corridor from 20 basis points to 50 basis points (Woodford 2001). Under the post-crisis condition of ultra-low (zero) interest rate, the central bank can control the interest rate and the amount of reserves simultaneously, by paying interest on reserves and setting the rate as the lower limit of market interest rate. Especially in the case of zero interest rate, if financial institutions are willing to keep excess reserves, this will be conducive to easing the inflationary pressure of quantitative easing (Keister and McAndrews 2009).

Theoretically, the income and cost of loans and deposits of the central bank should match, so the target interest rate is usually set in the middle of the interest rate range of deposits and loans; this is also called the equilibrium situation of policy interest rate (Woodford 2001). However, financial institutions often have to mortgage high-quality bonds in order to obtain financial support from the central bank, so the equilibrium deposit-loan interest rate range is actually not symmetric (Whitesell 2006). Following the global financial crisis, asymmetric deposit and loan interest rate range has become a new topic of discussion (Goodhart 2009). Many scholars have conducted substantial theoretical research on the impact of the central bank collateral mechanism (Bindseil and Winkler 2012), and on the effect of unconventional monetary policy and macroprudential policy in terms of the asymmetric interest rate corridor (Vollmer and Wiese 2016). It should also be noted that unless the policy target interest rate is determined under the guidance of rules (Berentsen et al. 2014), it will not be able to effectively curb the demand for liquidity. Even if the Eurozone or the UK were to adopt complete open market operation and interest rate corridor, deviation of the policy interest rate from the equilibrium level would lead to financial resource allocation distortion and financial crisis.

ii. Interest rate corridor mechanism, open market operation, and interest rate guidance ability of China's central bank

From the perspective of the policy framework, the interest rate system of China's central bank already has the function of "interest rate corridor" to some extent (Zhou 2013), and the interest rate operation mode is not very different from the mainstream international practices (BIS 2009). In particular, in 2015 China officially abolished the deposit-loan ratio requirement, improved the reserve assessment method, and attempted to build the SLF interest rate as the upper limit of the interest rate corridor; and from February 2016 the authorities expanded the regular open market operation from twice a week to daily, thus taking an important step in improving the interest rate corridor mechanism and open market operation. Both open market operation and interest rate corridor are important arrangements for the central bank to guide interest rates. In particular, liquidity adjustment is realized mainly through daily open market operations, a mode that was widely adopted by many countries before 1990. In addition, the upper and lower limits of the interest rate corridor play an important role in coping with unexpected shocks and stabilizing market expectations. In most cases, they are only "prepared for use." Open market operation and interest rate corridor are organically combined, and their coordination and mutual promotion can significantly improve the efficiency of currency operation.

From the perspective of the formation process, the interest rate corridor mechanism is mainly related to the progress of the payment system, and has little to do with the zero-reserve system. Some domestic scholars have misunderstood this mechanism. All countries with zero-reserve requirements require banks to keep a certain amount of clearing position in the clearing account when introducing a sizeable real-time payment system, which is similar to the assessment of reserve account. There are several reasons why countries might reduce reserves or implement the requirement of zero reserves. Besides the fact that reserves should not be overused as a monetary policy tool, if no interest is paid on the reserves, or the interest is extremely low, then their use is equivalent to taxing financial institutions and causes distortions in their behaviors. It is not conducive to the allocation of resources and the implementation of monetary policy (Feinman 1993). The Federal Reserve has also been trying to persuade Congress to agree to pay interest on the reserves of financial institutions (Goodfriend 2002). In the 50 years before 2008, the Fed's balance sheet was small, and its reserves were not large (in 2007, the average reserves were 43 billion US dollars, and the average excess reserves were 1.9 billion US dollars). Through the open market operation, the Federal Reserve can affect the amount of excess reserves, which then impacts the federal funds rate. After the beginning of the financial crisis, the Fed's balance sheet and reserves increased sharply due to the rescue of financial institutions and quantitative easing (the average reserves in the first half of 2012 were $100 billion, and the average excess reserves were $1.5 trillion). This made it more difficult for the Fed to influence the federal funds rate through the open market operation; that is, the efficiency of quantitative tools was reduced, forcing the US Congress to allow them to pay interest on reserves. Although the implementation of the reserve system will enhance the liquidity constraints of financial institutions and improve the central bank's ability to guide interest rates (Bindseil and Jablecki 2011), the complex requirements and frequent use of reserves will increase the exogenous shock on liquidity and market interest rate volatility. Therefore, in the context of fundamental changes in the way of the release of the monetary base in China with foreign exchange as the main channel, we should work hard to explore and improve the open market operation, interest rate corridor mechanism, and reserve management. In this way, through the coordination and cooperation of policy operation, we can effectively improve the market liquidity environment, as well as the central bank's interest rate guidance ability.

From the perspective of monetary price control and operation requirements of the interest rate corridor, the central bank must make clear the short-term policy target interest rate, take this as the core to determine the interest rate corridor range, and effectively carry out market interest rate guidance in line with the daily open market operation. Therefore, we should specify precisely the new short-term monetary policy interest rate and target level as soon as possible. While improving the reserve interest payment method and the re-lending (rediscount) arrangement including SLF, we should determine the appropriate interest rate corridor range, and form an open, transparent, and credible operation framework on interest rate corridor that can stabilize the expectation. At the same time, we need to further improve the primary dealer system of open market operation, expand the scope of open market operation and SLF trading object under specific standards, and promote the operation process. In this way, we can reduce the opportunities for market capital arbitrage and the liquidity impact amplification effect caused by market structure factors, and provide interest-rate guidance effectively. Based on the equilibrium policy interest rate, we should explore and improve the qualified collateral mechanism, carry out loan facilities following macro-prudential policies such as MPA to ensure the capital safety of the central bank, and effectively restrain the moral hazard of financial institutions.

4.1.4 Economic Stability, Financial Stability, and Broad Monetary Policy

Before the global financial crisis, central banks in many countries did attach great importance to financial stability and released financial stability reports when issuing monetary policy reports. However, because the traditional macroeconomic theoretical models do not regard financial friction as the main factor of economic cycle fluctuations, there was a strategic tendency to separate monetary policy and financial stability policy. Furthermore, many countries separated the micro-prudential supervision function of preventing financial risks from the central bank. Meanwhile, interest rate, as the only monetary policy tool, could effectively achieve inflation and output targets and did not need other policy operations. However, the global crisis has shown that the function of the financial sector is far beyond the understanding of the traditional theory. The macroeconomic adjustment under the great impact of the crisis is highly nonlinear, and the issue of the lower limit of zero interest rate has rendered the traditional interest rate tools ineffective, and incurred severe problems. Therefore, in the aftermath of the global financial crisis, monetary policy has placed more emphasis on coordination and cooperation with macro-prudential policies to promote financial stability and economic growth through unconventional policy measures. This is the most distinct change in monetary policy regulation strategy.

4.1.4.1 Macro-prudential Policy Framework and Its Coordination with Monetary Policy

I. Systematic Risk Prevention and Macro-prudential Policies

The traditional theory of monetary economics holds that price and output stability can automatically promote financial stability (Bernanke and Getler 2001). However, the financial crisis has posed a great challenge to this thinking. Financial institutions took excessive risks in a stable economic environment, rendering the financial system more fragile (Gambacorta 2009). Moreover, the negative effects of financial imbalance on the real economy far exceed the expectations of many developed economies (Mishkin 2011). Financial pro-cyclicality enlarges the fluctuation of the real economic cycle and exacerbates the instability of the financial system, resulting in continuous contraction of the economy in a vicious circle. The financial crisis caused a sharp rise in government debt (Reinhart and Rogoff 2009), threatening the stability of the financial system and exacerbating systemic financial risks. These problems have prompted academics and policy-makers to re-examine the existing monetary policy and financial regulatory framework.

The central bank needs to pay attention to financial stability and find prudent policy measures to control risks (Mishkin 2010). Traditional micro-prudential supervision can only control the risks of individual financial institutions. However, the interaction between financial institutions is external (Acharya 2009), such that the risks of various institutions can be transmitted to each other, and even a smaller risk impact may cause severe systemic events (Heider et al. 2015). Therefore, prudent management is required from an overall perspective; that is, it is necessary to build a macro-prudential policy framework.

In this context, developed economies such as the United States and the European Union have continuously improved their macro-prudential policies to solve problems of pro-cyclicality and "too big to fail" in their financial systems. Similarly, international organizations such as the IMF, BIS, FSB, and central banks of various countries have implemented a large amount of research and policy coordination on the macro-prudential policy framework. Generally speaking, macro-prudential policy tools can be divided into credit, capital, and liquidity policy tools (Claessens 2014). Credit policy tools mainly restrict the borrowers of financial institutions (e.g., loan-to-value ratio, LTV, debt-to-income ratio, DTI); capital policy tools focus on the safety of financial institutions (e.g., countercyclical dynamic capital supervision, leverage ratio supervision, balance sheet restriction); and liquidity policy tools mainly focus on the liquidity of financial institutions (e.g., liquidity coverage ratio, reserves, loan-to-deposit ratio). From the perspective of policy effect, a large number of studies show that macro-prudential policies can effectively maintain financial stability; credit tools such as loan-to-value ratio and debt-to-income ratio can effectively stabilize house prices and asset prices (Tressel and Zhang 2016); capital tools such as minimum capital requirements can effectively limit excessive increase in leverage ratio (Korinek et al. 2016); and liquidity indicators can effectively curb accumulation of liquidity risks (Cesa-Bianchi and Rebucci 2016).

II. Strengthening Policy Coordination, Exploring and Perfecting China's Macro-Prudential Policy Framework

In recent years, with the rapid development of the financial market, China's financial product system has become more complex, and there is a clear trend of comprehensive management. At the same time, in the process of an economic downturn, non-performing financial assets have gradually entered the risk exposure period. Financial markets are experiencing great fluctuations. Soft budget constraints and moral hazard constraints remain serious. Economic leverage risks are rising rapidly. Building a sound macro-prudential policy framework and strengthening coordination with other policies, such as monetary, fiscal, and taxation policy, are of considerable significance to prevent systemic financial risks and promote long-term and healthy economic development.

Under the quantity-based indirect monetary control mode, China's monetary control not only takes account of price indicators, but also pays more attention to the role of liquidity, credit quantity, and window guidance, which has a specific foundation in the practice of macro-prudential policies. In 2003, China took timely measures to prevent real estate credit risks, and avoided a real estate bubble by adjusting the mortgage ratio and interest rate leverage. In 2004, China implemented a differential deposit reserve system and classified credit policies, all of which reflected the idea of macro-prudential policies. In 2009, the PBC began to study the macro-prudential policy framework systematically, then in 2011 introduced a dynamic adjustment system for differential reserves, and in 2015 upgraded it to a macro-prudential assessment system (MPA). The original MPA provided a guide for banking financial institutions to strengthen self-discipline management in seven aspects, namely capital and leverage, assets and liabilities, liquidity, pricing behavior, asset quality, cross-border financing risks, and credit policy implementation; since 2016, off-balance-sheet financing has also been included in the macro-prudential assessment.

According to the new characteristics of capital flows, in 2015 foreign exchange liquidity and cross-border capital flows were brought into the scope of macro-prudential management, further improving the macro-prudential policy framework. Furthermore, in line with the changes in house prices and asset prices, while continuing to comprehensively use macro-prudential tools such as loan-to-value ratio (LTV) and debt-to-income ratio (DTI) to carry out countercyclical adjustment of the real estate credit market, in 2016 the PBC proposed the need to enhance the role of the two-pillar policy framework of "monetary policy + macro-prudential policy," and to proactively explore the coordination and cooperation between monetary policy and macro-prudential policy. In the future, based on lessons drawn from international experience, we should do a good job in the overall management of systemically important financial institutions, financial infrastructure, and financial comprehensive information statistics; reform and improve the financial regulatory framework so that it adapts to the development of modern financial markets; enrich the credit, capital and liquidity macro-prudential policy tools according to the national conditions; and conduct a large number of basic researches, especially on the macro-prudential tools for leverage ratio in real estate and financial markets.

It is also important to note that the relationship between monetary policy and macro-prudential policy has become a widespread concern in China. Traditional monetary policy has an important impact on financial stability, but is insufficient to maintain that stability. Therefore, to some extent, there is a substitution effect and complementarity between macro-prudential policy and monetary policy. That is, these two policies are not independent of each other, but affect each other and need close mutual coordination and cooperation (Shin 2016). Changes in monetary policy will affect market interest rates and cause changes in capital adequacy ratio, thus affecting macro-prudential policies. Macro-prudential policies will also affect monetary policies. By changing credit conditions such as capital requirements, macro-prudential policies can affect relevant interest rates and indirectly change monetary policy stance. They can also create additional operating space for monetary policies and affect their transmission efficiency. In addition, it is essential to coordinate macro-prudential policies with fiscal, micro-prudential, and other policies.

4.1.4.2 Unconventional Monetary Policy and Financial Stability

I. Responsibility of "Lender of Last Resort" and Unconventional Monetary Policy

Unconventional monetary policies include balance sheet expansion (quantitative easing), ultra-low (zero) interest rate policies, forward guidance, and negative interest rate policies (Borio and Zabai 2016). As noted by Fischer (2016c), during the financial crisis the Federal Reserve exercised the function of "lender of last resort" and provided liquidity to the financial market through various channels, such as lending to deposit insurance institutions when the market was under pressure, thus effectively reducing the impact of the crisis. The low interest rate policy performs well in reducing the unemployment rate and stabilizing the inflation rate (Fischer 2016b).

Unconventional monetary policy is necessary in times of crisis (Fischer 2016a); however, it has not met people's expectations in promoting post-crisis economic growth and moderate inflation (Borio and Zabai 2016). Due to the lack of coordination of structural reforms, the policy effect is not as good as expected; indeed, unconventional monetary policies may damage the credibility and policy reliability of the central bank (Borio and Zabai 2016), causing it to face greater political pressure and impairing its independence (Taylor 2016). In addition, the long-term use of unconventional monetary policies tends to lead to excess market liquidity, distort market risk appetite, and threaten financial stability and economic recovery (Gambacorta 2009). Moreover, unconventional monetary policies have exacerbated the spillover effect, making it more difficult for countries to coordinate monetary policies (Borio and Zabai 2016). Finally, central banks may also face losses. If an uncertainty shock occurs, monetary decision-making and exit will be more difficult (Borio 2016). For this reason, economists generally advocate that once the financial market is stable and the economy starts to recover, we should begin to withdraw unconventional monetary policies and realize the raising of interest rate and normalization of monetary policies. It also means to optimize the scale of the balance sheet of central banks. In fact, the Federal Reserve began to seriously discuss this issue as early as 2010 (Bernanke 2010). In recent years, the US economy has recovered significantly and is likely to return to a potential economic growth rate of 2% in the next year or two. When raising interest rates, gradually choosing an opportunity to shrink the balance sheet has become a policy direction for the Federal Reserve (Yellen 2016b, 2017).

II. Innovating and Perfecting China's Monetary Policy Tool System to Create a Good Financial Environment for the Transformation of Monetary Policy and Price Control Methods

The PBC has always attached great importance to the health of financial institutions. As early as the end of the last century, it resolved the problem of historical stock through unconventional online repair and emergency rescue methods of expanding the central bank's balance sheet and injecting foreign exchange reserves. It also adopted other methods, such as the introduction of international strategic investors to carry out joint-stock reform and listing, improve the corporate governance mechanism of financial institutions, and create a micro-financial foundation with strong competitiveness. At the same time, the PBC also emphasized the reforming principle of the buying mechanism. In this regard, the PBC further strengthened the capital and enhanced the capital constraint on banks through the capital market, while also giving attention to the sharing and recovery of rescue and reform costs, thus effectively avoiding moral hazard. Since then, the reform steps of China's state-owned commercial banks have generally been implemented along the stages of financial restructuring, establishing joint-stock companies, introducing strategic investors, and the public offering. This is of great significance for maintaining financial stability and improving macro-regulation, and has dramatically enhanced the authority and credibility of monetary control. The practice of these policies was also of great importance for the crisis relief programs of developed economies during the global financial crisis.

At present, China has entered a new normal in economic development, and there is a problem of how to balance macro-regulation and efforts in reform. Over-stimulated monetary and fiscal policies will not only fail to solve the deep-seated contradictions, but will lead to the solidification of structural contradictions. To maintain the so-called high economic growth with over-stimulation would bring a great deal of harm but no benefit. In this situation, zombie enterprises would not die, and backward production capacity would be difficult to exit. Given the recent over-exertion of short-term macro-control policies and the inadequate implementation and enforcement of supply-side structural reform measures, the proposal of a stable and neutral monetary policy recognizes that monetary policy has its boundaries, cannot deal with all issues, and cannot replace structural reform. The effective implementation of monetary policy requires the cooperation of other policies, especially the supply-side structural reform.

In addition, China is in a critical period of transition from a quantitative to a price-based monetary policy framework. Since the crisis, central banks in developed countries have been expanding their balance sheets and purchasing assets passively. Compared with them, the balance sheet of China's central bank has a relatively large space for adjustment and optimization in the context of the change of passive investment of foreign exchange. How to adjust the balance sheet structure of the central bank to further improve the effectiveness of regulating market interest rates merits further study. In the process of transforming to a price-based monetary control mode, we should actively explore the mechanism channels to optimize the balance sheet of the central bank, strive to improve innovative policy tools, and sort out the price-based interest rate tool system. While adjusting the asset scale and structure, we should also actively optimize the debt structure and consolidate the amount of equity capital. We should create favorable conditions for the transformation of monetary price control by creating a central bank balance sheet with an appropriate scale, reasonable structure, flexible operation, and controllable risks.

4.1.5 Monetary Policy Practice Promotes Theoretical Innovation

Given the close relationship between monetary and economic analysis theory on one hand, and policy-making on the other, real challenges have always been the most considerable driving force for the development of theory. If economic theory can make the sort of advances seen after the "great depression" and "stagflation" experiences, then it will enable us to have a deeper understanding of the mechanism of economic and financial operation, thus making the economy more stable and healthy and effectively avoiding the impact of financial crisis; in that case, the material losses suffered by the "great recession" will be negligible. Drawing on the lessons of more than 200 years of economic theory development, this can be said to be "the worry of growth." Of course, the pace of theoretical development and policy practice are not completely consistent. Policy practice is often slower than the theoretical progress in dealing with practical challenges. After all, according to Keynes (1936), "practical men are usually just slaves to the thoughts of some late economists." However, for this reason, and because "the most dangerous thing is not vested interests, but thoughts," it is vital that our academia, decision-makers, and market participants make joint efforts to track the theoretical frontier and better apply it to policy practice, to promote the realization of a better reality.

At the same time, we should note that China's policy practice is often ahead of the theoretical discovery. In fact, the development of theory is a slow process, a continuing evolution under the constant impact of reality. Moreover, all modern subjects of monetary economic analysis can always be traced to sources that date back decades or even hundreds of years. China's monetary policy practice is of great significance to central banks of developed economies and their development of monetary economic theories after the global financial crisis. However, as a newly developing and transitional economy, China's monetary policy still faces many challenges. First of all, compared with the situation in developed economies, the independence of China's central bank still requires improvement. For most countries, strengthening the autonomy and independence of central banks in monetary policy decision-making and operation has been the common experience for many years. In China, before the reform and opening up, banks, as cashiers of social funds, had long been subordinate to planning and finance; today, indirect monetary control in the modern sense has been in place for little more than 20 years (Zhang 2015). Therefore, China's monetary policy is in a relatively weak position in the macro-regulation system and could easily become the focus of contradictions. As evidenced by the implicit intervention embodied in the recent local debt replacement, the tendency to fiscalize financial functions has not yet been completely reversed. Secondly, the institutional framework of China's macro-regulation is still to be improved, and a macro-regulation system that meets the needs of the socialist market economy and the objective laws of the market economy is yet to be established. China's macro-regulation is still following the system used in the 1990s. Monetary policy and fiscal policy mainly serve industrial policy and economic growth, lacking the institutional guarantee of countercyclical control and macro-prudential management. Therefore, the Fifth Plenary Session of the 18th Chinese government Central Committee emphasized the need to "innovate and improve macro-regulation modes." In addition, the lack of effective coordination mechanism between the central bank and the financial regulatory authorities makes monetary regulation more difficult. The absence and offside of financial supervision are common, especially in the "feudal" supervision pattern; the functions of supervision and development are not separated; and the tendency of "macro-regulation of supervision behaviors" is often apparent. Under the condition of imperfect corporate governance, it is easy for financial institutions to expand their scale, increase their leverage, and eventually force the central bank to rescue them, resulting in macro-imprudence. Furthermore, China's monetary policy has been bearing a heavy burden, operating in the gap of stable growth, risk prevention, structural adjustment, and reform promotion. To further improve the efficiency of monetary policy regulation, substantial progress is needed in the reform of the relationship between the government and the market, the reform of state-owned enterprises, the relationship between the central and local governments, the financial supervision system, the macro-regulation framework, and the micro-subject corporate governance.

While we are trying to overcome various challenges through comprehensively deepening reform, it is necessary to summarize the valuable experience of China's monetary policy regulation and control so far, so as to refine the typical Chinese model of global growth to a theoretical height of universal significance. Of course, we should remain aware that even marginal theoretical innovation is challenging, and the dual complexity of theory and reality poses a huge challenge to decision-makers, which is an invaluable opportunity for all researchers. In particular, at a time when China has entered a new normal in terms of the economy, it has become our common historical mission for theorists and central bank researchers in the world's second largest economy to keep a close eye on the latest developments in international monetary and economic analysis theories, proactively promote theoretical innovation, better serve monetary decision-making, promote financial reform, and deepen supply-side structural reform through academic prosperity under the leadership of the Chinese government Central Committee and the State Council.

4.2 Transformation of China's Monetary Control Mode

As China's economy has transitioned from high-speed growth to high-quality development, China's monetary policy regulation mode should be changed from monetary-quantity-based to monetary-price-based regulation. A comprehensive review of the theory and international experience of monetary regulation mode and the transformation of China's indirect monetary regulation shows that with the acceleration and basic completion of interest rate marketization, as a result of the rapid development of financial innovation and disintermediation, the effectiveness of China's traditional quantitative monetary regulation is declining. Consequently, there is now an urgent need to switch to price-based regulation.

While the debate in western countries and western economics on monetary regulation mode, quantity or price, is based on a relatively mature and stable economic system, China is still an underdeveloped economy in the process of transformation, and its economic structure is unstable. The choice and transformation of money regulation methods must obey and serve high-quality development and transformation, a practice that is both entirely new, and more complex. For more than 20 years, China's indirect monetary policy practice has been faced with the constraints of excessive governmental attention to economic growth and budget soft constraint departments, imperfect financial supervision system, and insufficient depth of financial market. It is still necessary to deepen the development of financial market systems such as market micro-foundations, system guarantee, and product function. Furthermore, in order to deal with the liquidity shock and interest rate disturbance in a timely and effective manner, the central bank's interest rate decision-making space and policy operation autonomy under the monetary price control must be improved and guaranteed in the system. In the future, on the basis of coordinating the relations between reform, development, and stability, we should speed up reform-deepening measures, effectively alleviate various constraints, vigorously cultivate the benchmark interest rate system in the financial market, promote the transformation of monetary price control mode, and better promote the high-quality development of economy and finance in the new normal.

4.2.1 Interest Rate Marketization Reform

In October 2015, the PBC released the upper limit control on the deposit interest rate of financial institutions, marking the basic completion of nearly two decades of interest rate marketization reform. This was an important milestone in China's interest rate marketization and the entire history of financial reform. However, the deregulation of the deposit and loan floating interest rates does not mean that the central bank will no longer manage interest rates; rather, it will shift from administrative means to relying more on market-oriented tools and transmission mechanisms.

In theory, the interest rate reflects the price of capital, and the central bank is fully capable of influencing or even determining the market interest rate level. In practice, the central bank has an important influence on the interest rate formation mechanism and interest rate level in both interest rate regulation countries and interest rate marketization countries. Therefore, a complete expression of interest rate marketization should be that interest rates are jointly determined by monetary policy authorities and financial markets. The reform of interest rate marketization includes two dimensions: marketization of interest rate formation and marketization of interest rate regulation (Ji and Muhong 2014). The 12th Five-Year Plan for the Development and Reform of the Financial Industry explicitly regards "deregulation, formation, and adjustment" as the reform principle of China's interest rate marketization. With the lifting of the restrictions on deposit and loan interest floating rates, the goal of "deregulation" has basically been achieved. However, due to the immaturity of the pricing mechanism of financial institutions and the transmission of monetary policies, China has retained the benchmark deposit and loan interest rate while deregulating the deposit and loan interest rate regulation. In the future, China will make a large number of technical preparations in terms of "formation and adjustment." Indeed, China's interest rate liberalization is entering a new stage of deepening reform, with the marketization of interest rate formation and the regulation mechanism as the core.

At present, China's economy is in transition from the stage of high-speed growth to the stage of high-quality development, which requires us to take the new development concept as our guide. This means we should weaken the goal of GDP growth, and improve the total factor productivity and the quality and efficiency of growth, in terms of aspects of economic development such as quality transformation, efficiency transformation, and power transformation. As a mirror image of the real economy, finance must provide better service to that economy. In line with the evolution of economic development stages, financial promotion of real economic development should also shift from scale expansion to quality improvement, and financial regulation should reduce its reliance on quantitative goals and means. In particular, with the acceleration and basic completion of interest rate marketization reform, financial innovation and financial disintermediation have developed rapidly, financial market structure and financial products have become increasingly complex, and the effectiveness of traditional quantity-based monetary regulation and control has declined, becoming unable to meet the requirements of high-quality economic development. Therefore, in recent years, the PBC has repeatedly pointed out that the increased complexity of factors affecting the money supply mean that we should not pay too much attention to the change of M2, but should instead focus on the interest rate price index, and gradually promote the transformation of monetary price control mode. Since 2018, China has no longer announced the quantitative targets of M2 and social financing scale, which is not only an important step in the transformation of monetary policy regulatory framework, but also more in line with the policy requirements of high-quality economic development.

However, although China has played down the target of monetary quantity, it differs from central banks in developed countries in having greater autonomy in monetary decision-making. As the largest emerging developing transition economy in the world, China requires a monetary policy that not only provides necessary space for price integration and monetization, but also takes into account the needs of transition development and financial stability according to the reality of economic growth at different stages. For some time to come, the interference of double surplus should be considered, so that China's monetary policy always adheres to the multi-objective system while focusing on inflation (Zhou 2013). It can be seen that just as the "deregulation" of interest rate is a gradual process, due to the more complex constraints faced by China's monetary policy, the current conditions of "formation and adjustment" of interest rate and transformation to monetary price control are not mature. We should clarify our direction of reform through a comprehensive summary of China's monetary policy regulation experience, a full understanding of the necessity and urgency of the transformation of China's monetary regulation mode, and an in-depth analysis of the current practical constraints of the transformation of monetary regulation mode. This is of great importance to deepen the reform of interest rate marketization, optimize the allocation of financial resources through interest rate price leverage, and achieve high-quality economic development in the future.

4.2.2 Monetary Policy Quantity Control and Price Control

4.2.2.1 Theory and International Experience on Monetary Policy Regulation and Control

According to the specific operation target or intermediate target, monetary policy can be divided into quantity control and price control. In theory, the quantity and price of money are two sides of the same coin. Under the liquidity effect, the change of money quantity will affect the price adjustment, and the adjustment of money price will cause a corresponding change in quantity (Friedman and Kuttner 2011). Therefore, under the condition of sound development of the financial market and effective exertion of the price mechanism, to achieve the ultimate goals of monetary policy, such as price output, the policy effect of quantity control and price control should be equivalent. However, from the perspective of policy mechanism, monetary quantity control is mainly based on the macro aggregate relationship between variables. The policy effect is direct and distinct, but it is easy to distort the price mechanism and intervene micro-subject behaviors. Monetary price control relies on the fact that the microeconomic subjects adjust their own behaviors according to the macroeconomic signals, and play an indirect role through the price mechanism, which requires a high degree of market development and monetary transmission mechanism. The policy chain is long and the effect is not clear. It can be seen that the development of the financial market and the transmission mechanism of monetary policy have a significant impact on the effectiveness of different monetary control modes, which directly determines the regulatory framework of monetary policy and its transformation process. In particular, the breadth and depth of financial market development is closely related to the price formation (interest rate level) of financial products and the risk management ability of market subjects, which affects the effectiveness of monetary transmission and interest rate regulation mechanism, and is crucial to the choice of a country's monetary regulation and control mode. From the international experience, we can see that developed economies with sound financial system and unobstructed interest rate transmission mechanism of monetary policy mainly adopt the price control mode based on interest rate, while the monetary policy of emerging developing economies is mainly based on quantity control (Zhou 2004; Laurens et al. 2015).

Since the 1970s, driven by the increasing trend toward interest rate marketization, financial innovation and financial disintermediation have developed rapidly, and the importance of monetary policy credit transmission channels has undergone a dramatic decrease (Bernanke and Gertler 1995). The central banks of various countries have to modify their monetary statistics multiple times, while also constantly modifying their monetary supply targets. The controllability and measurability of the monetary quantity as the intermediate target, and the correlation effect with the final target, are not ideal (Mishkin 2009). The practical effect of monetary quantitative targeting has proved far from expected, as Friedman himself admitted (Nelson 2007). In fact, before the 1970s, the monetary policy of many countries was based on interest rate regulation (Bindseil 2004). However, in the late 1960s, the discretionary monetary policy adopted under the guidance of traditional Keynesianism led to painful "stagflation." This severely damaged the function of the financial market and the stable development of the economy, forcing all countries to accept the concept of monetarism. At first, the monetary policy of developed economies was mainly regulated by interest rate, a fact closely related to the history of the banking industry, in which central banks originated from traditional commercial banks and were already operating monetary policy in relatively mature and perfect financial markets. Driven by the wave of deregulation of interest rates and financial innovation, the breadth and depth of financial markets in various countries have been further improved, and the policy effect of monetary quantity control based on the theoretical premise of the stable monetary aggregate relationship is naturally deteriorating. As Gerald Bouey, fourth Governor of the Central Bank of Canada, put it, "we never give up monetary aggregates, but they give up us" (Mishkin 1999). With the completion of the reform of interest rate marketization, since the mid-1980s the major developed countries have generally turned to the monetary price control based mainly on interest rate, adopting a monetary policy framework that takes stabilizing inflation as one of the most important objectives and regulates short-term (overnight) market interest rate only under the guidance of certain rules (implicitly following Taylor's rule) (Blanchard et al. 2010; Bindseil 2016).

Because the impact of the global financial crisis severely damaged the function of financial markets, central banks quickly reduced the policy interest rate to a very low level. Due to the lower limit of zero interest rate, countries have to turn to unconventional monetary policy, in the form of quantitative easing (Borio and Zabia 2016). At the same time, the global financial crisis shows that price stability does not mean economic and financial stability. In the aftermath of the crisis, countries have generally strengthened the central banks' macro-prudential and systemic risk prevention responsibilities. From 2001 to 2006, similar to the zero-interest-rate and the quantitative easing policy of the Bank of Japan, quantitative targeting is only the second operation target of the unconventional monetary policies of various countries. To restore the function of the financial market and stimulate economic recovery, maintaining an ultra-low (zero) interest rate is still the most important operation target of the central banks of various countries (Bindseil 2004, 2016). In recent years, with the gradual stabilizing of the financial market and the strong recovery of the economy, major central banks of the United States, the United Kingdom, and Europe have started or attempted to raise interest rates, to shrink the balance sheet, and return to the normalization process of interest rate regulation.

4.2.2.2 China's Indirect Monetary Policy: Transformation from Quantity Control to Price Control

China's monetary policy practice came into line with modern mainstream thinking only about 20 years ago. Prior to that, the quantity-based indirect monetary control mode was restricted by objective factors such as the degree of development of China's financial market, and the poor interest rate transmission mechanism of monetary policy. In addition, subjective factors such as policy inertia and decision preference meant that the planned economy was more inclined to quantity control (Zhou 2004). In the past two decades, China has withstood the test of two massive external shocks: the Asian financial crisis and the global financial crisis. According to the changing reality of different stages of economic and financial development, China has flexibly carried out monetary regulation and control and successfully coped with the severe challenges of deflation, sustained double surpluses and excess liquidity, and the change of financial regulatory environment after the economy entered the new normal. The quantity-based monetary policy regulation has played an important and positive role in achieving steady and rapid economic growth and maintaining the basic stability of prices.

I. The Shift from Direct Planning Management to Quantity-Based Indirect Regulation

After 1949, under the planned economy system, China managed its economic operation mainly through planning with human intervention. Even after the reform and opening up, for a long time China did not establish a modern market-oriented macro-regulatory framework (Zhou 2013), nor a financial industry in the modern sense. Banks were major financial institutions, which mainly performed the role of social cashiers to supervise the use of funds. In the early years of that period, China attempted to guide the allocation of credit resources through interest rate and price leverage, and to improve the efficiency of capital use through "loan instead of appropriation." However, the price and allocation of financial resources were still carried out mainly through planning. Under the "unified" management mode, even the restructured professional banks were equivalent to the branches of the PBC (Zhang 2011). From 1984, when the PBC was formally charged with exercising the functions of the central bank, it regulated monetary credit mainly through methods of direct control such as cash issuance and credit scale management. However, with the establishment of the socialist market economic system and the development of the financial system, in 1994 the PBC began to narrow the scope of credit scale management, and announced the supply of money at different levels. In 1996, it officially took money supply as an intermediate target and turned cash issuance into a monitoring index. At the same time, China also unified the scattered inter-bank lending market into the national inter-bank lending market, vigorously developed the inter-bank bond market, and recognized it as an essential place for open market operation. As the inter-bank market belongs to the inter-bank wholesale market and its risk is relatively low, China took the lead in deregulating inter-bank lending and bond market interest rates. In 1998, marked by the cancellation of credit scale management and the restart of RMB open market business, China's monetary policy officially realized the transformation from direct regulation to indirect regulation based on quantity (Zhang 2015).

II. Monetary Policy Regulation in the Period of Deflation and Excess Liquidity

After the cancellation of credit scale control in 1998, the open market operation became the PBC's most important normalized monetary regulation method. In the context of deflation at that time, the base currency was issued through reverse repo. In 2000, the PBC introduced the positive repo business to absorb market liquidity, aiming at the rapid growth of the base currency and foreign exchange accounts due to the establishment of asset management companies and the divestiture of non-performing loans of banks. In the second half of 2001, responding to the situation of deflation at that time, the PBC carried out the reverse repo and a large number of cash bond buyout businesses, and increased the base currency investment (Dai 2003).

Following China's accession to the WTO at the end of 2001, at least since the second half of 2002, China's economy has gradually shaken off the impact of the Asian financial crisis and deflation and entered a new round of the rising cycle. In addition to the short-term impact of the global financial crisis, China has been facing a situation of double surplus and excess liquidity in the balance of payments for nearly a decade. Due to the restriction on the scale of bond assets that can be held by the central bank, in April 2003 the PBC officially issued central bank bills as the most important means to hedge liquidity. As the balance of payments surplus and excess liquidity imbalance continue to worsen, China has started to raise the deposit reserve ratio at frequent intervals, thus meeting its responsibility to freeze liquidity in depth, building the deposit reserve ratio into a conventional liquidity management tool matched with central bank bills issuance, rapidly locking in long-term liquidity, and effectively reducing the monetary multiplier and monetary credit expansion. At the same time, the PBC has also optimized the structure and rhythm of credit supply through re-lending (rediscount) and window guidance. In this way, combined with the increase in benchmark interest rates for deposits and loans and the steady and gradual appreciation of the RMB, the bank has effectively responded to the challenges and problems brought about by the long-term double surplus, and has better achieved the ultimate goals of monetary policies such as output prices (Zhang 2011).

III. Monetary Policy Regulation under the New Normal and Changes in Liquidity Pattern

Following China's success in coping with the impact of the global financial crisis, with the changes in factor endowments and the international economic environment China's economy has gradually entered a new normal, and the pattern of foreign exchange appropriation and excess liquidity that have long plagued China has changed. In 2011, the current account surplus as a proportion of GDP dropped for the first time, and since then it has remained within the internationally recognized reasonable range of less than 4%. Cross border capital presents a two-way flow trend. In 2012, the capital and financial account (excluding reserve assets) showed a small deficit for the first time since 1999. After the second quarter of 2014, when the foreign exchange reserve reached a stage high of nearly 4 trillion US dollars, the capital and financial account kept a deficit until the fourth quarter of 2016. The exchange rate fluctuated in two directions and remained stable at the basic equilibrium level. The PBC gradually reduced, and once basically withdrew from, regular intervention in the foreign exchange market. In this regard, in 2012 the PBC stopped issuing central bank bills and restarted reverse repo operations. Since 2013, it has carried out innovations in short-term liquidity management tools, including SLO, SLF, MLF, and PSL, and has improved the medium- and long-term supply mechanism of the monetary base. It has promoted the deposit-loan ratio and reserve assessment, adjusted the re-lending classification system, improved the central bank collateral framework, and expanded the open market operation from twice a week to daily. In this way, it has effectively ensured the basic stability of market liquidity, enhanced the ability to guide market interest rates, and created a suitable monetary environment for stable and rapid development of economy and finance, basically stable price level, and economic restructuring and upgrading (Zhang 2017).

IV. The Urgency and Necessity of Interest Rate Marketization, Financial Innovation, and the Transformation of Monetary Price Control Modes

As the monetary policy has shifted toward indirect regulation, the PBC has actively developed the financial market and relaxed interest rate regulation. In doing so, it achieved the marketization of interest rate in the financial market around 2000, realized the spread management mode of upper deposit interest rate limit and lower loan interest rate limit in 2004, and steadily pushed forward the reform of interest rate marketization through a gradual double-track system featuring Pareto improvement (Yi 2009a). China has effectively promoted the development of the money market and the improvement of the risk-free yield curve with a complete term through the issuance of the central bank bills, creating favorable conditions for promoting interest rate marketization and interest rate regulation (Zhang 2011). In addition, the Shibor benchmark interest rate system was formally introduced in 2007, and the downward floating space of mortgage interest rates was expanded in October 2008. However, the process of interest rate marketization reform in China has been relatively slow since 2004 under the heavy regulatory pressure of coping with excess liquidity and the impact of the global financial crisis.

China's monetary policymakers have long realized that monetary quantity control and price control are an interactive process. Whether the monetary quantity is reasonable will directly affect the efficiency of price transmission, while severe price deviation from the equilibrium level will inevitably lead to quantity distortion (Zhou 2004). Therefore, while focusing on quantity control, China's monetary policy attaches great importance to the role of interest rate and price mechanism and pays careful attention to the balance between "quantity" and "price" (Zhang 2015). As China's economic development has entered the new normal, the liquidity and outstanding funds for foreign exchange, as the main channels of basic currency investment, have undergone fundamental changes, thus greatly enhancing the initiative of the central bank in regulating liquidity, and providing the necessary macro conditions for accelerating the marketization of interest rates and the transformation of monetary price control. With regard to the marketization of interest rates, in June 2012 China allowed the deposit interest rate to rise for the first time. In July 2013, the loan interest rate regulation was basically lifted. Finally, in October 2015, the deposit interest rate floating limit was released.

In line with theoretical analysis and international experience, with the acceleration and basic completion of interest rate marketization reform, the innovation and disintermediation of China's financial market are developing rapidly. The boundaries between different financial products and currencies at different levels are becoming increasingly blurred; the demand for currencies is becoming more and more unstable; the stability of the relationship between M2 and output prices is deteriorating steadily; the measurability, controllability, and correlation with the real economy of currencies are clearly declining, and the traditional quantity-based monetary regulation is unable to meet the needs of the current monetary policy (Yi 2018a). In fact, China has long been aware of the problem of the M2 intermediate target. It began to introduce the social financing scale flow indicator in 2011, published the stock social financing scale data in 2015, and explicitly took it as a policy target in 2016. Although the statistical scope of social financing scale is wider and can provide more information, non-credit financing is more vulnerable to economic fluctuations and expectations, financial innovation and derivative financing methods are more difficult to grasp in a timely and accurate manner, the central bank cannot effectively control direct financing behavior, and the stock social financing scale as the asset side of financial institutions should theoretically be similar to M2 as the liability side. Consequently, social financing scale should not replace M2 as the intermediate target of new quantitative monetary policies. It is in this context that China ceased the announcement of specific monetary quantity targets in 2018, and the urgency of transforming to a monetary price control mode is increasing day by day.

It should be noted that after more than 20 years of market-oriented financial reform and quantitative indirect monetary control, China has basically met the necessary conditions for the transition to a monetary price control mode. In terms of the financial market, China's fixed income market ranks third in the world (corporate credit and bonds of financial institutions rank second in the world), with considerable market breadth and the necessary market depth (Pan 2016). In terms of monetary policy transmission mechanism, the interest rate sensitivity of China's microeconomic subjects has been significantly enhanced, the interest rate pricing and risk management capabilities of financial institutions have been significantly improved, the relationship between financial market interest rates and deposit and loan interest rates has become closer, and the interest rate transmission channels are increasingly unblocked and effective (Kamber and Mohanty 2018). In terms of interest rate operation mode, the PBC has conducted a great deal of technical preparation and theoretical research on liquidity management and market interest rate guidance (Niu et al. 2017). China's open market operation and interest rate corridor arrangement are not much different from the mainstream modes of foreign central banks (Zhou 2013).

4.2.3 *Practical Difficulties and Challenges in the Transformation of China's Monetary Price Control*

Since the reform and opening up, from the planned commodity economy to the final formal establishment of the socialist market economy system, the mode of national management of the economy has gradually changed from planned human intervention to macro-control based on the total amount. Learning from international experience, and applying innovation based on national conditions, will enable China to coordinate the relationship between reform, development, and stability, and thus establish and perfect its financial macro-regulation system (Zhou 2011). However, we must also realize that, notwithstanding the accelerated and basic completion of interest rate marketization, the rapid development of financial innovation and disintermediation, the increasingly complex structure and products of financial markets, and the urgent need for monetary policy to be transformed into price control, China is the world's largest emerging economy in transition. The major contradictions and characteristics of macro-regulation change in accordance with different stages of economic and financial development. The focus of policies also changes, and the policy effects of various types of monetary regulation are clearly different. The monetary policy practice that lasted for more than 20 years has left many deep-seated contradictions and problems in China's economy and finance, and these continue to restrict the effective function of the financial market and the smooth and effective transmission mechanism of interest rates. The transformation of the monetary price control mode cannot be achieved overnight.

4.2.3.1 Government Focus on Economic Growth, Large Number of Soft Budget Constraint Departments, Central Bank Monetary Policy Easy to Loosen, but Difficult to Tighten

Before 1998, the PBC's monetary and credit regulation was under pressure from local government investment impulses. In 1984, when the PBC began formally to exercise the functions of the central bank, it implemented the internationally accepted reserve system. At this time, under the credit scale management mode, the focus of the reserve system was to allow the PBC to control a considerable amount of credit funds and make structural adjustments. The credit scale was mainly managed by regional and project credit plans (Zhou 1993). However, the assumption of the credit scale management system is based on the premise that sufficient funds can flow to the central bank only through excess reserves, and the central bank adjusts the credit scale between regions, which is more in line with the actual situation of underdeveloped financial markets in the 1980s. With the development of lending markets in various regions and the diversification of financial tools, it became increasingly difficult for the central bank to effectively allocate credit funds. Since regions with small deposits still had loan quotas, loan plans often did not match actual deposits, so the central bank had to make additional loans to ensure their normal operation. Higher statutory reserve requirements also increased the pressure on professional banks towards re-lending. Moreover, the transparency of credit policies was poor, and the branches of the PBC were subject to local government interference. Therefore, the management of the credit scale could not effectively restrain the credit impulse, and credit plans were often broken through, which buried hidden dangers of economic overheating. It was against this background that in the early 1990s, with the establishment of the socialist market economy system, the PBC began gradually to shift from direct credit management to indirect regulation. In 1993, it centralized the right of re-loan issuance from branches to the head office of the PBC. In 1994, it stopped overdraft and special loans. In 1997, it decided to set up branch organizations across administrative regions to avoid interference from local governments. Finally, in 1998, it completely cancelled the management of credit scale and adopted instead indirect monetary regulation with the amount of money supply as the intermediate target (Yi 2009b).

Since the reform and opening up, in order to mobilize the enthusiasm for local economic development, China has formed a GDP-oriented "championship" growth model (Zhou 2007). Local governments promote economic growth mainly through infrastructure construction and development of the heavy chemical industry. At the same time, since the implementation of the land system "bidding, auction, and listing" in 2004, the land income has been completely owned by the local government. Urbanization and real estate investment have become important ways to promote the local economy and increase fiscal revenue. Infrastructure construction and heavy chemical industry investment rely mainly on local government platforms and state-owned enterprises, while real estate has the soft constraint feature of "too big to fail." Due to the government's excessive focus on economic growth, there are very many soft budget constraint departments in China, such as local financing platforms, state-owned enterprises, and real estate enterprises, which have strong internal driving forces for debt expansion to stimulate the economy (Ji et al. 2017). The overheating of the economy and the failure of credit scale management in the mid-1990s were closely related to local over-investment, which forced re-lending.

Since the second half of 2002, China's international balance of payments has maintained a large-scale double surplus. In order to ensure stable economic development, China should moderately reduce domestic investment. However, under the "championship" model, investment impulses in various regions cannot be effectively suppressed, which further aggravates the economic overheating and credit expansion in periods of excess liquidity, making monetary policies easier to loosen and more difficult to tighten. In fact, China has long recognized the disadvantages of the traditional growth model. At the end of 2006, the central government put forward the concept of "sound and fast" economic development. Having only recently escaped the shadow of deflation and SARS, the PBC emphasized the risk of excessive credit growth and strengthened real estate credit management. While moderately tightening and stabilizing monetary control through open market operations and reserve funds, the PBC was also proactively exploring macro-prudential policy measures. In 2004, the PBC implemented different deposit reserve systems for institutions with different asset quality and risk status; in 2005, it moderately increased the down payment ratio of different types of houses; in 2007, it launched the directional issuance of central bank bills with incentive compatibility.

Nevertheless, faced with the huge impact of the global financial crisis that broke out in 2008, China introduced a large-scale stimulus policy, and monetary policy shifted toward moderate easing. It should be noted that the necessary stimulus policies after the crisis have played an important role in stabilizing the financial market and promoting economic recovery. However, under the guidance of economic growth and the traditional growth mode, the means of stimulus policies are excessively adjusted, which makes it difficult to exit effectively, and aggravates the excess liquidity and overheating of the economy. Indeed, the PBC noticed the signs of excessive economic stimulus as early as the middle of 2009. Through the "dynamic fine tuning" of open market operation, it successively raised reserves and benchmark interest rates and gradually withdrew from the moderate easing policy in 2010. However, under the guidance of GDP growth targets and pressure from soft budget departments, credit demand remained robust. In particular, although the economy began gradually to enter a new normal from 2011, there was still a strong new round of stimulus expectations in the market. In order to break the expectations of easing policies of all parties, in the second quarter of 2013 the PBC reissued central bills and continued to carry out some expired 3-year central bills, actively communicated with the market, and successfully resolved the currency market fluctuations through open market operations and innovative policy tools.

Although China's potential output growth has tended to decline since the economy entered the new normal, in order to meet the policy needs of local government bond swap and to promote the development of weak links in the national economy, in 2014 the PBC created Pledged Supplementary Lending (PSL) to guide the reduction of financial market interest rates and loan interest rates through two targeted rate cuts and one interest rate cut. As the benefits of state-owned enterprises such as local government financing platforms and the real estate market have clearly declined, China has long been worried about deflation (Zhang 2015), and there is an expectation that all local policies will be significantly relaxed. Moreover, although China began to strengthen local government debt management in 2014, local governments have used PPP, industrial funds, government purchases, and other means to carry out a large number of hidden debts. In 2015 China experienced a stock market crash, and market fluctuations further exacerbated the worries of all parties about the economy. It was against this background that the PBC had to carry out five targeted rate reductions and five general rate reductions from 2015 to the first quarter of 2016. Moreover, in order to push forward the interest rate marketization reform and expand the floating range of deposit interest rates, the PBC has lowered the benchmark interest rate for deposit and loan on five consecutive occasions.

It should be noted that the optimization and adjustment of the economic structure and high-quality development require that monetary policy should remain stable and neutral, with no flooding of the traditional growth mode that relies on monetary and credit input. However, the interest rate policy is a macro monetary measure that reflects the price of capital. It cannot adjust structural problems effectively, and does not fully meet the needs of economic restructuring and upgrading. In particular, due to the rapid rise of hidden debts of local governments, the IMF (2017) calculate that in 2016 the leverage ratio of China's broad-based government departments considering hidden debts of local governments was 62.2%, which exceeded the European Union's warning line standard. Zombie enterprises and inefficient investment projects occupied a large proportion of financial resources, and the structural contradictions concealed by aggregation problems were even more prominent. The space of monetary policy is very limited, and the reserve ratio is its "sharp weapon," with a strong balance sheet effect and signal significance. In the situation that the downward potential growth trend and the economic cyclical decline interweave and overlap, a substantial reduction in the reserve requirement releases a strong signal of policy easing, which is obviously inconsistent with the stable and neutral tone of monetary policy. Therefore, the PBC compensates for the shortage of market liquidity mainly through reverse repo business, SLF, and MLF, and keeps the required deposit reserve ratio at a relatively high level. In particular, with the deepening of structural reforms on the supply side since the end of 2015, the PBC has insisted on holding the general gate of money supply, instead of making a general and directional lowering of the standard, only making a targeted reduction in January 2018 in line with the development of inclusive finance.

In addition, the soft budget constraint departments have squeezed out efficient private enterprise financing, due to the implicit guarantors' easier access to formal financial credit support, in order to reduce the credit premium (Ji et al. 2016). Although theoretically there is a "hard" budget constraint for any soft budget constraint problem, which can be made up by reasonable pricing (Luo and Hengfu 2014), if the price mechanism is completely relied on, the formal financing interest rate must rise to a level high enough to make up for the risk premium, which will push up the informal financing cost. Consequently, efficient private enterprises will face more severe financing constraints, which is not favorable to the stability of economic growth or the optimal allocation of resources (Ji et al. 2016). Therefore, after the floating restrictions on deposit and loan interest rates were lifted, China did not immediately turn to interest rate price control, but continued to control the excessive growth of debt and leverage ratio through quantitative methods such as reserve fund and broad credit.

4.2.3.2 Mishandling of the Relationship Between Supervision and the Central Bank, and Failure to Separate the Functions of Supervision and Industry Development

Before 1997, although China had a competent department in charge of the financial industry, there was no financial supervision in the modern sense. While the branches of the central bank were responsible for financial management, they were obviously constrained and restrained by local governments, and unable to focus on financial risks. In fact, the financial industry was in a state of mixed operation. Banks could directly issue loans to stock market participants, while speculation in the stock market was rampant and volatile. At the same time, the triangular debts of state-owned enterprises had seriously interfered with the normal financial order. Banks were forced to carry out a large number of high-yield speculative businesses in order to absorb the policy burdens in the manner of loans rather than appropriation. Around the country there was indiscriminate fund-raising, while the setting up of financial institutions and handling of financial businesses spread rapidly, severely interfering with the normal economic and financial order. In response to this, in July 1993 China began to carry out macro-regulation and rectification of the overheated economy. At the end of 1993, the Third Plenary Session of the 14th Chinese government Central Committee formally proposed the establishment of policy banks, turning professional banks into real commercial banks and implementing asset-liability ratio management. Modern financial supervision gradually took shape and was continuously strengthened. In particular, the 1995 Law of the People's Bank of China and Law of Commercial Banks clearly stipulate in legal form that the central bank is not allowed to overdraw funds and commercial banks are subject to proportional management. In 1996, China formally joined the Bank for International Settlements and promised to abide by the Basel Accord. The Asian financial crisis in 1997 made all parties attach great importance to financial risks. During this period, China successively set up special securities and insurance regulatory agencies, and the PBC was no longer responsible for the supervision of these industries. At the same time, in response to the abnormal overheating of the stock market caused by the illegal entry of a large amount of bank funds in 1996, the central government explicitly requested banks to withdraw all funds from the exchange market. Finally, the first national financial work conference, held at the end of 1997, formally established a modern financial supervision system with separate financial operations and separate supervision, which provided the necessary institutional guarantee to resolve the impulse of re-lending and to shift to indirect monetary regulation mainly based on quantity.

During the deflation period from 1998 to 2002, the PBC issued a large number of refinancing loans. The state also issued special treasury bonds to supplement the capital of state-owned banks and set up asset management companies to strip off non-performing loans. However, due to a large number of problems accumulated over a long period of time, excessive lending in the early stage, and weak risk awareness, the scale of non-performing assets in China's banking system was very large and capital adequacy was seriously insufficient. Some overseas institutions even pointed out that state-owned banks were close to the brink of technical bankruptcy. Banks were extremely reluctant to lend and the function of financial credit media was almost completely lost, which further aggravated deflation. It was not until the second half of 2002, after China had joined the WTO at the end of 2001 and fully integrated into the global division of labor, that China began to emerge from deflation and its economy began a strong upward trajectory.

In 2003, China separated the bank supervision function from the central bank, thus forming a "one bank, three committees" financial management pattern. However, the relationship between financial supervision and industry development has not been straightened out, and regulatory policies have always been inclined to the development of its own industry. In 2003, the PBC focused on the "online repair" of the financial system, carried out the reform of state-owned commercial banks with corporate governance as the core through the injection of foreign exchange reserves, and promoted the reform of rural credit cooperatives through the exchange of central bank bills by incentive compatibility. However, with the gradual digestion of the historical burden of financial institutions and the clear improvement in operating performance after the reform, the regulatory authorities gradually deviated from the prudent supervision of institutions and paid more attention to the development of its own industry. In particular, after the global financial crisis in 2008, the regulatory authorities placed more emphasis on finance to promote economic recovery, but failed to regulate bank credit supply effectively. In 2010, the growth rate of monetary credit greatly exceeded the target set at the beginning of the year. In response to this, in early 2011 the PBC introduced a dynamic adjustment mechanism for differential reserves, to monitor the scale of non-government financing and try to control the excessive growth of bank credit on balance sheets. However, due to the consideration of industry development and departmental interests, the regulatory authorities were still proactively encouraging financial innovation in order to avoid restrictions on reserves and credit scale. Furthermore, securities and insurance regulatory authorities were competing to relax regulatory requirements. As a result, financial innovation and shadow banking for credit scale regulation were developing rapidly. According to the Financial Stability Board (FSB), the proportion of China's shadow banking assets in GDP rose rapidly from 20% in 2011 to 31.2% in 2013, far faster than the monetary and credit growth over the same period.

Moreover, since 2014, the development of China's shadow banking has shown a trend of structuration and complication. Under the concept of industry development, the regulatory authorities did not pay attention to the overall systemic risk, and even reduced the regulatory standards for the development of the industry, resulting in "regulatory competition," regulatory arbitrage, and regulatory blank coexist. Consequently, the shadow banking structure became more complex, and the risk concentration more severe. In 2015, owing to the weak supervision of over-the-counter capital allocation and other violations, and the sharp fluctuation of the capital market, the PBC had to maintain the stability of the capital market by re-lending, and to stabilize the economic development by reducing the standard and interest rates. With the economic downturn and the gradual exposure of non-performing assets, banks had to increase the risk capital occupation and loan loss reserve. The "double drop" of non-performing loans was once an important goal of the regulatory authorities. For this reason, the regulatory authorities further encouraged innovation. Various micro-regulatory authorities lowered regulatory standards and formed a large number of regulatory vacuums. Shadow banking supervision was seriously insufficient. In particular, with the basic completion of interest rate marketization, bank indebted competition became increasingly fierce, and from 2014 financial disintermediation increased significantly (Li and Naifang 2017). In terms of capital sources, banks and non-bank institutions nest through inter-bank business, financial management, and so on, which makes the liability side extremely complex and aggravates the liquidity risk. In terms of asset utilization, the regulatory standards and risk weights of off-balance-sheet businesses such as asset management and inter-bank are relatively low, and the bank's actual capital and loan loss provisions are seriously insufficient. From 2014 to 2016, the credit scale of structured shadow banks increased rapidly, and evading supervision and regulatory arbitrage became an important driving factor (Ehlers et al. 2018).

As the multi-level nesting made financial transactions more complicated, the price of market products could not truly reflect the real credit risk premium, and the effect of interest rate transmission and interest rate regulation was greatly reduced. In the absence of necessary regulatory functions and good regulatory coordination, in order to control the credit expansion and financial risks of shadow banks, the PBC further strengthened its macro-prudential policy, upgraded the dynamic management of deposit reserve to macro-prudential policy assessment (MPA) in early 2016, and conducted countercyclical regulation on the broad credit scale, forming a "monetary policy + macro-prudential" two-pillar financial regulatory policy framework. In early 2017 and early 2018, off-balance-sheet financial management of banks and inter-bank certificates of deposit issued by banks with assets of more than 500 billion were included in the MPA assessment, further improving the macro-prudential policy system. The organic combination of monetary policy and macro-prudential policy not only creates a neutral and moderate monetary and financial environment for supply-side structural reform, but also prevents systemic financial risks and effectively maintains the stability of the financial system.

4.2.3.3 Factors Restricting the Pricing and Risk Management Capabilities of Financial Institutions, and the Transmission Efficiency of Interest Rate Policies

Before the 1990s, there was not a complete and unified financial market in China. With the recovery development of the banking system, the financial market also gradually developed, region by region. Since the mid-1980s, inter-bank lending markets set up in various regions of China to adjust the banks' capital surplus have played an important role in enriching the variety of transactions and improving the banks' efficiency. With the development of economy and finance, these inter-bank lending markets became more and more closely linked, and capital transactions became increasingly active. However, the situation varied greatly across different regions, and the degree of management was not consistent. Indeed, in the early 1990s scattered inter-bank lending markets became an important factor in the "triple chaos" of finance, short-term deposition, and long-term lending. For this reason, in early 1996 the PBC integrated the regional capital markets into a unified inter-bank lending market, effectively promoting the standardized development of the market and laying a good market foundation for the liberalization of inter-bank lending rate control and the opening of interest rate marketization reform that took place in July 1996. In the same year, while announcing that the money supply was the intermediate target, the PBC also began to try to conduct open market operations in the exchange bond market.

However, in February 1995, the "327 treasury bond futures" event had broken out, a result of deregulation and the serious lag of risk control compared with the expansion of market trading. The development of the exchange bond market almost stagnated, and a large amount of banks' funds in the exchange flowed illegally into the stock market, causing it to become extremely hot. Due to the limitation of the variety and quantity of bonds in the exchange market, after trying several transactions with a total amount of more than 2 billion yuan, the central bank had to stop the open market operation in 1996. Therefore, in 1997, the PBC established an over-the-counter inter-bank bond market based on the development experience of the international bond market, providing the necessary operation platform and solid market foundation for the open market operation (Dai 2003). Because of the restriction on the amount and scale of treasury bonds issued by the central bank at that time, when China resumed open market operations in 1998, it expanded its business to high-grade government-supported bonds such as policy-related financial bonds. While promoting the development of this kind of bond market, it also realized the marketization of bond market issuance and transaction interest rates.

As China faced excess liquidity from the second half of 2002, and especially after the reform of the exchange rate formation mechanism in 2005, the pressure of double balance of payments surplus further increased, and the central bank needed sufficient bond assets for liquidity hedging operations. However, as the finance department only considered its own financing needs in issuing treasury bonds, the term of those bonds was too long, the amount was too small, and the issuance was irregular; the breadth and depth of the treasury bond market could not meet the transaction needs of the central bank and financial institutions, so the central bank had to hedge its liquidity by issuing central bills. In view of the market development restriction caused by the strict control of corporate credit bonds by the National Development and Reform Commission and the Securities and Futures Commission, the PBC introduced short-term financing bonds and medium-term bills markets in 2005 and 2008 respectively. In 2007, an inter-bank market transaction consultation association was established to promote the standardized development of the bond market through market self-discipline, and to implement a registration system for the issuance of corporate debt financing tools. After the global financial crisis, drawing on international experience, the Shanghai Clearing House was established in 2009; this is now regarded as the central counterparty, further standardizing the development of the bond market.

The development of the inter-bank market has effectively pushed the relevant departments to loosen the over-strict market control, and in a very short time the size of China's bond market has risen to third place in the world. The inter-bank bond market has developed rapidly and has become the main body of China's bond market. It has played an important role in promoting interest rate marketization and unblocking the interest rate transmission mechanism. However, there are still problems in China's financial market, such as insufficient market segmentation and depth, which have impeded the effective formation of market interest rates and smooth transmission of monetary policies. The specific manifestations are as follows.

First, China's money market and bond market are still artificially divided. China's money market and bond market have always been separate, as the inter-bank and exchange markets respectively. Due to the obvious differences in market access and regulation between the two markets, the market price is clearly differentiated, which further encourages regulatory arbitrage in the market. In particular, the exchange market has a high credit risk premium, and the interest rate level and fluctuation are significantly higher than those in the inter-bank market, which interferes with market expectations and liquidity management by the central bank. For example, in recent years, the PBC has effectively guided the level of pledged repo interest rates of deposit-based financial institutions through the reverse repo, SLF, MLF, and other tools. In May 2017, it introduced the inter-bank fixing repo rate (FDR) and interest rate swap products with 7-day inter-bank fixing repo rate (FDR007) as reference interest rates. However, since the end of 2016, the prices of deposit-based financial institutions' pledged repo interest rates (such as DR001 and DR007) and all inter-bank market pledged repo interest rates (R001 and R007) have diverged, a phenomenon that also reflects the further intensification of market segmentation of different types of financial institutions due to the expansion of shadow banks and the concentration of financial risks.

Second, there are still strict access restrictions for financial market transactions, and the development of the interest rate derivatives market lags behind. Since the launch of the inter-bank bond market in 1997, the PBC has recognized the importance of the market transaction scale and variety, and of the derivatives market, to the formation of the market yield curve and the indirect monetary regulation, and has vigorously promoted the development of market participants, products, and derivatives innovation. However, access restrictions imposed by the micro-regulatory authorities are still too strict for financial entities to participate in the derivatives market. The derivatives market continues to be dominated by transaction types, and the development of financial products for price discovery and risk management lags behind. Internationally, the interest rate derivatives market, as the main means of risk management, has developed rapidly since the 1970s, with derivatives trading volume far exceeding the scale of basic assets. According to BIS statistics, in the first half of 2017 the transaction volume of interest rate derivatives for US dollar and Japanese yen bonds was US$ 156.2 trillion and US$ 40.8 trillion, respectively, equivalent to about 3.5 times the underlying assets of bonds. In 2017, China's interest rate derivative transactions reached a record high of 14.4 trillion yuan; however, this was still less than 20% of the total underlying assets of the bond market, and the depth of the market also requires improvement.

Third, the development of financial market products needs to be further enriched and improved. At present, pledge repo is the most important type in China's money market. The credit-based outright repo and market share of inter-bank lending are shrinking day by day. However, pledge repo requires the freezing of bond liquidity. Moreover, banks (especially large commercial banks) are the main source of market funds, and the exchange rate of bonds is low, which is not conducive to the discovery of bond market prices. Securitization of credit assets is an important way to effectively unblock the transmission of interest rates in financial markets and deposit and loan markets. Asset securitization, which was officially launched in 2005, was suspended due to the global financial crisis. After it was restarted in 2012, it was mainly based on corporate-credit-asset-backed securities, rather than internationally accepted mortgage or consumer credit. Consequently, the product information asymmetry became even more serious. The difficulty of estimating the default probability of products accurately, and of pricing them reasonably, was not conducive to the healthy and deepening development of the market (Xu 2015).

Fourth, due to the lack of pricing and risk management capabilities of financial institutions, there is still a dual system of interest rates. This is because the depth of the financial market is relatively limited, and the pricing and risk management capabilities of financial institutions are still insufficient. After easing the floating restrictions on deposit and loan interest rates, China continued to announce the benchmark deposit and loan interest rate as a transitional measure. Since banks in China have long relied on the deposit and loan benchmark interest rate for deposit and loan pricing and interest rate management, the retention of the deposit and loan benchmark interest rate is equivalent to a de facto two-track interest rate system (Yi 2018b). This will affect the transmission efficiency of the market interest rate to the deposit and loan interest rate and reduce the effectiveness of monetary price control.

4.2.3.4 Factors Affecting the Policy Autonomy of Interest Rate Regulation

The interest rate and exchange rate are the internal price and external price of money, respectively. Flexible adjustment of the exchange rate can effectively buffer external shocks and realize the final goals, such as output price. As a big country, China's monetary policy should focus on internal balance, such as output and prices, rather than external balance, and the external target of money should also obey the internal target. China's monetary policy adopts an intermediate arrangement of the limited opening of capital projects, managed floating of the exchange rate, and a certain degree of independence of currency, which ensures stable economic development in general. It is also an important experience of China's sound monetary policy (Xu 2017). However, with the deepening development of the financial market, the arrangement of the intermediate solution will become more and more unstable, and the corner solution will become the only stable arrangement (Yi and Xian 2001). As an economic safety valve and stabilizer, the flexible market exchange rate is an important condition for interest rate marketization and independent monetary policy (Yi 2013).

After the reform and opening up, in line with the reform of the financial foreign trade system, China implemented a foreign exchange retention system and established a foreign exchange adjustment market, and implemented the exchange rate dual-track system in which the official exchange rate and the foreign exchange adjustment market exchange rate coexist. In 1994 and 1996, China completed the exchange rate integration and current account opening, while the market-based managed floating exchange rate system and capital account opening were set as further reform goals. The Asian financial crisis in 1997 and the global financial crisis in 2008 delayed the pace of financial opening up (Zhou 2015). Nevertheless, since the launch of the reform of the RMB exchange rate formation mechanism in July 2005, China has continued to adhere to that reform, except for a period of short-term narrowing of fluctuations after the global financial crisis in 2008. In June 2010, China expanded the floating space of the RMB exchange rate further, and since then the floating space of RMB middle price has gradually expanded from 0.3 to 2%. In August 2015, China carried out the reform of the middle price formation mechanism of "closing rate + exchange rate of a basket of currencies."

Due to the sharp fluctuations in the stock market and other reasons, the growth of China's monetary base has been too fast since the second quarter of 2015. Coupled with the expectation of an increase in US interest rates, this has led to huge depreciation and capital outflow pressure. Therefore, at the end of 2015, China began to incorporate cross-border capital flows into the scope of macro-prudential policy, and in May 2017, the "countercyclical factor" was introduced into the middle price quotation model to reflect the macro fundamentals. With the improvement of the exchange rate and cross-border capital flow, the current relevant countercyclical adjustment policies have gradually returned to neutral. In September 2017, the collection proportion of foreign exchange risk reserve was reduced to zero, and in January 2018, the countercyclical factor of the middle price was adjusted to neutral.

Although the floating range of the RMB exchange rate rarely limits the level of the market-oriented exchange rate, expanding the former is still a signal to speed up the reform of the latter. In the long run, the RMB exchange rate is completely determined by market supply and demand and fluctuates cleanly, which has always been the goal of China's financial reform (Yi 2016). However, the breadth and depth of China's foreign exchange market are relatively limited, which to some extent also affects the formation of a reasonable and balanced exchange rate and the clean float (Guan 2018). Since the reform of the exchange rate formation mechanism in 2005, the PBC has done much work in expanding the participants and market variety of the foreign exchange market, and developing the foreign exchange derivatives market. It has successively introduced basic RMB foreign exchange derivatives such as forwards, swaps, currency swaps, and options. However, according to the requirement that finance must serve the real economy, China has always stressed the principle of real demand for RMB foreign exchange derivatives transactions, and all foreign exchange transactions must have a real and compliant trade or investment and financing background. There are still many restrictions on cross-border capital flows, and the direction of the net position of foreign exchange demand of enterprises does not change much under the condition of continuous current account surplus. Under the principle of real demand, banks only trade foreign exchange derivatives according to the foreign exchange trading positions of enterprises, and banks are risk-averse. The trading direction of the foreign exchange market, according to the foreign exchange demand of enterprises, is basically the same, which is not conducive to the discovery of foreign exchange prices. Judging from the experience of mature markets, if there is no moderate speculation, it is easy to affect the function of the foreign exchange market. The reason why offshore RMB forward (i.e., NDF) without principal delivery can be cleared at any time is that the market participants have both hedging and speculation, so the market has enough liquidity. Due to the limitation of the principle of real demand, the breadth and depth of the domestic foreign exchange market are still limited. According to BIS statistics, in April 2016 the onshore market accounted for only 36% of the global RMB daily average trading volume in the global RMB foreign exchange market, of which the onshore RMB daily average trading volume of spot and derivatives accounted for 43.6% and 32.3% respectively.

4.2.4 The Transformation of China's Monetary Price Control in the Stage of High-Quality Economic Development

Since 1984, when the PBC began formally to exercise its duties as the central bank, through unremitting efforts and exploration, China has gradually realized the first major transformation of its monetary policy regulatory framework, shifting from direct credit control to quantitative indirect monetary regulation. The degree of marketization of financial macro-regulation, and the role of the market in the allocation of financial resources, have gradually and continuously increased. Over nearly 20 years of effort the price of financial factors has gradually been liberalized, and with cancellation of the control of the deposit interest rate ceiling, the marketization of interest rates has been basically completed.

With the rapid development of financial innovation, and the increasing complexity of financial markets, the current monetary policy regulatory framework is facing the second major transformation, from quantity-based to price-based. The transition of the economy from high-speed growth to high-quality development is also a process of transformation and upgrading of China's resource allocation mode. This has changed from the artificial complement of the economic short board by quantitative means, to the promotion of the quality and efficiency of the economy through the marketization of the price mechanism. In 2018, China no longer set specific quantitative targets for M2 and social financing scale, but took it as an important monetary monitoring target, which also reflects the new changes in high-quality development requirements. However, due to the constraints of various factors, after the basic liberalization of interest rate control, China does not have the conditions to turn immediately to monetary price control.

The key to the "formation and adjustment" of interest rate is to deepen the development of the financial market system. Only a financial market with sufficient breadth and depth can form a reasonable interest rate level and smooth the interest rate transmission mechanism. It should be noted that although it is both necessary and arduous to strengthen governance and reorganization and institutional reform, for China the key and difficult issues are how to develop a financial market with a solid micro-foundation, unified market rules, and sound and effective functions; to truly let the market play a decisive role in the allocation of financial resources through the price mechanism; and to better play the role of the government through the marketization of price leverage. The question of how to deepen the market development and regulate the market operation in a market-oriented way has been a constant topic throughout the 40 years of reform and opening up, across different historical periods of economic development and macro-regulation. This challenge must also be addressed in the high-quality economic development stage. If it is not, then we will never escape from the vicious circle of "release causes chaos; constriction leads to death," or from the black-or-white problem between the market and the government.

4.2.4.1 Deepening the Development of Financial Markets and Improving the Formation Mechanism of Market-Oriented Interest Rates

It should be pointed out that the term "financial market" refers not only to a specific financial product market and its combination, but to a financial market system composed of financial market micro-subjects, financial system, and financial products. Deepening the development of the financial market should include at least three aspects, namely the micro-foundation, guarantee, and product system. In the process of transforming to a price control mode, the monetary policy must tackle the government's overemphasis on growth targets and soft budget constraints, financial market risks, deepening of financial functions, and reform of exchange rate formation mechanism, which are the concrete manifestations of development of the abovementioned three aspects.

The micro-foundation of the financial market comprises financial demand and financial supply. With regard to financial demand, the overemphasis on economic growth and the existence of soft budget constraint departments such as state-owned enterprises have led to excess demand for capital. The issuance of debt or loan financing through implicit guarantee does not depend on their own capital and how much money they have. In fact, the development of equity and of debt are not separated, and efficiency cannot be increased without capital constraint. Therefore, only when the government weakens the target of economic growth, exhibits financing behavior according to the principle of risk capital restriction and risk income matching under good corporate governance, and strengthens budget restriction, can the financing demand of market micro-subjects be more rational. Then, the monetary policy will no longer be under the pressure of forced expansion, and the market interest rate level can return to a reasonable level. The reform process of exchange rate formation mechanism is relatively slow, a phenomenon that is closely related to the traditional growth mode relying on foreign trade. With regard to financial supply, regulatory policies that pay too much attention to the development of the industry create a situation in which rigid payment is difficult to break and interest rate pricing cannot reflect the real credit premium. In that case, financial institutions pay more attention to scale expansion than to elaborate product management for diversified market demands. Only by comprehensively weighing risks and benefits, and providing diversified financial services around the market demand for capital, can financial institutions truly support the development of the real economy at a more reasonable price, and can monetary policy guide the behavior of financial institutions through the interest rate policy price mechanism, and realize the effective allocation of financial resources.

Turning now to the financial market system guarantee, because of the imperfect financial supervision system, the supervision departments do not really prevent risks according to financial functions and behaviors. More and more financial innovations are made to avoid regulation and regulatory arbitrage. While multiple levels of financial products increase financial risks, the interest rate level is superimposed with more unreasonable system costs rather than normal risk premiums, thus greatly reducing the efficiency of monetary policy interest rate transmission and policy effect.

Finally, regarding the development of the financial product market, while China currently has sufficient scale and breadth of financial market, the depth of financial market development is not yet sufficient, and the product function requires further improvement. Due to the defects of the financial system and the substitution of institutional access for product market development, a large number of so-called market innovations are more the products of regulatory competition and regulatory capture, while the truly market-oriented financial products (especially derivatives) with full price discovery and risk diversification functions are not abundant, and the interest rate pricing level and risk management ability of micro-finance subjects have never been truly tested by the market. Under a dual-track system of interest rates, which the benchmark interest rate for deposits and loans is still announced, the pricing of financial market products is mostly based on fixed interest rates. In the future, we should vigorously cultivate and improve the benchmark interest rate system of the financial market, represented by Shibor and treasury bond yields; provide a solid and reliable pricing basis for floating interest rate products; effectively enhance the pricing and risk management capabilities of financial institutions; and promote the deepening development of the financial market. The limited depth of the foreign exchange market (especially the foreign exchange derivatives market) is also closely related to excessively strict market control.

4.2.4.2 Deepening the Development of Financial Markets and Smoothing the Transmission Mechanism of Monetary Policy Interest Rates

Given the problems and challenges in China's financial market, such as the micro-subject of capital supply and demand, the financial supervision system, and the development of the financial product market, monetary policy has to rely on quantitative control measures while strengthening macro-prudential policies to ensure the stability of the financial system and the stable development of output prices. However, it should also be recognized that excessive reliance on quantity control will reduce the transmission efficiency of interest rates and the regulatory effect of monetary policies (Ma and Honglin 2014). Excessive reliance on structural policies is easy to exchange for price mechanisms, reducing the efficiency of financial resource allocation and the effectiveness of monetary policies (Yi 2006). Moreover, under the traditional monetary quantity control mode, the frequency of monetary quantity signals is relatively low, and the relevant chains of economic situation analysis, policy formulation, and policy operation are relatively long. In contrast, as financial market shocks disturb liquidity and interest rates more frequently, and monetary price control is more closely related to financial markets, this also requires that monetary policies should be adjusted in a timely manner according to changes in the financial markets; moreover, there is an urgent need to improve the central bank's interest rate decision-making space and policy operation autonomy, and to provide them with institutional guarantees. In order to meet the policy requirements of high-quality economic development, China must vigorously deepen the development of financial markets and accelerate the transformation of the monetary price control mode.

In the stage of high-quality economic development, the current reform measures in China can gradually alleviate various constraints and problems in the financial market, which is conducive to the transformation of monetary policy price control mode. With regard to the micro-basis of the financial market, based on regulating the financing behavior of local governments and the new Budget Law, since 2017 China has strengthened the governance and rectification of hidden debts of local governments; it has stressed the necessity of establishing a correct concept of political achievements, of weakening the orientation of local GDP assessment, and of strictly controlling the increase of local government debts, holding them accountable for life, checking the responsibility backward, and properly reinforcing budget constraints. At the same time, we should take the deleveraging of state-owned enterprises as the top priority, and do a good job in dealing with zombie enterprises. By putting the central and local financial and tax systems in order and deepening the corporate governance reform of state-owned enterprises, the budget constraints of China's micro-subject will be properly hardened, which is conducive to breaking the problem of rigid payment.

With regard to financial supervision reform, since 2017 China has strengthened its financial supervision, adopted the principle of penetration, strengthened supervision cooperation, and filled the supervision gap. As various supervision measures are gradually put in place, a large number of off-balance-sheet businesses will return to the on-balance sheet. While financial market risks are effectively mitigated, bank capital adequacy and reserves will face obvious constraints. China should also moderately reduce the statutory reserve requirements to reduce the reserve tax burden on financial institutions, and smooth the interest rate transmission mechanism. Of course, as China is still a developing country, it is inevitable that it will have to maintain a relatively high deposit reserve ratio for a long time.

In terms of the development of the financial product market, following further clarification regarding the main responsibility of financial supervision, the central bank will coordinate the development plan of the financial industry, the draft of important laws and regulations, and the basic system of prudent supervision, all of which will be conducive to the deepening development of the function of the financial market. In the future, according to the unified rules of market functions, we should adequately deregulate the unreasonable financial business; encourage financial innovation with the main purpose of trading technology and risk management ability; truly improve the pricing ability and risk management of financial institutions' products, thus creating the conditions to realize the integration of market interest rate and deposit and loan interest rate; clarify the short-term (overnight) policy target interest rate; and realize the transformation of monetary price control mode with the interest rate as the core.

Finally, with regard to the reform of the exchange rate formation mechanism, we should speed up and deepen the reform, and in future should deepen the development of the foreign exchange market. China should proceed according to the actual needs of economic and financial openness for a major country. Monetary policy should focus on domestic equilibrium and internal output price targets. It should speed up the reform of the market-oriented exchange rate formation mechanism; expand the flexibility and improve the tolerance of exchange rate fluctuations; truly play the role of the external economic stabilizer of the exchange rate; effectively improve the autonomy, effectiveness, and macroeconomic resilience of monetary policy; and create favorable external financial conditions for the transformation of monetary price control with the interest rate as the core.

4.2.5 *Accelerating the Transformation of Monetary Policy Regulation from Quantity to Price*

Theoretically, under the conditions of sound financial market development and sufficient and effective price mechanism, the policy effects of monetary policy quantity control and price control are equivalent. However, economic and financial realities have an important impact on the balance of "quantity" and "price" of money. The choice of a country's monetary regulation mode is closely related to its financial market development and monetary policy transmission mechanism. According to the practical experience of monetary policy regulation in developed economies, countries have generally experienced a cyclical process from the interest rate to quantity, and then back to the interest rate. The central banks of those countries started monetary policy operation in relatively mature and perfect financial market conditions. Although the monetarist experiment of monetary quantity targeting was only a fleeting phase in the more than 100 years of monetary policy practice of modern central banks, the transition process of monetary policy regulatory framework in developed economies shows that the choice of a country's monetary policy regulatory mode is closely related to its different stages of economic and financial development. In a situation where "stagflation" has severely damaged the function of financial markets, and the economy is mired in crisis, countries have to shift from interest rate regulation to a monetary quantity targeting system. Conversely, under the pressure of high inflation, countries have to release interest rate regulation. Financial innovations and the deepening development of financial markets have made the policy effect of monetary quantity control steadily worse. In terms of measurability, controllability, and correlation with the ultimate goal, interest rate-based monetary price control is obviously better than quantity control. Only then do countries return to interest rate regulation under certain rules. After the global financial crisis, the huge impact on financial markets and the constraint of zero interest rate lower limit forced countries to shift to unconventional quantity control such as quantitative easing. In recent years, with the gradual stabilizing of the financial market and the strong recovery of the economy, the smooth return to interest rate regulation and the gradual normalization of monetary policy have become the main direction of central banks' efforts.

Unlike the monetary policy of developed economies, which has always been conducted in the context of a relatively mature and stable economic system, that is, in what we call a high-quality economic and financial environment, China's financial system and monetary policy regulation originated from a planned economy, a brand-new and more complex policy practice. China's monetary policy, in its modern sense, has been in existence for little more than 20 years. In the early transitional period, the quantity-based indirect monetary policy regulation was in line with the actual situation of China's economic and financial development. It played an important and positive role in promoting the stable growth of output price and the transformation of the economy to high-quality development, and provided valuable policy experience. However, with the deepening of the financial marketization reform, especially the acceleration and completion of the interest rate marketization reform, the effectiveness of China's monetary quantity control is gradually declining under the impetus of the rapid development of financial innovation and financial disintermediation. Consequently, it is necessary to shift towards an interest rate-based price control mode. After 20 years of development, the function of China's financial market is increasingly sound, the transmission mechanism of the interest rate of monetary policy is smoother, and the interest rate operation modes such as the open market operation of the central bank and the interest rate corridor mechanism are basically complete. Hence China has the necessary conditions for the transformation to the monetary price control mode. However, just as the reform of interest rate marketization is a gradual process, the transformation of monetary control mode cannot be achieved overnight. In the practical process of transforming to the monetary price control mode, China's monetary policy has always been restricted by the government's overemphasis on economic growth and soft budget constraint departments, financial market risks, deepening of financial functions, and reform of exchange rate formation mechanism. There are still problems in the micro-foundation of the financial market, system guarantee, and product market development. Monetary policy is still reliant on the quantity control mode. With the acceleration of the overall deepening of reform and the effective easing of various constraints, the sufficient conditions for the shift to monetary price control will become more mature, and the transformation of China's monetary policy framework will be realized naturally.

The price mechanism is the core of the market economy. The essence of interest rate marketization is to let the market play a decisive role in the allocation of financial resources through the price mechanism, while monetary price control mainly based on interest rate allows government to better play its role in the financial field through price leverage. Therefore, accelerating the transformation of monetary policy regulation mode from quantity to price is precisely the policy requirement for high-quality economic development. In the future, we should emphasize optimization of the structure of quantity control, and focus on the coordination of monetary "quantity" and "price" control. We need to comprehensively consider the current situation of China as a developing country; take into account the need for reform, opening up, development, and stability; accelerate the promotion of various deep-seated reforms; and strive to do a good job in the technical preparation for the transformation of monetary price control mode. To ensure that the central bank is able to respond to liquidity shocks and interest rate disturbance in a timely and effective manner, its interest rate decision-making space and policy operation autonomy should be improved and guaranteed institutionally. According to the actual situation of economic and financial development and the actual requirements of structural optimization and adjustment, we should combine the short-term macro-regulation and long-term mechanism reform organically to gradually realize the integration of financial market interest rate and deposit and loan interest rate; vigorously cultivate the benchmark interest rate system in the financial market and promote the development of more floating-rate products; and clarify the short-term (overnight) policy target interest rate to improve the open market operation and interest rate corridor mechanism. We should also optimize the monetary policy tool system; scientifically carry out interest rate decision-making; effectively implement interest rate operation, so as to smoothly realize the transformation of monetary price control mode; and better promote the high-quality development of economy and finance under the new normal.

4.3 The Reform Process of Interest Rate Marketization in China

4.3.1 China Has Entered a New Stage of Deepening Interest Rate Marketization Reform

As early as 1993, China formally put forward the basic idea of interest rate marketization reform. After taking the lead in liberalizing inter-bank lending rates in 1996, the marketization of financial market interest rates was basically realized around 2000. The process followed the reform idea of liberalizing the money market and bond market interest rates first, and then gradually pushing forward the marketization of deposit and loan interest rates. In October 2004, the upper limit of loan interest rate and the lower limit of the deposit interest rate were liberalized, and the spread management mode was implemented. Since 2012, China has accelerated the pace of interest rate liberalization reform; the floating limit of loan interest rate was lifted in 2013, and since 2014 the upper limit of deposit interest rate has gradually expanded in line with the adjustment of the benchmark deposit and loan interest rate. In October 2015, the PBC released the control on the upper limit of deposit interest rate in commercial banks, marking the basic completion of nearly 20 years of interest rate marketization reform. This move represented a significant milestone in the interest rate marketization in China and in the whole history of financial reform.

In the process of interest rate marketization, we have done a great deal of technical preparation. First, with regard to the cultivation of the market-oriented interest rate mechanism, in September 2013 the market interest rate pricing self-discipline mechanism was established. In October 2013, a centralized quotation and release mechanism of the loan price rate (LPR) was established, and the inter-bank negotiable certificate of deposit business was started. Second, in terms of the construction of the benchmark interest rate in the financial market, in 2007 China established Shibor, the benchmark interest rate system of the money market. As early as 1998, the central bank restarted the RMB open market operation, and the open market operation interest rate started to become an increasingly important policy interest rate. Since the daily normalization of operation of the open market business in February 2016, the role of the open market operating interest rate as the short-term benchmark interest rate of the central bank has been gradually strengthened. To a certain extent, the system currently in use in China functions in the same way as an interest rate corridor. The interest rate of excess deposit reserve is regarded as the lower limit of the interest rate corridor, and the interest rate of SLF is regarded as the upper limit. There is little difference between the interest rate operation mode and the international mainstream practice.

However, China still retains the benchmark interest rate of deposit and loan, and there is a "dual-track" interest rate system between the interest rate of the financial market and the interest rate of deposit and loan. In contrast to the clear interest rate floating restrictions of the past, this is actually a "hidden" interest rate dual-track system. It has become an important direction for future reform, to steadily promote the integration of interest rates. After the basic deregulation of deposit and loan interest rates, China's interest rate marketization has entered a new stage of deepening reform, in which the formation of market-oriented interest rates and the control mechanism are at the core.

The existence of the dual-track system of hidden interest rates is manifested in three main aspects. First of all, the pricing of bank deposit and loan interest rates depends on the benchmark deposit and loan interest rate. For a long time, the pricing of deposit and loan interest rates in commercial banks mainly refers to the benchmark deposit and loan interest rate. The price is sticky, which is not conducive to market clearing. For this reason, coupled with the window guidance of the central bank and the control of credit scale, the deposit and loan interest rates will remain lower than the market interest rate level for a period of time. Second, the internal interest rate pricing management of commercial banks still adopts the dual-track parallel approach of deposit and loan benchmark interest rate and financial market interest rate. The loan interest rate pricing of financial institutions mainly refers to the loan benchmark interest rate, while the capital business mainly refers to the benchmark interest rate system of financial markets such as Shibor and national debt yield curve. Bank interest rate pricing management generally adopts two different internal fund transfer pricing (FTP) systems: deposit and loan interest rates and market interest rate. Due to the pricing habits of banks and customers, it is still very difficult to integrate the two FTP curves into a unified FTP curve under the condition that the central bank does not specify the short-term policy target interest rate. Third, the pricing management of bank deposit and loan interest rates still refers to the benchmark deposit and loan interest rate. Since lifting the restriction on floating loan interest rates in 2013, China has established a self-regulatory mechanism for pricing market interest rates. The pricing of bank deposits and loans is subject to the dual constraints of self-regulatory organizations and the window guidance of the central bank. In the evaluation of macro-prudential policy assessment (MPA), the degree of deviation of commercial banks' deposit and loan pricing from the benchmark interest rate is still considered as an important factor.

4.3.2 Impact of the Dual-Track System of Hidden Interest Rates on the Market Interest Rate System and Interest Rate Regulation

In theory, once the floating restrictions on deposit and loan interest rates are lifted, the relationship between market interest rates and deposit and loan interest rates should be closer. Meanwhile, with the funds outstanding for foreign exchange gradually declining and turning to negative growth, the central bank has regained the function of actively supplying and adjusting market liquidity. The necessity for, and urgency of, the transformation of monetary policy to price control have increased. In recent years, there have been obvious distortions in China's policy interest rates and financial market interest rates, mainly manifesting as follows.

First of all, the short-term interest rate in the financial market is not consistent with the change in the level of deposit and loan interest rates, and the efficiency of the interest rate transmission mechanism is still relatively limited. Monetary price control drives the adjustment of deposit and loan interest rates mainly through short-term interest rates in financial markets. Although the change of interest rate in China's financial market can affect the level of loan interest rate, the adjustment range of loan interest rate is relatively limited, due to the constant benchmark interest rate of deposit and loan, which weakens the effect of interest rate transmission mechanism. Consequently, the trend of loan interest rate lags behind the change of short-term interest rate in the financial market. For example, since the second quarter of 2018, the short-term interest rate in China's financial market has dropped significantly under various policies, such as the PBC's wide-range targeted rate reduction. However, the weighted average interest rate for general loans has not dropped significantly with the adjustment of the market interest rate, and it is only recently that it has shown a downward trend. Empirical research shows that there is a time lag of about half a year in the transmission of the interest rate from China's financial market to the loan interest rate. Although China's interest rate transmission mechanism is basically effective, it stands in stark contrast to the US commercial banks' immediate adjustment of the most favorable loan interest rate and other loan interest rates after a change in the federal fund interest rate.

Second, the financial market has unclear expectations regarding the central bank's interest rate policy and its adjustment. To some extent, this aggravates market fluctuations and weakens the effectiveness of interest rate regulation. After removing the floating limit of deposit and loan interest rate, the central bank should gradually weaken and finally completely cancel the benchmark interest rate means for deposit and loan. The current interest rate policy mainly refers to the interest rate adjustment of open market operation and other innovative policy tools. Although China's monetary policy has intensified its open market operations in recent years and guided the market interest rate by adjusting the operating interest rate, China does not yet clearly announce the policy target interest rate, the open market operations, or the interest rate adjustment of some innovative policy tools, and this lack of clarity could easily to weaken the effect of interest rate policy regulation. For example, since the second half of 2018 China has suspended open market operations many times; indeed, over one period of almost two months, from October 26 to December 16, it did not conduct any open market operations at all. Although these suspensions are mainly normal adjustments based on changes in market liquidity, the failure to provide clear interest rate policy signals to the market mean that they cause unnecessary speculation.

4.3.3 The Main Factors Restricting the Deepening of Interest Rate Marketization Reform

In developed countries, the interest rate policy is used mainly to guide the medium-to-long-term interest rate and deposit and loan interest rate level of the financial market through the short-term policy and interest rate regulation, so as to achieve the final goals of monetary policy such as output and price. However, there remain many deep-seated structural problems in China's economy, and it is difficult to fully achieve the goals of monetary policy through interest rate regulation alone. Therefore, at present, China still uses quantity control in parallel with interest rate regulation, and the regulation mode is gradually transforming from quantity control to price control. The deepening of reform of interest rate marketization still faces many constraints, such as the multiple objectives of China's monetary policy, limited in-depth development of the financial market, relatively backward formation mechanism of market-oriented exchange rate, and imperfect corporate governance of financial institutions. In addition, I would like to focus on the following two aspects.

First, there are still a large number of soft budget constraint departments in China, and the government interferes too much in the interest rate pricing behavior of financial institutions. Under the implicit guarantee of the government, many soft budget constraint departments, such as local government financing platforms and state-owned enterprises, occupy a large amount of financial resources, which aggravates the financing difficulty of private small and micro enterprises. Private enterprises are more efficient, but the information asymmetry and credit risk are relatively large, so their relatively high loan interest rate is also reasonable. However, under the policy guidance that "financing is expensive" for enterprises, the government blindly requires that the financing cost of private small and micro enterprises is reduced. Because the low loan interest rate cannot completely cover the capital cost and credit risk premium of private small and micro enterprises, financial institutions are less willing to lend. Consequently, private small and micro enterprises have to turn to the shadow banking system for financing, and the problem of expensive financing has still not been effectively solved.

Second, the statutory deposit reserve ratio is still relatively high, and monetary policy relies too much on quantitative control measures, reducing the transmission efficiency of interest rate policy. China's high statutory reserve requirement ratio is mainly to meet the need for policy response during periods of excess liquidity. Although the higher reserve ratio enhances the initiative of the central bank in liquidity management and market interest rate guidance, it also increases the reserve burden on financial institutions, which tends to distort the allocation of financial resources, reduce the sensitivity of deposit and loan interest rates to market interest rates, and further weaken the effectiveness of monetary price control. Since the mid-1980s, the central banks of major countries have shifted to the interest rate-based monetary price control mode, and countries have reduced the statutory reserve requirement (even the zero-reserve system) to improve the effect of interest rate regulation, which has a very enlightening significance for China. After the change of using funds outstanding for foreign exchange as the main channel of monetary base supply, at present, China relies mainly on quantitative structural tools such as MLF and PSL to expand the monetary base and money supply. In the future, as structural problems are gradually solved, we will reduce the reliance on quantitative structural tools. We will combine the reduction of reserve with the replacement of MLF and other tools, and carry out the monetary price control based on the interest rate according to the equilibrium interest rate level, so as to achieve, once and for all, the effect of "stabilizing growth, preventing risks, and promoting reform."

4.3.4 Suggestions for Deepening the Reform of Interest Rate Marketization

First, the short-term interest rate should be defined as the policy target interest rate of the central bank as soon as possible. Looking to the practice of major economies, even after the global financial crisis many central banks still focus on monetary price control, and the short-term interest rate is still the best policy target interest rate. Therefore, the short-term interest rate, another pricing benchmark, should be clearly announced at the earliest opportunity. This will undoubtedly help accelerate the exit from the old benchmark interest rate, the deposit, and the loan interest rate. Over the past period, the macro liquidity situation has changed greatly, and the central bank's liquidity management initiative has been significantly enhanced. As a result of the operation practice of recent years, the conditions for declaring "short-term policy target interest rate + interest rate corridor" as the operation framework of the new monetary policy are now basically mature.

Second, we should strengthen the construction of the interest rate pricing mechanism of commercial banks and realize the interest rate integration at a proper time. When defining the new target interest rate of short-term policy, a clear reform timetable should be drawn up. In view of the practical operational problems involved in the conversion of pricing benchmarks, a unified and detailed solution should be discussed and formulated to give the market a necessary buffer period, and we should promote the transformation of commercial banks' interest rate pricing mechanism in an orderly fashion. The market generally accepts the policy target interest rate target. For example, once the deposit and loan pricing has been fully adjusted in a timely manner according to the change of the policy target interest rate, it can announce at a proper time that the benchmark deposit and loan interest rate will no longer be published.

Third, we should deepen the development of the financial market and improve the yield curve of treasury bonds. Although China's financial market has sufficient breadth and the bond market ranks third in the world, there are still divisions between China's money market and the bond market; the development of the interest rate derivatives market lags behind; financial products are still to be enriched; and the depth of financial market development is limited. Consequently, there is an adverse impact on the reasonable formation of market interest rates and the transmission efficiency of interest rate policies. At the same time, China has a small number of short-term treasury bonds. Tax exemption only for the income of treasury bonds leads to insufficient liquidity in the treasury bond market. The role of the treasury bond futures market in price discovery and risk management is not yet fully played, and the treasury bond yield curve as the benchmark for pricing in the financial market still requires improvement. Therefore, in the future, in accordance with the unified rules of market functions, we will appropriately deregulate unreasonable financial business, encourage financial innovation focusing on transaction technology and risk management, truly improve the pricing ability and risk management of financial institutions' products, deepen the development of the treasury bond market, and improve the treasury bond yield curve.

In addition, China should accelerate all-round and in-depth reforms to optimize the target system of monetary policy, speed up the reform of the market-oriented exchange rate formation mechanism, improve the corporate governance of financial institutions, deepen the reform of state-owned capital management, and truly harden the budget constraints of local governments and state-owned enterprises. These measures will steadily push forward the "integration of two tracks into one" with regard to interest rates, and lead to the smooth realization of the reform objectives of transforming the monetary price control mode and deepening the marketization of interest rates.

Chapter 5
The Transformation of China's Financial Regulation Framework

5.1 Effective Financial Regulation

Since the international financial crisis, financial regulation policies have been a constant focal point in every field and society. Based on in-depth reflection on the crisis, major developed economies have been proactive in promoting financial regulation reforms, improving financial regulation standards, enlarging the scope of financial regulation, and comprehensively enhancing the power of financial regulation. Examples include the Dodd-Frank Wall Street Reform and Consumer Protection Act of the United States, the Financial Services Act 2012 of the United Kingdom, and MiFID II of the European Union. However, while such policies have improved the soundness of the financial system, they have also attracted criticism, as stronger regulation has stymied financial development and served the real economy. In June 2017, the United States' House of Representatives passed the CHOICE Act (A Bill Creating Hope and Opportunities for Investors, Consumers, and Entrepreneurs), which largely reverses the Dodd-Frank Wall Street Reform and Consumer Protection Act. At the same time, the US Ministry of Finance proposed the first report on the core principles of financial regulation, calling for deregulation of the banks.

Domestically, as China's economy enters the new normal, it is confronting a diverse range of risks, in the form of money shortage, Internet financial risks, stock market disasters, and bond market storms, among others, all of which reveal the deep deficiencies of China's financial regulation. It was in this context that the 13th Five-Year Plan proposed "reforming and improving the financial regulation framework that meets the development of a modern financial market." In the following sections, in an attempt to clarify the development process of financial regulation, I will discuss the framework of effective financial regulation from the perspective of economic and financial theories.

With the development of the financial market, financial regulation is also constantly evolving. The earliest forms of financial regulation were formed spontaneously by the market. For example, the Buttonwood Agreement, signed on Wall

Z. Xu, *Keep Reforming: China's Strategic Economic Transformation*,
https://doi.org/10.1007/978-981-15-8006-2_5

Street in 1792, marked the beginning of self-regulation and management of the securities industry in the United States. In 1907, private banker J.P. Morgan organized private banks to cope jointly with the financial panic; ultimately, this was to lead to the birth of the Federal Reserve. The Bank of England, the central bank of the United Kingdom, was founded as a private bank. However, with the increasing frequency and intensity of financial crises, especially after the "Great Depression," people realized that such crises could generate massive externalities, and economic and social costs. Market discipline alone cannot deal with market failures or prevent systematic financial risks. Theoretically, economists affirmed the importance of the public sector participating in financial regulation from the angle of weighing the profits and costs of regulation. In practice, to reduce the externalities of crises, the central bank derived the function of "lender of last resort," and began to supervise and scrutinize the operational activities of financing institutions, thus realizing the transition from private sector market discipline to public sector regulation.

After World War II, due to the prevalence of Keynesianism, financial regulation took "intense regulation with safety as the top priority," and implemented an overall strict financial control, which resulted in serious financial repression and efficiency loss. When Keynesianism was restrained by "stagflation" in the 1970s, financial regulation theories started to consider the limitation of financial control, and proposed theoretical explanations for the malfunction of regulation, such as supply–demand imbalance, rent-seeking, and regulatory capture. Western developed countries have since relaxed strict controls on the financial sector, veering toward "mild regulation with efficiency as the top priority," and pursuing financial liberalization. In the words of Alan Greenspan, former chairman of the Federal Reserve: "The least regulation is the best regulation."

With the outbreak of the international financial crisis in 2008, it became clear that the vulnerability of the financial system under soft-touch regulation exceeded both the micro-level risk management capability and the macro-level regulation ability. In the wake of the crisis, financial regulation theories have returned to the principle of "focusing on both safety and efficiency." There is a growing consensus on the importance of macro-prudential management, and a renewed understanding of the relationship between the central bank and financial stability.

Against this background, financial regulation theorists are seeking to answer the question: What kind of financial regulation system can pay equal attention to safety and efficiency, be strict and flexible, and effectively balance financial innovation and risk? In the following sections, I will consider this question from a range of different perspectives.

5.1.1 The Relationship Between Central Banks and Financial Regulation

Currency regulation and central bank control require the coordinated collaboration of financial regulation policies. According to the modern theory of money creation, the currency supply of the central bank is Outside Money, the currency created within the financial system is Inside Money, while currency regulation and control achieves its goals through influencing Inside Money with Outside Money. On the other hand, regulation policies act directly on financing institutions with high authority and rapid transmission, which have the power to bring about a dramatic adjustment of Inside Money. It, to a considerable extent, determines the effectiveness of monetary policy transmission. Since April 2017, China's financial authorities have introduced considerable regulation, which has caused the decline of the money multiplier and M2. It can be seen that, although the central bank can regulate Outside Money, without adequate regulation it cannot control the flow direction and use efficiency of that Outside Money, and cannot guarantee financial support for the real sector.

Furthermore, if the central bank is to perform its financial stability function, then it needs to obtain relevant financial regulation information. Minsky divides financing into three categories: hedge finance, speculative finance, and Ponzi firm. Hedge finance refers to the repayment of interest and principal based on the expected cash income of the financing entity. Speculative finance refers to financing subjects where the expected cash receipts only cover the interest; because they are not sufficient to cover the principal, it is necessary to borrow the new and old. A Ponzi firm is a financier whose cash flows cover nothing but the sale of assets or mounting liabilities. A stable financial system will inevitably be dominated by hedge financing. Introducing some investment models into a financial system dominated by hedge financing can improve its efficiency. To maintain financial stability, the central bank naturally assumes the rescue function of "lender of last resort," according to which it must have the ability to guide social financing to form a structure dominated by hedge financing in terms of law and management. This ability must be based on the central bank's understanding of the regulation information of various types of financing and related risks in the financial system. Through such understanding, we can better comprehend the "three overall plannings" stressed by General Secretary Xi Jinping, namely the overall planning of regulation of financing institutions and financial holding companies with systematic importance, especially the responsibility of prudential management of these financing institutions; the overall planning of regulation of critical financial infrastructures, including essential payment systems, clearing institutions, financial assets registration, and custody institutions, to maintain the sound and efficient operation of financial infrastructure; and the overall planning of responsibility for the comprehensive statistics of the financial sector, strengthening and improving financial macro-regulation, and maintaining financial stability through data collection covering the entire financial sector. We will also have a better understanding of the relations between macro-prudent management and the central bank.

In addition, in order that the central bank can carry out its functions as lender of last resort, especially in terms of providing rescues in times of financial crisis, there is a need for coordination and collaboration among financial regulation policies. The liquidity relief function of the lender of last resort gives the central bank an important position as the last defensive line of crisis rescue. In this regard, since the nineteenth century Bagehot's Rule has been an important guideline for central banks to provide liquidity assistance. According to this rule, the financing institutions with problems are the "weak minority," while most banks in the financial system are sound. Therefore, the central bank has neither the responsibility nor the need to provide free assistance for the small group of failing banks. As a result, this rule requires the central bank to act quickly and decisively in a liquidity crisis to prevent systemic risk from spreading. At the same time, it should guard against moral hazard by adhering to the principle of liquidity support for illiquid rather than financially troubled banks. Institutions with liquidity difficulties should provide high-quality collateral and should be charged punitive interest rates. If the central bank has not participated in regulation before the crisis event, and regulation information cannot be effectively shared, it is difficult for the central bank to know the asset status of the bank, making it harder to make accurate rescue decisions, and reducing efficiency. Under these circumstances part of the rescue is actually a transfusion to troubled financing institutions suffering insolvency, while the central bank's function as lender of last resort is simplified to that of a payment source, with severe moral risks.

5.1.2 The Regulation System Must Have Incentive Compatibility

For regulation to be effective, its goals must be clear and explicit. According to the Nobel prize-winning economist Holmstrom, and his collaborator Milgrom, when faced with multiple task objectives agents have an incentive to devote all their efforts to tasks where performance is easily observed, and to reduce or abandon efforts on other tasks. In China, the financial regulator often takes on the development function directly. Faced with the dual goal of regulation and development, the regulator will naturally tend to focus on areas where achievements will be more easily observed, while neglecting those regulation goals that are less visible. In the long run, regulation and construction are unified; that is, the financial system operates in a stable and efficient manner and effectively serves the real economy. However, in the short term, regulation and development may have inconsistent policy tendencies and conflicting goals, which will lead the regulator to focus on growth, rather than regulation. At the central level, regulation sectors consider greater significance to mean higher status. With the development and expansion of the industry as the internal driving force, there arises regulation competition in financial products with the same functional attributes and business applicability. Competition between regulators is not necessarily a bad thing. However, where there is a lack of unified regulation for the same financial products, regulation competition can easily evolve into a race to the bottom to lower regulation standards, so that "bad currency drives out good currency," which will inevitably damage the effectiveness of regulation and financial stability. Conversely, where there is unified regulation, competition among regulators will foster market development and the improvement of public services. Market vitality will be stimulated, which is conducive to the long-term growth and stability of the market. At the local level, the responsibility of local governments to mobilize more financial resources to serve local development may conflict with the function of financial regulation aimed at maintaining financial stability, especially prudential regulation. Local governments assume part of the prudential regulation function. However, the central government is responsible for the systematic risk of the financial system, and may therefore engage in administrative intervention at the local level, which is not conducive to the stability of the financial system.

It is also important that the power and responsibility in regulation should be on an equal footing. Economic studies have long recognized that regulation is the sum of the actions of regulators. The regulator may deviate from public interest goals for reasons of personal interest, resulting in a failure of regulation. First, there will be an imbalance of supply and demand in financial regulation. Financial regulation is a public good, but will not be provided by the regulator without cost and hesitation under the public interest. Second, rent-seeking exists in financial regulation. As long as the government intervenes in the allocation of resources through regulation, the private sector will find a way to rent, which reduces the efficiency of resource allocation. Third, financial regulation also involves capture; that is, regulation objects may capture regulatory institutions. Where regulation is the result of the influence of interest groups, there is a need for incentive compatibility to restrain the regulator's impulse to deviate from the public interest. This can be achieved through reasonable regulation division, strict accountability and penalties, salary, and other positive incentives, thus unifying the regulator's actions to the overall goal of financial regulation.

With regard to regulation division, according to the motivation theory the overall goals of financial regulation are divided among several regulators in such a way as to achieve a balance between regulation specialization and regulation of the whole economy. If there is a mismatch between power and responsibility in the division of labor, this will lead to severe distortion of incentives for regulatory institutions. Power without responsibility is often the abuse of power, while responsibility without power makes it impossible to achieve the goals of regulation. In terms of the management of financial risks before, during, and after a crisis event, if the central bank as lender of last resort and the deposit insurance as a risk disposition platform are separated from the day-to-day regulation before and during the event, not only will crisis rescue and risk disposition be inefficient due to information asymmetry, but there will also be a heightened risk of moral hazard, due to the fact that the regulator does not have to fully bear the rescue cost. Therefore, under the regulation division of incentive compatibility, the regulators responsible for crisis rescue and risk disposition often assume the day-to-day regulation function as well.

Taking deposit insurance as an example, originally, this served mainly as a "payment box," responsible only for reimbursing depositors after the event. However, this "payment box" model proved unsuccessful. Because there was no power of supervision before the event, the responsibility of deposit insurance was significantly greater than its power, making it difficult to cope effectively with regulation tolerance and the risk of moral hazard. Consequently, disposal cost was high, and the deposit insurance system was unable to dissolve financial risks in a timely and effective manner. Looking at the international development trend, the "payment box" model of deposit insurance was gradually overtaken by the "risk minimization" model with symmetrical power and responsibility. In this model, deposit insurance can implement different rates based on different levels of risk; it can offer lower rates to insurance institutions with more moderate risks, and apply higher rates to promote fair competition and build positive incentives. Moreover, deposit insurance can be given the function of early correction, with the power to inspect and intervene in the problem banks. In this way, it can achieve "early detection, early disposal" of financial risks before a bank becomes insolvent.

Turning now to the issue of accountability mechanism, because the financial regulator does not fully bear the cost of crisis and risk exposure caused by regulation errors, regulation incentives are insufficient, and the effort of regulation is lower than the optimal level. At the same time, even if the regulation system is transparent, the regulator may not strictly follow the law. The purpose of the accountability mechanism is to impose punishment on the regulator based on regulation errors and strengthen its regulation incentive. For example, the collapse of the HIH Insurance Group in Australia in 2001 was considered as a serious failure of regulation on the part of the Australian Prudential Regulation Authority (APRA), and there may have been a benefit transfer of political contributions. The Australian government set up a royal commission of inquiry to investigate, and many regulators were held accountable and removed from their posts.

Another important aspect of "integration of power and responsibility" and incentive compatibility is that pay levels for regulators must be reasonable and comparable to salaries for posts at the same professional level in the market. If the pay levels in regulatory institutions are lower than for comparable posts, regulatory institutions will suffer a loss of talent, and there will inevitably be a decline of regulation professionalism.

Finally, regulation policies should be open and transparent. Researchers such as Dewatripont and Tirole have applied the incomplete contract theory to financial regulation, pointing out that the regulator may deviate from public interest goals because it is easily influenced by political forces or captured by regulation. Therefore, the discretion of regulation policies should be matched with the independence of regulatory institutions. A regulator with substantial autonomy and the ability to internalize the interests of financial consumers into its target can be given more power to regulate. Conversely, if the regulator has weak independence and is subject to political pressure and the influence of interest groups, then the rule-based non-camera regulation system should be adopted to increase the transparency of regulation policies. This is also the theoretical basis of international regulation rules such as the Basel

Agreement. Incentive compatibility will be achieved through transparent regulation rules and will have specific embodiment in all phases of financial regulation development. For instance, Bagehot's Rule specifically requires that the liquidity assistance of the "lender of last resort" must take qualified collateral and punitive interest rates as the premises. Micro-prudential regulation requires that the total amount of risk (total assets) of financing institutions matches its risk tolerance (own capital) through apparent capital adequacy ratio. Macro-prudential regulation imposes higher regulatory requirements for financing institutions with systematic importance. A "Living Will" is required to be established. The regulation restraints will be enhanced based on the implicit protection of "Too Big to Fail."

5.1.3 The Balance Between Financial Regulation and Market Mechanism

The relationship between regulation and market is a controversial topic in financial regulation theory. The basic starting point of financial regulation is to complement the market, make up for market failure, and overcome the inherent defects of the market. However, in the course of the development of financial regulation theory and practice, it is difficult to establish a clear and explicit boundary between complementarity and substitution of regulation and the market, and to achieve a balance between them. Regulation is prone to both systematic financial risks in the absence of a remedy for market failure, and offside suppression of the market mechanism, leading to a loss of efficiency. In my opinion, accurate definition of the relationship between regulation and the market should be based on the big picture and regard financial regulation as a part of the financial governance system. It is also important to differentiate between the financial risks attributes, by going "small." In general, systematic financial risks should be dealt with by governmental regulation.

5.1.3.1 Financial Regulation is a Part of the Financial Governance System

Financial regulation does not exist in isolation; rather, it is an integral part of the financial governance system. The risk management of the financial sector comes from the internal control and external constraints of the financing institutions; specifically, internal control depends on corporate governance and its corresponding institutional arrangements, while external constraints include government regulation and market supervision. The overall goal of the financial governance system should be the achievement of financial stability through the cooperation of financial regulation and other marketization constraint mechanisms.

The lessons of the financial crisis have demonstrated that the stability and tenacity of financing institutions are the foundation for securing financial stability. Furthermore, the improvement of the corporate governance of financing institutions is conducive to the formation of effective decision-making, implementation, and checks and balances mechanisms. The requirements of risk prevention and control should be implemented in the daily operation and management. At the same time, clarifying the marketization withdrawal mechanism when financing institutions fail, including risk compensation and sharing mechanism; and strengthening the protection of depositors, can effectively prevent bank runs. These marketization constraints make it difficult to tolerate high leverage, low capital, or bad loans. They help to improve the robustness of financing institutions from the inside, and are often more effective than government regulation in micro and local risk prevention.

However, in practice in China, the marketization constraint mechanism is often not fully utilized, resulting in the complete reliance on financial regulation for risk management prior to the event. Then, when crisis occurs, the responsibility of the central bank as "lender of last resort" is unlimited.

With regard to corporate governance, financial regulation institutions often perform the functions of industrial authorities, focusing on how to manage enterprises rather than how to improve corporate governance. In recent years, regulation sectors of financing institutions have often appointed the senior managers of regulated institutions in the process of institutional access and risk disposal, leading to complicated human relations in regulation sectors and regulated institutions. This practice damages the independence of regulation and interferes with the personnel system reform of financing institutions. In addition, regulation sectors send institutionalized members to attend internal meetings such as the shareholders' meeting, the board of directors, and the board of supervisors, and express opinions to influence the performance of directors and supervisors. This interferes with the independent management of financing institutions. There is confusion and ambiguity, with potentially different requirements from multiple supervisors, regulation sectors, and shareholder units. Sometimes financing institutions can conform to no one at all, even leading to the formalization of regulation requirements such as capital constraint. In contrast, the *G20/OECD Principles of Corporate Governance* propose work that is beneficial to completing corporate governance, such as "providing guidance for financing institutions to establish and improve sound corporate governance structure, regularly evaluating corporate governance policies, measures and implementation, and requiring financing institutions to take effective measures and means for material defects." However, such work has rarely been undertaken in financial regulation.

From the perspective of risk disposal and market exit mechanism, in recent years China has experienced many defects and deficiencies in the allocation of financial risks. These are mainly embodied as the many disadvantages of administrative disposition modes of regulation sectors, and the restrictions upon the mechanism and functions of deposit insurance marketization disposition. First, when the duty of regulation is inconsistent with the disposal target, there will be a shortage of internal motivation for a prompt start of disposal. From the stance of the regulation sector, it is often desirable to delay the time of disposal after risks arise, so that often the best opportunity for disposal is missed. Second, due to the lack of a professional disposal platform, the marketization degree of risk disposal is not satisfying, and the disposal efficiency is low. A large number of delisted institutions are commonly "frozen but not dead, dead but not disposed." The "popsicle effect" of assets is on the rise, with clearing fees and losses mounting. Third, the lack of positive incentive and restraint mechanism can easily lead to moral hazard. Because regulation sectors do not cover the disposal cost, that cost is borne mainly by the state, resulting in weakened market constraints. It is easy to encourage or induce financing institutions to engage in malicious behavior. Fourth, all regulation sectors build their own rescue mechanisms, leading to fragmentation of disposal policies. This not only violates the basic principle of investors' risk-taking, but also is not conducive to breaking rigid payment. It is difficult to realize "self-rescue" when risks are exposed, so the institutions have no choice but to rely on the "lender of last resort" aid from the central bank.

5.1.3.2 Governmental Regulation Takes Defending the Bottom Line of Systematic Financial Risks as the Focus

Financial regulation theories have always differentiated systematic risks from non-systematic risks. Policies are also differentiated: governmental regulation mainly focuses on systematic financial risks, while non-systematic financial risks are dealt with by the self-discipline of the market. Bagehot's Rule requires the central bank to provide liquidity assistance in response to a systematic impact with liquidity shortage, not to save individual financing institutions. In other words, the "lender of last resort" is the savior of systematic financial risks. The market itself should clear non-systematic financial risks. According to the concept of double regulation (in which both prudential regulation and consumer protection are emphasized), prudential regulation is divided into macro prudence and micro prudence with systematic financial risks and non-systematic financial risks as the boundary to prevent systematic risks. The public sector always has to maintain the stable macro prudence of the financial system, while micro-prudential regulation can, to some extent, be left to the self-discipline of the market.

By distinguishing the risk attributes, governmental regulation takes the prevention of systematic financial risks and the maintenance of macro-financial stability as the key points, serving as the boundary between regulation and market determined by "safety and efficiency". On the one hand, when non-systematic financial risks occur, the surplus of financial risks is limited and poses a smaller threat to financial security. As a result, we should mainly use micro and prudent compliance regulations, which rely more on the self-discipline of the market to take part in regulatory duties. The marketization approach of deposit insurance is used for risk disposal, which can give full play to the market mechanism of survival of the fittest and foster the right market discipline. On the other hand, if the risks are systematic financial risks, then risk prevention must be kept to a minimum. Given the considerable spillover and socio-economic costs of systematic uncertainties, crisis relief and risk management require more than deposit insurance. The central bank's function as the "lender of last resort" is required, and the involvement of financial funds might also be necessary. Government departments need to make available a significant amount of social resources, and to intervene deeply. As a result, in the regulation before and during the event, except for the requirements of micro-prudential regulation, the prevention of systematic financial risks requires the application of countercyclical measures to reduce the risk of contagion. The requirements for macro-prudent management that are "Too Big to Fail" must be restricted. It demonstrates the integration of power and responsibility and the incentive compatibility of risk management before, during, and after the event.

5.1.4 Regulation Must Balance Financial Innovation and Risk Prevention Effectively

The recent global financial crisis demonstrated that if financial innovation lacks a sound institutional environment, it can easily become separated from the real economy and embark on a road of blind expansion and blind development. Innovation for its own sake, and the "conceptualization, bubbling" financial innovation outside the real economy will result in products without source or root. They may thrive for a period, but when prosperity declines, not only will they be useless for promoting economic development, but they will also bring about disaster for both the financial industry and the real economy.

As an essential system to support the healthy development of financial innovation, financial regulation adopts a differentiated response to different forms of financial innovation. First, we should differentiate prudential regulation from non-prudential regulation. For the businesses and institutions that fall under non-prudential regulation, we should strictly execute the rules to ban the so-called financial innovation that violates regulation by engaging in bank businesses that should be under prudential regulation, such as the capital pool business developed by some P2P platforms in recent years. Second, financial regulation should target in particular those financial products that evade regulation or have regulation interest arbitrage. For example, the innovative financial products of some financing institutions are described as the development of direct financing, but are actually alternative credit products in other forms. Funds are invested in restricted areas, for the game of macro control. Third, for financial innovations that have real innovation value and whose functional attributes are the same as those of existing financial services and products, unified regulation rules should be imposed following the principle of functional regulation, such as the current information management products. Fourth, for financial innovations that are currently difficult to locate accurately, we can refer to international attempts at sandbox regulation. Regulators should improve risk awareness. There should be an emphasis on prediction and planning, instead of taking action only after problems occur. Fifth, given the rise of the Internet, the regional attributes of financial services are getting progressively weaker. We should further straighten out the regulation relationship between the government and the market, and between the different levels of government, so as to ensure the efficient and coordinated operation of the central and local government, thus defending the bottom line of preventing systematic financial risks.

5.2 The Optimal Option: Enriching the Financial Committee with Matrix Management

In recent years, China has experienced many and frequent financial risks. The fundamental reason for this is the prominent contradiction between the development trend of comprehensive management in the financial industry and the financial regulation system. Given that the trend of comprehensive management is irreversible, the reform should aim at establishing a modern financial regulation system that can adapt to this trend, and should never return to separate management. In order to enhance the authority and effectiveness of financial regulation coordination and strengthen the penetrability and unity of the significant measures of financial regulation under the premise of avoiding the shock of institutional integration, the fifth National Financial Work Conference took the decision to establish the Financial Stability Development Committee of the State Council. Experience at home and abroad shows that under the regulation system of separation and fragmentation, coordination exists only at the top level, but not between macro-prudential management and systematic financial risk prevention. Consequently, risk prevention and control remain powerless and ineffective. Therefore, to achieve the reform goal under the condition that the institutions are stable, there is a need for substantial integration of business lines, so that the financial commission can play a more critical role than the joint mechanism of financial regulation coordination and the crisis response group. According to our research, based on a balance between the urgency and complexity of reform, and the overall goal of improving stability, the optimal solution is a combination of drawing lessons from relevant experience at home and abroad, and enriching the financial commission with matrix management.

5.2.1 "Two Transboundary Operations and Four Separations"

In recent years, transboundary operations in the Chinese financial industry have germinated rapidly. There has been a return of the "three chaotic phenomena," and a high rate of frequency of financial risks. The fundamental reason for this is that there are salient contradictions among the development tendency of comprehensive management in the financial industry, the regulation system, and mechanisms of financial business separation. The regulatory power of financial regulation is too weak, and there is a lack of macro-prudential policies. There is an urgent need to strengthen the horizontal policy coordination among various units to improve the macro-prudential management system.

First of all, financing institutions conduct expansions through transboundary operations. Under the regulation system that assumes business separation, the different standards of cross-industry investment policy and the lack of any standard covering how financial holding companies and entity enterprises deal with finance have promoted the practice of cross-industry investment. As a result, holding companies and local financial groups have expanded too quickly; most central enterprises and some private enterprises have taken advantage of capital advantages to participate in or hold a variety of financing institutions, showing a clear trend from real to virtual.

In addition, there is interest arbitrage of transboundary operations in financial businesses. The lack of functional and penetrative regulation, and the difference in the regulation standards of similar financial products, has driven the rapid online and offline development of all kinds of cross-industry, cross-market, multifunctional, and long-chain asset management products. Cross-market flows of capital and risk have intensified.

Furthermore, there are separations in financial infrastructures. All industries develop, register, and settle infrastructures of the financial market and financial statistics systems independently, and according to diverse data standards. Information gathering is difficult, and the leverage ratio and overall financial risks base are unclear.

The functions of financial stability are also separated. The central bank is not involved in everyday regulation, while the financial stability function is reduced to a bailout payment box. The inequity of power and responsibility leads to time-consuming and inefficient rescue and disposal, as well as moral hazard. If regulatory institutions establish guarantee rescue funds for various industries, then it is difficult to safeguard deposit insurance. At the same time, it is hard to clarify the boundaries of responsibility of institutions involved in transboundary operations and business risk disposition.

Similarly, with regard to financial consumer protection, the one bank the three committees set protection institutions independently for consumers (investors). Consumer protection agencies involved in transboundary operations of financial businesses shuffle their duties. Moral hazard leads to the nonfeasance of consumer protection, while illegal fund-raising online and offline, fraudulent advertising, and other misleading consumer activities are widespread and uncurbed.

Finally, the resources for regulation are limited. In local financial management sectors, most of the personnel have no economic or financial educational background or experience of the financial industry. In recent years, there has also been a noticeable loss of regulation talents in central regulation sectors. In the context of a shrinking supply of professional talents, the practice of separate regulation for separate businesses has scattered and divided regulation resources, preventing their deployment in a centralized way, thus aggravating the contradiction of insufficient supply of human resources.

5.2.2 Building a Financial Regulation System Compatible with Comprehensive Management

Some people regard comprehensive management as a monster, and advocate returning to separate operation, through the introduction of strict legislation and severe penalties. This is a wrong understanding, and one that is out of step with the times.

In fact, comprehensive management is not only an inevitable trend of economic globalization, but also an inevitable requirement of financial liberalization and marketization. To serve the development of the real economy under the background of economic globalization the financial service demands of enterprises are increasingly comprehensive and diversified, including diversified financing channels, personalized risk management tools, and convenient means of payment and transaction. Only through comprehensive management of financing institutions can they meet these diverse demands through a "one-stop" service. Furthermore, to effectively enhance the competitiveness of the financial sector, the status of the financial market is constantly improving, and financial disintermediation has become a global trend. It is therefore inevitable that the financial industry will choose to improve its competitiveness to effectively integrate all the financial markets and financial forms, thus maximizing synergies.

It should also be noted that comprehensive management itself does not magnify risks; rather, it is the maladjustment of regulation that is the source of risks. Theoretically, comprehensive management is conducive to the diversification and reduction of risks. "Putting eggs in multiple baskets" can be achieved through business diversification in comprehensive management, which should lead to synergies, high efficiency, and low risk; however, it will also bring higher management costs of cross-industry operation and face the constraint of scarce cross-industry professional talents. Since the 1980s, the development of science and technology has dramatically improved the efficiency of financial activities, amplified the benefits of business collaboration, and reduced the management costs of cross-industry operations, thus promoting comprehensive management as an irreversible development trend of the financial industry. This has raised challenges to the regulation system based on business separation, under which regulatory institutions perform their duties. Due to the shortage of financial regulation professionals across industries, it is not very easy to achieve comprehensive regulation that is compatible with comprehensive management. Indeed, at the root of the risk that led to the subprime crisis was not comprehensive management, but outdated, fragmented regulation. Some of the United States' commercial banks, such as Washington Mutual, ran into trouble because of bad loans in their traditional banking business, not because they were in the securities business with transboundary operations. Investment banks, such as Bear Stearns and Lehman Brothers, operate very little commercial banking, and their exposure to risk stems from their exposure to securities. However, one of the crucial causes of the crisis was the regulation prohibiting the payment of interest on demand deposits, which restricts the competition of banks on demand deposits based on the principle of business separation regulation. This regulation is an important reason why shadow banks such as money market funds have replaced a significant amount of demand deposits, leading to rapid expansion and risks. With specific reference to China, when the business separation regulation system causes financial repression within the system, out-of-system risks can get out of control. The regulation system under business separation has the attributes of feudal separationist rule. In order to reduce and control risks within each jurisdiction, strict access control is generally implemented, while financial repression within the system drives the demand for social financing underground. In the past, the regulation sector turned a blind eye to these high-risk and unregulated financing activities, which eventually led to the "three chaotic phenomena" of finance outside the system.

Finally, it is impossible to eliminate risks by restricting comprehensive management, since this will only create new risks. Restriction of comprehensive management is a typical misunderstanding of "replacing regulation with access." Restricting business access will not eliminate risks, and financing institutions may choose higher risks in any business they engage in. Regulation should focus on how to reduce risk motivation rather than on setting up market barriers. After the crisis, many countries implemented financial regulation reforms that improved regulation rules and risk prevention mechanisms, but did not overturn the general pattern of comprehensive management. In 1933, the United States passed the Glass-Steagall Act to constrain the diversified operation of the American financing institutions; however this was based on a wrong understanding of the lessons from the Great Regression. The subsequent Latin American debt crisis, savings and loan crisis, and other financial crises proved that it was impossible to eliminate risks by restricting comprehensive management. With the rise of financial liberalization in the 1980s, the Financial Services Modernization Act of 1999 finally recognized the de facto general management trend. After the subprime crisis, The Dodd-Frank Act (Volcker Rule) continued to conform to that trend, mainly by adjusting the form of comprehensive management and strengthening risk prevention and control. Without financial regulation system reform, any attempt to return to business separation through draconian laws will lead only to more regulation avoidance and risky behavior.

5.2.3 *Matrix Management: The Optimal Option for Financial Regulation System Reform*

Following a decision by the fifth National Financial Work Conference, China established the Financial Stability Development Committee of the State Council (hereinafter referred to as "the Financial Committee"). This was a major step aimed at enhancing the authority and effectiveness of financial regulation coordination, and strengthening the unified penetrative major measures of financial regulation under the premise of avoiding the institutional shock of institutional integration and the uncertainty of effectiveness. The conference also decided that the Financial Committee

Office should be within the People's Bank of China, and strengthened the PBOC's duties of macro-prudential management and prevention of systematic risks.

Drawing lessons from the experience of regulation coordination at home and abroad, China has established a financial regulation coordination joint mechanism and a crisis response group. Before the financial crisis, major economies had set up similar top-level coordination mechanisms; for example, the UK established a tripartite committee among the Ministry of Finance, Bank of England, and Financial Services Authority. The experience of these coordination mechanisms in dealing with financial risks shows that if the Financial Committee implements only pure top-level coordination, it cannot solve the fundamental contradiction of the inability of business separation regulation to adapt to comprehensive management under the current system. Financial risks prevention and control is still powerless and ineffective.

First of all, simple top-level coordination cannot deal with risks in a timely manner. Financial risks in the modern financial market have the features of rapidity, tensibility, high frequency, and intensity. Simple top-level coordination extends the decision-making chain by overlapping each other, and the layer upon layer transmission of information reduces the decision-making efficiency, which is incompatible with the risk prevention requirements of timely decision-making and decisive execution. At the same time, the upward shift of responsibility leads to management mistakes and costs borne by the top institutions, which will inevitably aggravate the responsibility shifting of regulatory institutions. Before this financial crisis, the United Kingdom adopted a "three-for-one" regulation system. In addition, as mentioned above, a tripartite committee was established among the Ministry of Finance, Bank of England, and Financial Services Authority as a simple top-level coordination mechanism to enhance information communication and coordination. However, this did not prevent the run on the Northern Rock Bank that occurred in 2007. Because the Bank of England, as the lender of last resort, failed to obtain timely and accurate daily regulation information through the tripartite committee, it was unable to intervene at an early stage and missed the "golden window" for crisis rescue. As a result, the financial system suffered a confidence shock that endangered overall financial stability.

Furthermore, simple top-level coordination lacks professional support close to the market and cannot guarantee scientific and effective decision-making. Under the simple top-level coordination mechanism, the top-level institution lacks the professional and comprehensive evaluation ability of the financial market, institution, product, and business, and still relies on the existing regulatory institutions to provide necessary information and the basis for policy judgment. When regulatory institutions disagree, it is bound to become a higher-level wrangling platform. After the multi-layer processing of relevant information, the final decision often lacks the professional support close to the market, and the scientific effectiveness cannot be guaranteed. For example, during a crash in 2015, China introduced a number of rescue measures, attempting to deal with all the problems with just one method. Some of the measures apparently lacked professionalism; they were inconsistent with the actual situation of the market, and made wrong expectations of the market response. Not only did they fail to achieve the goal of stabilizing the market, but they actually had a negative impact on market liquidity and confidence, making it more difficult to rescue the market.

In addition, regulation implementation under the simple top-level coordination mechanism actually lacks coordination. The Financial Committee cannot coordinate the implementation of decisions in some key areas without practical action on the implementation level. For example, in the practical work of dealing with illegal fund-raising, it is difficult to balance the dual goals of financial consumer protection (behavioral regulation) and maintaining the safety of financing institutions and the financial system (prudential regulation). There is also a question as to how macro-prudential and micro-prudential regulation can achieve coordination and cooperation at the tool level to strengthen regulation and avoid the "risk of risk disposal" caused by the impact on the macro liquidity environment. In the regulation of cross-market and cross-industry financial products, there is no clear way to strengthen the overall planning and coordination of regulation sectors of business separation and truly realize penetrative regulation. Furthermore, the implementation of regulation lacks overall planning and coordination, and is conducive to the continuation of the scattering of regulation resources under business separation, thus exacerbating the conflict of insufficient supply of professional talents and constraining the effectiveness of regulation.

Consequently, substantial integration of business lines is needed to achieve the reform goal under the condition that the organization remains basically stable. In this situation, the Financial Committee can play a more important role than the joint financial regulation coordination mechanism and the crisis response group. First, professional support germane to the market should be provided for the Financial Committee's top-level decision-making. Second, we should provide the Financial Committee with an important focus on overall planning and coordination at the executive level, and truly achieve functional regulation and comprehensive regulation through the full integration of business lines. Third, we should integrate regulation resources and give full play to the professional ability of regulation professionals.

According to our research, based on internal and external experience, the optimal approach will be to enrich the Financial Committee with matrix management. In this way we can adhere to the general principle of seeking progress while keeping performance stable. Such an approach can achieve the reform goal to the greatest extent with the least shock and reform cost, establish the macro-prudential policy framework, and realize the effective coordination of prudential regulation and behavioral regulation. At the same time, it leaves room and makes preparation for further reforms and improvement in the regulation system.

Matrix management involves the construction of a horizontal organizational management system on the vertical organizational management structure to form a criss-cross, vertically-oriented, horizontally-supplemented, compact, accountable, and effective matrix management system, which is convenient for information sharing, overall decision-making and coordinated implementation. Since the 1950s, matrix management has been widely used in the internal management of large international organizations (such as Goldman Sachs and Morgan). On the vertical line, through the establishment of a number of regional headquarters, these institutions can manage the regional administration, personnel, evaluation, and motivation, in order to fully adapt to local needs for business, encourage the local team to proactively, and give rapid responses to local market situations. On the business line, they command with the headquarter business as the core. For example, according to differences in the nature of the business, Goldman Sachs has set up four lines of investment banking: institutional customer service, long-term investment and loan business, and investment management business. Each line of business has several sub-lines, which are respectively responsible for the coordination of different businesses. In this way, the group realizes the specialization and standardization of all kinds of business, and centralizes the unified management of the company's resources.

Matrix management is also widely used in government governance (including financial governance). As a multilateral international organization, the Financial Stability Board (FSB) set its plenary session as the highest decision-making level on the vertical line. The members include the financing sectors of member economies, the central banks, the people in charge of regulatory institutions, chairmen of the leading international financial standard-setting institutions, and the senior representatives of international financial organizations. Specific financial stability work remains the responsibility of individual countries. In the business line, a number of transnational specialized sub-committees of the plenary session each hold clearly differentiated responsibilities; these include the State Regulatory Commission (SRC), State Commission of Assessing Vulnerability (SCAV), State Commission of Standard Implementation (SCSI), and State Commission of Budget and Resources (SCBR). At the same time, thematic working groups comprising personnel from member states are set at horizontal latitudes, each with specific responsibility for a specific field or task.

Based on relevant experience at home and abroad, the matrix management framework in our preliminary phase can be constructed as follows. First, the current overall framework of "one bank, three committees, and one bureau" remains unchanged on the vertical line, while the Financial Committee is set above it. Second, a number of specialized committees are set up under the Financial Committee, responsible for horizontal information sharing of major policies, overall decision-making, and coordination of implementation. The chairman should be the principal person in charge of "one bank, three committees, and one bureau," and the deputy governor of the People's Bank of China. Related departments and bureaus of "one bank, three committees, and one bureau" are also involved. Secretariats of specialized committees, set up under the People's Bank of China (the Financial Committee Office), undertake the daily work of the specialized committees.

5.2.4 The Reform Achievement of Matrix Management

After the financial crisis, based on profound reflection on the lessons learned, major economies launched reforms in financial regulation systems. The mainstream approach has been to set up top-level coordination agencies, strengthen the financial regulation function of the central bank, strengthen overall planning and coordination in business lines across sectors, and centralize the use of regulation resources. These measures in essence coincide with the philosophy of matrix management. Hence, enriching the Financial Committee with matrix management is in line with the measures taken in reforms of financial regulation systems. We can achieve the same ends by using different methods. It is an inevitable choice to draw fully on international experience and lessons, and make full use of China's "late-development advantage."

First of all, major economies have established cross-sector committees responsible for top-level coordination, strengthened the financial regulation functions of the central bank, and clarified the core position of the central bank in macro-prudential management and the prevention of systematic financial risks. These measures are in line with the idea of enhancing overall planning and coordination through matrix management.

In the United Kingdom, the Financial Policy Committee (FPC) is set under the Bank of England. In the United States, the Financial Stability Oversight Committee (FSOC) covers all major financial regulation sectors. The European Union has established the European Union Systemic Risks Board (ESRB), made up of representatives from the central bank systems of EU member states. The central banks of various countries not only participate in top-level coordination as important members, but also generally take charge of macro-prudential management and systematic financial risks prevention.

In 1997, the United Kingdom completely rejected the separation of micro-prudential regulation from the Bank of England. It turned the Bank of England into a "super central bank," integrating monetary policy, macro-prudential, and micro-prudential regulation. A Monetary Policy Committee that is relatively independent but also closely connected is set under the Bank of England. The Financial Policy Committee and the Prudential Regulation Committee are responsible for monetary policies and macro-prudential planning, and micro-prudential regulation respectively.

In the United States, the Dodd-Frank Wall Street Reform and Consumer Protection Act specifically enhanced the financial regulation functions of the Federal Reserve, making it responsible to decide on and execute the macro-prudential advice from the Financial Stability Oversight Council (FSOC). The Federal Reserve coordinates and regulates financing institutions and financial infrastructures with systematic importance, and is in charge of systematic risk disposition with units such as federal deposit insurance companies. As the umbrella-type regulator, the Federal Reserve can directly regulate bank holding companies and has the right to directly regulate their subsidiary corporations. At the same time, it mainly regulates state member banks and foreign banks. The Bureau of Consumer Protection set under the Federal Reserve is in charge of the overall coordination and enhancement of financial consumer protection. In the European Union, a single regulatory system covering all Eurozone members, and those EU member countries outside the Eurozone that chose to join the system, provides the European Central Bank with its role as the highest regulator in the banking industry. Its responsibilities encompass macro-prudential and micro-prudential regulation, and it directly regulates banks with systematic importance. So far, about 129 banks with systematic importance are under the direct regulation of the ECB. Its assets account for about 82 percent of Eurozone banks' total assets. The ECB also has the right to regulate any banking institution directly at any time.

Second, major economies universally reinforce the overall planning and coordination across sectors in the business line, which is similar to the horizontal dimension of matrix management. Taking the United Kingdom as an example, in addition to the Financial Policy Committee (FPC) that is responsible for overall planning of macro-prudential regulation, the Prudential Regulation Authority (PRA), responsible for micro-prudential business, and the Financial Conduct Authority (FCA), in charge of behavioral regulation, form the "double peaks." In this system, the Financial Policy Committee is the commander and decision maker, while the "double peaks" are executors, taking orders and suggestions from the FPC. A number of cooperation memoranda have been signed between the "double peaks," and the overall planning and coordination mechanism of the horizontal business line, including the establishment of the Joint Data Management Committee, the Regulation Joint Meeting and the Dispute Settlement Meeting, being responsible for the regular coordination and cooperation in data sharing, double regulation and dispute settlement of "double peaks".

Third, all major economies highlight the collective planning and utilization of financial regulation resources, which is similar to the resource integration in the horizontal dimension of matrix management. The regulation in the United Kingdom does not implement the "double peaks" concept rigidly and mechanically; nor does it implement dual regulation in a uniform way. Instead, it starts from the perspective of coordinating the use of regulation resources. The de facto uniform regulation for small financing institutions that do not have systematic effects is implemented by the Behavioral Regulation Bureau. The reason is that prudential regulation "focuses on the big but not the small." Financing institutions with relatively small systematic influence are not guaranteed sufficient attention and resource investment in regulation. However, the Behavioral Regulation Bureau has a relatively balanced allocation of resources for small- and medium-sized institutions, and micro-prudential and behavioral regulation can be implemented simultaneously. In Germany, the Bundesbank has long been entrusted by relevant financial regulation institutions to undertake daily regulation, on-site inspection, and information collection of the bank. This is because the relevant regulation sectors lack sufficient manpower and branch establishment. It coordinates available regulation resources from a comprehensive perspective and carries out relevant work with assistance from the Bundesbank, drawing on its strengths in terms of manpower and branches.

5.3 Chaotic Phenomena in the Financial Market and the Urgency of Reform

In recent years, China's financial market has been subject to many and frequent risk events, which have highlighted the urgency of preventing and defusing risks. The Chinese government Central Committee has proposed that it will take about three years to win the battle against major financial risks. While there is widespread awareness of the urgency of tackling risk, differing perceptions of the underlying causes of risk mean that prescriptions vary. The task of clarifying the root cause behind the risk chaos, and of unifying the ideological understanding, requires consideration of not only whether the financial market can adhere to the correct direction of development of regulation reform, but also the overall situation of national financial security and stability, and more importantly, the strategic transformation of high-quality development of the Chinese economy in the new era. In the current chaotic financial environment, the coordinating role of the central bank should be extended and strengthened. In the next stage, under the framework of the Financial Committee, we will explore ways to better realize the central bank's "three overall plannings" and effectively coordinate the comprehensive regulation reform programs of prudential regulation and behavioral regulation on the basis of responsibility for macro-prudential regulation. We need to address regulation weaknesses and win a tough battle to defend the bottom line against systematic financial risks.

5.3.1 Understanding the Problems of Business Separation and Mixed Operation

Currently, the off-list business of financial institutions is rampant, and the alienation of inter-bank business is an important manifestation of the chaotic phenomena in the financial market. Some people hold that the crux of the chaotic phenomena lies in mixed operation. Therefore, regulation reform should include a crackdown on mixed operation, or even a return to the earlier business separation. In essence, this view is the traditional concept of "business separation means financial safety, while mixed operation means financial crisis;" however, this concept is based on three common misunderstandings or mistakes.

The first mistake is regarding mixed operation as the "original sin" of financial crisis. The battle between business separation and mixed operation started in the Great Regression in the 1930s in the United States. Under the combined action of political and social demands, mixed operation was considered the root of financial crisis, and this view eventually led to the birth of the Glass-Steagall Act. Subsequently, however, there arose ever increasing evidence to show that the act was based on a misreading of financial crisis. Merton Miller (1996), a Nobel Prize winner in economics, has argued that the business separation requirement is a provision based on a completely wrong interpretation of historical facts, that it weakens the ability of the banking industry to reduce risks by providing diversified services, and harms the interests of investors. In fact, mixed operation is the inevitable result of the development of the financial system. As in most other industries, it is the internal requirement of economies of scale and economies of scope, while its own internal driving force is derived from the progress of science and technology. Indeed, it is an inevitable choice that conforms to the trend of historical development, and to the change from quantity to quality. Since the 1980s, science and technology have advanced rapidly, and interest rate marketization reform has expanded dramatically. The products, tools and organizational structure of the financial market have been further optimized, and the pace of innovation has been continuously accelerated. Informatization and integrated operation have gradually become the trend. At the same time, with the deepening of economic globalization, in order to adapt to the fierce global competitive environment, it is also necessary to provide a full range of financial services to multinational enterprises. Hence, mixed operation is the result of the development of economic globalization, and the progress of science and technology, which promotes the operation efficiency of financing institutions. This trend itself is the concentrated embodiment of financial deepening and efficiency improvement. The key question is whether the financial regulation framework design and talent team construction can keep up with the development pace of the financial system.

The second misconception is that business separation helps "divide and govern" risks, thereby improving financial competitiveness and maintaining financial security. Paradoxically, although the Glass-Steagall Act was designed to reduce risks through strict business separation, it did not prove safe for the American banking sector; rather, the long stranglehold it placed on business exacerbated risks. The savings and loan crisis of the 1980s was second only to the Great Regression and financial crisis of the 1930s. The crisis was ostensibly caused by the narrowing of interest rate spreads over the marketization, which led to a rise in risk appetite and an overexposure to real estate. However, another critical background was that, faced with a large number of shunt savings of monetary funds and the de facto impact of loan business operation of securities companies, thrift institutions, as the banking institution most limited by the Glass-Steagall Act, were not capable of providing comprehensive services for clients to assuage the impact of interest margin shrinkage, and finally stepped on the road of no return—high-risk real estate financing. In fact, in the years after the act was implemented, the financial industry in the United States was in a rough condition. Banking systematic crisis occurred almost every 20 or 30 years. The number of bank failures peaked in 1984, after the great depression. Moreover, operation under business separation depressed the international competitiveness of the United States' banking industry, so that in the 1970s and 1980s the international big banks were mainly concentrated in Japan and Germany. This was an important background to the decision to abolish the Glass-Steagall Act in 1999, and replace it with the Financial Services Modernization Act.

As for the third mistake, from the perspective of historical development period, one might assume that the international financial regulation reform after the crisis represented a return to the circle of "business separation—mixed industry—business separation." In fact, the Dodd-Frank Act passed by the United States after the crisis shows no hint of the tendency to return to business separation, as seen after the Great Regression in the 1930s, with the exception of some provisions on restrictions and isolation of proprietary trading under the "Volcker Rule." As Bernanke pointed out in The Courage to Act, mixed operation in itself is not a problem, while fragmentation in regulation under business separation in the United States is a real one. Elaborating on and underlining this point, Geithner wrote in Pressure Test that "The United States' regulation system under business separation is riddled with loopholes and rivalries and full of looming intrigue, yet no one is responsible for the stability of the entire system."

From the perspective of China's practice, the fact that regulation under business separation and mixed operation did not adapt to the development trend was the main reason behind interest arbitrage of regulation and massive financial chaos. Compared with other countries, except for regulation arbitrage in the context of business separation, where regulation for each business differs, but has the same function, interest arbitrage of regulation in China is more serious, due to deep-seated reasons such as institutional mechanisms. For a long time, influenced by the thinking on the planned economy, China's regulation sector has been accustomed to regard itself as the leading sector of the industry. The goals of regulation and development are not differentiated. Although many financial innovation products are consistent in nature, regulation competition in the cross-functional business areas of the same financial products is not necessarily a bad thing. However, under the trend of "emphasizing development and neglecting regulation," regulation competition on the premise of lack of unified regulation for the same financial products is likely to evolve into a race to the bottom in terms of regulation standards, leading to a situation in which "bad currency drives out good currency," and damaging the effectiveness of regulation and financial stability.

Taking the asset management business as an example, the trust plan of trust companies and the asset management plan of financing institutions such as securities companies and funds are essentially the trust business of "entrusted by people and financing for people," but the market access conditions and regulation standards they face are quite different. For the channel business, the trust company deducts 1‰ to 3‰ of the venture capital, while asset management plans deduct only a few tenths of a percent of venture capital, and fund subsidiaries have no net capital requirements at all.

Furthermore, regulation under business separation causes market segmentation, leading to insufficient market competition and severe damage to the efficiency of resource allocation. Taking corporate credit bond issuance as an example, the international market generally requires the public offering to be registered or examined by the government, while private offering can be exempted from registration. However, China is composed of multiple sectors to register or audit of company credit bonds. There is no distinction between public and private offerings in terms of rigor of management, while specific rules for multiple sectors are not unified and penetrative regulation cannot easily be implemented. This creates more difficulties for the issuing entity to follow, while also leaving room for rent-seeking, which disrupts the market order and greatly reduces the efficiency of market resource allocation.

In addition, regulation under business separation creates artificial separation between regulation personnel in terms of knowledge and professional skills. This is not conducive to improving the professionalism or effectiveness of regulation. During the wave of reforms that separated financial regulation from the central bank in the 1980s and 1990s, the most common argument was that business separation regulation helped to improve the professionalism of regulators. From the perspective of the building of China's financial regulation team, the original intention of separating the China Insurance Regulatory Commission from the People's Bank of China in 1998, and the China Banking Regulatory Commission from the People's Bank of China in 2003, was to strengthen industrial regulation, specifically to avoid the conflict between the central bank's monetary policy (rescue capacity) and financial regulation. However, this view was relevant only to a particular historical stage. Nearly 20 years of practice showed that the central bank has no right to regulate but does hold the liability for rescue. Such an inequity between power and responsibility makes it hard to cope effectively with regulation tolerance and moral risks, leading to high disposal cost and the incapacity for prompt prevention of and useful solutions for financial risks. Moreover, regulation professionalization is not the same as specialization, and the requirements continue to evolve, changing with each historical stage. Faced with the practical reality of entering mixed operation in the financial industry, the professionalization of regulation requires not only that personnel have expertise in specific financial fields, but also that the system itself is capable of grasping market dynamics and regulation rules. Currently, China's regulation team suffers from a shortage of such talents, while the knowledge system of regulation personnel lags behind. In sharp contrast, the staff of the market institutions have become very familiar with the core and operation mode of business separation regulation and are able to realize arbitrage of interest among different industries. It is closely related to both the off-the-counter capital allocation business that caused the stock market crash in 2015, and the various capital management plans that led to the insurance disaster in 2015 and the debt disaster in 2016.

5.3.2 *Understanding the Problem of the Entry of Private Capital*

It has been argued that some recent chaotic phenomena, such as the tunneling of financing institutions by major shareholders, are the evil result of introducing private capital. According to this view, private capital should be restricted, if not driven out altogether. In fact, however, this view does not look through the phenomenon to see the essence, and it is this failure that leads to misinterpretations and misunderstandings.

In terms of phenomena, it is certainly true that there were both some large private financial enterprises and some ordinary private enterprises behind the various kinds of chaotic phenomena in the early stage. At that time a few private enterprises, driven by interests, took advantage of the lacunae and loopholes of regulation to engage in false capital injection, circular capital injection, related transactions and other illegal behaviors, and "hollowed out" financing institutions.

However, in essence, the introduction of private capital is not the root of the chaotic phenomena. Rather, the most significant cause was the co-existence of "replacing regulation with access" regulation segmentation, and "no action, no accountability" in regulation sectors of business separation. Recent examples of such phenomena include the behavior seen after the merger and acquisition of private capital and the reorganization of middle- and small-sized financing institutions, when some people abused the rights of major shareholders to fully control the operation and management of those institutions, resulting in a lack of any real governance. Through the hidden channels of private equity and commercial factoring companies in the banking sector, funds were diverted to the parent company and its affiliates, causing the financing institutions to be gradually "hollowed out." What is more alarming is that in the course of the outbreak of risk events, local governments, provincial associations, local banking regulatory bureaus, and other relevant sectors failed to either detect or deal with them in a timely manner. Viewed in the context of the system, this problem is still under the pattern of business separation regulation, where regulation is governed by itself. The departmentalist concept and behavior distortion caused by the feudal domain-style regulation thinking have led to the narrow understanding of regulation responsibility as "taking care of one's own business." As a result, certain problems have become inevitable, such as market segmentation, "access over regulation," "approval over regulation," and "development over regulation."

In addition, it is important to note that regulation under business separation has different capital regulation rules to financing institutions. First, business separation regulation lacks penetration. Regulation sectors are concerned only with their own liabilities, rather than the source and utilization of funds. Taking "the Battle of Baoneng and Vanke" in 2016 as an example, Baoneng successfully acquired 25% of Vanke for 43 billion yuan through various financial channels and the organization of various kinds of leveraged funds, chiefly the nested use of asset management plans, thus becoming the largest shareholder. The diverse range of acquisition finance, including funds, banks, securities, and insurance, involved many different financial sectors. From a penetrative point of view, the whole acquisition was an equity investment with debt funds, which is clearly against common sense and obviously risky. However, from the perspective of regulation under business separation, all the small and medium-sized insurance companies involved were compliant. In fact, in addition to the equity allocation of Qianhai Life Insurance Co., Ltd., to meet the CIRC's requirements of "not breaking the 30% red line and ensuring adequate capital," a series of high-risk operations, such as pledge and financing of affiliated companies behind the scenes, did not fall within the regulation scope. However, the CSRC regulates only where market takeovers raise issues of compliance, while other issues are not within its regulatory scope, thus leading to the absurdity of de facto high risk but formal compliance. Second, regulation under business separation cannot implement effective penetrative regulation to the complex stock rights structure of financing institutions, nor identify illegal behaviors such as false and circulating capital injections, unreal capital and "invisible shareholders." Some financing institutions have complex equity relations and many levels of shareholders. They often use the complex equity structure as a cover to realize "bridge capital increase" and self-inject capital to cover the fact of unreal capital. Furthermore, some enterprises take advantage of blind zones of regulation under business separation, gaining shareholdings of financing institutions through a large number of shadow shell companies. Such behavior leads to the disappearance of the equity relationship in the legal sense in the core company and most affiliated financing institutions. Consequently, they can become de facto "invisible shareholders" to evade regulation.

In fact, the phenomenon of "controlling by insiders" or tunneling by major shareholders is not unique to private capital. Rather, it is a common issue in the management of modern companies. The key to solving the problem is not to treat capital with different attributes differently, but to treat it equally and implement consistent market access, regulation, and exit requirements. Looking to international practice, in both Anglo-American and continental law systems the regulation requirements for the shareholders of financing institutions emphasize qualification and compliance, rather than discrimination and restrictions on certain capital attributes. Based on a misunderstanding of the nature of chaotic phenomena, some people blindly deny the positive significance of private capital entering the financial sector, instead regarding private capital as unambiguously bad. Instead of emphasizing the problem of regulation, they tend to limit the qualifications of capital attributes by ways of financial repression. This runs counter to general laws of development and the spirit of the 19th Chinese government National Congress, which emphasized that "the market should play a decisive role in the allocation of resources."

5.3.3 Understanding the Issue of Illegal Fund-Raising in the Financial Field

According to some commentators, the recent problematic phenomenon of illegal fund-raising can be traced in part to immoral Internet financing institutions. In response to this perceived problem, they advocate a system of license plate management with "territorial regulation, territorial disposal." In essence, this view follows the old road of closure and rigidity, and is therefore incompatible with the "dialectical thinking, bottom-line-thinking" put forward at the 19th Chinese government National Congress.

On the one hand, from the perspective of dialectical thinking, regulation under business separation tends to lead to financial repression within the system, which in turn leads to an explosion of more distorted mixed operations outside the system. International practice has shown that there is a strong sense of territory in the regulation system under business separation. This leads not only to regulation fragmentation, but potentially to a "beggar-thy-neighbor" approach that creates artificial regulation loopholes and causes financial risks to other sectors, while the overall financial risks are not controlled, or may even be worsened. In China, due to political, legal, social, and other factors, regulation sectors under business separation tend to be more conservative, often placing too much emphasis on the bottom line of risks within the jurisdiction. This restricts or even stifles normal financial innovation activities, pushes the social financing demand outside the system, and ignores or even promotes the explosive growth of mixed businesses outside the system. On the surface, it may appear that many informal financial risks are in the system, but in practice, financial risks are proliferating and unregulated outside the system. To make matters worse, in the event of an outbreak of risk, regulation sectors under business separation may use their jurisdictional radius as an excuse for evasiveness. In recent years, the outbreak of cases of Internet financial risks such as "Ezubo" have offered typical examples of out-of-system chaotic phenomena brought about by regulation under business separation. Owing to the repressive regulation concept of "taking care of only their own responsibilities," these Internet financial innovations, which might have met the demand for inclusive finance, cannot be integrated into the regular operation of the financial system. Given the extreme mismatch between the illegal benefits and the cost, the temptation is high to take the risk and turn it into a Ponzi scheme. This extreme asymmetry between incentives and constraints caused by regulation loopholes is not so much a moral hazard as a perverse incentive and indulgence caused by regulation system distortion. The financial repression brought about by the regulation system under business separation directly endangers the metabolic process of the financial system, hinders financial innovation, and amplifies moral hazard.

Furthermore, from the perspective of Bottom-Line-Thinking, the Internet has no territorial significance, making it difficult to manage. Illegal fund-raising is not a geographical risk; rather it is a systematic financial risk, or even a social risk. The essence of Internet finance is still finance, hence it carries all the risks of the traditional financial industry while also facilitating cross-industry and cross-region activities. At the same time, risks become more hidden, contagious, widespread, and sudden. The registration place of institutions is often inconsistent with the business place, and the sources of funds and assets are also inconsistent, which poses a challenge to "territorial regulation, territorial disposal." Moreover, these illegal fund-raising activities are often under the guise of inclusive finance. The victims are usually members of the public without financial expertise and identification ability, and the social impact can be enormous. However, under the "territorial regulation, territorial disposal" regulatory mode of separation and fragmentation, management sectors and regulation sectors of local governments are restricted within their jurisdictional radius, without sufficient power or resources, and without foresight for regulation policies and tools. Before the event, there is a lack of strict control over the access of Internet finance qualification. During the event, there is a late response to the occurrence of risk. After the event, there is a lack of coordination and collaboration in risk disposition, and even evasiveness. These have become the deep-level systematic sources of the chaotic phenomena in preliminary illegal fund-raising.

Internationally, there are very many lessons regarding "territorial regulation, territorial disposal," most prominently from the United States. For a long time, financial regulation patterns in the United States were famous for fragmentation, complication, and administrative localization, which severely restricted the regulatory ability of federal and local regulatory institutions. In 2005, before the subprime crisis, only 20% of all subprime mortgages in the United States came from banks and thrift institutions under the regulation of federal regulatory institutions, 30% came from non-bank subsidiaries under federal regulation, and the remaining 50% came from mortgage companies chartered by the states and almost outside of regulation. Only a few states, such as Massachusetts and North Carolina, had adequate regulation on non-bank mortgage loans, while most had little or no regulation due to lack of resources and political support. Also, with regard to Internet finance, it is difficult to distinguish prudential regulation from behavioral regulation. This presents a new challenge to hold the bottom line for systematic financial risks. Some Internet financing institutions were initially established as small-loan companies, but they are mainly targeted to implement behavioral regulation. Nevertheless, in recent years, some small-loan companies have used Internet technology to take deposits from the public, quickly reaching out to the rest of the country, and are likely to be systematic in the event of an outbreak of risk. In this sense, if we are to deal effectively with the problem of illegal fund-raising in Internet finance, there is an urgent need to set up an agency that is fully responsible for coordinating behavioral regulation and prudential regulation.

The aforementioned chaotic phenomena fully reflect the urgency of financial regulation system reform, whether the target is the mixed operation without practical regulation constraints, or the early regulation failure and the current regulation chaos owing to the improper behaviors of some private capital, or the illegal fund-raising under financial repression. All of these chaotic phenomena expose the institutional contradiction whereby the regulation system has failed to adapt to the development trend of mixed operation. Driven by technological progress and the deepening function of the market in allocating resources, the development trend of mixed operation of the financial industry is irreversible. The direction of the reform should therefore be to establish a modern financial regulation system that is adequate, instead of going back to the mode of "closed, fragmented and land-locked." In fact, since the international financial crisis regulation reforms have not returned to the so-called old way of business separation. On the contrary, methods such as the establishment of a top-level coordination mechanism, enhancing the financial regulation functions of the central bank, ameliorating the coordination of behavioral regulation and prudential regulation, and utilizing regulation resources in an overall and collective manner have all come under consideration as means to establish a comprehensive regulation framework in the context of a mixed industry, led by the central bank and integrating prudential and behavioral regulation. Taking the United Kingdom as an example, in 1997 it put an end to the separation of micro-prudential regulation from the Bank of England, which became a "super central bank" integrating monetary policy, macro-prudential management, and micro-prudential regulation. This move was in order to adapt to the practical need to strengthen unified regulation in the operation of a mixed industry. The same is true of the Federal Reserve's expansion of regulation power after the crisis.

Looking specifically at China, we have the concept of the "three overall plannings," proposed at the fifth plenary session of the 18th Chinese government Central Committee; the decision of the fifth National Financial Work Conference on the establishment of the Financial Committee; and the sound monetary policy and the dual-pillar regulation framework of macro-prudential management proposed at the 19th Chinese government National Congress. All of these show that the direction of regulation reform is to strengthen central bank coordination, improve the system, strengthen weak links, and close loopholes, rather than return to the old way of business separation.

In the current environment of frequent financial turmoil, it is necessary to further strengthen the central bank's overall planning role, rather than simply maintain its role in coordination. In the next stage, under the framework of the Financial Committee, we will explore ways to better realize the central bank's "three overall plannings" and to effectively coordinate the comprehensive regulation reform program of prudential regulation and behavioral regulation on the basis of responsibility for macro-prudential regulation, so as to complement the weak points of regulation and win a tough battle to defend the bottom line against systematic financial risks.

References

Acharya, V. 2009. A theory of systemic risk and design of prudential bank regulation. *Journal of Financial Stability* 5 (3): 224–255.
Ahearne, A. G., and N. Shinada. 2005. Zombie firms and economic stagnation in Japan. *International Economics & Economic Policy* 2 (4).
Anginer, D., et al. 2014. How does competition affect bank systemic risk. *Journal of Financial Intermediation* 23 (1): 1–26.
Arslan, Y., and C. Upper. 2017. Macroprudential frameworks: Implementation and effectiveness. BIS Papers No. 94.
Ball, L., J. Gagnon, P. Honohan, and S. Krogstrup. 2016. What else can central banks do? Geneva reports on the world economy. 18th Geneva Report.
Basu, P., M. Gillman, and J. Pearlman. 2012. Inflation, human capital and Tobin's Q. *Journal of Economic Dynamics and Control* 36 (7): 1057–1074.
Bayoumi, T., et al. 2014. Monetary policy in the new normal. IMF Staff Discussion Notes.
Bernanke, Ben S. 2016. *The courage to act: A memoir of crisis and its aftermath.* China Citic Press. (In Chinese)
Benes, J., and P. N'Diaye. 2004. A multivariate filter for measuring potential output and the NAIRU: Application to The Czech Republic. IMF Working Paper Series, No 04/45.
Berentsen, A., A. Marchesiani, and C. Waller. 2014. Floor systems for implementing monetary policy. *Review of Economic Dynamics* 17 (3): 523–542.
Bernanke, B., and M. Gertler. 1986. Agency costs, collateral, and business fluctuations. Proceedings, Federal Reserve Bank of San Francisco.
Bernanke, B., and M. Gertler. 1995. Inside the black box. *Journal of Economic Perspectives* 9 (4): 27–48.
Bernanke, B., and M. Gertler. 2001. Should central banks respond to movements in asset prices? *American Economic Review* 91 (5): 253–257.
Bernanke, B. 2010. Federal Reserve's exit strategy. Testimony before the Committee on Financial Services, U. S. House of Representatives, Feb., 10th.
Beveridge, S., and C. Nelson. 1981. A new approach to the decomposition of economic time series into permanent and transitory components with particular attention to measurement of the business cycle. *Journal of Monetary Economics* 7: 151–174.
Bindseil, U. 2004. *Monetary policy implementation.* New York: Oxford University Press.
Bindseil, U. 2014. *Monetary policy operations and the financial system.* Oxford University Press.
Bindseil, U., and A. Winkler. 2012. Dual liquidity crises under alternative monetary frameworks. ECB Working Paper Series, No. 1478.

Z. Xu, *Keep Reforming: China's Strategic Economic Transformation*,
https://doi.org/10.1007/978-981-15-8006-2

Bindseil, U., and J. Jablecki. 2011. A structural model of central bank operations and bank intermediation. ECB Working Paper Series, No. 1312.

BIS. 2009. Monetary policy frameworks and central bank market operations. Market Committee, May.

Blanchard, O., G. Dell'Ariccia, and P. Mauro. 2010. Rethinking macroeconomic policy. *Journal of Money, Credit and Banking* 42 (S1): 199–215.

Blinder, A., M. Ehrmann, M. Fratzscher, J. Haan, and D. Jansen. 2008. Central bank communication and monetary policy: A survey of theory and evidence. *Journal of Economic Literature* 46 (4): 910–945.

Böhm-Bawerk, E. von. 1884, 1890. *Capital and interest. A critical history of economic theory*, translated with a preface and analysis by William Smart, London: Macmillan.

Borio, C., and A. Zabai. 2016. Unconventional monetary policies: A re-appraisal. Bis Working Papers.

Borio, C. 2016. Revisting three intellectual pillars of monetary policy. *Cato Journal* 36 (2): 213–238.

Borio, C., and A. Zabai. 2016. Unconventional monetary policies. BIS Working Paper, No. 570.

Brown, J. R., G. Martinsson, and B. C. Petersen. 2012. Do financing constraints matter for R&D? *European Economic Review* 56 (8).

Caballero, R. J., T. Hoshi, and A. K. Kashyap. 2008. Zombie lending and depressed restructuring in Japan. *American Economic Review* 98 (5).

Campbell, J. 2013. Odyssean forward guidance in monetary policy: A primer. *Economic Perspectives* 2013 (5): 130–138.

Carney, M. 2013. Monetary policy after the fall. Speech at Eric J. Hanson Memorial Lecture, University of Alberta.

Cesa-Bianchi, A., and A. Rebucci. 2016. Does easing monetary policy increase financial instability? NBER Working Paper, No. 22283.

Christians, L., and T. Fitzgerald. 1999. The band pass filter. NBER Working Paper, No. W7257.

Claessens, S. 2014. An overview of macroprudential policy tools. IMF Working Paper, No. WP/14/214.

Cooley, T., and G. Hansen. 1989. Inflation tax in a real business cycle model. *American Economic Review* 79 (4): 733–748.

Dai, Genyou. 2003. Practice and experience of the open market operation of the People's Bank of China. *Journal of Financial Research* 2003 (01): 55–56. (In Chinese)

DeJong, D., and C. Dave. 2007. *Structural macroeconomics*. Princeton: Princeton University Press.

Dewatripont, M., and J. Tirole. 1994. *The prudential regulation of banks*. MIT press.

Didier, Tatiana, Hevia Constantino, and Schmukler Sergio. 2011. How resilient were emerging economies to the global crisis? World Bank Policy Research WP 5637, No. April, 2011.

Domanski, D., and V. Sushko. 2014. Rethinking the lender of last resort: Workshop summary. In *Rethinking the lender of last resort*, vol. 79, ed. BFI Settlements, 1–9. Bank for International Settlements.

Ehlers, T., S. Kong, and F. Zhu. 2018. Mapping shadow banking in China. BIS Working Papers, No. 701.

Eichengreen, et al. 2003. Currency mismatches, debt intolerance, and original sin. NBER Working Papers, vol. 10036, 121–170. English Translation, London: Macmillan.

Francesco, F., et al. 2015. Exchange rate pressure in Angola. NOVAFRICA Working Paper Series wp 1502.

Feinman, J. 1993. Reserve requirements: History, current practice, and potential reform. *Federal Reserve Bulletin* June.

Feldstein, M. 2005. Structural reform of social security. *Journal of Economic Perspectives* 19 (2) (Spring, 2005): 33–55.

Fischer, S. 2016. Why are interest rates so low? Causes and Implications [R].

Fischer, S. 2016a. The lender of last resort function in the United States. Speech at the Conference of The Lender of Last Resort, Washington, D.C., Feb., 10th.

Fischer, S. 2016b. Reflections on macroeconomics then and now. Speech at 32nd Annual National Association for Business Economics Economic Policy Conference, Mar. 7th.
Fischer, S. 2016c. Low interest rates. Speech at the 40th Annual Central Banking Seminar, Federal Reserve Bank of New York, Otc. 5th.
Fisher, I. 1933. The debt-deflation theory of great depressions. *Econometrica* 1 (4): 337–357.
Friedman, B., and K. Kuttner. 2011. Implementation of monetary policy. In *Handbook of monetary economics*, vol. 3, ed. B. Friedman, and M. Woodford, 1345–1438. Amsterdam: Elsevier.
Friedman, M. 1968. The role of monetary policy. *American Economic Review* 58 (1): 1–17.
Furfine, C. 2003. Standing facilities and interbank borrowing: Evidence from the Fed's new discount window. *International Finance* 6 (3): 329–347.
Furman. 2014. The fifth anniversary of the American recovery and reinvestment. View the Council of Economic Advisers' Report, Feb. 17th.
Gaballo, G. 2013. Good luck or good policy? *Journal of Economic Dynamics and Control* 37 (12): 2755–2770.
Gali, J., and T. Monacelli. 2005. Monetary policy and exchange rate volatility in a small open economy. *Review of Economic Studies* 72: 707–734.
Gambacorta, L. 2009. Monetary policy and the risk-taking channel. *BIS Quarterly Review* (December): 43–53.
Goncalves, C., and A. Carvalho. 2009. Inflation targeting matters: Evidence from OECD economies' sacrifice ratio. *Journal of Money, Credit and Banking* 41 (1): 233–243.
Goodfriend, M. 2002. Interest on reserves and monetary policy. *Federal Reserve Bank of New York Economic Policy Review* 8 (1): 77–84.
Goodfriend, M., and B. McCallum. 2007. Banking and interest rates in monetary policy analysis. *Journal of Monetary Economics* 54 (5): 1480–1507.
Goodfriend, M., and R. King. 1997. The new neoclassical synthesis and the role of monetary policy. In *NBER Macroeconomics Annual*, 231–283.
Goodhart, C. 2009. Liquidity management. Paper for the Symposium on Economic Policy for the Information Economy, Federal Reserve Bank of Kansas City.
Greenspan, A. 2002. Issues for monetary policy [R].
Guan, Tao. 2018, Developing the foreign exchange market is the key to deepening the exchange rate reform. *China Forex* 2018 (01): 28–29. (In Chinese)
Gurley, J. G., and E. S. Shaw. 1955. Financial aspects of economic development. *American Economic Review* 45 (4).
Gust, C, K. Johannsen, and D. Lopez-Salido. 2015. *Monetary policy, incomplete information, and the zero lower bound*. Board of Governors of the Federal Reserve System, Finance and Economics Discussion Series, 2015-099.
Hayek, F. A. 1935. *Prices and production*, 2nd ed. Routledge and Kegan Paul.
He, Fan, and Zhu He. 2016. Strategies for dealing with Zombie Enterprises. *China Finance* 2016 (13): 25–27. (In Chinese)
He, D., and H. Wang. 2012. Dual-track interest rate and the conduct of monetary policy in China. *China Economic Review* 23 (4): 928–947.
Heider, F., M. Hoerova, and C. Holthausen. 2015. Liquidity hoarding and interbank market rates. *Journal of Financial Economics* 118 (2): 336–354.
Hirsch-Kreinsen, Hartmut. 2011. Financial market and technological innovation. *Industry and Innovation* 18 (4).
Hodrick, R., and E. Prescott. 1997. Postwar US business cycles: An empirical investigation. *Journal of Money Credit and Banking* 29 (1): 1–16.
Holmstrom, B., and P. Milgrom. 1991. Multi-task principal-agent analyses: Incentive contracts, asset ownership and job design. *Journal of Law Economics & Organization* 7 (Special Issue).
Hornby, L. China changes tack on 'Social Credit' scheme plan. *Financial Times.*
Hoshi, T., and A. K. Kashyap. 2004. Japan's financial crisis and economic stagnation. *Journal of Economic Perspectives* 18 (1).

Hsu, Po-Hsuan, Xuan Tian, and Yan Xu. 2013. Financial development and innovation: Cross-country evidence. *Journal of Financial Economics* 112 (1).

Iacoviello, M., and S. Neri. 2010. Housing market spillovers. *American Economic Journal: Macroeconomics* 2 (2): 125–164.

IMF. 2008. World Economic Outlook. October.

IMF. 2017. 2017 Article IV consultation. IMF Countries Report, No. 17/326.

Issing, O. 2005. Why did the great inflation not happen in Germany? *Federal Reserve Bank of St. Louis Review* (March/April): 329–336.

Powell, J. H. 2014. Monetary policy accommodation, risk-taking, and spillovers: A speech at the global research forum on international macroeconomics and finance, Washington, D.C., November 14, 2014. *Speech* 8 (61): v–vi.

Jaskowski, M. 2015. Should Zombie lending always be prevented? *International Review of Economics and Finance* 40.

Ji, Min, and Niu Muhong. 2014. Establishing the anchor of central bank policy interest rate expectations. *China Finance* 2014 (09): 19–22. (In Chinese)

Ji, Min, Yan Baoyu, and Li Hongjin. 2017. Leverage ratio structure, level and its relationship with financial risk. *Journal of Financial Research* 2017 (02): 1–25. (In Chinese)

Ji, Yang, Tan Yuyan, and Huang Yiping. 2016. Dual finance system and interest rate liberalization. *Economic Research Journal* 2016 (06): 45–57. (In Chinese)

Justiniano, Alejandro, Giorgio Primiceri, and Andrea Tambalotti. 2011. Investment shocks and the relative price of investment. *Review of Economic Dynamics* 14 (1): 101–121.

Kahn, G. 2009. Beyond inflation targeting. *Federal Reserve Bank of Kansas City Economic Review* 94 (3): 35–64.

Kahn, G., and A. Palmer. 2016. Monetary policy at the zero lower bound. *Federal Reserve Bank of Kansas City Economic Review* (First Quarter): 5–37.

Kamber, G., and M. Mohanty. 2018. Do interest rates play a major role in monetary policy transmission in China? BIS Working Paper, No. 714.

Keister, T., and J. McAndrews. 2009. Why are banks holding so many excess reserves. *Federal Reserve Bank of New York Current Issues in Economics and Finance* 15 (8): 1–10.

Keynes, J. M. 1936. *The general theory of employment, interest and money.* New York: Macmillan Cambridge University Press.

Keynes, J. M. *A treatise on money: The pure theory of money.* London: Macmillan

Kiyotaki, N., and J. Moore. 1997. Credit cycles. *Journal of Political Economy* 105 (2): 211–248.

Klee, E., Z. Senyuz, and E. Yoldas. 2016. *Effects of changing monetary and regulatory policy on overnight money markets.* Board of Governors of the Federal Reserve System, Finance and Economics Discussion Series, 2016-084.

Kool, C., and D. Thornton. 2015. How effective is central bank forward guidance? *Federal Reserve Bank of St. Louis Review* 97 (4): 303–322.

Korinek, A., and A. Simsek. 2016. Liquidity trap and excessive leverage: Dataset. *American Economic Review* 106 (3): 699–738.

Kydland Finn, E., and C. Prescott Edward. 1977. Rules rather than discretion: The inconsistency of optimal plans. *Journal of Political Economy* 85 (3): 473–491.

Kydland, F., and E. Prescott. 1977. Rules rather than discretion. *Journal of Political Economy* 85 (3): 473–491.

Kydland, F., and E. Prescott. 1982. Time to build and aggregate fluctuations. *Econometrica* 50 (6): 1345–1370.

Laubach, Thomas, and John C. Williams. 2016. Measuring the natural rate of interest redux. *Business Economics* 51 (2), 57–67

Laubach, Thomas, and John C. Williams. 2003. Measuring the natural rate of interest. *The Review of Economics and Statistics* 85 (4): 1063–1070.

Laxton, D., and R. Tetlow. 1992. A simple multivariate filter for the measurement of potential output. Technical Report, No. 59, Bank of Canada.

Laxton, D., P. Isard, H. Faruquee, E. Prasad, and B. Turtelboom. 1998. Multimod Mark III the core dynamic and steady-state models. IMF Occasional Paper No. 164, p. 30

Levine, Ross. 1997. Financial development and economic growth: Views and agenda. *Journal of Economic Literature* 35 (2).

Li, Hongjin, and Su Naifang. 2017. Financial innovation, financial disintermediation and credit money creation. *Research on Financial and Economic Issues* 2017 (10): 40–50. (In Chinese)

Linde, J., F. Smets, and R. Wouters. 2016. Challenges for central banks? Macro models. Sveriges Riksbank Working Papers, No. 323.

Liu, Bin. 2016. *Dynamic stochastic general equilibrium model and its application*, 3rd ed. China Financial Publishing House. (In Chinese)

Liu, Z., J. Miao, and T. Zha. 2016. Land prices and unemployment. *Journal of Monetary Economics* 80 (C): 86–105.

Lucas, R. 1976. Econometric policy evaluation: A critique. *Carnegie-Rochester Conference Series on Public Policy* 1 (1): 19–46.

Lucas, R. 1972. Expectations and the neutrality of money. *Journal of Economic Theory* 4 (2): 103–124.

Luo, Changlin, and Zou Hengfu. 2014. Discussion on soft budget constraint. *Economic Perspectives* 2014 (05): 115–124. (In Chinese)

Ma, Jun, and Wang Honglin. 2014. Theoretical model of transmission mechanism of policy interest rate. *Journal of Financial Research* 2014 (12): 1–22. (In Chinese)

Ma, Jun, Cheng Lin, and Xie Wenhong. 2018. China's global influence in green finance. *Tsinghua Financial Review* 2018 (12): 56–58. (In Chinese)

Ma, Yong. 2015. Empirical research on the transparency of China's monetary policy. *The Journal of World Economy* 2015 (09): 3–28. (In Chinese)

Mankiw, G. 2006. The macroeconomist as scientist and engineer. *Journal of Economic Perspectives* 20 (1): 29–46.

McKinnon, Ronald I. 1973. *Money and capital in economic development*. Washington DC: Brookings Institution.

McKinnon, Ronald I. (ed). 1976. Money and finance in economic growth and development. Essays in Honor of Edward S. Shaw. *Business Economies and Finance* 8, New York, Basel.

Merton, Robert C. 1992. Financial innovation and economic performance. *Journal of Applied Corporate Finance* 4 (4).

Miller Merton, H. 1996. The social costs of some recent derivatives disasters. *Pacific-Basin Finance Journal* 4 (2).

Minsky, Hyman. 1982. The financial fragility hypothesis: Capitalist process and the behavior of the economy. In*Financial crisis*, ed. Charles P. Kindlberger and Jean-Pierre Laffargue. Cambridge: Cambridge University Press.

Mishkin, F. 1997. The causes and propagation of financial instability. In *The maintaining financial stability in a global economy*, Federal Reserve Bank of Kansas City Proceedings, 55–96.

Mishkin, F. 2009. *The economics of money, banking and financial markets*. Pearson Education.

Mishkin, F. 2011. Monetary policy strategy: Lessons from the crisis. NBER Working Paper, No. 16755.

Mishkin, F. 2010. Monetary policy flexibility, risk management, and financial disruptions. *Journal of Asian Economics* 23 (3): 242–246.

Myrdal, G. 1939. *Monetary equilibrium*. Glasgow: William Hodge.

Nelson, E. 2007. Milton Friedman and U. S. monetary history: 1961–2006. *Federal Reserve Bank of St. Louis Review* 89 (May): 153–182. New York, Feb., 26th.

Nikolsko-Rzhevskyy, A., D. Papell, and R. Prodan. 2014. Deviations from rules-based policy and their effects. *Journal of Economic Dynamics and Control* 49 (C): 4–17.

Niu, Muhong, Zhang Lina, and Zhang Xiang. 2017. Interest rate corridor, interest rate stability and regulation cost. *Journal of Financial Research* 2017 (07): 16–28. (In Chinese)

Nomura Securities. 2013. China's rising financial risks. Research Report. (In Chinese)

OBR. 2011. Estimating the output gap. OBR Briefing Paper, No. 2.

Okun, Arthur M. 1962. Potential GNP: Its measurement and significance. Reprinted as Cowles Foundation Paper 190.
Pan, Gongsheng. 2016. *Reform and development of China's bond market, understanding the 13th five-year plan.* China Renmin University Press. (In Chinese)
Pescatori, Andrea, and Jarkko Turunen. 2016. Lower for longer: Neutral rate in the US. *IMF Economic Review* 64 (4).
Pigou. A. C. 1917. The value of money.*Quarterly Journal of Economics* 32 (1): 38–65
Powell, J. 2016. Discussion of the Paper 'Language after Liftoff'". Speech at the 2016 U. S. Monetary Policy Forum.
Reinhart, C., and K. Rogoff. 2009. *This Is different: Eight centuries of financial folly.* Princeton: Princeton University Press.
Reinhart, C., and K. Rogoff. 2011. From financial crash to debt crisis. *American Economic Review* 101 (5): 1676–1706.
Roberts, John. 2014. Estimation of latent variables for the FRB/US model. Federal Reserve Board FEDS, Working Paper No. 2014-46 (November).
Samuelson, P. 1955. *Economics.* 3rd ed. New York: McGraw-Hill.
Shackleton, Robert. 2018. Estimating and projecting potential output: Using CBO's forecasting growth model. Congressional Budget Office, Working Paper.
Sheng, Songcheng, and Liu Xi. 2015. *On the coordinated promotion of financial reform.* China Citic Press. (In Chinese)
Shin, H. 2016. Macroprudential tools, their limits, and their connection with monetary policy. In *Progress and confusion: The state of macroeconomic policy*, ed. O. Blanchard, R. Rajan, K. Rogoff, and L. Summers. Cambridge: MIT Press.
Sims, C. 2004. Limits to inflation targeting. In *The inflation-targeting debate*, ed. B. Bernanke, M. Woodford, 283–308. Chicago: Chicago University Press.
Smithin, J. 2003. *Controversy on monetary economics.* Edward Elgar.
Song, Li, Niu Muhong, Cao Yujin, and Li Shigang. 2016. Research on China's leverage ratio. National Research Institute Working Paper. (In Chinese)
Stiglitz, J., and A. Weiss. 1981. Credit rationing in markets with imperfect information. *American Economic Review* 71 (3): 393–410.
Svensson, L. 2011. Inflation targeting. In *Handbook of monetary economics*, 3rd ed., ed. B. Friedman, M. Woodford, 1237–1302. Amsterdam: Elsevier.
Svensson, L. 2012. Evaluating monetary policy. In *The Taylor rule and the transformation of monetary policy*, ed. E. Koening, R. Lesson, G. Kahn, 219–245. Stanford: Hoover Press.
Kenc, T., F. P. N. Erdem, and B. Ünalm. 2016. Resilience of emerging market economies to global financial conditions. *Central Bank Review* 16 (1): 1–6.
Tan, Yuyan, Tan Zhibo, Huang Yiping, and Hu Yongtai. 2017. The investment crowding out effect of Zombie Enterprises: Evidence based on Chinese Industrial Enterprises. *Economic Research Journal* 52 (05): 175–188. (In Chinese)
Taylor, John B. 1993. Discretion versus policy rules in practice. *Carnegie-Rochester Conference Series on Public Policy* 39 (1): 195–214.
Taylor, J. 1999. A historical analysis of monetary policy rules. In *Monetary policy rules*, ed. J. Taylor, 319–348. University of Chicago Press.
Taylor, J. 2014. The role of policy in the great recession and the weak recovery. *American Economic Review* 104 (5): 61–66.
Taylor, J. 2015. Getting back to a rules-based monetary strategy. Presentation at the Shadow Open Market Committee Conference, March 20th.
Taylor, J. 2016. Can we restart the recovery all over again? *American Economic Review* 106 (5): 48–51.
Taylor, J., and Williams, J. 2011. Simple and robust rules for monetary policy. In *Handbook of monetary economics*, 3rd ed., ed. B. Friedman, M. Woodford, 829–859. Amsterdam: Elsevier.
Taylor, J., and V. Wieland. 2016. Finding the equilibrium real interest rate in a fog of policy deviations. Hoover Institution Economics Working Papers, No. 16109.

Thornton, D. 2004. The fed and short-term rate. *Journal of Banking and Finance* 28 (3): 475–498.
Timethy, F. Geithner. 2015. *Stress test: Reflections on financial crises*. China Citic Press. (In Chinese)
Tressel, T., and Y. Zhang. 2016. Effectiveness and channels of macroprudential policies: Lessons from the Euro Area. IMF Working Paper, No. WP/16 /04.
Vollmer, U., and H. Wiese. 2016. Central bank standing facilities, counterparty risk, and OTC-interbank lending. *North American Journal of Economics and Finance* 36 (C) L: 101–122.
Whitesell, W. 2006. Interest rate corridors and reserves. *Journal of Monetary Economics* 53 (6): 1177–1195.
Wicksell, K. 1898, 1936. *Interest and prices: A study of the causes regulating the value of money.*
Williams, J. 2016. Whither inflation targeting? Presentation to the Hayek Group, Reno, Nevada, Sep. 6th.
Williamson, S. D. 1989. Restrictions on financial intermediaries and implications for aggregate fluctuations: Canada and the United States, 1870–1913. *Nber Macroeconomics Annual* 4: 303–350.
Woodford, M. 2001. Monetary policy in the information economy. Paper for the Symposium on Economic Policy for the Information Economy.
Woodford, M. 2003. *Interest and prices*. Princeton: Princeton University Press.
Xu, Zhong. 2015. Hot issues in the development of China's bond market and their understanding. *Journal of Financial Research* 2015 (02): 29–35. (In Chinese)
Xu, Zhong. 2017a. A comprehensive understanding of prudent and neutral monetary policy. *Tsinghua Financial Review* 2017 (03): 16–19. (In Chinese)
Xu, Zhong. 2017b. China's corporate governance problems urgently need to be solved. *Financial News*, 2017–04–17(010). (In Chinese)
Xu, Zhong. 2017c. Deleveraging in China requires orderly market clearing. *Social Science Weekly* 2017–06–15(001). (In Chinese)
Xu, Zhong. 2017d. Four "Hard Bones" for reform in the new era. *Money China* 2017 (12): 36–38. (In Chinese)
Xu, Zhong. 2017e. Government debt is likely to exceed the debt warning line. *China Real Estate* 2017 (14): 9. (In Chinese)
Xu, Zhong. 2017f. How to improve local fiscal incentive and restraint mechanism. *China Business Times*, 2017–12–27(003). (In Chinese)
Xu, Zhong. 2017g. How to improve local fiscal incentive and restraint mechanism. *China Industrial and Commercial Times* 2017–12–27(003). (In Chinese)
Xu, Zhong. 2017h. Macroeconomic impact of excessively rapid housing price rise. *China Finance* 2017 (17): 49–51. (In Chinese)
Xu, Zhong. 2017i. Practical experience of China's prudent monetary policy and international frontier of monetary policy theory. *Journal of Financial Research* 2017 (01): 1–21. (In Chinese)
Xu, Zhong. 2017j. Reform is the only way to prevent financial risks. *Zi Guang Ge* 2017 (01): 24–26. (In Chinese)
Xu, Zhong. 2017k. Solutions to the symptoms and root causes of deleveraging. *Finance Economy* 2017 (11): 20–22. (In Chinese)
Xu, Zhong. 2017l. The key to effective capacity cutting. *China Finance* 2017 (12): 18–21. (In Chinese)
Xu, Zhong. 2018a. "Ming Gu Shi Zhai" and state-owned capital management. *China Business News* 2018–01–08(A10). (In Chinese)
Xu, Zhong. 2018b. A correct view of further opening up of the financial industry. *Shanghai Business* 2018 (04):11–13. (In Chinese)
Xu, Zhong. 2018c. Challenges for big technology companies to get involved in finance. *Manager' Journal* 2018 (12): 11. (In Chinese)
Xu, Zhong. 2018d. Discussion on effective financial supervision system. *Tsinghua Financial Review* 2018 (08): 16–18. (In Chinese)
Xu, Zhong. 2018e. Financial regulatory policies must respect market rules. *Entrepreneurs' Daily* 2018–09–10 (A03). (In Chinese)

Xu, Zhong. 2018f. How to make financial regulation more effective? *Entrepreneurs' Daily* 2018–10–08 (A04). (In Chinese)

Xu, Zhong. 2018g. How to understand China's economy and related reforms after the 19th national congress. *Shanghai Finance* 2018 (02): 1–4. (In Chinese)

Xu, Zhong. 2018h. Interpretation of the reform plan of deepening the reform of party and state institutions on the financial supervision system, the first quarter of 2018. *Trends in IMI Research* 2018: 459–461. (In Chinese)

Xu, Zhong. 2018i. Modernization of China's financial system and national governance system in the new era. *Economic Research Journal* 53 (07): 4–20. (In Chinese)

Xu, Zhong. 2018j. Modernization of China's financial system and national governance system in the new era. *Social Sciences Digest* 2018 (09): 48–51. (In Chinese)

Xu, Zhong. 2018k. Promoting high-quality development by implementing new development concepts. *China Development Observation* 2018 (01): 13–14. (In Chinese)

Xu, Zhong. 2018l. Strengthening the real economy and defusing financial risks. *United Times* 2018–08–31 (004). (In Chinese)

Xu, Zhong. 2018m. Systematic rediscussion on the relationship between fiscal and finance. *Entrepreneurs' Daily* August 20, 2018 (A03). (In Chinese)

Xu, Zhong. 2018n. Systematic rediscussion on the relationship between fiscal and finance. *Entrepreneurs' Daily*, August 27, 2018 (A03). (In Chinese)

Xu, Zhong. 2018o. Systematic rediscussion on the relationship between fiscal and finance. *Entrepreneurs' Daily*, 2018–09–03 (A03). (In Chinese)

Xu, Zhong. 2018p. The construction of financial system should be embedded in the modernization of national governance system. *China Business News*, 2018–08–09 (A11). (In Chinese)

Xu, Zhong. 2018q. The establishment of bond financing support tools for private enterprises is a major policy innovation of the central bank. *China Securities Journal*, 2018–10–23 (A02). (In Chinese)

Xu, Zhong. 2018r. The key to the overall controllable hedging of external risks of China's economy lies in deepening reform. *China Business News*, 2018, 2018–07–02 (A11). (In Chinese)

Xu, Zhong. 2018s. The path of gradual financial opening is more in line with China's reality. *21st Century Business Herald*, August 17, 2018 (004). (In Chinese)

Xu, Zhong. 2018t. The path of gradual financial opening is more in line with China's reality. *Enterprise Observer* 2018 (09): 20–21. (In Chinese)

Xu, Zhong. 2018u. The transition to high-quality development depends on institutional competition. *Beijing Daily*, 2018–03–26 (013). (In Chinese)

Xu, Zhong. 2018v. Transformation of China's monetary control mode at the stage of high-quality economic development. *Journal of Financial Research* 2018 (04): 1–19. (In Chinese)

Xu, Zhong. 2019a. Responding to demand management with the idea of reform. *Modern SOE Research* 2019 (05): 41–44. (In Chinese)

Xu, Zhong. 2019b. There are four major problems in some policy documents: Why do they avoid difficulties? *Honesty Outlook* 2019 (02): 62. (In Chinese)

Xu, Zhong, Cao Yuanyuan, and Tang Yingwei. 2017. Promoting the reform and development of financial market by opening to the outside world. *Tsinghua Financial Review* 2017 (11): 16–18. (In Chinese)

Xu, Zhong, Guo Lian, and Feng Yinnuo. 2018a. Sustainable development of green finance. *South China Finance* 2018 (10): 3–14. (In Chinese)

Xu, Zhong, Ji Min, and Li Hongjin. 2018b. Monetary policy with yield curve as operational target: Historical experience and policy reflection. *International Economic Review* 2018 (05): 91–103+6. (In Chinese)

Xu, Zhong, Ji Min, and Li Hongjin. 2018c. Theoretical basis and discussion of yield curve regulation policy. *Economic Perspectives* 2018 (08): 106–118. (In Chinese)

Xu, Zhong, and Jia Yandong. 2019. Natural interest rate and China's macro policy choice. *Economic Research Journal* 54 (06): 22–39. (In Chinese)

Xu, Zhong, and Jia Yandong. 2019. Comprehensive measurement of China's potential output and its policy implications. *Journal of Financial Research* 2019 (03): 1–17. (In Chinese)

Xu, Zhong, and Li Hongjin. 2019. Term selection of policy target interest rate under the mode of monetary price regulation. *Studies of International Finance* 2019 (03): 3–12. (In Chinese)

Xu, Zhong, Niu Muhong, Xu Xin, and Tang Xiaoxue. 2018. Research on the development direction of modern financial system in the new era and related issues. *New Finance Review* 2018 (05): 78–102. (In Chinese)

Xu, Zhong, Zhang Xuechun, Cao Yuanyuan, Tang Yingwei, and Wan Tailei. 2017. Promoting the reform and development of financial market by opening to the outside world. *New Finance Review* 2017 (05): 135–160. (In Chinese)

Xu, Zhong, and Zou Chuanwei. 2018. What can and cannot Blockchain do? *Journal of Financial Research* 2018 (11): 1–16. (In Chinese)

Yellen, J. 2016a. The outlook, uncertainty, and monetary policy. Speech at the Economic Club of New York, New York, Mar., 29th.

Yellen, J. 2016b. The federal reserve's monetary policy toolkit. Speech at Symposium on Designing Resilient Monetary Policy Frameworks for the Future, Aug., 26th.

Yellen, J. 2016c. Macroeconomic research after the crisis. Speech at 60th Annual Economic Conference, 14 Oct. 2016.

Yellen, J. 2017. The economic outlook and the conduct of monetary policy. Speeches at the Stanford Institute for Economic Policy Research, Jan, 19th.

Yi, Gang, and Tang Xian. 2001. A theoretical basis for the "Angular Solution Hypothesis" of exchange rate regime. *Journal of Financial Research* 2001 (08): 5–17. (In Chinese)

Yi, Gang. 2006. Macroeconomic policy and market allocation of resources. *Caijing* 2006 (03): 22–23. (In Chinese)

Yi, Gang. 2009a. Interest rate liberalization in China in the past three decades. *Journal of Financial Research* 2009 (01): 1–14. (In Chinese)

Yi, Gang. 2009b. China's monetary policy in 30 years of reform and opening up, 30 years of reform in China. China Development Press. (In Chinese)

Yi, Gang. 2013. The advantages and disadvantages of interest rate liberalization and current interest rate situation in China. *China Finance Forum Research Weekly* 2013 (219). (In Chinese)

Yi, Gang. 2016. Continue to deepen exchange rate reform. *Capital Markets* 2016 (04): 8. (In Chinese)

Yi, Gang. 2018a. Monetary policy review and outlook. *China's Finance* 2018 (03): 9–11. (In Chinese)

Yi, Gang. 2018b. *Transcript of Questions and Answers at the Sub-Forum of the Boao Forum for Asia Annual Conference 2018*, www.pbc.gov.cn, 11 April 2018. (In Chinese)

Zhang, Jie. 2011. *The structure and changes of China's financial system.* China Renmin University Press. (In Chinese)

Zhang, Ping. 2015. The challenge of deflation mechanism to Chinese economy and stabilization policy. *Economic Dynamics* 2015 (04): 4–11. (In Chinese)

Zhang, Xiaohui. 2011. The choice, use and innovation of monetary policy tools under the condition of balance of payments surplus, www.pbc.gov.cn, 24 March 2011. (In Chinese)

Zhang, Xiaohui. 2015. The development, challenges and prospects of monetary policy. *China Finance* 2015 (19): 28–30. (In Chinese)

Zhang, Xiaohui. 2017. Review and prospect of monetary policy. *China's Finance* 2017 (03): 12–15. (In Chinese)

Zhou, Lian. 2007. Research on promotion tournament model of local officials in China. *Economic Research Journal* 2007 (07): 36–50. (In Chinese)

Zhou, Xiaochuan. 1999. Some problems in debt-to-equity swaps. *Comparison of Economic and Social Systems* 1999 (06): 3–5. (In Chinese)

Zhou, Xiaochuan. 2004. Some problems to be paid attention to improve the Transmission Mechanism of Monetary Policy, www.pbc.gov.cn, 14 April 2004. (In Chinese)

Zhou, Xiaochuan. 2011. Establishing a financial macro-control system in line with China's national conditions. *China Finance* 2011 (13): 9–13. (In Chinese)

Zhou, Xiaochuan. 2013. The main characteristics of China's monetary policy since the new century. *China Finance* 2013 (02): 9–14. (In Chinese)

Zhou, Xiaochuan. 2015. Speech at the Boao Forum for Asia Annual Conference 2015, www.pbc.gov.cn, 2 April 2015. (In Chinese)

Zhou, Xiaochuan. 2016. Grasping many target monetary policies: Perspective of China's transformation economy. Speech in Michel Camdessus Central Banking Lecture, www.cbc.gov.cn, June 23, 2016. (In Chinese)

Zhou, Zhengqing. 1993. *Research on China's monetary policy*. China Financial Publishing House. (In Chinese)

The manufacturer's authorised representative in the EU is Springer
Nature Customer Service Centre GmbH, Europaplatz 3, 69115 Heidelberg,
Germany. If you have any concerns regarding our products, please
contact ProductSafety@springernature.com

Printed and bound by CPI Group (UK) Ltd, Croydon, CR0 4YY
30/09/2026
02225453-0015